Ebenezer Bain

Merchant And Craft Guilds

A History of the Aberdeen Incorporated Trades

Ebenezer Bain

Merchant And Craft Guilds
A History of the Aberdeen Incorporated Trades

ISBN/EAN: 9783744723978

Printed in Europe, USA, Canada, Australia, Japan

Cover: Foto ©ninafisch / pixelio.de

More available books at **www.hansebooks.com**

Merchant and Craft Guilds

A HISTORY

OF

THE ABERDEEN INCORPORATED TRADES

BY

EBENEZER BAIN

EX-MASTER OF TRADES HOSPITAL

"VIS UNITA FORTIOR"

ABERDEEN
J. & J. P. EDMOND & SPARK
1887

TO

THE CONVENER, MASTER OF HOSPITAL,

OFFICE-BEARERS, AND MEMBERS

OF

The Seven Incorporated Trades

OF ABERDEEN,

THIS VOLUME IS MOST RESPECTFULLY

INSCRIBED.

●

PREFACE.

WHILE holding office among the Seven Incorporated Trades of Aberdeen a few years ago, I had frequent opportunities of scanning their interesting old records and other documents, and I had not gone far in my perusal of them until I discovered that they contained a considerable amount of material fitted to throw light on the trading customs, and the social and religious life of the community from the fifteenth century downwards.

It was also an agreeable surprise to find that, notwithstanding the many vicissitudes through which so many of our local institutions have passed, the records of the Trades, including the documents belonging to the monastery of the Trinity Friars, were in an excellent state of preservation ; and it occurred to me that, as a new generation has now arisen, having little in common with the old burgher life, a historical account of these ancient societies might prove acceptable, not only to the existing members of the Trades, but to many others who take an interest in the different phases of early burgh life.

In estimating the position which these craft guilds held in the community, it is necessary to bear in mind the large proportion of the population that came within their jurisdiction. The families, journeymen, apprentices, and servants, as well as the craftsmen themselves, were all subject to the authority of the deacons and masters of the different crafts, and amenable to the laws and statutes enforced under the powers conferred by

Royal Charters, Seals of Cause, and Acts of Council ; and taken at a moderate computation, these classes would represent about two thirds of the whole community. The history of the craft guilds, therefore, ought in no small measure to reflect the conditions of life among the great bulk of the industrial classes ; and if this volume helps to a better understanding of the guild life of our own community my object in collecting the historical information in this volume will be fully accomplished.

To the many friends who have assisted me in various ways I take this opportunity of returning my best thanks, more particularly to Mr. P. J. ANDERSON, Secretary of the New Spalding Club; Mr. A. M. MUNRO, of the Aberdeen Town House ; and Mr. J. P. EDMOND, and to the CONVENER, MASTER OF TRADES HOSPITAL, DEACONS, and BOXMASTERS of the various Trades who so readily afforded me access to the books and documents under their charge. To Mr. ANDREW J. GIBB, Mr. E. W. JAPP, Mr. C. CARMICHAEL, and Mr. GEORGE WATT, I am also indebted for assistance in connection with the plates and drawings.

E. B.

ABERDEEN, *October*, 1887.

CONTENTS.

PART III.

THE SEVEN INCORPORATED TRADES.

PART I.

MERCHANT AND CRAFT GUILDS.

CHAPTER I.

INTRODUCTORY.

In tracing the origin and development, and in ascertaining the true character and influence of the different classes of trade guilds that up to a recent period played so important a part in the industrial and social life of almost every town and village in Europe, many difficulties have had to be encountered. There has been no lack of antiquarian and historical research, but much of the material necessary to satisfactory inquiry has disappeared, and, in consequence, there has been considerable difference of opinion in regard to their true scope and functions. Most writers on the subject frankly admit that, to a considerable extent, they have been groping in the dark, while several have evidently taken up a preconceived theory or idea, and manipulated their historical material accordingly. The death of Toulmin Smith, in the midst of his elaborate work of research among the ancient Guilds of London and England, is a matter for deep regret, but he has left behind him a vast amount of material which has greatly helped to throw light on the darkness with which the early history of communities has been surrounded. Lugo Brentano, of Aschaffenburg, Bavaria, has also pursued his researches into this interesting subject with a success that none have been able to excel ; and from the works of these writers, as well as from the writings of such standard historians as Hallam, Froude, Freeman, and others, much interesting information may be gleaned.

Considering the important part that religious, commercial, and industrial Guilds have played in civilised life for so many centuries, it is a matter of surprise that so little attention has been given to them by historians, compared with the attention given to records of dynasties, ruling families, great battles, and civil and religious revolutions. Most of our historians content themselves with mere incidental references to the industrial life of the people, not so much from any desire to ignore it, but mainly from a want of reliable historical data to work upon. The history of any period, or nation, and especially of towns must necessarily be incomplete which does not take full cognisance of its Guild life, so intimately associated is it with the religious, the social, the inner, and common life of the people. In the Guild life we can trace civilisation to its cradle. In very early times these Guilds or associations were like the people themselves, rude and simple in their organisation, but they all sprang from the one common instinct of men seeking strength by union or combination. As civilisation developed, the Guilds developed; they changed in character and scope as new wants arose, and adapted themselves to the continual and progressive march of civilisation. The modern combinations of to-day, such as friendly societies, trades unions, and trading companies of all kinds, are but a further development of ancient Guild life, rendered necessary by the freer, broader, and more enlightened ideas of modern times.

A considerable amount of valuable information has been collected by successive Royal Commissions that have inquired into the history of the London Guilds. Mr. Herbert, the laborious librarian of the Corporation of London, made a very exhaustive inquiry, and his information has been largely supplemented by the reports furnished by the various Livery Companies. It is necessary, however, to bear in mind that these reports were prepared for a special purpose, and historical impartiality has at times been sacrificed for the purpose of serving the particular end in view. But, with the knowledge of this tendency before us, we can easily extract sufficient material of a reliable character from the reports of these Royal Commissions to serve our present purpose; and with regard to the points on which such eminent historians as

Hallam and Freeman, Brentano and Toulmin Smith differ, we must be content to leave them until further inquiry and research has thrown more light upon them.

In the etymology of the word *guild*—or *gild*, as the German authorities prefer to spell it—we have some light thrown on the origin of the institution. *Gild*, or *geld*, is Old English for a set payment or contribution, from *zeldan* or *zyldan*, to pay (from which the present word *yield* is derived); the primary meaning being payment, and the company of those who paid becoming known by this chief title to membership. Thus, also (according to the *Encyclopædia Britannica*) *gilde*, Danish and Low German, in the sense of a contributory company of this kind ; *gjalda* or *gildi*, Icelandic, a payment, and *gildi*, also meaning a banquet. In the opinion of some authorities the word thus derived is better spelt without the *u*, but a colour is given to the ordinary modern form of Guild by deriving it (as in Wedgewood's English Etymology) from the Welsh or Breton, *Gouil*, a feast or a holiday—*gwylad*, keeping a holiday. In Aberdeen down to quite a recent period the word was uniformly spelt *gild*.

The name Guild has been almost exclusively applied in Scotland to the associations or organisations formed by the merchant class of the community. The Craft-associations were simply designated by the name of the particular craft to which their members belonged, such as, " The Weavers," " The Bakers," " The Wrights," &c. In more recent times they were spoken of as " The Weaver Trade," " The Baker Trade," &c., while it is quite a common practice now to style them "Weaver Incorporation," " Baker Incorporation," and so on. The word Incorporation was brought into use in connection with the Craft-Guilds when the craftsmen in a particular town incorporated themselves together under a deacon-convener, and established a Convener Court, or Convenery, to look after matters that were common to all the different crafts. Thus we may speak of " The Aberdeen Incorporated Trades," or "The Incorporated Trades of Aberdeen," but in speaking of an individual trade it would have been far more appropriate if the name which is used on the continent and in many parts of England had been adopted, namely, "The Guild of Weavers ; "

and we should then have had the appropriate title of "The Aberdeen Incorporated Craft-Guilds," a designation that would have been understood wherever Guilds are known.

Summing up the result of his inquiry into the origin of all the different classes of Guilds, Brentano states that "the family appears as the first Gild, or at least as the archetype of Gilds. Originally its providing care satisfies all existing wants, and for other societies there is, therefore, no room. As soon, however, as wants arise which the family can no longer satisfy— whether on account of their peculiar nature, or in consequence of their increase, or because its activity grows feeble—closer artificial alliances immediately spring forth to provide for them in so far as the State does not do it. Infinitely varied as are the wants which call them forth, so are naturally the objects of these alliances. Yet the basis on which they all rest is the same; all are unions between man and man, not mere associations of capital like our modern societies and companies. The cement which holds them together is the feeling of solidarity, the esteem for each other as men, the honour and virtue of the associations, and the faith in them—not an arithmetical rule of probabilities indifferent to all good and bad personal qualities. The support which the community affords a member is adjusted according to his wants—not according to his money state, or to a jealous debtor and creditor account. In short, whatever and however diverse may be their aims, the Gilds take over from the family the spirit which held it together and guided it; they are its faithful image, though only for special and definite objects." Here we have the essential difference pointed out between the Guilds in their earlier forms, and the associations and combinations of modern days; and in proportion as the Guilds became mere money-making institutions—in some instances, embarking upon industrial and commercial undertakings—in so far did they fall away from their original character and constitution. As a rule they invested their money in land in the immediate neighbourhood of towns, hence the wealth and influence which many of them acquired. It is roughly estimated, for instance, that over one half of the land on which Aberdeen is built is held by the Incorporated Trades of Aberdeen, while the enormous wealth of the London Craft

Guilds is in a great measure due to the purchase of land on which modern London is built.

The Greek and Roman Empires both furnish examples of Guilds bearing a strong resemblance to the Mediæval Guilds of Europe. Much controversy has taken place as to whether or not the Mediæval Guilds were a survival of the Roman *Collegia opificum*. In his notes to " Cicero de Senectute," Mr. Reid says that the resemblance of the *Collegia* to the London Guilds is, in many respects, not excluding that of hospitality, very striking ; and in his " History of the Middle Ages " Mr. Pearson remarks that, " in spite of the English names under which we know them, it is pretty certain that they only continued the old Roman *Collegia* of the trades ; " while Dr. Mommsen directs attention to a letter from Pliny to Trajan, and the Emperor's reply thereto, respecting the establishment of a Guild of smiths *(fabri* or *fabbri)* at Nicomedia. Among the Greeks, too, in the second and third centuries B.C., associations known as *Eranoi,* or *Theasoi* existed ; and although Professor Newton, of the British Museum, contends that these associations were distinctly religious communities, and not in any sense Craft Guilds, there are others who consider that they were not so strictly confined to matters of religion as Professor Newton endeavours to make out. One writer mentions that the *Eranoi* were numerous at Rhodes, in the islands of the Archipelago, at the Piræus, and in other important places. These societies, he adds, partook more nearly of the character of the Mediæval Guilds than those of the Romans. The members paid contributions to a general fund, aided one another in necessity, provided for funerals, met in assembly to deliberate on their affairs, and celebrate feasts and religious sacrifices in common. Strict rules against disorderly conduct were enforced by fine, and he who did not pay his yearly quota to the society was excluded unless he could show cause by poverty or sickness. " Some of these societies," he goes on to say, " concerned themselves with religion, others with politics and commerce ; in the cause of liberal, as opposed to official, religion they appear to have done good service. In both the Greek and Roman Guilds we find the same motives at work—weakness seeking the power of numbers to resist oppression ; and the affinity which those possessing the same occupation and the same interests have in each other." These are the underlying forces that have operated in all countries, and in all ages, in bringing Guilds into existence, and are sufficient to account for the existence of the *Eranoi* in Greece contemporary with the *Collegia* of the Romans ; and, further, they are sufficient to explain how, although the *Collegia opificum*, or Artisans' Guilds, are found as late as the code of Justinian, we have, fifty or sixty years later in the 6th century, says the writer already quoted, a record of a soapmakers' craft in Naples (letter of Pope Gregory the Great) ; also that the Guild in the towns of Italy should begin to show a new life in the 10th century (Hegel). They also explain why in England we find, from the 7th to the 10th century, other Guilds actively in existence, while in Norway they were instituted in the 11th century. These societies "may thus have one history in China, another in India, another in Greece or Rome, another in Europe of the Middle Ages ; the like needs all require the same kinds of help, and develop institutions which, amid whatever diversities of outward garb, will substantially fulfil the same end." Mr. E. A. Freeman is one of those who are of opinion that no actual connection can be traced between the ancient *Collegia* and the Guilds of the Middle Ages. "The gap between the Roman and English periods is hidden," he says, "by the blackness of darkness which shrouds our settlement in Britain, and which, to those who have eyes, teaches much more clearly than any light could what the nature of that settlement really was. Had there been any continuity between the institutions of the two periods, that blackness and darkness could hardly have been." The question of continuity, however, is not of the first importance. We need not be so much concerned about the continuity as with the fact that institutions similar to those which existed in many parts of Europe and in our own country in the Middle Ages, existed at the time of the Roman Empire ; and of that fact there can be no doubt whatever.

Guilds have been divided into three classes—Religious or Social Guilds, Merchant Guilds, and Craft Guilds—but the distinction must be regarded as more of a general than of a precise nature. They each partook, to a more or less extent, of the character of the other. Religious or Social Guilds were, in some instances, Merchant and Trade Guilds ; while Merchant and Trade Guilds were always associated—especially the earlier Guilds—with religious observances and religious rites and ceremonies. And, in the same way, the Merchant Guilds and the Craft Guilds were interwoven with each other, the one overlapping the other in their aims and objects. The further back we go, the more do we find the religious element predominating in all Guilds ; and in countries where religious influence most predominated, we also find that the Guilds possessed in proportion a larger share of the religious element. In pre-reformation times especially, in Merchant and Craft Guilds alike, the religious element is a strongly marked feature of their constitution. Each Guild had its patron saint ; its ordinances provided for statutory religious observances ; attendance at church or mass was made obligatory on the members ; and in most of the larger Guilds there was a regularly appointed chaplain to conduct services at the stated meetings, and to look after the spiritual interests of the members and their households. Brentano holds that the first societies formed " were the sacrificial unions, from which, later on, the religious Guilds were developed for association in prayer and good works. Then, as soon as the family could no longer satisfy the need for legal protection, unions of artificial family members were formed for this purpose, as the State was not able to afford the needful help in this respect. These Guilds, however, had their origin in direct imitation of the family. Most certainly none were developed from an earlier religious union ; as little were the Roman *Collegia opificum* from the Roman sacrificial societies, or the Craft Guilds from the Guild Merchants, or any Trades Unions from a Craft Guild."

The Merchant Guilds in Mediæval times had always, more or less, an aristocratic leaning. They associated themselves with the ruling powers much more than the Craftsmen did. A general opinion, and that adopted by the Royal Commission of 1882, is " that originally the Guild Merchants was an association of the owners of the land on which the town was built, and of owners of estates in the neighbourhood. Many of the patrician families engaged in business pursuits in the towns, and became in this way associated with the Merchant Guilds. Eventually, however, the aristocratic municipality had, in almost every case, to give way, though in some instances not till after a long and fierce struggle, to the general body of the citizens as represented by the more plebeian Craft Guilds. In London the victory of the popular party had become assured as early as the reign of Edward II." Even to this day, with the exception, perhaps, of London, we see a closer association between the Merchant Guilds and the municipalities than there exists in the case of the Craft Guilds. The latter, on account of the supervision they had to exercise over their own members in all matters connected with their crafts, had to form independent associations ; while the Merchant Guilds, having more general interests and possessing a wealthier class of members, became more closely associated with the governing bodies.

When communities first began to take form there was no definite dividing line between the merchants and craftsmen. The craftsmen were admitted to equal privileges with the merchants if they were possessed of land of a certain value within the territory of the town. Almost everywhere the craftsmen traded in the raw material with which they worked, the separation between the trader or merchant and the handicraftsmen being a gradual process. When referring to the causes that separated the two classes, Brentano speaks in anything but flattering terms of the Merchant Guilds. "By the enjoyment of power," he says, " the descendants of the Frith Guild (from which the Merchant Guild sprang) became proud, ambitious, and tyrannical. The freer and more independent the burghers became, and the less they needed assistance from the general body of the crafts for the defence of liberties acquired, and the obtaining of fresh ones, the greater was the degree in which this degeneration of the original noble spirit seems to have taken place." The fight for supremacy was often keen and bitter. Many a bloody fight took place in towns on the Continent. For instance, at Magdeburg in the year 1301 ten Aldermen of the Craft Guilds were burned alive in the market place. After the Cologne weavers had lost "The Weavers' Battle" against the ruling families on November 21, 1371, thirty-three weavers were executed ; and on the day after, houses, churches, and monasteries were searched ; all craftsmen who were found concealed were murdered ; and, lastly, eighteen hundred of them were exiled with their wives and children, and their hall was demolished. Reference will afterwards be made to the many conflicts that took place in Aberdeen when we come to deal with the Aberdeen Trades. In London the struggle ended in the complete victory of the Craft Guilds. So completely did they obtain the mastery that, in the time of Edward II., no person —whether an inhabitant of the city or otherwise—could be admitted to the freedom of the city unless he were a member of one of the trades or mysteries. In Norton's "Commentaries of London" we find it recorded that "in the 49th Edward III. an enactment passed the whole assembled commonality of the city, by which the right of election of all city dignitaries and officers, including members of Parliament, was transferred from the ward representatives to the trading companies."

In nearly all the oldest towns throughout Europe we find that the Guilds preceded the more extended governing body for the community generally—that, in fact, the Guilds existed prior to the formation of Town Councils or municipalities. Many of the Guilds had charters of confirmation or recognition from the Crown prior to the time that regular charters were granted to the burghs as such. In some instances the two might have come together; but the records of the oldest towns in England, and in Scotland also, show that the power of regulating the special trading privileges was merely delegated by the Crown to the local governing bodies when the latter were brought into existence. Discussing this particular point, Hallam, in his " View of the State of Europe during the Middle Ages," refers to the acuteness of Thierry in discovering the origin of the communities in the north of France. " Thierry," says Hallam, " deduces them from the old Teutonic institution of Guilds or fraternities by voluntary compact, to relieve each other in poverty or to protect each other from injury. Two essential characteristics belonged to them : the common pay-

ment and the common purse. They had also in many instances
a religious, sometimes a secret ceremonial, to knit more firmly
the bond of fidelity. They became as usual suspicious to
Governments, as several capitularies of Charlemagne prove.
But they spoke both to the heart and to the reason in a voice
which no Government could silence. They readily became
connected with the exercise of trades, with the training of
apprentices, with the traditional rules of art. We find them in
all Teutonic and Scandinavian countries, they are frequently
mentioned in our Anglo-Saxon documents, and are the basis of
those corporations which the Norman Kings recognised or
founded." It is also true, as Hallam remarks further on, that
the Guild was in its primary character a personal association;
it was in the State, but not the State; it belonged to the city
without embracing all its citizens; its purposes were for the
good of the fellows alone. But while they did not embrace all
the citizens, those outside them had no separate or independent
municipal or corporate existence. And to this conclusion it is
evident that Hallam comes in the end, when he says —
" From the private Guild possessing already the vital spirit of
faithfulness and brotherly love, sprang the main community;
the body of citizens bound by a voluntary but perpetual
obligation to guard each other's rights against the thefts of the
weak and the tyranny of the powerful."

The nature and objects of the Guilds support the view that
they were established in the earliest stages of civilisation. As
self-protection is the first instinct of the individual, so we also
find it to be the case with groups of individuals. No sooner
did the art of a craft become known, than the instinct of protection and self-preservation by means of common counsel and
combined action asserted itself. Rude and elementary though
these associations must have been originally, they rapidly improved in organisation; they became possessed of wealth and
property; and formed the basis of the wider and more popular
forms of government for the inhabitants generally. And, to a
considerable extent, the same spirit or desire for protection is
manifested in newly formed communities in our own colonies.
Protection is their infant cry, as protection has been the infant
cry of all new countries and peoples over the civilised world.

During the reign of Richard II. an inquiry was made into the origin and development of Guilds, and although much of the record thus made has been lost, portions have been brought to light again by the Early English Text Society. An important result of that inquiry was confirmation of the opinion that "the Trade Guilds have in all countries attracted more attention than the rest, on account of their wealth and influence. They were of two orders—Guilds-Merchant and Craft Guilds. The Guild Merchant arose in this way. The same men who had possession of town lands were frequently also traders, and the uncertain state of society in early times naturally caused them to unite for protection of their trade interests in a *gilda mercatoria*, which made internal laws akin to those of other Guilds. The success of their private interests enlarged their influence, and when the towns and boroughs obtained confirmation of their municipal life by charter, they took care to have it included that the men of the place should also have their Guild Merchant. Thus these Guilds obtained the recognition of the State; in their origin they had been as other Guilds, partaking especially of the character of Peace Guilds; but now the citizens and the Guild became identical, and what was Guild law often became the law of the town." In great cities such as London and Florence, says Norton, we do not hear of the Merchant Guild; there the separate occupations or crafts early asserted their associating power and independence, and the Craft Guilds gradually took a place in the regulation of the town government. Many Craft Guilds, the heads of which were concerned in the government of the commune, are found in Italy between the 9th and 12th centuries. "But in England and the north of Europe, the Guilds Merchant during this period, having grown rich and tyrannical, excluded the landless men of the handicrafts; those then uniting among themselves, there arose everywhere by the side of the Guilds Merchant, the Craft Guilds, which gained the upper hand in the struggle for liberty in the 13th and 14th centuries."

This was more especially the case on the Continent, where severe struggles were frequent between the inhabitants and the municipalities established by this class of Guilds, but in almost every case the general body of the citizens, as repre-

sented by the more plebeian Craft Guilds, threw off the power
of the Merchant Guilds. These Merchant Guilds do not appear
to have ever obtained much hold in this country. Even in
London it is doubtful if they ever had a predominating influence in the municipality. The Bishop of Chester, a recognised
authority on the constitution of the municipality of London,
says :—" During the Norman period London appears to have
been a collection of small communities, manors, parishes,
churchsokens, and guilds held and governed in the usual way ;
the manors descending by inheritance ; the church jurisdictions
exercised under the bishop, the chapter, and the monasteries ;
and the guilds administered by their own officers and adminis-
tering their own property ; as holding in chief of the king, the
lords of the franchises, the prelates of the churches, and even
the aldermen of the guilds, where the guild possessed estates,
might bear the title of barons. It was, for the most part, an
aristocratic constitution, and had its unity, not in the municipal principal, but in the system of the shire."

CHAPTER II.

CONTINENTAL GUILDS.

In a series of papers obtained by the Royal Commission of 1880 from different authorities on the Continent on the origin and development of Guilds in France, Belgium, the Netherlands, Switzerland, Germany, Austria, Norway, Sweden, Italy, Spain, Portugal, Russia, and Turkey, much valuable historical information is to be found; and a brief summary of their main historical features may be given for the purpose of showing the striking resemblance that exists between the Continental Guilds and the Craft Guilds in our own country. One of the most interesting papers is that furnished by M. E. Levasseur, of the French Institute, on the Guilds in France, where at the close of the 12th century the Trades had in most of the large towns their organised Corporations. The Hundred Years' War proved very disastrous to the Corporations, and although there was a revival of them from 1450 to 1550, many passed out of existence altogether. In 1673 an ordinance was issued by which all trades were formed into communities, and at this time the number of Corporations was again increased, the system of Trade and Craft Guilds becoming in the municipality the recognised mode of industrial organisation until the Revolution of 1789, when, by an Act of the *Assemblée Constituante*, the regimen of Corporations was finally made to give place to the system of free labour. Before admission to the Corporations it was necessary to have been received as master, the qualification for which was the execution of a masterpiece, and its acceptance by a jury. In most of the trades the candidate before attempting the masterpiece had to show that he had served for a certain term as a journeyman. In many trades the number of freemen *(maîtrise)* was limited by statute, and, with few exceptions, admission to the freedom could only be made where there was a vacancy. The king

could under certain circumstances make grants of the freedom
of any of the Corporations, and these, being sold to the highest
bidders, considerably augmented the Royal revenues. Although
the sons did not necessarily succeed their fathers, nevertheless,
in almost all the Corporations they enjoyed special privileges,
such as exemption from the masterpiece, reduction of the fines
payable on admission to freedom, dispensation from the pro-
bationary clause, and right of admission by special favour on a
vacancy arising, in preference to the other journeymen. In a
small number of Corporations the sons alone, or with them the
sons-in-law and some other relations, were allowed to succeed.
But membership in the Trade Guild was always conditional on
the exercise of the trade. After the suppression of the Corporations in 1791 the State took possession of their real property,
refunding to the freemen a part of their freedom fine, and
charging itself with the winding-up of their affairs. At one
time some of the French Guilds were very wealthy. Besides
the common fund, they owned property consisting of houses
which served as meeting places, or the headquarters of the
Corporations; but in the 18th century they fell into decay, and
the liquidation of their debt, which was not completed until
1789, absorbed the whole of their funds.

Several valuable papers were furnished regarding the Guilds
of Italy. "The Craft Guilds *(Corpi d'arte)* in Italy," says
Allessandretti, "are of great antiquity, and, in addition to
their original purpose, more especially during the mediæval
period, they acquired a purely political character." In the
Middle Ages they served to counterbalance the power of the
nobles; but in course of time, owing to reforms effected by
the State, this became less necessary, and the associations
(sodalgia) in question "devoted themselves to the regulation
of their crafts and the performance of friendly offices to their
members." The right of entry into a Corporation was not
hereditary, but was conferred on any one actually following
the trade, provided that he was of good reputation and character. The craftsmen were divided into apprentices and masters,
with occasionally the intermediate grade of journeyman; and
before passing from one grade to another, a period of service
was at least necessary, and more commonly the production of

a masterpiece was also required. The Craft Guilds also formed in most cases religious brotherhoods, who chose for themselves a patron saint whose effigy they bore on their standard. As they came into existence first in Italy, so also they appear to have been the first to disappear. From the time that they began to lose sight of their primary purpose, and to undertake industrial enterprises on a large scale, they began to decline. The Italian economists of the eighteenth century frankly pronounced themselves opposed to the *regium* of Corporations of Arts and Misteries, which were finally abolished in Tuscany in 1847, in Naples in 1821, and in Lombardy, Venetia, and Parma in 1813. But, although legally abolished, several of them still survive, especially at the ports and frontier towns. At Genoa, for instance, there still exists the Corporation of the "cadrai" or bumboat men (vivanduri), in whom is vested the right of selling eatables to the ships in the port; the "calafati" (calkers) of the canal, whose duty it was to remove and stow in the warehouses all the merchandise; the porters (imballatori), barrel porters (barillari), box carriers (cassari), and the porters at custom-houses or free ports—a society somewhat similar to the Pynours or Shore Porters of Leith and Aberdeen. The by-laws of all the Guilds were originally taken from one model, which was in great part based on the Communal Ordinances. Every Corporation had its chief or master, "capo," "ill massaro," a vice-master, "sotto massaro" or syndic, and two assistants who acted as the Syndic's Deputies. No citizen could aspire to the Council and Magistracy, or any public office, unless affiliated to one or other of the Corporations or Colleges. As Lucca had what was known as a Guild of the Seven Arts (the same number as now exist in Aberdeen), it will be of interest to quote entire what is said regarding them :—

They existed from very ancient times, and were inaugurated in the 12th century. Of one, entitled the Guild of the Seven Arts (*intillotata Delle sette Arte*), which included all the arts concerned in the building and finishing of a house, we have records which go back to the year 1194. The origin of others was considerably less ancient, but it is certain that there was no handicraft, trade, or profession in Lucca which had not at one time or another a society or company where its members might meet. The administration of these societies varied according to the times. Their chief object was originally the imposition on the members of certain trade regulations, but with their growth or reorganisation they acquired the aspect of religious associations, recreative assemblies, or mutual aid societies, while interference with the trade in most cases either became a secondary consideration or was altogether neglected. By the law of 1808 these harmless societies were legally suppressed, but on the downfall of the Napoleonic rule a few of them recovered their former standing, and resumed the possession of their property. This remnant of the ancient Coporations, reduced in number and activity, and limited to the performance of certain devotional functions, have survived to the present day. Judging from those statutes which remain to us, the old societies in Lucca had a great variety of regulations, but in none of them is it expressed that the right of membership descended from father to son. Sometimes, however, to a son who followed his father's trade (*Il mestiere paterno*), and wished to enter the Guild of which his father had been a member, certain advantages were conceded.

In Portugal nearly all the trades were organised as societies (*embandeirados*). Under one flag and one patron saint were united several trades. Each band chose one or more representatives, amounting in all to 24, who were elected annually, and forming together a corporation known as " The House of the 24 ; " they chose from amongst themselves the judge of the people, their notary ; and the trades, which in Lisbon were four in number, formed part of the Council and assisted at its deliberations, though their vote was not of equal weight with that of the municipality.

The Guilds in Holland were abolished in 1798. The right of membership was not hereditary *qua talis*, but was dependent upon the actual practice of the craft or trade. The freedom of the town was also a condition precedent to admission to a Guild. The children born in lawful wedlock to a free citizen were, from the moment of their birth, free citizens likewise. " Burgerrecht," however, was obtainable in more ways than one, and he who had it not by birth-right might petition the magistrates of the town to be pleased to grant him the freedom. Citizens thus created were called " cooked " burghers. After the suppression of the Guilds, the funds in a few instances were allowed to remain in their possession, and were administered for charitable purposes by a committee under the inspection of the local authorities. By a decree issued in 1820, it was directed that the money should be employed for the support, in the first place, of necessitous ex-members of the former Guilds and their widows and children, and in the next place, of other indigent craftsmen.

Special interest attaches to the information supplied concerning the Guilds in Germany on account of an attempt, begun in 1881, to revive a number of their ancient privileges. The Guilds, or Zünfte and Innungen, were abolished in 1859-60, but a reaction was caused by the fact that on account of the removal of the old laws and customs new evils sprang into existence. A large number of young men established themselves in business with neither the requisite technical knowledge nor a sufficiency of capital, and, consequently, were soon obliged to go into liquidation. The adherents of the old system made use of the stagnation of trade caused by the crisis in 1873 as a ground for demanding a revision of the statutes relating to trade. In consequence of this agitation a change was made in the commercial laws of Germany, by which the system of Guilds and masterpieces became again operative, though not compulsory. Owing to this change, by the spring of 1883, no fewer than 500 Guilds were re-founded and their statutes registered by the Courts. The right of membership in Germany is not hereditary, but is acquired by fulfilling the necessary conditions—the apprentice test, the three years' " wanderzeet," and the masterpiece. When the original Guilds were abolished they had little property to dispose of, and it was never looked after.

The first Guild ordinances granted in Norway are dated 4th Nov., 1682, but the Guilds were in existence in very early times. The members were required to be thoroughly trained in all manual skill and dexterity belonging to their trade. On the one side were exclusive privileges connected with the pursuit of their industry ; and, on the other, all approach to an alliance with other organised bodies was forbidden. In the country districts, industries were as a rule only free in the case of the most necessary crafts, such as the tailors, the shoemakers, the blacksmiths, and the carpenters. In the towns the manual industries were affiliated to a particular Guild composed of freemen, journeymen, and apprentices, and to pass from one grade to another, it was necessary after a certain period of

c

service in the subordinate position to produce a "masterpiece."
In 1839 it was decreed that no new Craft Guild might be
established, and that every Guild should be abolished when all
the masters or freemen admitted to the Guilds previous to 1840
were dead, or the survivors were agreed to dissolve the Guild.
Craft masters are now compelled to enter into a written contract to teach any apprentice they may take, which contract
must not last more than five years, and to provide at the same
time for his perfecting himself in the trade, so that at the end
of his apprenticeship he can exhibit the above-named voluntary
masterpiece or test work. The insignia, plate, cash, and
furniture owned by the Guilds have been given, some of it to
the public museums, and the remainder sold. There are still,
however, voluntary associations of craftsmen who, even now,
appear in religious processions with banners and the emblems
of their craft displayed.

Russia seems to have been as far behind in the matter of
Guilds as in everything else. The Guilds in that country
were founded in the first instance in the 18th century, in the
reign of Catherine the Great. They did not spring up con-
currently with social progress, but by legal enactment. They
are not a national institution, and have not the characteristics
of those in Western Europe. In instituting the Guilds, we are
told by Professor Yanson that the Empress wished to encourage industry in the towns by granting a quasi-monopoly, their
introduction being in fact a political measure. The principle
of the Russian legislation is that persons applying for membership must have previously exercised a trade in order to qualify
themselves. Admission to the Guilds in Russia is free, on
compliance with the following conditions :—(1) Service of three
years as a journeyman ; (2) age must be not less than 21 ; (3)
the applicant must possess sufficient means to open a shop ;
and (4) qualify as a "master" by showing a specimen of his
work.

CHAPTER III.

THE LONDON GUILDS.

THE London Guilds or Livery Companies are the oldest Craft and Merchant Guilds in Europe. According to the Report of a Royal Commission that inquired into their condition in 1834, they were in their original constitutions not so much trading societies as trade societies, instituted for the purpose of protecting the consumer or the employer against the incompetency or fraud of the dealer or the artisan; and also for protecting the workman trained to his art, according to notions of early times, by preventing his being undersold in the labour market by an unlimited number of competitors. Further, the Companies acted as domestic tribunals—adjudicating, or rather arbitrating, between master and man and settling disputes. They were also in the nature of benefit societies, from which the workmen, in return for the contributions which they had made when in health and vigour to the common stock of the Guild, might be relieved in sickness or when disabled by the infirmities of old age. In all these respects they formed a model after which the Guilds throughout England and Scotland were formed.

The London Companies were originally almost wholly Craft Guilds; and one of the most striking features in their history is the mastery which at a very early period they obtained in the municipality of the city. Even to this day the Guilds of London possess more power and a greater control in the municipal government than in any other city in the world. Two causes led to this mastery. They were invested with the sole right of conferring the freedom (in nearly all other places the granting of the freedom was vested in the governing body or municipality); and they early became possessed of great wealth, and, as a natural consequence, exercised a powerful influence among the general body of citizens.

The London Guilds were thus able to assert and maintain their independence to a far greater extent than the Guilds throughout England and Scotland; they preceded the constitution of the city itself, and never lost their original power and influence. "England," says Brentano, "must be considered as the birthplace of Guilds, and London, perhaps, as their cradle. At least there is documentary evidence that the constitution of the city was based upon a Guild." The London Guilds still retain much of their predominance in regard to municipal affairs; and no small amount of their present troubles is due to the fact of their having clung too tenaciously to the ancient rights and privileges they possessed. They have not been wise in their day and generation in yielding up the controlling power they exercised in connection with the government of the city. They have stubbornly refused to conform to the reforming spirit of the age; and there is now every probability that the hand of reform will be applied more drastically than it would have been had they been less tardy in reading the signs of the times. A keen struggle of a double character seems to be impending. On the one side, the citizens of London will make every effort to obtain as large a slice of the enormous wealth of the Companies as they can; and, on the other, the London Companies will struggle to retain as much of their ancient power and influence as possible. Into these questions, however, we have no desire to enter; it will be sufficient for our purpose to give a brief sketch of those great companies with the view of assisting us to understand the nature of the Guilds which were formed after the model of the early London Guilds. It may be here noted that the name Livery Company was adopted in consequence of the members of the governing bodies wearing elaborate robes or livery, the members who were entitled to wear these robes coming to be known as liverymen.

The Royal Commission which was appointed in 1880, consisting of Lord Derby, the Duke of Bedford, Lord Sherbrook, Lord Coleridge, Sir Richard Cross, Sir Nathaniel Rothschild, Sir Sydney Waterlow, Alderman Cotton, Mr. Albert Pell, Sir Henry James, Mr. J. B. Firth, and Mr. Thomas Burt, had authority to enquire into the circumstances and dates of the foundation of the Companies, the objects for which they were founded, and how far these objects had been carried into effect; and into any Acts of Parliament, charters, trust deeds, decrees of Court, or other documents founding, regulating, or affecting the said Companies. They were also empowered to inquire into the constitution and governing bodies of the Companies, and the mode of admission of freemen, liverymen, and other members; to ascertain the extent and nature of the property of, or held in trust for or by, the Companies, both real and personal, and the mode in which the property is managed and the income is expended. The powers of the Commission were fully exercised, and it is to the credit of the Guilds that they loyally responded to the demand made upon them for information, which they had hitherto been exceedingly jealous of affording. Five huge blue books were filled with the results of the labours of the Commission, containing a vast amount of interesting and valuable historical matter.

There is a remarkable blank in history respecting the period between what may be termed the Roman London, and the London of the thirteenth century. An attempt has been made to trace an unbroken connection between the two periods, but the attempt has been only partially successful. It is only from the rudimentary municipal constitution which Alfred planted that any connection can be traced with the mediæval and modern Corporations. We have already referred to the Craft Guilds that were undoubtedly in existence among the Romans themselves; but it is only from the similarity of the Guilds known in the mediæval period that we can even assume that the Romans founded them in this country. There is no positive trace of a connection between them, at least so far as London is concerned, and great diversity of opinion exists among historians on the point.

As the Craft Guilds and Merchant Guilds were the germ of the municipalities of Europe, so were they also the germ of the municipality of London. In Scotland the connection maintained between the Guilds and public bodies was of a very fragmentary character, and of slight account compared to what exists in London. At the present day, notwithstanding the alterations which have taken place on the constitution of

the Companies of London, the body known as the Common
Hall, and which is composed of members of the Livery Companies, continues jointly with the Court of Aldermen to elect
the Lord Mayor and certain other important civic functionaries;
while for five hundred years, up to the year 1835, membership of
a City Company was compulsory before full citizenship of the
city of London could be enjoyed. The difference in this respect
between the London Guilds and the Guilds in Scotland is very
marked. The power of granting the freedom was very early
conferred on the Town Councils in Scotland; the Crafts Guilds
simply tested the qualifications of the applicants; but in
London the Guilds both tested the qualifications and granted
the freedom.

In the London Guilds there have always been three grades
of membership—(1) simple membership, the possession of the
freedom which makes a "freeman" or "freewoman;" (2)
membership of what is called "the livery;" and (3) a place on
the "court" or the governing body. The freedom of the
Companies has been obtainable in two ways—(1) by apprenticeship; and (2) by patrimony, the latter mode accounting for the
fact that so many of the freemen and liverymen of London are
not *bona fide* craftsmen. A system of apprenticeship, however,
was an essential element in the Guilds in their earlier history.
All apprentices had to serve with a freeman for a period of
seven years, at the end of which time they were admitted to
the freedom of the Company. The "liverymen" are simply a
superior grade of freemen, consisting (1) of craftsmen who
are employers of labour, and (2) persons of some wealth and
position who have joined the Companies by patrimony or by
purchase, and who need not necessarily be craftsmen. The
number of liverymen is limited, an Act of the Court, dated
27th July, 1697, being still in force, to the effect "that no
person shall be allowed to take upon himself the clothing of
any of the 12 Companies unless he have an estate of £1000;
or of any of the inferior Companies unless he have an estate
of £500." In some cases as much as £100 has to be paid by an
individual who is "called" to the livery. At the present day
a person joining one of the leading London Companies as a
freeman by purchase might, in his progress from the position

of a mere freeman to full membership, have to pay upwards of £300 in fees and fines. Apart from their privileges and position in connection with the municipal government of London, freemen and the widows and orphans of freemen are entitled, in the case of poverty and in old age (1) to be received into the almshouses of the Companies which have almshouses: and (2) to pensions and casual relief out of the trust funds which have been left to the Companies for that purpose. They are also relieved out of the general income, i.e., that part of the Companies' income which is in the eye of the law not trust income. Liverymen and their widows receive pensions varying from £50 to £150 a year.

The Companies, while they exercise a considerable amount of control in the municipal affairs of London, have through their courts or governing bodies the entire control of their own affairs, the appointment of their officials, the management of their property, the admission to the freedom, livery, and court, the administration of their charitable trusts, the appointment of incumbents to the Companies' livings, and of the masters of their schools. Although the municipality of London can now confer the freedom irrespective of the Companies, the Corporation possesses a very slight, hardly more than a nominal, control over the Companies. In short, they retain full possession of, and control over, their enormous property, valued by the Royal Commissioners several years ago at not less than fifteen millions sterling, and which it was calculated would in the course of twenty years be increased to twenty millions if the existing rate of accumulation continued.

The London Guilds are at present divided into two classes, namely, twelve Great Companies — the Mercers, Grocers, Drapers, Fishmongers, Goldsmiths, Skinners, Taylors, Haberdashers, Salters, Ironmongers, Vintners, and Cloth Workers, and sixty-two minor Companies; but some of the so-called minor Companies are wealthier than their great neighbours. The total membership is only something like 10,000, about 1500 of whom form the Courts of the Companies. On an examination of the register for 1882 it was found that "the liverymen, from whom the members of the Courts are selected, are a body consisting of persons following professions, persons engaged in commerce, or persons who have retired from business. A considerable number are men of eminence; and many members of the House of Commons are liverymen. The Aldermen who represent the City belong to the several Companies, and are Common Councilmen."

The admission by patrimony has produced a most striking effect on the membership of the liveries and the constitution of the courts. Where a family has continued prosperous from generation to generation, and its members were able to join the liveries, they very soon came to possess a position of paramount influence. A remarkable instance of this is to be found in the case of the Mercers' Company, the court of which is recruited from a livery of 97, on which certain families are represented by as many as 9 or 10 members. Before leaving this part of the subject it may be of some interest to state that the Royal Commission, to which reference has been made, recommended that the State should intervene (1) for the purpose of preventing the alienation of the property of the Companies ; (2) securing the permanent application of a considerable portion of the Corporation income to useful purposes ; and (3) declaring new trusts in cases in which a better application of the trust income of the Companies has become desirable.

The London Companies do not now pretend to be bodies of craftsmen. One of their leading members, Alderman Cotton, informed the Commission that for 400 years the larger number of the members did not pretend to have followed the crafts of their Companies ; and from this fact he argues that "any forced devolution of their funds in aid of such trades would be a gross injustice." The corporate or non-trust income—that is, income apart from revenue from bequests, and mortifications—amounts to about £600,000 per annum, £175,000 of which is spent on " maintenance," £100,000 on entertainments, and about £150,000 on benevolent objects. £40,000 a year is paid to the members of the governing bodies as " court fees," and £60,000 on salaries. The highest fee paid for attendance at a meeting is five guineas, and the lowest half a guinea ; and in some cases as much as £300 a year is paid to one individual. The salaries are also on a liberal scale. The clerks receive about £700 a year, and the higher officials from £1500 to £2000.

The entertainments given by the Companies, and which cost £100,000 a year, are of two kinds—(1) banquets to the liveries, and (2) dinner parties which take place on the days on which the courts meet. In the larger Companies two or three of the former kind are held annually, while numerous entertainments are given to persons of eminence and royal personages both at home and from abroad. In addition to the £150,000 spent out of the corporate revenue on benevolent objects there is a trust revenue of about £200,000 available for similar purposes. Out of this large sum £85,000 is applied for the relief of old and decayed members, about £15,000 less than is spent on entertainments, and within £25,000 of what is required for salaries. The Companies have been wisely bestirring themselves for some time back in educational matters. They support between thirty and forty schools, chiefly middle class and classical. The City and Guilds of London Technical Institute is also supported by the Companies, and is doing a large amount of good work in promoting technical education throughout the kingdom.

CHAPTER IV.

THE CRAFT GUILDS IN SCOTLAND.

In Scotland, Merchant and Craft Guilds sprang up and flourished for over four centuries to as great, if not indeed a greater, extent than in any part of Europe. The burgh and other records of Edinburgh, Glasgow, Dundee, Aberdeen, Stirling, and other places, as well as the legislative enactments of the Scottish Parliament and the charters granted by successive sovereigns, afford abundant evidence of the important part they played in the civil, commercial, and industrial life of the burghs. Whether or not they sprang up spontaneously in Scotland or were introduced from the Continent or from England, it is impossible to say, although there is no doubt of the fact that at different periods in the early history of the country considerable numbers of craftsmen were brought into Scotland from abroad. But it is at least clear that these associations found a congenial home among the Scottish people. All the early acts and ordinances extant of these associations bear remarkable evidence of the outstanding national characteristic, thrift; and although the primary object in forming the associations was the protection of trading privileges, the making of provision for old age, dependants, and for poor brethren has always been a prominent characteristic. The members helped each other in sickness, in poverty, in infirmity, and in preserving the morals of the community, and until quite recent times performed all the functions of provident and insurance societies, burial clubs, annuity associations, and such like organisations. And it is not going too far in the direction of self-laudation to say that in no country were the virtues of thrift and forethought in providing for the proverbial "rainy day" more marked than in Scotland; whilst it is an equal pleasure to record that among the burghs in Scotland there are none that exhibited these virtues in a greater degree than Aberdeen. This will appear later on when we come to deal with the financial position and progress of the Aberdeen Trades.

The Craft Associations in Scotland had, as can be readily understood, all a strong family likeness. Their privileges were almost identical; they had all the same battle to fight with the Merchant Burgesses in regard to their relative rights —Edinburgh, Glasgow, Dundee, Aberdeen, Perth, and Stirling having all common indentures or agreements entered into about the same period after prolonged conflicts and legal contests; and each of the Crafts had a constitution and governing body as nearly alike as possible. A history of the development of the one is therefore very much a history of the others, and as the Aberdeen Crafts will be dealt with fully, it is not necessary to give anything but a brief general statement of the Crafts in a few of the leading towns

In Edinburgh there are twelve Incorporated Trades (at one time there were fourteen)—namely, Goldsmiths, Skinners, Furriers, Hammermen, Masons, Tailors, Bakers, Fleshers, Cordiners, Weavers, Waulkers, and Bonnetmakers. In Glasgow there are fourteen Trades—Hammermen, Tailors, Cordiners, Maltmen, Weavers, Bakers, Skinners, Wrights, Coopers, Fleshers, Masons, Gardeners, Barbers, and Dyers and Bonnetmakers. A curious speculation has arisen about the number of the Crafts in each burgh, both in this country and on the Continent. In Edinburgh and Glasgow there were fourteen; in Aberdeen and Stirling seven; and it is conjectured that, in granting and confirming the deeds of incorporation, the authorities had prominently in their minds the scriptural number of seven, or a multiple thereof! The Glasgow Trades House or Convener Court is composed as follows:—The Hammermen, Tailors, and Cordiners, a Deacon and five assistants; Maltmen, their visitor and five assistants; Weavers, their Deacon and four assistants; Bonnetmakers and Dyers, their Deacon and one assistant; the Bakers, Skinners, and Wrights, Coopers, Fleshers, Masons, Gardeners, Barbers, each their Deacon and three assistants, being in all fifty-four in number. The office-bearers consist of a Deacon-Convener and collector. In 1882 the Trades House and

Trades had a total revenue of £23,233 19s. 5d., their stock amounting to close upon £500,000.

In Stirling there are seven Incorporated Crafts, three "tolerated communities," and an "*omnium gatherum.*" The seven Crafts are—Hammermen, Weavers, Tailors, Shoemakers, Fleshers, Skinners, and Bakers; and the three tolerated communities—Maltmen, Mechanics, and Barbers. The "*omnium gatherum*" is an association similar to the Aberdeen Pynours or Shore Porters. The total funds belonging to the Stirling Trades amount to between £3000 and £4000.

There are eight Incorporations in Perth—Hammermen, Glovers, Bakers, Shoemakers, Tailors, Fleshers, Wrights, Weavers. In few if any of the burgh councils were the Craftsmen so strongly represented as in Perth. By a resolution of the Convention of Burghs held in Edinburgh in 1658 the number of craftsmen in the Council was fixed at 13, the members of the Guildry in the Council remaining as before. This was the origin of the combination known as the "Beautiful Order" that ruled in the town till the Burgh Reform Act. There are neither Seals of Cause nor Charters in existence, and the Town Records before 1600 are reported to be illegible. The records of the Convener Court consist of only one book— the minute-book at present in use; and none of the Incorporations have documents of the early centuries of their history. According to the tradition of the Glovers they had a charter from William the Lion; and the Hammermen Incorporation, which ranks as the premier Incorporation, claims a no less ancient origin.

When King James VI. visited Perth in 1617, among the amusements provided for him were the "Sword Dance" by the Glovers, and the "Egyptian Dance" by the Bakers; and at the visit of Charles I. in 1633 the monarch was received with great honours—the Glovers and other trades taking part in the festivities. On that occasion the "Sword Dance" was again performed. The dancers, thirteen in number, dressed in green caps, silver strings, red ribbons, white shoes, with bells about the legs, schering rapiers in their hands, and all other abulziment, danced the "Sword Dance" with many difficult knotts and *allafallajessa*, five being under, and five above upon their shoulders ; three of them dancing through their feet, drinking of wine, and breaking of glasses among them, which " God be praised," says the old record, " was acted and did without hurt and skaith to any, which drew us to great charges and expenses, amounting to the sum of three hundred and fifty merks, yet not to be remembered because we was graciously accepted by our Sovereign and both estates to our honour and great commendation." When Queen Victoria visited Perth in 1842 a glover, dressed in one of the dresses that were worn in 1633, walked in the procession of the citizens with the cap on head and the bells jingling with every step. The Hammermen Incorporation include Goldsmiths, Sword Slippers, Saddlers, Blacksmiths, workers in the different metals, and Watchmakers. The Glovers and Skinners form one Incorporation, and the Wrights include Masons, Glaziers, Bookbinders, and Barbers.

In Dundee there are nine Trades incorporated, namely, Bakers, Shoemakers, Glovers, Tailors, Bonnetmakers, Fleshers, Hammermen, Weavers, and Waulkers (Dyers). There is also an Incorporation of " The Three Trades," consisting of Wrights, Masons, and Slaters, but the Convener is elected by the Nine Trades. These form what is called the General Fund Court, but each trade has its own individual court for the management of its funds. The fees of admission to the General Fund are—£2 10s. for a member's son or son-in-law ; and £10 for extraneans. The Convener is a member of the Harbour Board, and also sits at all the principal Trusts in the city. The Dundee Trades are not wealthy, the entry money into the individual Incorporations being trifling.

In the larger burghs in Scotland the Crafts continued to flourish under the altered condition of local government to a remarkable degree. They have now, it is true, changed their character, and a number of the associations have little accumulated stock ; but they still perform many useful functions, and have a future before them in the direction of encouraging technical and secondary education among the industrial classes, which would still further extend their usefulness. Some of them are already moving in this direction ; but there is abundant scope for greater exertions and development in this respect. There is an obvious lack in the present day of organised effort for the promotion of technical instruction among young craftsmen. When a lad leaves school to commence his apprenticeship he is to a very large extent left to his own resources, and allowed to pick up a knowledge of the scientific side of his trade as best he may. And in the hurry of production, comparatively little attention is paid to the training of the head as well as the hands—to giving the apprentice a knowledge of the technical and scientific part of his business as well as the purely mechanical. This gap must be filled, and there are no institutions so well fitted to undertake systematic effort in this direction as the craft associations which in the past made the proper training of apprentices one of their first duties. Writing recently on the necessity for a scientific organisation of our industries, which the changed conditions of the time render indispensible to their prosperity, Professor Huxley puts the case thus :—" I do not think I am far wrong in assuming that we are entering—indeed, have already entered—upon the most serious struggle for existence to which this country has ever been committed. The latter years of the century promise to see us embarked in an industrial war of far more serious import than the military wars of its opening years. On the East the most systematically instructed and best informed people in Europe are our competitors ; on the West an energetic offshoot of our own stock, grown larger than its parent, enters upon the struggle possessed of natural resources to which we can make no pretension, and with every prospect of soon possessing that cheap labour by which they may be effectually utilised." Here is a field large enough for all the spare energies and available means of all our craft associations throughout the country ; and a remembrance of what they owe to their forefathers in many respects ought to be a stimulus to their heirs and descendants to do more even than they are doing for the rising generation.

PART II.

THE RISE OF THE ABERDEEN CRAFTS.

CHAPTER I.

SPECIAL PRIVILEGES OF CRAFTSMEN.

THE great change which has taken place in the municipal government of Aberdeen during the last half century renders it somewhat difficult for the present generation, living under new jurisdictions, new laws, and new conditions and customs, to realise the place and position occupied by the craft associations for over four centuries. The power which they possessed and the jurisdiction they exercised in virtue of Royal Charters, Acts of Parliament, and Acts of Council, were far more extensive than is generally supposed. Their monopoly of trading privileges, so far as their own handicrafts were concerned, was but one thing. They were much more than mere industrial or trading societies; they had a far wider scope. They embraced a rigid supervision of the whole conduct of the individual; all the journeymen, servants, and apprentices in the town, as well as the members proper, came within the jurisdiction of the deacons and their courts. Each craft acted as its own parochial board; they were the only friendly and benefit societies in existence, and to a certain extent members were assisted by loans out of the general funds to carry on their business. It will be readily understood, therefore, that as the individuals connected with the craft associations, both directly and indirectly, formed by far the largest proportion of the population for over four hundred years, the history of these societies cannot fail to assist in throwing light on the habits, customs, and

general mode of living of the people from the twelfth
century down to within less than half a century ago.   Under
the jurisdiction of these associations the individual gave up
almost all freedom of action on religious and social, as well as
trading, concerns; and the different acts and statutes passed
in these associations, and to which we will refer more in detail
as we proceed, will illustrate the extent to which individual
or personal liberty was voluntarily resigned in favour of the
common weal.

The early history of the Craft Guilds or associations in
Aberdeen is to some extent traditional.   We have evidence of
the existence of special trading privileges as far back as the
twelfth century, but it is not until well into the fifteenth
century that the public records give us any direct information
of the existence of organised bodies of craftsmen.   Deacons
or Masters of the Craft are known to have been general in all
the leading burghs in Scotland about 1424, but it is impossible
to fix the precise date at which any particular Craft formed
an association with "ane wise man of the Craft" at its head.
The introductory chapters which have already been given on
Merchant and Craft Guilds both at home and abroad, should
assist in throwing some light on that period of the history of
the Aberdeen Crafts which may be considered traditional—
the period embraced between the date when trading charters
were first granted to the town, down to the time when
mention is made of their functions and privileges in the Burgh
Records.

The earliest charters granted to Aberdeen had reference to
trading privileges solely.   Charters confirming the town in
the possession of its property came at a much later date; in
its infancy the town only sought protection to hold its market,
and carry on its small trading concerns freely and peaceably.
In 1196, William I. (King William the Lion) granted the
following charter to burgesses in and north of Aberdeen :—

William, by the grace of God King of Scots, to all good men of his
whole land greeting, Know all men present and to come, that I have
granted, and by this my charter have confirmed to my burgesses of Aberdeen, and to all the burgesses of Moray, and to all my burgesses dwelling
to the north of the munth (?) [the Grampian Hills] their free hanse, to be
held where they will, and when they will, as freely and peaceably, fully

and honourably, as their ancestors in the time of King David, my grand-father, had their hanse freely and honourably. Wherefore I strictly forbid anyone to trouble or disturb them therein, on pain of my full forfeiture.

By this charter it is evident that similar privileges had been granted during the reign of David I. (1124-53), but it is not improbable that these privileges had been granted without any formal written charter. In point of fact, charters in writing were scarcely known in the North of Scotland at this period, their introduction taking place in the reign of David's brother, Alexander I.

King William also granted "speciall fredomes to the whole burgesses of Scotland," one of these being that no prelate, earl, baron, or secular person shall presume to buy skins, hides, or such like merchandise, but that they shall sell the same to merchants or burgesses within whose sheriffdom and liberty the sellers of such merchandise dwell; and also that the merchandise aforesaid and all the other merchandise shall be presented at the mercet and mercet cross of burghs and there " preofferit " to the merchants of the burgh " effectuoaslie " without fraud or gyle, and the custom thereof be paid to the King. By two separate charters, King William confers similar privileges to the burgesses of Aberdeen specially, giving them also exemption from tolls and customs in all markets and fairs within the Kingdom. Both these charters are dated Aberdeen, 1179.*

It will be observed that these charters were granted to " my burgesses " generally. Here we find the starting point with regard to both merchant and craft associations. This is the basis on which the superstructure rests, and unless this fact is kept clearly in view it will be impossible to understand the growth and development of the merchant and craft associations known as Guilds or Crafts. The rights conferred are conferred generally, and the distinctions between the

---

* It may be mentioned in this connection that King William's name is very closely associated with the Aberdeen Trades. In the earlier part of his reign he erected a palace (the site of which would be about the foot of the present Exchange Street), which was afterwards gifted to the monks of the Holy Trinity. This palace, at which King William occasionally took up his residence, became the property of Dr. William Guild, and was gifted by him to the Incorporated Trades in 1633. In an inventory of the furniture in this edifice, taken at the time it came into possession of the Trades, there are mentioned King William's chair, King William's table, and his picture, all of which are still extant. Fuller reference to the old Trinity monastery will be made in a subsequent chapter.

D

privileges of the merchants and the craftsmen arose gradually, before being recognised by law or royal charter. When we keep this cardinal fact before us as to the general nature of the original gifts of right to trade and other privileges, we can trace not only the development, but the causes of all the various conflicts and differences that arose as the towns increased in importance, and advanced in their ideas of government and the relative rights of citizenship.

The word burgess, which has, it is said, a Roman origin, simply meant a citizen or inhabitant. Burgesses were the legally recognised inhabitants of a place, hamlet, or village, or any considerable collection of families—groups of individuals who, by trade and the use of handicrafts, were seeking to maintain an independent existence, and not be entirely subject to the nobles and chieftains of the land. The conditions and privileges of burgess-ship have varied in different periods and in different parts of the kingdom, but, in its simple and original form, it meant a legally recognised inhabitant and nothing more.

In the twelfth century, when the first recognition of burgesses by the Crown in Scotland took place—or at least of which there is any record—the villages and towns in Scotland were both few in number and scantily populated. Previous to that, they had not been deemed worthy of special recognition; it was only when the inhabitants became sufficiently numerous to be of service to the king in times of emergency that they were recognised, and that the right to trade and protect themselves against invasion was granted. The earliest towns have been well described as a "mere bit of land within the lordship, whether of the king or some great noble or ecclesiastic, whose inhabitants, either for purposes of trade and protection, came to cluster together more closely than elsewhere." Thus the granting of trading privileges and protection in the possession of any property they might acquire, came to be the first means of knitting the burgesses together, first into a body known in some parts of the country as the Frith Guild, formed for the purposes of order and self-defence; and next as a Guild for defending and protecting their means of livelihood as well as their lives. As time wore

on, the burgesses divided themselves into two classes. The merchant class, as Hallam says, "gradually concentrated themselves on greater operations of commerce, on trades which required a larger capital, while the meaner employments of general traffic were abandoned to their poorer neighbours." Motley, in his history of the Dutch Republic, also gives an excellent description of the rise of towns, which may, with remarkable accuracy, be applied to burghs in this country:—
"By degrees the class of freemen, artisans, and the like, becoming the more numerous, built stronger and better houses outside the castle gates of the ' land's master,' or the burghs of the more powerful nobles. The superiors, anxious to increase their own influence, favoured the progress of the little boroughs. The population, thus collected, began to divide themselves into Guilds. These were soon afterwards erected by the community into bodies corporate ; the establishment of the community, of course, preceding the incorporation of the Guilds."

Much confusion has arisen in attempting to make out that the Craft or Trade Guilds sprang out of the Merchant Guilds. Neither in Scotland nor anywhere else was this the case. Both had the one common origin, and the division or separation into distinct classes, having distinct and separate interests at stake in the community, was simply the natural outcome of their conflicting interests. The confusion on this point has chiefly arisen from the fact that in some places merchant trading was more extensively carried on than handicrafts ; but as a matter of fact there were more instances of an exactly opposite nature, where the craftsmen became and were known to be associated into Guilds before the merchants. Originally they both belonged to the one general class designated as burgesses, and only became separated when their particular interests began to conflict. It is a simple case of development. First, the general body of burgesses loosely brought together ; then followed the grant of rights and privileges; then arose combinations in each class for the defence of the privileges pertaining to their particular branch of trade or industry. But at no time were the crafts under the control of the merchants. The merchant burgesses, it is true, had greater influence in the Town Councils than the craftsmen, as was the case in Aberdeen, but the one class of associations did not spring from the other; they all sprang into existence on account of the trading privileges granted to the general body of the burgesses or inhabitants.

On 12th February, 1222, a charter, of which a translation follows, was granted to Aberdeen by Alexander II. :—

Alexander, by the grace of God King of Scots, to the bishops, abbots, earls, barons, justiciars, sheriffs, provosts, officers, and all good men of his whole land, clergy and laity, greeting. Know all men present and to come that I have granted and by this my charter have confirmed to my burgh and to my burgesses of Aberdeen, the rights and privileges that my predecessors granted to the burgh and to the burgesses of Perth, that is to say to hold their market on Saturday in every week. And I have rightly given my sure protection to all good men who shall come to that market. And I forbid anyone wrongously to inflict injury or annoyance or inconvenience upon them while coming to market or while returning, on pain of my full forfeiture. I also strictly forbid any stranger merchant to buy or to sell anything within the Sheriffdom of Aberdeen outwith my burgh of Aberdeen, in despite of my protection. But stranger merchants are to bring their merchandise to my burgh of Aberdeen, and there sell the same and receive their money. If, however, any stranger merchant shall, in despite of my protection, be found within the Sheriffdom of Aberdeen buying or selling anything, he is to be apprehended, and kept in custody, until I shall have declared my pleasure regarding him. I likewise strictly forbid any stranger merchant to cut his cloth for sale in the market of Aberdeen, save from the day of the Ascension of our Lord to the Feast of St. Peter's Chains; between which terms it is my will that they cut their cloth for sale in the market of Aberdeen, and there buy and sell their cloth and other merchandise in common with my burgesses in like manner as my proper burgesses : saving my rights. I likewise ordain that all who dwell in the burgh of Aberdeen, and wish to take part with my burgesses in the market, take part with them in paying my dues, whose men soever they be. I likewise forbid the keeping of any tavern in any town within the sheriffdom of Aberdeen, save where a knight is lord of the town and dwells therein; and there no tavern save one only is to be kept. I likewise grant to the same, my burgesses of Aberdeen, that they have their Merchant Guild, the waulkers and weavers being excluded. I likewise strictly forbid anyone dwelling outwith my burgh of Aberdeen within the Sheriffdom of Aberdeen to make or cause to make cloth, dyed or shorn, within the Sheriffdom of Aberdeen, save my burgesses of Aberdeen who are of the Merchant Guild, and who take part in paying my dues with my burgesses of Aberdeen; with the exception of such as had hitherto their charter securing this privilege. Wherefore I strictly forbid anyone within the Sheriffdom of Aberdeen to presume to make cloth, dyed or shorn, on pain of my full forfeiture. If, however, any person's dyed or shorn cloth shall be found made in despite of this protection, I command my Sheriff to seize the cloth, and to do therewith as was the custom in the time of King David my great grandfather. I likewise strictly forbid any stranger outwith my burgh at Aberdeen to buy or to sell hides or wool, save within my burgh of Aberdeen. All these privileges and usages, however, I grant, and by this my charter confirm to them, without prejudice to the privileges and free usages which before this grant were bestowed on other burghs and burgesses within the bailiwick of Aberdeen. Moreover, I strictly enjoin my baillies of Aberdeen to render aid to my burgesses of Aberdeen, and rightly to maintain them in possession of the foresaid true usages of the burgh. And I forbid anyone to make bold wrongously to trouble my foresaid burgesses, in despite of the foresaid reasonable laws and usages, on pain of my full forfeiture.

In the curious exception made in the above charter regarding waulkers and weavers—an exception that is also made in charters granted by Alexander II. to Perth and Stirling—we have an indication that the merchants even at that early period had been desirous of securing the monopoly of dealing or selling, and of confining the craftsmen to the exercise of their particular crafts. The same exclusion was attempted during the reign of Edward I. in London, Winchester, Marlborough, Oxford, and Beverley, and are the first indications that we have of the long-standing conflict between the more plebeian crafts and the more wealthy merchant burgesses. In all countries, the weavers, and their fellow craftsmen the waulkers or dyers, were the first to make their existence known as a combined body, and it is thus interesting to note that in Scotland, as far back as the thirteenth century, they were specially mentioned in a charter excluding them from the same privileges as the Merchant Guild.

King Robert the Bruce granted six charters to Aberdeen, all of a more or less trading character. The first was a charter granting to the community the charge of keeping the forest of Stocket ; by the second he granted the privilege of holding the Trinity Fair in the town ; and by the third, which is dated Berwick, 10th December, 1319, he confirmed the burgesses in the property of the burgh, along with the mills, waters, rivers, fishings, small customs, tolls, courts, weights and measures, and all other liberties granted by His Majesty's predecessors. This charter is looked upon as the fundamental charter of the town.

In 1336, a portion of Edward's army, under Sir Thomas Roscelyn, laid Aberdeen waste. It was pillaged and burned by the English invaders, and some years elapsed before it recovered from the devastation. King David, who had been abroad at the time of his father's death in 1329, came to Scotland in 1341, and, along with his consort Johanna, paid several visits to Aberdeen, where he also held his first Parliament. It was about this time that he granted several charters to the town, confirming the burgesses in all their property and privileges, and it was also during his reign that the newly-restored town came to be called New Aberdeen. From this period trade began to develop with considerable rapidity. In the *Rotuli Scotiæ* there is frequent mention made of Aberdeen merchants obtaining passports to England to barter their commodities ; and the customs paid at this period also show that, compared with other towns in Scotland, Aberdeen must have been an active trading centre.

The mention of New Aberdeen recalls the fact that there are in the " archives " of the Aberdeen Trades several interesting documents pertaining to the trades in Old Aberdeen, showing that so far as trading privileges were concerned the two burghs acted independently. These documents include a translation of the charter granted by James IV. in 1498 in favour of the Right Rev. Father in Christ William Elphingston, Lord Bishop of Aberdeen, etc., etc., for his great services as Ambassador to England, France, Burgundy, and Austria, and for his other important, faithful, and useful labours for the good of the commonwealth, by which the village of Old Aberdeen is confirmed in the privileges of an Episcopal City and University, and erected into a free burgh of barony, holding of the said Bishop Elphingston and his successors, Bishops of Aberdeen, who are to have power of appointing a provost, baillies, and other magistrates ; and the burgesses thereof are allowed to buy and sell wines, wax, cloth, woollen, and linen or any other merchandise ; and to exercise the occuations of bakers, brewers, fleshers, fishers, and craftsmen of any other trade ; to have a cross and market-place, and a weekly market every Monday, and two public fairs—one on the Monday before Pasch (or Easter), to be called Skeir

Thursday's fair, and the other on St. Luke's day, to continue for a week. This Charter, which is dated Linlithgow,
21st August, 1498, was confirmed by an Act of Parliament of
Charles II., passed on 20th May, 1661. There is also a charter
granted by the Right Rev. Father in God George Halyburton,
Lord Bishop of Aberdeen, to the Trades of Old Aberdeen,
which confers upon them several privileges, and grants them
the liberty of erecting lofts for themselves in the Cathedral.
This charter is dated the Episcopal Palace, Old Aberdeen, 20th
April, 1684. A charter was granted by George I. confirming
all previous charters, and directing the town of Old Aberdeen
to be held as a barony of the Crown as coming in place of
the Bishops of Aberdeen, dated at St. James's, 19th February,
1719.

It was under these early charters that the craftsmen began
to form their associations. One of the first Acts of the reign of
James III. was to the effect that " no man of craft use merchandise be himself, nor sell merchandise either by himself, nor his
factors, nor his servants, unless he leave and renounce his craft
without colour or dissimulation." Thus the merchants and the
crafts were driven apart, and each had to form associations for
the protection of their particular privileges. As towns grew
in size, craftsmen of the same calling multiplied, and having
interests in common, it was natural for them to associate
together for the promotion of their mutual interests. Reading
and writing were unknown accomplishments among craftsmen,
and all interchange of ideas and information had to take place
by "word o' moo." When, therefore, they had interests in
common to protect they were compelled to meet and form
combinations of some sort. Out of such meetings the formation of private fraternities or societies, composed of the members
of the same handicraft, was an easy step. "Such private
societies existed long before the members sought public
recognition by the authorities, and before the magistrates of
the Royal Burghs had the power conferred upon them to
bestow exclusive privileges upon craftsmen." (Warden's
" Burgh Laws.")

When the crafts began to assume a position of importance
in the burghs, the Legislature took more particular cognisance

of them; and for their better organisation and "conduction," the second Parliament of James I., held at Perth, passed the following Act on 12th March, 1424 :—

It is ordainit that in ilk toune of ye realm, of ilk sundrie craft used yairin, be chosen a wise man of ye craft, and be consent of ye officer of ye toune, ye qlk shall be holdine Deacon or master over the rest for ye tyme, to governe and assaye all workis yat beis made be ye craftsmen of yat craft, sua that ye kingis leidges be not defraude and skaithed in tyme to cume as yai have been in tymes bygone threw untrue men of the craftes.

This is the first mention of deacons in an Act of Parliament. Previous to the passing of this Act the craftsmen appear to have elected their deacon without asking the consent of the "chief officier of the toune," perhaps for the good reason that in many of the burghs there was no chief officer at this period in existence. Three years after the passing of the above statute, another was passed which plainly indicates that the deacons and the crafts had been assuming more power than was deemed desirable. This Act emphatically declares :—

Whereas the statutes made in former Parliaments anent Deacons or crafts in the burghs of the Kingdom tended to the hurt and common loss of the whole kingdom, the King, with the advice of the three estates of the realm, has revoked the said statutes and wholly annulled them, forbidding in time to come the election of such deacons by the craftsmen in any burghs of the kingdom, or the exercise by them though otherwise elected of the duties of deacons, or the summoning of their customary assemblies which are believed to resemble meetings of conspirators.

The Act then proceeds to specify the duties to be performed by the Wardens who were to be chosen by the Councils :—

It is statute and ordanit that men of Crafts within burrows shall have for a year to come of every Craft a Warden chosen by the Councill of the burgh, who, with counsel of other discreet men unsuspected, assigned to him by the said Councill shall examine and appryze the matter and the workmanship of ilk Craft, and sett it to a certain price, the whilk if any breakes, the said Warden shall punish the said breakers in certain pain, whom, if he punish not, the Alderman, Bailies, and Councill of the burgh shall punish them in certain pain ; whom if they punish not, the king shall have a certain pain of that burgh. The pain of the breakers of the price shall be escheat of the samen thing of the whilk the price beis broken, to be applied, the one half to the Warden of that Craft, and the other half to the common work of that burgh where it beis seen most expedient. The pain of the Pryzer, if he be negligent and punish not shall be in the unlaw of the Burrow Court as oft as he beis convict culpable, and fallyse, shall be applied for the half of the common purse of the town, and of the other where it beis most expedient to the work of the town. The pain of a Alderman, Bailies, and Councill of the Burgh that beis negligent in punishing of the Warden as oft as the default, shall be in ten pounds to the king, and shall be raised after that they be challenged and convict by the Chamberlain and his deputes, the whilk ordnance shall be extended to Measons, Wrights, Smiths, Taylors, Weavers ; and all others likewise generallie who has fees and handling shall be prysed as is before said, and attour to landward jurisdictions, ilk Burrow shall pryse in the Burrows, and punish the trespassers as the Wardens does in the Barronies, and if the Barron does not the Sheriff shall punish the Barron, and if the Sheriff does not they shall be in Amerciament to the King. And the Aldermen, Bailies, and Councill in Burrows shall inquire ilk month at least if the Warden of the Crafts pryse will and punish ye trespassers, and if any man complains of over great price or breaking of the price made or sett to the Alderman, Bailies, and Councill that they punish the pryser and gar the party complaining be assized under the pains aforesaid.

The above Act furnishes a striking illustration of what may be called the State regulation of industry instituted in the fifteenth century and continued down to very recent times. Wages were regulated, the price of manufactured goods of all kinds, from the penny loaf to a salmon barrel, fixed, the number of journeymen and apprentices strictly limited, and the quality of the work inspected. All these matters were subject to the control of the local authority and the craft associations acting under Royal Charters, Acts of Parliament, and Acts of Council.

It is evident from the numerous Acts passed at this period that the craftsmen had a hard time of it. No sooner was the election of deacons legalised, and the powers they were entrusted with put into operation, than the associations of craftsmen were condemned as conspiracies " of general prejudice to the kingdom," their gatherings denounced as "meetings of conspirators," and the election of deacons declared illegal. About 1457, however, the crafts seem to have taken the law into their own hands, and elected their deacons without obtaining the consent of the governing body of the town. An exemption had been made in the case of the goldsmiths of Edinburgh, who were authorised to appoint " ane officiar " to inspect all work and see that it was up to a certain standard ; and, taking advantage of this case as a precedent, the craftsmen throughout the country generally continued to elect their deacons in despite of the statute that was passed putting them down "in all tym cuming." This, however, was soon put a stop to. In 1491, the office was again abolished, because it was "understood by the king and the three estaits that the using of Deacons of Crafts in Burghs is richt dangerous, and as they use the same, may cause trouble to the leiges by convening together and making laws of their craft contrary to the common profit, whereby when one leaves work another dare not finish it," and "it is statute that ilk sik deakons sall cease for ane yeir, and have no power but to examine stuffe and warke wrocht by the craft ; that measons and wrichtes and uther men of craft wha statutis that they sall have fee alsweill for the halie daie as for the wark day sall be indicted as common oppressors and punished accordingly." For a time the craftsmen were less aggressive towards the Town Councils ; but as they gradually increased in numbers and influence in the communities, they commenced a long series of conflicts, the history of which, as far as Aberdeen is concerned, will be given in a subsequent chapter.

Very severe punishment was imposed upon craftsmen when they ventured to act independently or in any spirit of antagonism to the Town Council. For instance, on 18th May, 1484, we find that in Aberdeen, "ye alderman, baillies, and consale, becauss thae have foundin grete fault in ye craft of ye cordiners at yis tym, thae have put down ye deyknis of ye said craft, annuland al powaris that yai gef to thaim of befor, and will, fra hyncefurth, tak ye correction of thaim all in tym to cum, and to punyss thaim after yair demerits yt sal be committed in tym cummand."

The office of deacon-convener was never formally recognised by law in the same manner as that of the deacon. A convener of deacons is first heard of when the crafts had to combine for their common interests against what they considered encroachments in their privileges by the merchant class of burgesses. The first mention of a deacon-convener in Aberdeen occurs in connection with the Common Indenture in which George Elphinston, saidler, is designated as deacon-convener ; but, for reasons not far to seek, the Town Council of

that period do not appear to have looked on the office with
any degree of favour. An effort was made in 1591, as the
following extract from the Council Register will show, to put
down the office altogether, but the craftsmen seem to have
paid little heed to the edict, as they continued after a brief
interval to elect their convener as before :—

3rd November, 1591—The said day in the terms assignat to David
Castell, deacon to the wobsteris, Alexander Steven, deacon to the baxters,
William Spence, deacon to the cordinaris, Andrew Watsou, wricht, alleg-
ing him deacon to the wrichts, and Gilbert Blak, deacon to the couparis,
for thamselffis, and in name of the remauent deacons of the craftis of this
burgh to exhibit and produce before the prouest, baillies, and counsall
sic power authoritie and right granted be thame either be the Acts of
Parliament, or yit giffin to thame be His Grace, or any of his majesties
predecessoris, or be the magistrates and counsall of the said burgh to elect
and cheis ane deacon of deaconis, or deacon-convener, to assemble and
convene the haill crafts of this burgh, with certification that gif thai
failziet to produce the same this day the prouest, baillies and counsall
shall proceed against the said deacons for electing of the said Alexander
Steven, deacon-convener, and against the said Alexander for accepting,
exercising and using of the said office, as disturbers of the common weal,
quhytness, and peace of this burgh, contravenaris of his Majesties Acts of
Parliament and usurpairs of authoritie and power upon them to cheis and
have a deacon-convener prohibitt be his grace's lawis, and discern them to
have done wrang thereanent. And the sadis deaconis to desist and ceas
fra all cheising and electing of ony to be deacon of deacons or deacon-
convener to the craftis of this burgh hereafter, and the said Alexauder to
desist and cease frae all using and exercising of his said office in ony tym
coming, as the craft and ordinance set down thereanent upon the 27th of
October last by past at lynth does testify—The persons of the counsall
after calling they are to say, Alexander Rutherford, prouest, etc., being
all personallie present in the counsall hous, causit call all the saidis deacons
out the tollboyth window to compere this day before thaim to the effect
aforesaid and thay being oft tymes callit nane ane compearit except the
said Alexander Stevin, present deacon-convener to the saidis craftis, and
the saidis David Castill, deacon to the wobsteris quha being desired be
the counsall to satisfy the desire of the said ordinance maid upon the said
27th of Oct. for producing before them the power, authoritie, and right
which they and the saidis crafts had giffen and granted to them be Actis
of Parliament or be his Grace or his Hines predecessors or yet be the
magistrates of this burgh to elect and cheis ane deacon of deaconis, or
deacon-convener, and to produce whatsomever right they had giffane
thame power and authoritie to that effect (gif they any had) the said
Alexander Stevin, present deacon-convener to the saidis craftis, and the
said David Castell, deacon to the wobsteris, compearing personallie for

themselffes, aud in name of the remanent deaconis of the craftis of the saidis burgh, producit nathing for satisfyeing of the dyett according to the ordiuance of the said Act of Counsall of the date aforesaid ; And therefore the Provost, Baillies, and the persons of the Counsall foresaid have faud that the deaconis of the craftis of this burgh have done wraug in electing of the said Alexander Stevin, deacon of deacons, and deacon-couvener to thaim, and the said Alexander in the using and exercising of the said office without any power, right, or authoritie giffen or grantit to him to that office either be Actis of Parliament or be His Majesties predecessors, or yet be the magistrates of this burgh. And therefor descernit and ordainit the saidis deacons to desist and ceas frae all cheising and electing off ony deacons off deacons or deacon-convener, and the said Alexander Stevin fra all using and exercising of the said office in tym cuming.

For eight years after this deliverance, there is no mention of a deacon-convener being appointed, but, as will be seen from the following list, there is an almost unbroken line from 1587 down to the present day :—

LIST OF DEACON-CONVENERS, 1587—1886.

George Elphinston,	saidlar,	1587
Alexander Stiven,	baker,	1591
Gilbert Blak,	couper,	1599
George Elphinston,	saidlar,	1600
Gilbert Blak,	couper,	1601
John Mercer,	saidlar,	1612
Do.	do.	1613
George Bruice,	saidler,	1614
Andrew Watson,	wright,	1615
Gilbert Blak,	couper,	1616
James Gregory,	saidler,	1617
John Mercer,	saidler,	1618
Do.	do.	1619
Do.	do.	1620
James Gregorie,	saidler,	1621
Hew Anderson,	goldsmith,	1622
Do.	do.	1623
George Bruice,	saidler,	1625
John Mercer,	saidler,	1626
Thomas Gardyne,	tailzour,	1627
Alex. Chalmer,	couper,	1628
Thomas Garden,	tailzour,	1628
George Bruice,	saidler,	1629
John Mercer,	saidler,	1630
Thomas Gardine,	taylour,	1631
Thos. Robertsone,	cordoner,	1632
Hew Anderson,	goldsmith,	1633
William Ord,	wright,	1634
Thos. Robertsone,	cordiner,	1635
James Chrystie,	taylour,	1636
George Pyper,	wright,	1637
William Ord,	do.	1638
George Pyper,	wright,	1639
William Ord,	do.	1640
James Chrysty,	taylour,	1641
Thomas Clerke,	weaver,	1642
William Anderson,	couper,	1643
Patrick Annand,	baker,	1644
William Anderson,	goldsmith	1645
Do.	do.	1646
Do.	do.	1647
Alex. Williamson,	baker,	1648
Alex. George,	smith,	1648
John Malice,	couper,	1649
Alexander Clerk,	weaver,	1650
William Anderson,	goldsmith,	1651
George Moreson,	tailour,	1652
Do.	do.	1653
William Anderson,	couper,	1654
Patrick Murray,	baker,	1655
Alex. Cruickshank,	couper,	1656
William Christy,	goldsmith,	1657
Do.	do.	1658
Alexander Clerk,	weaver,	1659
William Scot,	wright,	1660
Do.	do.	1661
Walter Melvill,	goldsmith,	1662
William Chrystie,	goldsmith,	1663
Do.	do.	1664
Do.	do.	1665
Alex. Ettershank,	couper,	1666
Robert Lindsay,	goldsmith,	1667
Do.	do.	1668
Alex. Ettershauk,	couper,	1669

William Scot,	wright,	1670	George Robertson,	shoemaker,	1727
William George,	smith,	1671	William Smith,	taylor,	1728
Alexander Charles,	wright,	1672	Do.	do.	1729
Robert Clerk,	weaver,	1673	William Chrystall,	wright,	1730
George Rosse,	pewterer,	1674	Do.	do.	1731
Alex. Galloway,	goldsmith,	1675	William Smith,	taylor,	1732
James Blinshell,	weaver,	1676	Do.	do.	1733
James Shand,	couper,	1677	Alexander Forbes,	goldsmith,	1734
Do.	do.	1678	Do.	do.	1735
Alexander Idle,	cordiner,	1679	Robert Smith,	blacksmith,	1736
Do.	do.	1680	Do.	do.	1737
William Scott,	goldsmith,	1681	Patrick Barron,	wright,	1738
Do.	do.	1682	Do.	do.	1739
James Shand,	couper,	1683	John Auldjo,	baker,	1740
Alex. Patersone,	armourer,	1684	Do.	do.	1741
Alexander Idle,	schoomaker,	1685	John Sim,	couper,	1742
James Shand,	couper,	1686	Do.	do.	1743
John Wobster,	couper,	1687	John Auldjo,	baxter,	1744
John Leslie,	weaver,	1688	Do.	do.	1745
Alexander Scott,	glover,	1689	James Smith,	sadler,	1746
Patrik Whytt,	hookmaiker,	1690	Do.	do.	1747
James Smith,	blacksmith,	1691	John Auldjo,	baxter,	1748
Patrik Whytt,	hookmaker,	1692	John Sim,	cooper,	1749
William Phanes,	tailour,	1693	Do.	do.	1750
William Coutts,	wright,	1694	William Johnston,	pewterer,	1751
Patrik Whyt,	hookmaker,	1695	Do.	do.	1752
James Douglas,	baiker,	1696	James Smith,	sadler,	1753
John Chrystie,	tailour,	1697	Do.	do.	1754
Patrik Whyt,	hookmaker,	1698	George Donaldson,	weaver,	1755
William Coutts,	wright,	1699	Do.	do.	1756
James Douglas,	baiker,	1700	John Thom,	blacksmith,	1757
Patrik Whyt,	hookmaker,	1701	Do.	do.	1758
William Coutts,	wright,	1702	George Forbes,	baxter,	1759
Patrik Whyte,	hookmaker,	1703	Do.	do.	1760
James Douglas,	baiker,	1704	James Norie,	taylor,	1761
Patrik Whyte,	hookmaker,	1705	Do.	do.	1762
John Findlay,	couper,	1706	Colin Allan,	goldsmith,	1763
James Simpsone,	tayleor,	1707	Do.	do.	1764
Robert Smith,	tayleor,	1708	Patrick Durward,	baker,	1765
David Speedieman,	glover,	1709	Do.	do.	1766
Gilbert Moir,	couper,	1710	George Donaldson,	weaver,	1767
David Speedieman,	glover,	1711	Do.	do.	1768
John Findlay,	couper,	1712	William Duncan,	wright,	1769
William Lindsay,	goldsmith,	1713	Do.	do.	1770
Patrick Gray,	wright,	1714	George Davidson,	cooper,	1771
Do.	do.	1715	Do.	do.	1772
James Simpsone,	taylior,	1716	John Tower,	cooper,	1773
Do.	do.	1717	Do.	do.	1774
Alexander Smith,	cordoner,	1718	Robert Mackie,	skinner,	1775
Do.	do.	1719	Do.	do.	1776
James Simpson,	tailior,	1720	David Shirriffs,	wright,	1777
George Walker,	goldsmith,	1721	Do.	do.	1778
Do.	do.	1722	James Clark,	taylor,	1779
John Walker,	goldsmith,	1723	Do.	do.	1780
Do.	do.	1724	Thomas Taylor,	wright,	1781
James Simpson,	tayloir,	1725	Do.	do.	1782
George Robertson,	shoemaker,	1726	John Tower,	cooper,	1783

John Low,	taylor,	1784	Alex. M'Kenzie,	weaver,	1836
Do.	do.	1785	Do.	do.	1837
William Donald,	baker,	1786	James Topp,	baker,	1838
Do.	do.	1787	Do.	do.	1839
Alex. Hutcheon,	shoemaker,	1788	Alex. M'Kenzie,	weaver,	1840
Do.	do.	1789	Do.	do.	1841
John Wallace,	baker,	1790	James Clyne,	shoemaker,	1842
Do.	do.	1791	John Leslie,	weaver,	1843
Alex. Hutcheon,	shoemaker,	1792	Do.	do.	1844
Do.	do.	1793	Chas. Playfair,	gunsmith,	1845
James Clark,	taylor,	1794	Do.	do.	1846
Do.	do.	1795	William Murray,	wright,	1847
William Michie,	wright,	1796	Do.	do.	1848
Do.	do.	1797	Hugh Sutherland,	glazier,	1849
George Craig,	shoemaker,	1798	Do.	do.	1850
Do.	do.	1799	Robert Watson,	wright,	1851
Arthur Farquhar,	do.	1800	Do.	do.	1852
Do.	do.	1801	John Fraser,	shoemaker,	1853
John Leslie,	goldsmith,	1802	Do.	do.	1854
Do.	do.	1803	John Fyfe,	tailor,	1855
Alex. Thomson,	cooper,	1804	Do.	do.	1856
Do.	do.	1805	George Donald,	glazier,	1857
John Webster,	weaver,	1806	Do.	do.	1858
Do.	do.	1807	James M'Kenzie,	baker,	1859
David Reid,	wright,	1808	Do.	do.	1860
Do.	do.	1809	Robert Beveridge,	weaver,	1861
John Webster,	weaver,	1810	Do.	do.	1862
Do.	do.	1811	Robert Thomson,	tailor,	1863
William Douglas,	shoemaker,	1812	Do.	do.	1864
Do.	do.	1813	James Berry,	optician,	1865
William Nicol,	tailor,	1814	Do.	do.	1866
Do.	do.	1815	James Mitchell,	baker,	1867
William Douglas,	shoemaker,	1816	Do.	do.	1868
Do.	do.	1817	William Allan,	cabinetmaker,	1869
William Milne,	glazier,	1818	Do.	do.	1870
Do.	do.	1819	Daniel Laird,	tailor,	1871
Alex. Harper,	baker,	1820	Do.	do.	1872
Do.	do.	1821	Alexander Adam,	cooper,	1873
James Robb,	wright,	1822	Do.	do.	1874
Do.	do.	1823	James Abel,	baker,	1875
William Smith,	glazier,	1824	Do.	do.	1876
Do.	do.	1825	John Mitchell,	weaver,	1877
Andrew Affleck,	shoemaker,	1826	Do.	do.	1878
Do.	do.	1827	Alex. Robertson,	plumber,	1879
Alex. Mortimer,	baker,	1828	Do.	do.	1880
Do.	do.	1829	Peter Raeburn,	baker,	1881
David Carter,	hammerman,	1830	Do.	do.	1882
Do.	do.	1831	David Byres,	weaver,	1883
Alex. M'Kenzie,	weaver,	1832	Do.	do.	1884
Do.	do.	1833	Andrew Robb,	gunsmith,	1885
Alex. Cooper,	saddler,	1834	Do.	do.	1886
Do.	do.	1835			

CHAPTER II.

THE CRAFTS AND THE CHURCH—BEFORE AND AFTER THE REFORMATION.

ANY inquiry into the history of the craft associations in Aberdeen would be incomplete which did not take into account their relation to the church, both before and after the reformation; and the extent of its influence in determining their character, aims, and constitution. It may at first sight appear a somewhat far-fetched notion to say that the pageants and religious processions of the pre-reformation period helped in no small measure to bring about the combination of the craftsmen in the community under appointed leaders. But such undoubtedly was the case. These pageants, religious ceremonials, and miracle plays, constituted nearly all that the artizan classes of that early period had in the way of instruction either in religion or literature, recreation, and social intercourse, and when each separate body of craftsmen was called in to combine for the purpose of finding banners, ornaments, and other paraphernalia, they at the same time were naturally led to combine for more secular purposes, such as the protection of their trade privileges, the establishment of schemes for mutual aid in sickness and old age, and for kindred objects. In other respects, such as the light it throws on the origin of dramatic performances, and the nature of the influence exercised by the ecclesiastics, the connection between the church and the crafts in Aberdeen during the fifteenth and sixteenth centuries opens up an interesting field of inquiry, and few towns, either in England or Scotland, possess records so well fitted as those of our own ancient burgh to throw light on this somewhat obscure period in the history of the social and religious life of our country.

The ecclesiastics of the fifteenth century had a strong influence among all classes of the burgesses; and in the Town

Council, such as it then was, their influence was paramount. So far as the craft burgesses were concerned, the first burgess fee imposed was in the nature of a contribution to the church, generally a gift of wax "to decore" the altars, while nearly all the fines for breaches of the ordinances of the town went to the same destination.   The duties imposed on the citizens, nominally by the Town Council, but in reality inspired by the ecclesiastics, embraced not only the religious and moral conduct of the citizens, but extended to the regulation of their amusements and pastimes.   This influence was specially manifest in connection with the pageant and miracle plays, common throughout nearly the whole of Europe for over two centuries. Much though these performances have been condemned by a class of modern writers, it ought to be borne in mind that in giving them countenance the ecclesiastical authorities of the Roman Catholic Church encouraged them mainly as a means of impressing upon an ignorant people the fundamental doctrines of Christianity.   Supernatural displays and the use of rude imagery were the only means then available for teaching the people.   But while in their original design these plays were looked upon as sacred and devotional exercises, in course of time, they rapidly degenerated into gross buffoonery of sacred subjects and scriptural characters.   In the time of Gregory the Great (the twelfth century) the priests were in the habit of commemorating the passion of Christ by processions, choruses, chants, and dialogues, and gradually the laity were introduced to take part in them.   "The custom of representing miracle plays at certain church festivals and on other great occasions spread itself over the length and breadth of the land ; the custom was almost as universal as the celebration of the church festivals themselves.   During the fifteenth century these exhibitions had made such progress that nearly every large city had its own company of performers, generally composed of the various trade corporations, and the king himself and many of the nobility kept among their retainers complete companies of players who often went about from place to place giving performances.   They continued to be as common and popular as ever during the sixteenth century even after the regular drama had been developed, and did not cease to be represented in England till at least the beginning of the seventeenth century." [Keltie's " British Drama."]

The reference made to the various trade corporations taking part in these processions and plays is fully borne out by what occurred in Aberdeen. As early as 1440 a leader was appointed, called the Abbot of Bon-Accord, to conduct the play of Halyblude at Wyndmylhill, the eminence now known as the Porthill. His appointment is noted in the Council Register as follows :—

13th May, 1440—Curia Gilde tenta per prepositum in pretorio Burgi de Abirdene xiij die mensis Maij Anno Domino millesimo quadringentesimo et xlmo. Item, eodem die, per commune consilium concessus fuit Ricardo Kintor, tunc Abbati de Boneacord, vnus burgensis futurus faciendus, ad libitum suum quandocunque ipsum presentauerit pro expensis suis factis et faciendis in quodam ludo de ly Haliblude ludendo apud ly Wyndmylhill.

Two years after this appointment the following edict was issued, calling on the craftsmen to appear annually at "the offerand of our Lady" at Candlemas :—

Thir craftes underwritten sal fynd yearly in ye offerand of our Lady at Candlemas thir persounes underwritten, yat is to say—
                    The Littistaris sal fynd,
    The Empriour and twa Doctouris and alsmony honeste Squiares as
                            thai may.
        The Smythis and Hamermen sal fynd
    The Three Kingis of Culane and alsmony honeste Squiares as thai
                            may ;
                    The Talzoures sal fynd,
    Our Lady, Sancte Bride, Sancte Helene, Joseph and alsmony
                    Squiares as thai may.
                    The Skynnares sal fynd,
    Twa Bischopes, four Angels, and alsmony honeste Squiares as
                        they may.
        The Wobstares and Walkares sal fynd,
    Symion and his disciples and alsmony honeste Squiares, &c.
                    The Cordonares sal fynd,
    The Messyngear and Moyses and alsmony honeste Squiares, &c.
                The Fleschowares sal fynd,
    Twa or four Wodmen and alsmony honeste Squiares, &c.
            The Brethren of the Gilde sal fynd,
    The Knyghtes in harnace and Squiares honestely arait, &c.
                    The Baxtaris sal fynd,
    The Menstrals and alsmony honeste Squiares as they may, &c.

E

In one of his caustic notes, Joseph Robertson points out that the tailors are the only craftsmen who were not enjoined to find "honest" squires! The minstrels which the bakers had to find are often referred to in the Council Register, and seem to have been maintained in a somewhat similar manner to the chaplains of the altars in the kirk :—

28th January 1500.—The said day, it was statut, ordanit, and grantit be the alderman, balyeis, and maist part of the consal and comunite present for the tyme, that Jonhe and Robert, thar comone menstralis, sal haue resonabile diets, sevralie, throw the nichtbors of the towne ; And gif ony persone, or personis, refuss to resaue thame to thar dietis, it sal be lesum to them to gif to the said menstrals xij d. one the day, bat [both] for meat, drink, and wagis, for simpile folks.

13th January 1504.—The said day, the alderman and counsale grantit thame avand, in the townis nayme, to Davy Theman, foure markis, vsuale money of Scotlande, for the kepin of thar comon horelege and knock, and for ane vnce and [half] vnce of siluer, quhilk he put in the comon armes of the tovne, gevin to thai comone menstralis, quhene thai passit to our souerane Lordis marage, at the tounes comand ; quhilk thai grauntit to pay to the said Davy.

21st January 1509.—The said day, the borgh fundin be Robert Piper and Johnne Piper, comon menstralis, upoun David Ines, for the wranguiss withhaldin fra thame of thar dietis yerly, and thar fie, was fundin awaile; and for the quhilkis, it was deliuerit be ane suorne assis, Cristofer Prat, forspekar, that the said David was in ane amerciament of the court, and aw to pay to thame yerly xviij d. : Nothwithstanding, the alderman and baillies defalkit ij d. yerly ; and say the said Dauid sall pay to the said menstralis xvj d. yerly.

22nd January 1535.—The said day, the prouest and counsale, in name of the haill tovn, tharof thar exprest comand and chais, gevin and grantit to thame, convenit, an l elect Johnne Tulidelf and Wille Murray, to [be] the tovnis comond menstralis, during the tovnis vill ; Quhilk personis sall serve the guid tovn, as use hes bene in tymes bigane ; and sall pas every day, thro all the rewis and stretis of the guid tovn, at five hours in the morining, and betuix aucht and nyn at evin ; quhilk thai suore to do lelie and trulie : ffor the quhilk, thai [sal] haue ther dalie meit of the nychtbors of the guid tovin, annd, ilk day, of euery burgess of gild, they eit with xvj d., and of euery craftisman xij d. ; and sal pas thro all this tovin, and slip na man ; and quha refuss to gif thame meit and drink, sall gif them dobble vaigis ; and quhen they get doble vagis, they sal lef that day on the vaige, and pas to na man for meit and vaig that day.

24th November 1574.—The said day the haill counsale being warnit to this day, ordaint Johnne Cowpar to pas everie day in the mornyng, at four houris, and everie nycht at viij houris at ewyne, throw all the rewis of the

toune, playand vpon the Almany quhissil,* with ane servand with him,
playand on the taborine, quhairby the craftisman, thair servandis, and all
utheris laborious folkis, being warnit and excitat, may pas to thar labouris,
and fra thar labouris in dew and convenient tyme ; and ordains the said
Johnne to haff for his stipend and fee, yierlie, twa shilling of euerie burges
man, and xviijd. of euerie free craftisman, at four termes in the yier, Candilmes, the Ruid day, Lammes day, and Alhallow day ; and the first terme
to begyn at Candelmes next to cum, and that upon his gud seruice, endur-
ing the consellis will.

On the 30th April, 1445, " it was concludit, statute, and
ordanit be the comoune counsale and mony others of the gilde
for lettying and stancheying of diuerss enormyities done in tyme
bigane be the Abbits of this burgh callit Bone Acorde that in
tyme to come thai will give na feis to nae sic Abbotis ;" and it
was " sene speedful to tham that for this instant yher thai will
haue nae sic Abbot, bot thai will that the Alderman for the
tyme and a balyhe quham that he will tak til him supple that
faute." But this arrangement, which would suggest that
the Council were jealous of the influence exercised by these
functionaries, did not last long. On 8th May, 1496, " the
alderman, balyeis, and consale present for the tyme at the
Womanhill for uphaldin of the ald louabill consuetud, honor,
consalacion, and plesour of the burghe like as has bene usit in
tymes of thair worthie and honarabill progenitouris, chesit
Thomas Leslie and Robert of Cullane conjunctlie Abbats and
Priors of Bonaccord tile vyse and exerce the said office this
instant yer ; and granted to pay theme v. marks of the
common guds this tyme tuelf months."

It was also ordained by the alderman and council in 1484
that " the talzeours and al utheris craftismen within the toune
sal in tyme to cum beyr thare takyinis of thare craft apon
their beristis, and thare best aray on Candlimes day at the
Offerand ; and quha that contervenis and dois nocht sal tyne
their fredum for a yer." It was also ordained that each
craft should have a standard :—

23rd January, 1496.—The saide day, it was statut and ordainit be the
alderman, bailyeis, and consale, for the honor and defenss of the tone, that
everie craftsmen within the burghe sale ger mak ane standart for thar
craft.

* *Almany quhissil*—German whistle.

And on 12th January, 1512, it was ordained by the magistrates that "every craft within this towne sall have a pair of torcheiss, honestlie maid of four pund of wax, to decoir and worschip the sacrament on Corpus Christi day and at the Fest of Pasche, at the Resurrexioun, at Youle, and at all utther tymes quhen neid is to the honor of the towun; and ordainns all frie and unfrie to loit and scot and pay their part tharto as thai ar extendit to, be the deknys of thair craftis."

The exact nature of these plays and pageants remain shrouded in a good deal of obscurity. They have frequently been held up to ridicule; and many are the lampoons, rather unmerited, that have been made upon them. These lampoons, however, have served a very useful purpose. They supply us with interesting material as to the character of the plays which would not otherwise be in existence. Take for instance the following quotation from the "Popish Kingdom" describing the ceremonies of Corpus Christi day in Coventry :—

Then doth ensue the solemne feast of Corpus Christi Day,
Who then can shewe their wicked use, and fonde and foolish play?
The hallowed bread, with worship great, in silver Pix they beare
About the Church, or in the Citie passing here and theare.
His armes that beares the same, two of the welthiest men do holde,
And over him a Canopey of silke and cloth of golde
Foure others use to beare aloufe, least that some filthie thing
Should fall from hie, or some mad birde hir doung thereon should fling.
Christes passion here derided is, with sundrie maskes and playes,
Faire Ursley, with hir maydens all, doth passe amid the wayes :
And, valiant George, with speare thou killest the dreadful dragon here,
The Devil's house is drawne about, wherein there doth appere
A wondrous sort of damned sprites, with foule and fearefull looke,
Great Christopher doth wade and passe with Christ amid the brooke :
Sebastian full of feathered shaftes, the dint of dart doth feele
There walketh Kathren, with hir sworde in hande, and cruel wheele :
The Challis and the singing Cake with Barbara is led,
And sundrie other Pageants playde, in worship of this bred,
That please the foolish people well, what should I stande upon
Their Banners, Crosses, Candlesticks, and reliques many on,
Their Cuppes, and carved Images, that Priests, with count'nance hie,
Or rude and common people, beare about full solemlie?
Saint John before the bread doth go, and poynting towardes him,
Doth shew the same to be the Lambe that takes away our sinne :
On whom two clad in Angels shape do sundrie flowres fling,
A number great of sacring Belles with pleasant sounde doe ring.

The common wayes with bowes are strawde, and every streete beside
And to the walles and windowes all, are boughes and braunches tide.
The Monkes in every place do roame, the Nonnes abrode are sent,
The Priestes and schoolmen lowde do rore, some use the instrument.
The straunger passing through the streete, upon his knees doe fall ;
And earnestly upon this bread, as on his God, doth call.
For why, they counte it for their Lorde, and that he doth not take
The forme of flesh, but nature now of breade that we do bake.

In a MS. by Archdeacon Rogers, who died 1569, and who saw the Whitsun Plays at Chester, we have the following interesting description (Harlean MSS.):—

The manner of these playes weare, every company had his pagiant, or p'te, which pageants weare a high scafolde with 2 rowmes, a higher and a lower, upon 4 wheeles. In the lower they apparelled themselves, and in the higher rowme they played, beinge all open on the tope, that all behoulders might heare and see them. The places where they played them was in every streete. They begane first at the Abay gates, and when the first pagiante was played, it was wheeled to the highe crosse before the Mayor, and so to every streete, and soe every streete had a pagiant playinge before them at one time, till all the pagiantes for the daye appoynted weare played, and when one pagiant was neere ended, worde was broughte from streete to streete, that soe they mighte come in place thereof, excedinge orderlye, and all the streetes have their pagiantes afore them all at one time playeinge togeather ; to se w'ch playes was great resorte, and also scafoldes and stages made in the streetes in those places where they determined to playe their pagiantes.

The manner of which playes was thus : they weare divided into 24 pagiantes according to the companyes of the Cittie & every companye brought forthe their pagiant which was the cariage or place which they played in. And thei first beganne at the Abbaye gates, and when the firste pagiante was played at the Abbaye gates then it was wheled from thense to Pentice, at the hyghe Crosse, before the Maior, & before that was donne the seconde came,—and the first went into the Watergate Streete, from thense unto the Bridge Streete, and so one after an other, till all the pagiantes weare played appoynted for the firste daye, & so likewise for the seconde & the thirde daye—these pagiantes or carige was a highe place made like a howse with 2 rowmes, beinge open on the tope—the lower rowme theie apparrelled & dressed themselves, & the higher rowme theie played, & thei stoode upon VI wheels, & when they had donne with one cariage in one place theie wheled the same from one streete to another.

In the records of the Guild of Smiths in Chester some amusing entries are to be found of expenses incurred in connection with the plays, such as :—

1451.—It' payed for vj skynnys of whitleder to godds garment. xviij^j

It' payed for makyng of the same garment . . . . . x^d

1553.—It' payd for v schepskens for gods & coot for makyng . iij^s

1498.—It' payd for mendyng a cheverel for god and for sowyng of gods kote of leddur and for makyng of the hands to the same kote . . . . xiij

1490.—It' a cheveral gyld for Ihe.

1565.—pd for payntyng & gyldyng (inter alia) gods cote.

pd for a gyrdyll for god . . . . iij^d

1501.—It' pd ffor a newe sudere for god . . . . vij^d

1560.—Item for a selldall for god . . . . xij^d

The devil seems to have been an unusually well got up character, as the following items of expenses incurred for his habiliments will show :—

1451.—Item payd for the demon's garment makyng & the stof . v^s iij^d ob.

Item payd for collyryng of the same garment . . . . viij^d

1477.—Item for mendyng the demons garment (inter alia)

Item for newe ledder to the same garment . . . . . xxij^d

1494.—Item paid to Wattis for dressyng of the devells hede . . viij^d

1490.—Item the devyls hede (repaired)

1498.—It' paid for peynttyng of the demones hede (inter alia)

1567.—Item payd for a stafe for the demon. . . . . iiij^d

In his "Curiosities of Literature," D'Israeli also gives amusing anecdotes by way of illustrating the rude character of the performances and the ridiculous blunders that resulted from ill-managed machinery. "In 1437 when Conrad Bayar, Bishop of Metz, caused the mystery of the Passion to be represented on the Plain of Veximel near that city, God was an old gentleman, named Nicholas Neufchatel, of Touraine, curate of Saint Victory of Metz, and who was very near expiring on the cross had he not been timely assisted. He was so enfeebled that it was agreed another priest should be placed on the cross the next day to finish the representation of the person crucified, and which was done ; and at the same time the said Mr. Nicholas undertook to perform the Resurrection, which, being a less difficult task, he did it admirably well. Another priest, whose name was M. Julu de Nicey, curate of Metrange, personated Judas, and he was like to have stifled while he hung on the tree, for his neck slipped ; this being at length luckily perceived he was quickly cut down and recovered."

Joseph Robertson, in his "Book of Bon-Accord," enters into an interesting speculation regarding the Candlemas Day pageants in Aberdeen which will be read with interest. He says:—"The Emperor, who appears in the spectacle of 1442, was probably Augustus; and he differed little, perhaps, from the Monarch, who, in the procession which welcomed Queen Margaret in 1511, was figured

> rydand under croun,
> Richt awfull, strang, and large of portratour,
> As nobill, dreidfull michtie campioun.

The 'Doctors,' it may be conjectured, were representatives of the Jewish sages, with whom Christ disputed in the Temple. The 'Three Kingis of Culane,' or Cologne, are the same with the personages commemorated by Dunbar, in 'The Queen's Reception':—

> And syne thow gart the Orient Kingis thrie
> Offer to Chryst with benyng reverence
> Gold, sence, and mir with all humilitie,
> Schawand him King with most magnificence.

These are the wise men or shepherds, who came from the east to welcome the infant Saviour; the eldest, Melchior, who appeared bowed down with years, and wearing a long beard, offered gold; franckincense was the gift of Gasper, who was represented as a beardless youth; and Balthasar, who presented myrrh, was figured as a gigantic Moor or negro, with a large flowing beard. I cannot offer any explanation of the group of The Virgin, St. Bride or Bridget, St. Helen, and Joseph; the latter personage was believed to be advanced in age and of a crabbed temper; perhaps the Flight into Egypt, a favourite subject in such spectacles, was represented. St. Bridget, who flourished in the fourteenth century, was designated *Sponsa Christi*, and her book of revelations was held in great esteem. We may pass the two Bishops and four Angels, personated by the Tanners, without any other remark than that among the productions of Bale is enumerated, 'Of the Councils of the Bishops, one comedy.' At the festivals celebrated at Aix, in Provence, Simeon was represented with a mitre and cap, carrying in his left hand a basket of eggs; but no notice is taken of his disciples. Indeed, there is more reason to conjecture that the scene delineated was that which occurred in the house of Simon the leper, in Bethany, when Mary Magdalen annointed the feet of the Saviour, and his disciples were displeased.   Moses was generally depicted with horns—an irreverend absurdity, arising from an error in the vulgate translation of the Scriptures; the Messenger is a name frequently given to the Archangel Gabriel, and the incident figured on this occasion was probably the appearance of the Angel of the Lord in a flame of fire, out of the midst of a bush on Mount Horeb.   The Woodmen, provided by the Butchers, were perhaps Satyrs, such as were exhibited at the baptism of James VI., and by the witty agitation of their tails so highly offended the English embassy.   The Brethren of Guild were charged with, it is likely, the most costly part of the show, the Knights in armour ; and the Bakers were burthened with the provision of the Minstrels, who, as we gather from Dunbar, were dispersed through the pageants, ' blawing to the sky.' "

It was in connection with these pageants that the first orders of precedence were established among the different bodies of craftsmen, a matter which appears to have given the magistrates no small amount of trouble.   The earliest statute with regard to the order in which the craftsmen were to walk in the procession is as follows :—

30th January, 1505.—The said day, it was fundin by the ald lovabile consuetud and rite of the burgh, that in the honor of God and the blissit Virgin Mary, the craftismen of the samyn, in thar best aray, kepit and decorit the procession one Candilmes day yerlie ; quhilk auld and louable consuetud, the prouest, baillies, and counsale, riplie avisit, ratifeit, and approvit the said rite ; and atour statut and ordanit that the said craftis-men and their successoris, sale perpetualie in tyme to cum, to observe and keipe the said procession, als honorabily as they can : and they sale, in order to the Offering in the Play, pass tua and ij togidr socialie ; in the first the flesseris, barbouris, baxturis, cordinaris, skineris, couparis, wrichts, hat makars and bonat makars togidr, walcaris, litstaris, wob-staris, tailyeouris, goldsmiths, blacksmiths, and hammermen ; and the craftismen sal furnys the Pageants ; the cordinaris, the Messing ; wob-staris and wolcaris, Symeon ; the smyths and goldsmiths, iij Kingis of Cullane ; the listaris, the Emperor ; the masons, the Thrie Knichts ; the talyouris, our Lady, Sanct Brid, and Sanct Elene ; and the skynners, the Tua Bischopis ; and tua of ilke craft to pass with the pageant that thai furnyss to keip thair geir ; and gif ony persone or persouns happinis to failze and brek ony poynt befor writin, and beis convictit tharof, sale pay xl sh. to Sanct Nicholas werk, and the balzeis unlaw unforgiven : ande to the obseruing and keping of the samyn, ale the said craftismen was oblist, be thair handis uphaldin.

This order did not give satisfaction to the skinners. They rebelled against being mentioned after the cordiners, and on 28th May, 1507, " the provest and bailyis statut and ordanit that all skynaris sall gang before the cordinaris in al process- ions, baitht at Candelmes play and utheris processions that accordis thame to gang in." The statute of 1505, however, was reenacted in 1510 in exactly the same terms, and the skinners had to go back to their old place. It was not, however, until 1531, that a definite order was established. This order, as will be seen from the following extract, was fixed in conform- ity with the order observed in Edinburgh :—

Curia Balliuorum burgi de Abirden tenta in pretorio eiusdem vigesimo secundo die mensis Maii anno Dni millesimo quingentesimo trigesimo primo per magistrum Andream Tulidef baliuum.

The said day it was statut and ordanit be the prouest bailyeis and coun- saile pnt for the time conforme to the auld lovabill consuetudis and rytt of this burgh and of the nobill burgh of Edinburgh of the quhilkis rite and consuetude the forsaid prouest has gottin copy in write. That is to say that in the honoʳ of God and the blessit Virgyne Marye the craftismen of this burgh in thair best array keipe and decoir the procession on Corpus Cristi dais and Candilmes day als honorabillye as thai can every craft wᵗ thair awin baner wᵗ the Armes of thair craft yʳin. And thai sal pas ilk craft be thame self tua and tua in this ordour. That is to say in the first the flescharis, and next thame the barboʳis, nixt thame skynaris and furrowris togidder, nixt thame the cordonaris, nixt thame the tailyoʳis, efter thame the vobstaris, valcaris, and litstaris togidder, nixt thame the baxtaris, and last of all nrest the Sacramēt passis, all hemermen, that is to say, symthis, wchtis, masonis, cuparis, sclateris, goldsmythis, and armouraris. And every ane of the said craftis in the Candelmas procession sall furniss thair pageaue conform to the auld statut maid in the yeir of God jaj vc and x yris [1510], quhilk statut was maid wᵗ the aviss of the haile counsaile and appvit be the craftismē of the toune for the tyme for thame and thair successoris. And oblist thame to the keping of the samyn vnder the pane of xl ss and the bailyeis vnlaw unforgevin to be vptakin of thame that beis absent but ane resonabill causs fra the said processioun, or that makkis trubill or perturbatioun yʳin. To the quhilkis they wer oblist be thair handis vphaldin in iugement. And the prouest, bailyies, and counsale put for the tyme ratifeis and approvis this pnt statut

aud the painis contenit y'in to be kepit iuviolablye in all maner in tyme
cuming.   The craftis ar chargit to furneiss their pangeanyis vnder
written :—

> The flescharis Sanct Bestian aud his trūmatouris.
> The barbouris Sanct Lowrance and his trūmētouris.
> Skynnaris Sanct Stewin and his tormētouris.
> The cordinaris Sanct Martyne.
> The tailyeouris the Coronatioun of Our Lady.
> Litstaris Sanct Nicholess.
> Wobstaris walcaris and bonet makaris Sanct John.
> Baxtaris Sanct Georg.
> Wrichtis messonis sclateris and cuparis The Resurrectioun.
> The smithis and hemmirmen The Barmen of the Croce.

An important change in the character of these displays
took place in 1508, when the Abbot and Prior gave place to
" Robyne Huyd and Litile Johnne."   In the month of May of
that year it was ordained that " al personis that ar abill within
this burghe salbe reddy with their arrayment made in grene
and yallow, bowis, arrowis, brass (?), and all uther convenient
thingis according thairto to pass with Robyne Huyd and Litile
Johnne all times convenient thairto, quhar thai be requirit be
the saidis Robyne and Litile Johnne ; " and in the following
month a more explicit ordinance was passed :—

17th November 1508.—The said day, the prouest, bailyeis, counsaill, and
comunitie of the said burghe, representand the haill body of the samyne,
warnit be the hand bell, ale in ane voice considerand, riplie avisit, for the
auld rit and lovabile consuetud of the said burgh, vsit and perseurit all
tymes bigaue, past memor of man, in the honor of thar glorius patron
Sanct Nicholaice, statut aud ordainit, that all personis, burges, nichtbouris,
and inhabitaris, burges sonnys, habill to ryd, to decor and honor the towne
in thar array conveinant therto, sall rid with Robert Huyid and Litile
Johne, quhilk was callit, in years bipast, Abbat and Prior of Bonaccord,
one every Sanct Nicholaice day, throw the towne, as use and wont has
bene, quhen thai war warnit be the said Robert Huyde or Litile Johne, or
ony ane of theme ; and giff ony man haffaud taks of watris, fischeingis,
landis, or ony pensioun or proffit of the toune, habill to rid, beaud warnit,
be the saidis Robert Huyd or Litile Johne forsaid, and will nocht ryd, and
beis convict tharintill be ane suorne assiss of the said burgh, [thai] sall
tyne thar takis, pensiounis, and proffitis that thai haue of the said burghe,
and salbe secludit, removit and uterlie expellit fra ale takis, pensionis,
proffitis, quhatsumever thai have of the said burgh, in tyme to cum ; without ressonable causs schawin and propinit to the prouest, bailyeis, counsaill, Robene, and Litile Johne, obefoir, and be considert be thame to be

lauchfull impediment and excuss quharthrow thai mycht not ryd ; and the personis havand na takis of the said burghe, beand warnit be the said Robert Huyd or Litile Johnne, and will not rid, sall pay xx shilling to Sanct Nicholas werk, and viij sh. to the bailyeis unlaw vnforgevin.

With the exception of the following protest from the deacon of the Hammermen, the order of precedence established in 1510 seems to have been faithfully observed for a number of years after the change in the nature of the displays took place :—

21st June, 1538.—The sayd day, Walter Hay, goldsmyth, dekyne of hemermen, comperit in judgment, and complenit to the balyes, allegiand wrang don to thaim be the armeraris, in usurping of their place in the processioun of Corpus Xri, this day, and ganging behind thame, agains the comond ordinance and statute of this nobill burght, and all the borrowis within this realm ; requyrand thaim for remeyd of law ; protesting, gyf thai refusit, that it be lesum to call the said armerars befor gugis sperituall or temporal, and for remeid of law.

Whether this "wrang don to thaim be the armeraris" was put right the Council Register sayeth not. A still more serious dispute regarding the order of procedure arose in 1554, when the deacons of the wrights, masons, coopers, and slaters complained against the smiths and hammermen for not keeping their proper place. Judgment was given in favour of the hammermen, against which judgment the other four crafts protested. The following minute (Council Records) regarding this dispute is doubly interesting from the fact that it contains the name of William Jamesoune, grandfather of George Jamesone, the Scottish Vandyk. The artist's father was also a mason, the register of indentures stating that he served his apprenticeship with Andrew Bethleam. He is described in his indenture as "Androa Jamesoun, sone naturall to umq^{ll} Wilzeam Jamesoune." The minute also contains one of the few references made in the Records to a deacon of the mason craft :—

21st May, 1554.—The said day, Andro Bisset, dekin of the wrychtis, William Jamesoune, dekyne of the masonis, and Jerome Blak, dekin of the cowperis, comperit in jugement, and exponit to the bailies, quhow that Johnne Jenour, thair officiar, at thair command, and chargit thame, and thair haill craftis, to pass in order upoun Corpus Xri day now approacheand, in the processioun, by the ald maner and ordor ; that is to say, to pass be$^-$ thame selffis; and with the sklateris, all togidder, havand ane honest baner and Pagane of thair awin, immediatlie befor the smythis and vtheris hamyrmen ; quhair thai had wont to gang, with the said smythis, as thai allegit, all togidder, under ane baner and Pagane; and producit ane statitut maid theruppone, of the dait the xxii day of May, the yeir of God m. vc. xxxi yeir : And Williame Robertsone, dekin of the smythis, comperit in judgement, and allegit thai war in vse of gangging be thame selffis in the said processione, vnder thair awin baner, hindmaist and nixt the Sacrament, and the saids wrychtis, masouns, cowperis, and sklaiteris to proceid togidder befoir thame, under ane baner and pegane, separat fra the saids smythtis, and producit ane statitut maid therupon, of the dayt the xiij day Junii, the yeir of God m. vc. xxxiij yeris : And the baillies decernit and ordaint the last statitut to be observyt and keipit, under the panes contenit in the same, becaus thai all wer present, and consentit therto, and oblist thame to obserf the same, as the said statitut proportis at lyntht : And the saidis wrychtis, masonis, cowperis, and sklayteris protestit that quhat the baillies dois or decernis this day, anent the ordor forsaid, mak na dirogacioune to the forsaid statitut first maid, producit be thame in judgement, bot that thai may haf thair ald prevelege observit, and for remeid of law, quhen tyme and place requiris : and Alexander Kempt, dekyne of the bexteris, allegit imlykwyiss, that thai ar put by thair rowme and ordour vsit obefor, and protestit sicklyk, that quhat be done this yeir be the baillies, anent the said ordor, hurt thame nocht in tym cumyn.

To illustrate the strictness with which the ordinances of the town with regard to these processions were enforced, we give the following extracts from the Council Register :—

3rd February, 1502.—The saide day, Johne Rede, wobster, John Williamson, &c., ilkane of thame was convict be ane suorne assise, Alexander Reid forespeker, because thai did nocht it that accordit thame to do one Candilmese day, in the Passioun, efter the auld honerabill and lovabill consuetude of the burghe, and for the quhilkis thai war in ane amerciament of the court, and to amend as law will, and forbere in tym to cum, because thai pretentit thame to precede and pass in the place of the processione, quha the tailzeours had vyss to pass tymes bigane.

3rd February, 1510.—The said day, Thomas Meldrum, William Patonsone, Andro Jonsone, younger, John Allane, and Richard Wricht, was, ilkane of thame, in amerciament of court, be thae avin toung condemit, because thai passt not in the procession of Candilmes day to decoir the samyn, and tile amend as law wile, and forber in time to cum.

5th February, 1523.—The same day, Johne Pill, tailzeour, wes convikit be his awin toung grant maid in jugement for the dissobeing of David Anderson, bailze, becaus he refusit to pas in the Candilmess processioun with his taikin and sing of his craft in the place lemit to his craft, and in likwiss for the mispersoning of the said Dauid Andersoun, the merchandis of the said guid toun, in calling of thame Coffeis, and bidding of thame to tak the salt pork and herboiss in thair handis ; for the quhilk the prowest and hail [councel] chargit the said Johne, he beand oblisit in jugement be his hand wphaldin thair deliuerance, to cum on Sonday that next cumis in the tyme of hiemes, barfut, and bairheid, with an candle and ane pund of wax, and offer the samyn to thair patroun Sanct Nicholace, and sit doun humelie on his kneis, besikand the prowest and guyd toun to ramyt his forsaid falt, an inobedience doyne to the bailze, and to bring on his briest the usit taikin of his craft, that is to say, ane pair of patent sheris ; and gif euer the said John committis ony siclik falts in tym cumin, to pay to Sanct Nicholas wark x merkis but remissioun.

The sayd day, tha provest, with the aviss of the haill counsell present for the tym, fund and delyverit, that the craftismen of the said burgh had failzet in the observing and keeping of the lovabill auld statut, maid be their predecessoris, with the consent of the haill craftismen, in the honoring and decoiring of the procession on Candilmes day, because thai that wer absent for the maist part, and that thai that wer present, buyr nocht the taikins of thar craft, eftir the forme of the said statut : And ordanit the bailyes to wptak thair vnlawis of the absent, and thai that failyeit in the bering of thair taikins, to amend in tym cuming, vnder al payne contenit in the auld statut, to be uptakin by ramissioun.

5th June, 1553.—The said day, the dekyn and haill craft of the smyths wer convickit, be ane suorne assis, for the disobeying of the baillies in refusing contempurindlie to gang in ordour in the procession of Corpus Xris day last bipast, befor the sacrament, as thai yied in ordor, the yier immediately bypast ; and the baillies war maid quit, be the said asses, of all strublens of the said craft ; and it was gevin for dome.

The year 1555 saw the extinction of Robin Hood and Little John. An Act of Parliament was passed which "statute and ordanit that in all tymes cumming na maner of ,persoun be chosin Robert Hude nor Lytill Johne, Abbot of vnressoun Quenis of Maij nor vtherwyse nouther in Burgh nor to land-wart in ony tyme to cum and gif ony Prouest, Baillies, counsall, and communitie, chesis sic ane Personage as Robert Hude, Lytill Johne, Abbottis of vnressoun, or Quenis of Maij within Burgh, the chesaris of sic sall tyne thair fredome for the space of fyve zeiris, and vtherwyse salbe punist at the Quenis grace will, and the acceptar of sicklyke office salbe banist furth of the Realme. And gif ony sic persounis sic as Robert Hude, Lytill Johne, Abbottis of vnressoun, Quenis of Maij, beis chosin outwith Burgh and vthers landwart townis, the chesars sall pay to our Souerane Lady x pundis, and thair persounis put in waird, thair to remane during the Quenis grace plesoure. And gif ony

wemen or vthers about simmer treis singand makis perturbatioun to the Quenis liegis in the passage throw Burrows and
vthers landwart townis the wemen perturbatouris for skafrie
of money or vtherwyse salbe takin handellit and put upon the
Cukstulis of everie Burgh or towne."

This Act of Parliament led to serious trouble, not only in
Aberdeen but throughout Scotland.   In Aberdeen the craftsmen appear to have been the leading raisers of tumult, as the
following interesting entries in the Register fully set forth:—

4 May 1562.—The said day, John Kelo, belman, wes accusit in jugement for the passing throw the rewis of the tounn, with the hand bell, be
oppin voce, to convene the haill comunite, or sa mony thairof as wald convene, to pass to the wood, to bring in symmer upoun the first Sonday of
Maii; contraveinand the actis and statutis of the Quenis Grace, and Lordis
of Consel; epperandlie to raiss tumult, and ingener discord, betuix the
craftismen and the fre burgesses of gild, and the saidis craftesmen to dissobey and attempt aganis the superioris of the toun, gif it stud in thair
power, as the saidis prowest and baillies ar informit; the said Johnne
having na comand of the saidis prowest and baillies to do the same; and
inlykwyss, Alexander Burnat, alias Potter, wes accusit for passing throw
the toun with ane swech, to the effect and occasioun aboun wrytin; quhilk
Johne and Alexander confessit the samyn, alleigand thai did the samyn of
na ewill mynd, but conforme to the auld wse, and be comand of Johnne
Grant, quha is ane fre burgess, and brother of gild; and had done na
wrang tharin, as thai allegit: And the said Johne Grant inlykmaner beand
accusst for giffing command to the saidis Johnne and Alexander, as is
aboun wrytin, and passing throw the toun, fortifeing and menteining
thame as he mocht, to the effect forsaid, grantit and approwit the same,
and denyit ony wrang done be him thairintill: Quhilk mater wes put to
the decisioun and knawleg of the assiss aboun wrytin, [consisting of
twenty-one persons] chosin, suorne, and admittit in jugement; quhilk
accepit the said mater on thame, and efter consultacioun and considera-
cioun, ryplie awisit, enterit in court, and fand and deliuered all in ane
voce, be the moutht of Gilbert Menzes, elder, chancellar of the said assiss
for the tyme, that the saidis personis had grytlie wrangit in the comitting
of the said enormitie and heyt atemptat, but the awiss of the prowest,
baillies, and superuris of the toun; quhairfor thai, and ilkane of thame,
wer in amerciament of court; and that wes gevin for dome, and the
modificacion of the amendis referrit to the discretioun of the consell;
quhilk thaireftir being deulie convenit, discernit and ordanit the saidis
persones to compeir vpoun Sonday nixt cums, within the paroche kirk,
and thair, immediately eftir the preching, in presens of the congregacioun,
grant thair said offens as done throw ignorance; and, upoun thair kneis,
ask God and the congregacioun forgifnes, and obleist thame selfiss, thair

opinlie, that gif thai be convickit for sic offens in tym cuming, to tyn thair fredome, proffit, and privilege of this guid toun, and to be seperat and exulat fra the societie tharof, frathensfurtht ; and quha of thame dissobeyis the said ordainnce, to incur the samyn pane, but fauor or request to be hard on the contrar.

14 May 1565.—The said day, Johnne Kelo, belman, maid faytht, in jugement, that he, at comand of the prowest and baillies, past on Setterday was viij dais, viz. the v day of Maii, the rewis and gettis of this toune, be oppen voce, and maid inhibitioune to all burges men, craftismen, and all utheris, inhabitantis and induellaris of the said toune, that nane of thame tak upone hand to mak ony conventioue, with taburne plaing, or pype, or fedill, or have anseinges, to convene the Quenis legis, in chusing of Robin Huid, Litill Johnne, Abbot of Ressoune, Queyne of Maii, or sicklyk contraveyne the statutis of parliament, or mak ony tumult, scism, or conventione.

The said day, James Marsar, Lourens Marsar, Mathow Guild, Thomas Huntayr, and Androw Wysman, wer convickit for the cumyng throw the toune, upon Sunday last wes, eftir none, with ane menstrall playand befor thaim, throch the Gallowgett, in contemptioune of the townis actis and proclamaciouns maid obefoir, and breaking of the actis of parliament, and contravening of the saim ; quherfor thai wer put in amerciament of court, and were ordanit to remane in the tollbuth, quhill thai find sourtie for fulfilling and satisfeing of the emends to be modifyt be the consell.

18 May 1565.—The sayd day, the consell present for the tyme, being convenit to decern anent the emendis and punyshment of James Marsar, Lourens Marsar, sadlar, Mathow Guild, armerar, Andrew Wysman, cordinar, and Thomas Huntar, cutlar, quhilk are convickit for contempning and dissobeying of the townis actis and ordinans obefor, and contravening of the actis of parliament : The counsall, reply adwysit, considering the said attemptat, and ground quharof the same proceidit, to be to genir schism and discord within the burgh, dischargit the saidis personis of their fredome, and fra all exercitioune of their crafts, conform to the act of parliament ; and ordanis publict proclamacioun to be made heirupoun ; and the consell alsua statut and ordanit, with consent of the haill toun present for the tyme, that na craftisman be maid fre for sewin yeirs to cum, except fremenis sonis.

The James and Lawrence Mercer, Matthew Guild, Thomas Hunter, and Andrew Wiseman, mentioned in the foregoing extracts were all leading craftsmen in the city at this period, and took a prominent part in connection with the Common Indenture entered into a few years after for removing the differences that had arisen between the craft and merchant burgesses. Matthew Guild, armourer, or "sweird slipper," as he was more commonly described, was the father of Dr.

William Guild, and Jean Guild, wife of David Anderson of Finzeauch, well known for their benefactions to the Trades and to the citizens generally. Matthew had also another son, named William, who was slain in 1584, two years before the doctor was born. The elder William was buried in St. Nicholas Churchyard, the record simply mentioning that he was "slain by John Leslie, son to James Leslie, burgess."

The close connection between the craftsmen and the religious ceremonies of the church prior to the reformation proved very disastrous to a number of their associations throughout the country. Many of their societies were put down "on suspicion of being superstitious foundations" and their property seized by the crown; in fact, the reformation shook the whole system of Guilds to its foundation, more particularly in England. By an Act passed in the reign of Edward VI. all money devoted by "any manner of corporations, guilds, fraternities, companies, or fellowships of mysteries, or crafts" to the support of a priest, obits, or lights, was vested in the king; and under the same Act, the property of "all fraternities, brotherhoods, and guilds, being within the realm of England and Wales, and other the king's dominions, and all manors, lands, tenements, and other heriditaments belonging to them, or any of them, other than such corporations, guilds, fraternities, companies, and fellowships of mysteries, or crafts, and the manors, lands, tenements, and other heridaments pertaining to the said corporations, guilds, fraternities, &c.," were handed over to the crown. Mr. Toulmin Smith describes this seizure as "a case of pure, wholesale robbery and plunder, done by an unscrupulous faction to satisfy their personal greed under cover of law. No more gross case of wanton plunder is to be found in the whole history of all Europe. No page so black in English history."

Nothing, however, like the same wholesale appropriation of funds and property devoted to the purposes of religion by the guilds took place in Scotland at the time of the reformation such as occurred in England. But the records of the Aberdeen Trades show that they suffered to some extent in a similar way. Previous to the reformation each trade had its own patron saint, each of the wealthiest of the crafts maintained a chaplain, and paid so much yearly both individually and collectively, for "decoring, upholding, and repairing the altars within the parish kirk," and for supplying "imagerie, vestments, and towels, chandeliers, desks, lights, and all manner of ornaments required to the glory of God." These payments were rigorously exacted, and if any of the crafts failed in their duty in this respect they were summoned before the Town Council to answer for their derelictions. On one occasion (in the year 1495), the cordiners (shoemakers) of Aberdeen were summoned before the Town Council for refusing "meyttis, drynkis, and sustentatioun" to that "discrete mane, Shir Alexander Gray, chaplane of Sanctis Crispini and Crispinianis altar, situat within ye parroche kirk of yis burghe." The appeal by this worthy and "discret manne" for redress, is worth giving in full :—

The said day (26th September, 1495) comperit ane discrete mane, Shir Alexander Gray, chaplane of Sanctis Crispini and Crispiniauis altar, situat within ye parroche kirk of yis burghe, and producit and shewit ane autentyrie Instrument under the subscriptioune of Shir Johnne Striveling, notar public, and seile of Thomas Fyf, makin mentione and schewin that ye houest and faithful mene of craft, cordonars of the said burghe, with ane consent and assent in the honour of God Almichtie, the blissit Virgine Mary, Sancts Nicholas, Santis Crispini and Crispiniani and al Sanctis, had chosen and taken ye said Shir Alexander thair perpetuale Chaplane to mak ministracioune of dyvine seruice at the said altar as efferis ; for the quhilk they were bundin to sustene the said Chaplane honestlie as efferis, in meyttis, drynkis, and sustentatioune circualie, be sevin of ye best and worthaist of the said craftismene, ilkane ane day in ye oulk, ande payand to him xls. usual monie of Scotland, yeirlie for his fie, of uyiris, ye remanent of ye craft, as in ye samyn mair fullie is contenit ; quhilkis instrument, seyne and understandin, ye haill cordonaris lauchfullie warnit, callit and comperit, the said chaplane humlie meynt him to ye aldermen, bailzies and counsale, yt he wantit his fie and pairte of his dietis in the oulk, besehing thame for remede of law ; quhilk peticoune ye said aldermen, bailzies aud counsale and diuerss of the communitie, understandin richtness and consonant to resone express consent and assent of ye best and worthaist of ye said craft, ordanit, fand, and delyverit ye said evident of availe and ye saids craftismen to sustene ye said Chaplane honestlie eftcr ye tenour of ye samyn ; and maide and ordanit Thomas Meldrum and William Ranisone, dekyns and maisters of ye said craft, in that parte, to compell and distrinzie thair nichtbouris craftismen and cordonaris to the sustentatioune of thair said Chaplane eftcr ye tenoris of his evident.—*Council Register, vol.* vii.*, p.* 660.

F

Again in 1591, the alderman and baillies found fault with the cordiners for refusing to "sustain" their chaplain, and "ordainit Williame Scrimgeur, officiar, to pass with Shir Jonhne Litster, chaplan of Sanctis Crispini and Crispiniani, altar with ye dekyns of ye cordonaris and causs him to be pait and content of his fee of al ceruies bigane efter ye tenor of his warrande documentis maide to him yairupon aucht to him be ye haill craftismen of ye cordonair craft, within yis burght, and to charge thame tile obey thar dekyns yairvintill according to justice."—*Council Register, vol.* viii., *p.* 82.

As to what became of the altars, stalls, and property which the crafts had contributed to the kirk very little is known. When the protestant religion was established the churches were found to be divested of all the altars and carved work nothing remaining but the bare walls. The craftsmen evidently had their suspicions of who had appropriated the church property, as the following extract from a summons served upon the magistrates will show. The summons was at the instance of the Trades against the Magistrates of Aberdeen requiring them to answer before the Privy Council of Scotland to a charge of "dilapidating, alienating, and appropriating to themselves for their own use, profit and emolument, the Common Good, lands, revenues and property of the Burgh : and of continuing the magistrates in a few families by electing themselves from father to son for three or four generations,' more particularly—

(1) For disposing, dividing, and sharing among themselves, the lands of Tullies, Bogfairlie, Gardens, Brotherfield, Countesswells, Hazelhead, Shetocksley, Forresterhill, Rubislaw, Kingswells, and Cruves, all belonging to the Common Good of the Burgh.

(2) For sharing among themselves the whole plate, furniture, and plenishing of St. Nicholas Church extant at the alteration of religion, viz. :— 8 chandeliers, of fine silver ; 8 chalices, and other patens, 2 eucharists, 1 steip (font), 1 cresie (lamp), with a silver stock ; 6 altar spoons, and 2 censers of fine silver, amounting to 40 pounds weight of silver in whole ; also, 52 brass chandeliers, a great latron of massey brass within the choir, wherein the Evangel (gospel) was read, in form of the pelican and her birds, weighing 520 lbs. of fine brass ; also, 5 new stands of Kapis (copes), of fine gold, and 3 inferior ones ; also, 10 stands of fine mass cloths of gold, crimson, green, black, and purple velvet, starred with gold with thin chesables ; several other fine latrons belonging to the various altars, &c. ; also, a pair

of fine organs, complete and perfect; also, 10 pairs of hangings before the various altars, of crimson velvet and satins, drapped with gold and golden letters, &c.

(3) Also, 8 great oak trees in the churchyard cut down, and with the rest of the foregoing articles, applied to their own uses.

(4) For selling great pieces of artillery belonging to the town, such as *lang meg*, yettings, double and single falconers, double slings, slings, &c., together with ammunition belonging to the same and sharing the price among themselves.

(5) Also, a great chain of iron and shipmasts linked together with the branders thereof, which was for going across the harbour to protect the shipping.

(6) Also, materials provided for repairing the blockhouse.

(7) Sharing the profits arising from the town's marking irons (for stamping measures, &c.), and from the keep of the shore.

(8) Also, the yearly income from the town's seals.

(9) Selling a quantity of fine wainscotting, and a great deal of other materials purchased for public works, and dividing the proceeds among themselves.

(10) Sharing among themselves the profits arising from the town's customs.

(11) Also, the profits of the handbell.

(12) Also, 1200 merks raised from the inhabitants to buy lead to theich the north aisle of the kirk.

(13) Also, an impost of 1000 merks raised upon false pretences, and so parted.

(14) Selling 3000 pieces of fine hewn freestone for building the pier head and quay, and parting among themselves the proceeds.

(15) Also, £40 of the poor's money, so parted.

(16) Another impost, or tax, of 4500 merks, so parted.

(17) Also, another of 3200 merks.

(18) Also, the sum of £8000 belonging to the community.

(19) Allowing the Bridge of Dee to fall into disrepair and appropriating to themselves the funds destined for its support.

(20) Also, the Tolbooth steeple dilapidated in like manner, and

(21) Allowing the Town's Commonties to be destroyed by permitting them to be torn up, occupied, and cultivated by individuals, suffering them to burn heather, cut down wood, &c., to the great injury of the poorer class of the community, &c., &c.—*Convener Court Papers.*

The records are silent as to whether the Trades were successful in the action; the probability is they were not. The property had gone whence it had little chance of returning.

After the change of religion the connection between the crafts and the church underwent a radical alteration; but the

influence of the pageants was long visible in the processions
that were held upon fixed holidays, when the craftsmen turned
out with the banners and insignia of their crafts, finishing
the day in jollity and feasting. An indication of the change
that took place is apparent in an ordinance passed in October,
1587, on which day "it was devysit, statute, and ordanit be the
prouest, bailleis, and counsall of this guid toune, and ratifet
and apprevit be the haill toune, alsweill craftsmen as burgessis,
being lauchfullie warnit to this day, &c., that all maisteris of
housholdis alsweill craftismen as burgessis sall repair to the
paroche kirk, keep and observe the sermonis and prechingis on
the oulk dayis, to wit, Tuysday and Thuirisday, of heiring of the
wourd of God and Christis Evangell trewlie prechit, in all
tyme heirafter under penaltie of twa s. to be uptaken of ilk
burgess, and xii d. of the craftisman absent fra the sermone
the saidis dayis without lauchtfull excuiss of infirmities, seik-
niss, or absence of the toune ; and heirunto the haill craftismen,
alsweill burgessis, voluntarlie obliest tham selfiss, being particularlie inquirit be Gilbert Mengzes, prouest, and consentit
therto, prowyding that this act be extendit onlie to maisteris
of househaldis."   And, again, in 1588, owing to the " cauldness
enterit in practiss of a gryt numer of inhabitants professing
Christ, and be gaming and playing, passing to the tavernis and
ailhoussis, using the tred of merchandise and handie labour in
tyme of sermone on the oulk day," it was ordained that there
should be paid by " everie householder and his wyff, burgessis
of Gild, for thair remaining fra the sermon on the Sabbath day
xiii s. iiii d., and for thair remanin ilk oulk day tua s.; and for
everie craftsman houshalder and otheris inhabitantis for thair
remaining fra the sermonis on the Sabbath day sax s. viii d.,
and everie oulk day xii d., and in caice ony merchant or
burgess of gild be find within his merchand buith efter the
ringing of the third bell to the sermone on the oulk day to
pay sax s. viii d."   This "gude and godlie statute made ebefoir"
was ratified in 1598, and in the following year all " brither of
gild and craftsmen alike " were specially enjoined " that in
all tyme theirafter thair suld be a pastyme day oulklie,
to vit, every Mononday, quhairon it suld be lesum to all the
laboraris of the ground within this realm to do thair awin

business, and navayes to be answerabill to thair maisteris that day, for eschewing of the prophanatioun of the Sabbath day, quhilk hes been prophanit be the laboraris of the ground of the meaner sort be schearin of their cornis, and doing of their uther handis labour, be occasion that na lassour was given to thame in all the oulk be thair masteris for doing thareof, being then occupeit in thair masteris service."

Following the example set by the Town Council the individual craft associations passed rigid statutes for the observance of the Lord's Day, and went the length of ordering that no Papists, Quakers, or heretics should be eligible for office, "but only those of the sound Protestant faith." That this ordinance was acted upon is evident from the following minute in the books of the shoemaker trade :—

17th October, 1674.—The said day George Troup is electit and chosin ane maister to the traid, in choiss and plaiss of Thomas Mylne quho culd not carrie office, in respeck of his professione, being ane quaiker, being also refusit be the Deacon Convener Court to be ane member thereof.

The kirk-session had also summoned this same Mr. Mylne before them, in order to check and, if possible, to turn the current of his zeal into its former channel; but Mylne was impervious, and with considerable skill he maintained and defended the propriety of strictly adhering to his newly-embraced creed. Certain ministers of the gospel were appointed to commune with him thereanent, but they soon found that neither their presence nor their arguments were of any avail. At last the Kirk Session found it impossible to make any impression "whatsomever" on Mr. Mylne, and they allowed him to go without further molestation.

From the following extract it would appear that Mylne had been at times twitted by his brethren of craft regarding his being a Quaker :—

23rd Feb., 1674.—The said day Thomas Mylne, having given in ane bill of complaint against Alexander Idle for some scandalous speaches spokin against him, which wer verified and prowin, therfor the traid ordanit the said Alex. Idle to acknowledge his transgression, and to enact himselff not to transgress in the lyk, nor speak any scandalous or opprobrious speaches to the said Thomas in tyme comeing under the pain of four punds *toties quoties* conforme to ther ancient actis."—*Shoemakers' Records.*

The burial of the dead and the use of mort-cloths were also matters which formed the subject of frequent disputes and arguments between the craftsmen, the Council, and the Kirk. The following "solemn contract and agreement" was entered into in 1649, with the view of settling all differences, each trade being furnished with a copy of the deliverance for their guidance :—

Att Aberdeen, the ninteenth day of December, one thousand six hundred and fourty nine years, in presence of the Provost, Bailies, and Councill, conveened for the time, they are to say, Alex. Jeffray, Provost ; George Morison, George Culline, John Jeffray, and Waltor Cochran, Bailies ; Thomas Melvill, Dean of Gild ; and Thomas Boyes, Thesauror ; Mr. Thomas Gray, Mr. Robert Farquhar, Andrew Burnett, Mr. William Moir, Mr. Alex. Forbes, Alex. Watson, Gilbert Menzies, James Smith, Andrew Guiddeall, Patrick Murray, Baxtor ; and William Scott, Wright. The said day forsomeikle as by Act of Generall Assembly and the laudable practice of this kingdom the burying within kirks is now abolished, and persons of all sorts and ranks are buried in the kirkyards and other publick parts appointed for burials, and seeing thereby within this burgh many persons of mean quality who are buried in the ordinary place of burying cannot attain nor be able to satisfy and pay for their lairs according to the old rate as was erected for the burials within kirks afore : And the Deacon-Conveener, in name of the haill Crafts of this burgh having particularly supplicate the Councill for an ease of the said burialls, as also the said Deacon-Conveenor, in name of the saids Crafts having desired that the Councill would be pleased to appoint some of their number to meet with the Deacons anent the taking away of any difference that has thir sundry years been in this town occasioned by the Crafts, their separating themselves from the brethren of Gild and remanent inhabitants of the burgh in not making use of the common mort-cloath of the town, and intending to have an mort-cloath of their own, and now being sensible of the prejudice, they were willing to give in their mort-cloath to the Thesaurer, which they intended to have used, and only to make use of the common mortcloaths of the town as the rest of the inhabitants doe, if it should please the Councill to show courtesie of the price and rent of burialls, and of the said mort-cloaths. Whilk the Councill having taken to their consideration and having heard the reports of those that were delegate to speak with the Crafts, and being willing to compose all difference in so far as may be and to show the inhabitants such ease as is reasonable, decerned and ordained the rate and prices of burialls and of the mort-cloaths in time coming to be att the rate and prices after-following, viz. :—That every person of whatsomever rank of what sort or quality soever they be within this burgh who shall be buried in the south side of the kirk, and in the north side within thirty foot to the church wall who shall be carried upon staves shall pay for their lairs three pound, and for every one that shall be carried under men's arms the sum of twenty shillings for ilk ane. And declares that the rest of the bounds in the kirkyard lying on the north side of the kirk being thirty foot from the kirk wall shall be free and any who please to lye there shall pay nothing for their lairs if they be poor and have not means. And the prices of the mort-cloaths to be as follows, viz. :--The price of the best velvet mort-cloath for persons of age three pound, of the second velvet mort-cloath for persons of age fourty shillings, the price of the best velvet mort-cloath for bairns twenty shilling, and of the second velvet mort-cloath for bairns to be ten shilling. The price of the mort-cloaths of blac cloath as well of these which were in the town's possession before as mort-cloaths to be given in by the Crafts for persons of age to be twenty shilling, and for bairns to be ten shilling. And in testimony of the Crafts their contentment with the prices above written they gave in their mort-cloaths of black cloath to be keeped by the thesaurer, and obliged themselves to make use of the common mort-cloaths in all time coming according as the rest of the inhabitants of the burgh doe, and that att the prices and rates above written. It is specially declared that the prices of lairs above written shall no ways be extended to those who shall have any tombs or lair-stones to lye upon graves, but the Councill shall sett down the prices therein as occasion and the quality of the persons shall require. Likewise if it shall fall out that the town shall have occasion of buying and erecting of an common houfe and buriall place by the churchyard, it shall be lawfull to the Councill to alter the prices of burialls and lairs in the said houfe as necessity shall require. And the Provost and Baillies for themselves and in name of the Councill, and also the Deacon-Conveenor and haill remanent deacons of the Crafts for themselves, and in name of the rest, in testimony, &c.—*Convener Court Papers.*

About the beginning of the seventeenth century the deacons on behalf of their respective crafts petitioned the Town Council for permission to erect "dasks" or lofts in the parish church of St. Nicholas, the prayer of which was granted after the following fashion :—

16th May, 1638.—Ye quhilk daye aneut ye petitionne given in to ye Provest, Bailzies, and Counsell be George Farquhar, deacone of ye cordiners of this burt., for hymselff and in behalfe of his bretherene, ye haill maisteris and friemene of ye said craft, makand mentionne that for decernment of the paroche kirk of this burghe, they intend, God willing, with permissione and lycence of ye Magistrats and Counsell, to build and erect ane dask in ye said kirk, foreagainne ye southmaist dor of ye auld kirk, at ye secunde pillar fra the wast gavel of ye said kirk, in the southsyd therof, till it cum to ye pillarr narrest the said gable, desyir therfor that warrand and lycence beis given for building and erecting of ye said dask at ye pairt forsaid, as at mair lengthe wes contenit in ye said

petitioune. Quhairwith ye saids Provest, Bailzies, and Counsell advysin
and haveing passit ye said paroche kirk, sein and considderat ye pairt
foirsaid quhair they desyir to build ye dask, thay find the petitioune
ressonable, and thairfor gives and grauts lycience and tolerance to ye said
petitiouners to big ane dask for ye vse of the bretherene, maisteris, and
friemene of ye said craft, at ye pairt assigned, provydeing that ye samen
beis built assweille for decernement as for ye vse of the petitiouneris, be
aduyce of ye Mr of Kirk Workis, and all he sall give ordour and directioune
for that effect.—*Council Register, vol.* lii., *p.* 378.

In addition to having seats in the parish kirk, the Trades
maintained seats in the Trinity Chapel until it was sold in
1793 ; while the Bakers, who were almost all Episcopalians,
erected a loft in old St. Paul's. In 1740 the crafts resigned
their right to the seats in the parish kirks, a minute to the
following effect being passed by the Convener Court, and subsequently endorsed by the individual trades :—

16th June, 1740.—The Convener Court, considering the several Acts of
the corporations of the Trades of this burgh concerning the seats and lofts
belonging to the Trades of this burgh in this old and new churches, they
unanimously ratifie, homologat, and approve the same, and grant warrant to
the convener, in conjunction with the deacons and paymasters of the
several corporations to renounce and assigne in favour of the Magistrates
and Town Council of this burgh with the powers to them and their successors to sit and dispose of the same to any persons they please in time
coming. But with preference always to any freeman who shall incline to
take seats or lofts pertaining to that trade whereof they are members.
And in consideration that the Magistrates and Council pass from any
bygane rents that may be claimed for the said seats and lofts for the time
bygane, the Court hereby earnestly recommend to their successors and to
the haill trades to contribute generously towards the repair of the old
church how soon the same shall be begun to be repaired. But in case
the seats and lofts in the old church shall happen to be removed at repairing thereof, the Court recommend and appoint the same to be removed
to no worse place, but may be altered for the better, beautifying the
church.—*Convener Court Book.*

Thus ended the direct connection between the craftsmen
in their collective capacity and the church, a connection that
had subsisted in one way or other for over three centuries.

CHAPTER III.

DIFFERENCES AMONG THE MERCHANT AND CRAFT BURGESSES.

IN a previous chapter some account was given of the early differences among the craftsmen. For a time these differences were lost sight of on account of the disturbing effect of the wars with England. About 1430, Scotland became so much depopulated by the wars with England, that it was found necessary to import craftsmen from France and Flanders. In 1431, King James, "to augment the common weil, and to cause his lieges increase in mair virteus, brocht mony nobill craftsmen out of France and Flanders, and other partes—for the Scottis were exercit in continuell wars frae the time of King Alexander the Third to thay days. Thus were all craftsmen slane be the wars." James V. had also to plenish the country with craftsmen from France, Spain, Holland, and England. Pitscottie tells us that "some of these were gunners, wrights, carvers, painters, masons, smiths, harness-makers, tapesters, broudsters, taylors, cunning chirurgeons, apothecaries, with all other kinds of craftsmen that might bring his realm in policy, and his craftsmen apparel his palaces in all manner of operation, and necessaries, according to their order, and gave them large wages and pensions yearly." The depopulation of the country by the wars with England also told severely on the common good of the burghs. In 1491 the third Parliament of King James, "holden at Perth, 18th March," passed the following Act, in which the deacons are asked to furnish a statement to the Chamberlain of Scotland of all monies received from craft burgesses in payment of their freedom :—

It is statute and ordainit anent the Common Good of all our Sovereign Lord's Burrows within the Realme that the said Common Good be observed and kept to the common profit of the town, and to be suspended (expended) in common and necessary things of the burgh with the advice and councill of the town for the tyme : and Deacons of crafts where they are, an inquisition yearlie to be taken by the Chamberlain of expenses and disposition of the samen.

When the country became more peaceful the burgesses again began to differ among themselves as to their relative rights and privileges. We have already seen that in the earliest trading charters granted to Aberdeen the weavers and fullers were excluded from the Merchant Guild, and in the reign of James III. a general statute was passed enacting that every craftsman " aither forbeare his merchandise or els renounce his craft " without any colour or dissimulation, under the pain of escheat of his merchandise ; and again, in the reign of James IV., the Convention of Royal Burghs enacted that " na craftesman sall vse ony maner of merchandise within the burgh, but occupy his awin craft under the pains contenit in the Actis of Parliament." But, notwithstanding these statutes, there were always differences of opinion as to what was meant by the " use of his awin craft." The wrights, for instance, claimed the right to import timber, the shoemakers to deal in leather, the skinners and glovers to deal in hides and skins, and so forth ; and in these disputes the Town Councils, being dominated by the merchant influence, showed little favour for the craftsmen. In this respect Aberdeen was a notable example. The Dean of Guild was a member of the Town Council *ex-officio* ; he collected all the burgess dues not only from merchant burgesses, but from trade burgesses, and handed them over to the Common Good ; and this coalition with the alderman and baillies naturally aroused the jealousy of the more plebein but more numerous craftsmen. The craftsmen, at certain periods of the town's history, contributed as liberally as the merchants to the Common Good, and naturally they held they were entitled to a proportionate representation in the Town Council. Frequent disturbances were the result—disturbances that were at this time common in most of the burghs in Scotland. A specially severe encounter between the merchants and craftsmen of Edinburgh led to the passing of an Act in the reign of Queen Mary (1555) which again abolished the office of deacon. Shortly before the passing of this Act the Edinburgh magistrates had passed a law encroaching on the craftsmen's special rights and privileges, and this new infringement, says Campbell in his "Cordiners of Glasgow," roused the resentment of the deacons of the Trades to such an extent "that they at once resolved to let it be clearly understood that they were in no mood to submit, but were determined to obtain redress, and that speedily." They accordingly proceeded to the Town-House, where, apparently with the intention of overawing the magistrates, they drew their swords. In this object they were disappointed and were themselves seized and overpowered by an armed force, and thereafter imprisoned. The craftsmen then assembled to rescue their deacons ; but, on the matter beginning to assume a serious aspect, it was put an end to by the interposition of the Regent Arran.

In few burghs in Scotland was the war between the two classes of burgesses waged with such bitterness as in Aberdeen. The Act of 1555, giving the Magistrates the power of appointing deacons of the crafts, gave great dissatisfaction, and in the following year a "special gift" was obtained from Queen Mary restoring to the craftsmen the power to elect their own deacons, and bestowing other privileges, with the object of removing "the dissensions, public and private hatred and contention of our merchants and craftsmen dwelling within our burghs."*

But while this charter strengthened the position of the craftsmen in Aberdeen, it did not, as might be supposed, tend to lessen the friction between them and the merchant burgesses or Guildry. On the contrary, disagreements became more frequent and more bitter. The composition paid to the Common Good, the relative rights and privileges of the two classes of burgesses, and their representation at the Town Council, all in turn formed matters of dispute and controversy. In reference to the question of representation it may be here explained that at the end of the fourteenth century the management of the public affairs of the burgh was vested in the hands of an Alderman and four

* See Appendix.

baillies who were chosen " with the consent and assent of the whole community of the burgh ; " but this, apparently popular, mode of election existed in name only and not in practice. The Magistrates were for a long period practically self-elected, and the management of the public affairs of the town fell into the hands of a few leading families, who took care to exclude all who did not meet with their approval. Meanwhile the craftsmen had increased in number, and through their associations they began to act more vigorously. By an Act of Parliament passed in 1460 craftsmen had a right to take part in the elections, it having been then enacted that " Ilk craft shall choose a person of the same craft that shall have voice in the said election of officebearers for that time," and this right they determined should be fully recognised. They were just beginning to feel their strength, and to realise the usefulness of their associations, each with its duly appointed deacon and set of officebearers. They had to bear " Scot and lot, watch and ward " the town, and they claimed to have a voice in the election of the governing body. And to enable them to carry on their agitation for more control in the management of the town's affairs, they incorporated their associations under a Deacon-Convener and Convener Court. The Town Council evidently did not like the new office-bearer, and in 1591 declared the office illegal and the election unconstitutional. The jealousy of the Council with regard to the Convener can easily be understood. The crafts- men had become more numerous than the merchants ; they had obtained privileges independent of the Town Council ; and the Deacon-Convener must have occupied a position of no small influence in the community. The whole population at this period, it may be observed, was about four thousand, and as the members of the free craftsmen numbered several hundreds, they, with their journeymen, servants, apprentices, and families must have represented a large proportion of the total population.

Not the least serious element of dispute was the composi- tion or dues charged for making freemen. When trading privileges were first granted, no special arrangement existed with regard to the sums paid for burgess-ship. A freeman was simply bound to pay "Scot and lot, to watch and ward the town;" and, as will be seen by the Acts of Parliament already quoted, the sums collected were to be spent upon the "common warkis of the toune." These dues formed one of the chief sources of the town's revenue, and, along with the grants of lands and fishings made by the Crown, constituted what, to this day, is known as the Common Good.

The disputes about the composition arose when the Crafts began to exact entrant dues to their own associations. The Council held that these entrant dues interfered with the dues exacted for the freedom ; while the Crafts maintained that the entrant dues to their own associations were used for eleemosynary purposes, and for protecting the craftsmen in the exercise of their special trading privileges. The craftsmen had no objection to undergo "scot and lot" for the maintenance of the "Common Warkis," but they also claimed the right to institute funds of their own, to provide for their own poor, and to combine for the protection of their own special rights and privileges. It was, in short, the old familiar warfare of the more plebeian crafts fighting for political power and the maintenance of their rights against their richer and more powerful brethren. And this warfare continued, to a greater or less extent, from the end of the fifteenth century down to the passing of the Burgh Reform Acts.

In 1579 the dispute about the composition, and the admission of members to the Crafts who had not duly passed the Council, reached an acute stage. A number of craftsmen were arrested and fined for " breaking the Acts and ordinances of the town," in sums ranging from 40 shillings to ten pounds Scots ; and "the counsal being convenit for the maist pairt within the counsal-hous, reasoning upone the exorbitant and gryt compositions takin be the deconis of the craftes of this burght fra craftesmen and breder of the craft in admytting thame fre of their craft aganis thair prevelegeis, statut, devysit, and ordanit, that in all tyme cuming the decain of everie craft sall present the person of craft creven to be admittit free of the said craft to the deines of gill of this burght as ane worthy and qualificit craftismen to be admittit be the toune free of his craft efter diligent tryell and

examination of thair habilitie be the said craft ; and that the
decanis of thair craft sal nawayis compone witht thame quhill
the person creven to be admittit free of the craft first compone
with the said deines of gill, and to be admittit free be the
toune, the maisterstick of the persone to be admittit being
exhibit and producit in judgement ; and giff ony decain heireftir contraveinis this present ordinance, and acceptis the
contrair of the premises the contravener to pay als mekil to
the deniss of gill of this burght of his awn purss as he
happenit to tak for the composition of the craft."—*Council
Register, vol.* xxix., *p.* 879.

Two years after the passing of this statute something very
much resembling modern " boycotting " was resorted to in the
case of a number of leading craftsmen who were disturbing
" the bowels of the burgh."   Johne Duncan, Ion Roray,
talyeouris ; James Bannerman, baxster ; and Patrick Leithe,
armourar, were charged with having purchased law burrows
against the Provost, Baillies, and Council, " intending thairby
to leive within this burght without any correctioun or ordour "
Leithe promised to become obedient, but with regard to the
others, " the counsell, seeing the forenamed three persons
within this burght and bowills thairof, continuallie refusing
all dutiful obediens of their superiouris and magistrates under
the Kingis Majestie to the evill of the guid burght, gif remeid
were nocht provydid for correcting of the saidis licentious
persones, and to avoid the evill example and company of the
saidis three persones, it was ordanit, consentit, and grantit to,
that na burgess of gild suld set ony dwelling-houss or butht
to ony of thame, nor keep secretis witht thame, or gif thame
ony labour or manual execretions of thair craft in tyme
cuming, in respect thai are discharget of thair fredome and
fundin be the decretis producit unprofitabill neeboris of the
Commoun Weltht of this bught, resors of upror, sesine, and
divisioun withtin the bowallis thairof unto the tyme they
come to obedience of our Soueran Lordis lawis and lauchfull
statutes of this brught, and be receavit be the magistrates
thairof quharinto the hail bredrene of gild consentit bot [with-
out] ony contradictioun."—*Council Register, vol.* xxx., *p.* 612.

Meanwhile the craftsmen were diligently collecting funds to

"prosecute their causs" against the Guildry, and the Council
deemed it necessary to "mak ane oulklie (weekly) stent and
contribution to be uptaken of everi burgess of gild sua that
the samen exceed nocht twa shillings of ilk persone at the maist,"
this collection to be used in defending themselves against
what were regarded as encroachments by the craftsmen.

In 1581 the Aberdeen craftsmen took a bold step. Immediately after James VI. came to the throne they joined with the
craftsmen of Edinburgh, Dundee, and Perth in applying for a
new charter of privileges, and succeeded in obtaining an important confirmation of previous rights and liberties, along with
an extension of their right of dealing in merchandise. The
Act of 1555, which deprived the Crafts of the power to elect
their Deacons and conferred it on the Town Councils, was
specifically repealed. With the object of "removing all public
and private dissensions, hatreds, and contentions between
merchants and craftsmen, and for certain other reasonable
causes," the charter declares:—"We repone them to use and
have Deacons of Crafts who shall have vote in choiceing of
officers of Burrows and shall elect and admitt all kinds of
Craftsmen within Burgh to use and exerce their craft if they
be fund able therefor. And they shall Siclyke hear the
compts of the common good and be parts of the Auditors
thereof; and they shall conveen and make priviledges statutes
and ordinances above the said Craftsmen for keeping of good
order amongst them, and sustentation and Intertainment of
Gods service, and said use and exerce all maner of merchandize within our said Realme, and outwith the same as they
shall think most expedient to their greatest commoditie, with
all and sundrie priviledges and liberties and faculties granted
to them by our most noble progenitors, or whereof they have
been in possession in times bypast, notwithstanding the said
Act of Parlt. or whatsoever pains contained therein, anent the
whilks we be thir present dispenses. Attour we be thir
present ratifys and approves all priviledges, liberties, and
faculties, given and granted by our most noble progenitors to
the saids Craftsmen in all times bypast, to be used and exerced
by them in the same form, force, and effect, in all times coming
as they possess the same off before, &c."

The Aberdeen Magistrates were very much displeased with the craftsmen for joining with their brethren in Edinburgh, Perth, and Dundee in applying for this gift, and immediately took steps to punish the ringleaders among the craftsmen. A number of them were summoned to appear before the Magistrates and Council, when they admitted that they had rashly and unadvisedly approved of the purchasing of the new "pretendit" privileges, expressed their contrition for engendering uproar, schism, tumult, and sedition betwixt them and their superiors, the Provost, Baillies, Council, and Free Burgesses of Guild, and consented, as the following minute bears, to pass therefrom:—

25th August, 1581.—The said day thir craftismen vnderwretin that is to say Mathow Guild, armorar, Lowrens Marsar, George Elphinstoun Arthour Hill, Hew Johnnstoun, sadlaris ; Patrik Hay, Goldsmyth, George Nesmyth, Patre Leithe, Androw Meille, smythtis ; Patre Wilsoune, Lourens Bell, Pewteraris ; Richart Williamsoune, Williame Allane, Culteltaris; Gilbert Blak, Robert Sanders, cowparis ; Johnne Rora, Thomas Spensar, Alexr. Patersone, David Henrie, George Keir, Johnne Barnis, Johnne Knycht, Talzeouris; and Patrik Straquhyn, Baxter; comperit all personallie in Jugement and being aduysit with yame selffis efter retfull deliberatioun and consultatioun and grantit and confessit yat yai had raschly and onaduysatly apprevit in jugement the purchasing of ye new pretendit preuilege obtenit of ye kyngis maiestie and lordis of secreit counsale agains ye freedom, libertie, and common weill of ye frie burgessis and Brethren of gild of yis burt, quhilk yai understand now tendis to engener vproar, schism, tumult, and seditioun, betuixt yame and yare superiouris and magistrates the prouest, Ballies, Consale, and frie burgessis of gild of yis burt, and yairfor war content to leave ye samen and pas yairfra, and to leif upon yair awin Craftis and vocatioun only, according and conforme in all poyntis to ye approbatioun, consessioun, act, and ordinance maid be ye remanent craftismen of yis burt, upon ye fourtene day of August instant and ratefeit and apprevit ye samen in all poyntis and obleist yameselffis and war sworne néuir to cum in ye contrair yairof and put yame in will fur the said assisting and adhering to ye said new preuilege, craving pardoun and forgifnes yairof, and obleist yameselves neuir to do ye lyk in tym cuming bot to be subjectit to all obedience of ye said prouest ballies and consale and to leif at quyatnes upon yeir Craftis and vocationis alanerlie in all tyme cuming. And renuncit ye said preuilege and all uyir preuilege and letters purchest or to be purchest be yame perpetually in all tym cuming.—*Council Register, vol.* xxx., *p.* 494.

The Council, however, could not undo the King's Charter, and the promises they exacted from the craftsmen that it would not be acted upon, do not appear to have restored anything approaching an amicable understanding. In 1582 the representatives appointed by the craftsmen to vote at the annual election of magistrates, declined to take any part in the proceedings, a step that brought matters to a crisis, and forced the Council and Guildry to the conclusion that some definite mutual agreement must be arrived at without further delay. The following is the entry in the Council Register bearing on the refusal of the craftsmen to take part in the election, a refusal which in a measure led to the important negotiations narrated in the next chapter :—

1st October, 1582.—The saide day the craftismen eftir following, that is to say Andrew Will, George Elphinstoun, Patrik Hay, Mathew guild, Alexr. Patersone, David Watsoun, Johne Sanders, Cordinar ; Thomas Cuik, Cordeuar ; Arther Hill, Alexr. Donaldsone, Alexr. Stevin, James Wysman, Johne Wricht, being oppiulie inquirit be calling of ye suit roll be yair names in speciall to gif thair wote in chesing and electing of ye provost, bailies and officiaris of yis burt. according to the comoun order and consuetude of yis burt. obseruit in tymes by past, whilkis anserit everie ane particularlie be yame selffis personalie present yat yai wald gif na wote nor electioun of ye saidis juges and officiaris quhill yai be restorit to yair libertie and adjoint to ye Societie of uyiris fremen of this burt, and ye actis gif ony be maid yair anent annullit andyair foir refusit to nominat ony persone to exerce ye said office and tuik act and instrument yairupon ; and siclyk Robert Mengzes, baillie, in name of ye toun tuik act and instrument yairupon and protestit yat yai be not hard to haif vote in tyme coming becaus efter yair present refuse without just occasioun.— *Council Register, vol.* xxx., *p.* 722.

CHAPTER IV.

THE COMMON INDENTURE.

THE year 1587 was a memorable one in the history of the Guildry and Crafts in Aberdeen. Something approaching a dead-lock in the management of the affairs of the burgh had been brought about by the conflicts and disputes between the merchant and craft burgesses, and, with the view of arriving at a better understanding, it was arranged to hold a conference or a " commoning " :—

22nd June, 1587.—The said day the counsaill convenit for ye maist part with ane certain number of the brethrene of gild aduysing upoun ye articulis given to ye Prouest, Bailleis, and Counsaill be ye deaconis of ye crafts for them selffis and remanent craftsmen of ye said burght desyring sum preuileges to be granted to thame according to ye saidis articulis, the Counsaill, with consent of the brethrene of gild, thought it guid that thair sal be som commoning haid thairanent with ye saidis deaconis or twa or thre for ye saidis craftis appointit and nominat for ye haill haueing comissioun of ye saidis craftis at twa houris after nowne to continue within Sanct Nicholas Kirk. And for yat effect the counsaille and brethrene of gild nominat Alexr. Cullane, David Mengzes, Baillis and Alexr. Rutherfurd to meit at the hour foirsaid, and have commouing vpoun ye saidis articulis with sic as sal be chosin be ye craftismen aucthoresit with their comissioun to see and consider gif ane vniformite may be haid betwixt the brethrene of gild and thame, and to report agane quhat beis done the morne to ye effect the counsaill may consult yair anent. With prouisioun that ye commoning be na wayis preiudiciall to the richtis, preuilegeis, liberteis, and imuniteis of ye haill brethrene of gild and all actis and constitutiones of yis burght nor zit to the civill actionis and caussis depending presently befoir ye lordis auent ye saidis preuilegeis betwixt the saidis provest, bailleis, counsaill and brethrene of gild on ye ane part, and ye saides craftsmen on ye other part.—*Council Register, vol.* xxx., *p.* 218.

The preliminaries having been satisfactorily arranged, and the craftsmen having appointed George Elphinstone, saddler, Alexander Robertson, baxter, and John Duncan, tailor, as their commissioners, the Common Indenture or "The Aberdeen Magna Charta," as it came to be called, was formally ratified upon the 6th day of August, 1587, with all the serious solemnity befitting such an important event. We are told that "the haill town being lauchfullie warnit to this day be the hand-bell passand thro' the haill rewis of the town, quhairupon the bearer made faith in judgement, to the effect underwritten; and being conveenit for the maist part, representant the haill body of the town, compearit personally in judgement ane worshipfull man maister Alexander Cheyne, parson of Suaw, commissar of Aberdene, oversman in the action and matter underwritten, and produced the decreet and appointment given in and pronounced betwixt the bretheren of gild of this burgh and craftismen of the same burgh, concerning all contests and debates betwixt the saids brethren of gild and craftismen for avoiding of the said debates whilk has been amang them in time bygane, and there desirit the saids brethren of gild and craftismen, being conveenit for the maist part, to affirm the samen, and to grant to the registration thereof in the buikes of this present auditore; whilk being openly read in judgment, the saids brethren of gild and craftismen ratifyit and affirmt the same, and consentit and agreit all in ane voice, without contradiction to the registration of the said appointment in the said buikes, that execution may pass thereupon in form as effeirs; in respect whereof the saids baillies ordaint the same to be done, and to be registrate in the buikes of this present auditore, to have the strength of ane confest act and judicial decreet, and excutorials of poinding and horning to pass thereupon in form as effeirs, and interpont their authority thereto to the effect forsaid, and monisht the saids brethren of gild and craftismen to underly and fulfill the samen in all points."—*Council Reg., vol.* xxxii., *p.* 233.

Under this agreement the mode of admitting craftsmen to the freedom was strictly defined, and the composition rates fixed as follows:—" Giff the entrant be the eldest son of any free burgess, or zit the eldest son of ane free craftisman that hes past their prenticeship within the said burgh of Aberdene, he sall be free with the craft for the bancate only; bot the rest of merchants sons, or free craftismen's sons that hes past their prenticeship within the said burgh of Aberdene, sall pay forty shilling o'head, with the bancate also befoir, allenarly; and all prentices learning within the said town, and zet being ane forane, or born out of the said town, as also they that are not freeman's sons, suppose they be born within the town, sall pay ten marks overhead with the bancate, for their freedums, to the deacon and bretheren of their craft; sicklike outlands craftismen that are notht born burgesses sons or freemen's sons of the said burgh, neither hes past prenticeship within the same, but has learnt their craft in ony uther place not within the town, they sall pay to the deacon and maisters of their craft for their freedom, at the least twenty marks money forsaid with the bancate as said is; and decerns the composition of the money forsaid for the freedum, as is above expreamt, to be delivert and payt to the deacon of the craft, he to be answerable for the twa parts of the same to the dean of gild and to deliver the same to him for to be wared and bestowt upon the aid, support, and help of the common charges of the town, according to the directions to be given be the provost, baillies, and council of the said burgh to him thereanent; and the third part of the said composition, with the bankates foresaid, to be distributit and bestowt at the pleasure of the deacons of the craftis and their brethern foresaids freemen of the said burgh."

The other conditions of the agreement related chiefly to respective trading privileges of the two classes of burgesses, and to the number of representatives the craftsmen were to have at the election of the office-bearers in the Town Council. In regard to the latter it was decreed that "it sall be liesome to the said craftismen to choise sax persons of their awin number zearly, to be upon lyitis, of whom the concil sal choise twa thereof zierly, who sall have place with the rest of the ordinary auditors to hear and see all and sundry the town's compts, baith of property and causualitys."

The Common Indenture was confirmed by Royal Charter granted by James VI., dated at Faukland, the 16th of July, 1617, and was again ratified by an Act of the Scottish Parliament held at Edinburgh on the 28th of January, 1633.*

---

* For full text of the Indenture, see Appendix.

The much-desired peace "within the bowells of the burgh," which was expected to follow the solemn enactment of the Common Indenture, was, however, of very short duration. Several of the deacons, in their defiance of the Town Council went the length of admitting craftsmen "free of their craft" before they were presented to the Council, an offence which led to the following sentences being pronounced, and an ordinance passed that deacons who ventured to do so in future would be fined £20 Scots for each offence :—

19th May, 1591.—The said day the prouest, bailleis, and counsall, modefeit the unlawis of the deaconis of the craftis vnderwretin quha war convict obefoir for receawing and admitting craftismen frie of their craftis respective vnderspecified, befoir thay war made frie of the toun be ye prouest, baillies, and deanis of gild theirof, express against the statutis of ye toun, ye ald preuileges grantit to yame, and contrar ye tenor of the appoyntment decreit and contract maid betuix the actis of thair convictiouns of the dait the xvii. day of Maii instant, at lynth proportis as eftir follows :—That is to say—Alex. Ronaldsone, deacon of the baxteris, to fyve merks ; Johne Sanderis, deacon of the cordoneris, to fyve merks ; Androw Lesly, deacon of the websteris, to fyve merks. And this day being assignit to Mathow Guild, deacon of the hammermen, and to Johne Dauidsone, deacon of the tailzeoris, to produce befoir the prouest, baillies, and counsalle, ane warrand of the deanis of gild, and prouest, baillies, and counsalle of this burght, to mak Adame Gordone frie of the craft of the hammermen, and the said Johne Dauidsone, for receaving of Androw Riddell, frie of the said tailzeour craft, and sua doing did na wrang in receaving and admitting of the saidis persones, nathing being producit be ye said Mathow and Johne to preiff the samen, quairfor thay war convict and put in amerciament of Court for transgressing of the said contract, and ilkane of thame tua unlawis modefeit to fyve merkis, and ye deanis of gild was ordanit to uplift thair unlawis, and the prouest, baillies, and counsall deuysit statut and ordanit that giff ony deaconnis of the craftis of this burght sal be convict theireftir for receaving and admitting of ony persone frie of thair saidis craftis befoir thay be presented, receavit, and admittit be ye toun and maid frie be ye deane of gild, that the deacone convict herein sall incur the unlaw of tuentie pundis als oft as thay happen to be convict, to be payit to the deanis of gild without ony diminutioun. And the persone admittit be thame befoir he be admittit be ye toun neuer to be receawit nor admittit burges nor frie of the toun, and yat na craftisman be maid frie bot be compositioun of ten merkis at ye leist.—*Council Register*, vol. **xxx.**, *pp.* 1110, 1111.

Fresh differences also arose regarding the election of the Magistrates, and in 1592 a sanguinary conflict took place be-

tween the commoners, who had assembled in Greyfriars Kirk
under the Deacon Convener, and Lord Huntly with the county
Barons and 250 men.   The following memorandum, entitled
" Anent the common cause betwixt the town and trades, anno
1592," appears in the Trades Records :—

> The great division betwixt the Commonalties and the Magistrates of
> Abd. was in the year of God 1591 and 1592, whereupon proceeded for the
> Magistrates great trouble.   Upon Wedensday before Michaelmass Even,
> it came to blood, the Commons being in the Gray-frier Kirk be the Con-
> veener to the election of the Magistrates that year, and Huntly with the
> County Barons being in the town att the Michaelmass Court where through
> the Laird of Balquhayne with the Lord Huntly with his accomplices whilk
> being convened together all in arms about the number of 250 or thereby,
> and of our commons about the number of 15, and there was, the said day,
> Alexr. Rutherfourd being Provost for the time, caused James Laing bell-
> man thereby goe through the town to inhibit and forbid under the com-
> mand of the said Provost that no common man of the said burgh should
> wear armour upon that day because it was the day of the election under
> the pain of the highest that might be laid to their charge, and so upon
> Wednesday it came to blood before the Grey-friers Kirk.   There was of
> 15 there, six hurt and three or four Magistrates hurt and others, and
> William Johnston Reader, son to the goodman of Standing Steenes being
> shott by two shotts the one by Thomas Buik and the other by Thomas
> Nicolson who was on the Magistrates part.   Whereupon proceeded a great
> plea in Edr, more as six score of Commons were summoned that confisca-
> tion of the cas was remitted to the decision of four Lords of Councill, the
> ministers, and four burgesses, the King to be oversman, who decreed that
> remains as yet.

On the 27th September a solemn " consultation " between
the Magistrates and the Commons of the town was held, when
the blood on both sides was " remitted."   This " act of great
solemnity " is also recorded in the Trades Books as follows :—

> The consultation betwixt the Magistrates and Commons of Aberdeen
> was held with great solemnity, first att the Womanhill, thereafter passed
> both parties to the Kirk and heard the sermon, and thereaftor came to
> the Mercatt Cross and drank ilk ane with others ; the blood on both
> sides being remitted ilk ane embraced others, the government of the town
> being decerned by decreet arbitrall to be this year as follows :—Thomas
> Menzies, of Durn, Provost ; William Menzies, George Forbes, William
> Gray, Mr. Patrick Cheyne, Bailies ; Richard Irvine, Dean of Gild ; and
> David Cargill, Thesaurer.

In 1595 it was agreed to appeal to the Convention of
Royal Burghs in regard to the differences about the election

of the Provost and Magistrates. The craftsmen "agreet that the Commissionaris of burrowis in thair nixt Conventioun generall sauld discuss and discerne quhou mony crafts sall have voit in the electioun of the provest, baillies, and vther publict officemen of this burght in all tyme to come, by an attour, the four craftsmen on the auld and new counsallis. Whereupon the saidis craftsmen for themselffs and their successors submitted thaim selffis to the saidis commissionaris of burrowis, renounce all vther jurisdiction and judgement, and oblesing thaim and their forsaidis to stand and abyd at the discreit sentence and determination of the saidis commissionaris of burrowis theiranent bot reclamation or again calling quhilsumever." In July of the following year (1596) the Convention met in Aberdeen, when there appeared before them Thomas Menzies of Durn, provost, and Alexander Rutherford, commissioners for the burgh on the one part, and " Matthew Guyld, dekin of the Hammermen ; John Kempt, dekin of the Baxters ; Johne Merser, Saidler, Alexander Stevin, Baxter, procurators ; having power of the remnent deykins and brethern of the craftes of the said burght, and submitted themselves to the amicable decision of the Commissioners anent the difference and question betwixt the saidis partis concerning the number of the craftismen of the said burght quilk sall have voit yeirlie in the election of the magistrates of the samen at the feist of Michaelmas." After due deliberation, and with the consent of both parties, the Convention discerned and ordained—

That in all tyme cuming, yeirle and ilk yeir, the tyme of the electioun of the said magistrates thair salbe twa craftsmen of the auld counsal, and twa of the new counsall, with the six deacons of crafts of the said burght allanerlie, quhlk salbe ten persons iu number for saids craftis, and ua mae to have voit in the yeirlie chosing, at Michaelmas, of the provest, baillies, dean of gild, and theasurer ; and in case ony of the saidis ten personis sall happen to be absent the day of the electioun, it sall be lessum to the remanent of the saidis craftis hauing voit in the electioun, as said is, and being present to chois and put ane qualified persone or persones in place of thame that sall happen to be absent to have voit as gif the personnes absent war personallie present ; and gif it sall happen ony of the provest, baillies, dean of gild, theasurer, and consal of the said burght, auld and new (by the said craftismen), quhilkis sall not exceed the number of threttie personnes by the provestes, or woit, quilk mackis threttie ane voittis in the haill for the part of the gild brethern to be absent the said time of the election ; in that case it shall be lesum to the said provest, baillies, dean of gild, theasurer, and consal quha salbe present to elect another person or personis according to the number of them that salbe absent to gif voit at the said electioun in and be all thingis as gif they had been all present that hes voit ordinarlie ; and this decreet they discern and ordain to be registrat in the buikis, etc.—*Council Register, vol.* xxxvi., *p.* 565.

The ten office-bearers of the Crafts who were thus empowered to vote at the election of the Provost and Magistrates came to be known among their brethren as the " X." They had, as the following minute of the Convener Court shows, to vote " solid," in accordance with the decision of a majority of their own number :—

25 Sept., 1671.—The said day the haill Deacon Convener Court all with ane consent and assent strictly statuts and ordains that in all tymes hereafter it shall be observed be the Deacon Convener, haill deacons, and the tua councillors who shall goe up yearly to the election of the magistrates and council, shall be all of one mind and shall voice all alike in electing of the said council as the major part of them shall ordain, and put in the Deacon-Convener's mouth for that effect according to old use and want that so there be no alteration nor breach of their ten voices (called the *X.*) in any manner or way, but to stand firm and sure to all future ages under infamie and perjurie. And any who shall contravene hereunto be holden and reputed infamous, and no ways to have society nor correspondence with his traid, nor voice at their meeting, nor benefit of the hospital, until he supplicate and give the Deacon Convener Court satisfaction as they shall ordain. And sicklike, if it be found that any be refractory or disobedient therein the Deacon Couveuer to have full power to put off that person or persons, and put on another of that trade in his place for voicing in the said election as said is. And this Act to stand unalterable in all time coming as the laws of the Medes and Persians.—*Convener Court Book.*

The two Trades Councillors had also to vote " together as one man." When any matter affecting the Trades came before the Council for consideration, the Convener Court had to be consulted by the Trades Councillors, who were then instructed to give their vote according to the decision of the Court. The method of procedure was laid down as follows :—

23rd September, 1672.—The said day it is strictly statute and ordained by the haill court unanimously that whoever the two Councillors be who shall sit upon the Council for the traids that they, nor neither of them, shall give their voice in anything which shall be agitate in the Council concerning the traids in general, or any traid in particular, anent their liberties or any other public interest, until they first acquaint the Deacon Convener and remanent Deacons for the time, and after their advice and information given by them thereanent, that both the said Councillors shall conform themselves thereunto, and give their voice unanimously as they shall be advised or enjoined to do. And if any of the said two Councillors shall transgress and contravene herein shall have no voice in his Court until he supplicate the same, and give the members thereof for the time satisfaction as they shall ordain.—*Convener Court Book.*

The Deacon-Convener, unless specially appointed by the Trades as one of their representatives, had no vote *ex officio*. He simply attended, along with the " X.," and marked the voting list for the Trades' representatives. On one occasion a Trades Councillor was fined £10 Scots for not attending the meetings of the Council, and was also debarred from the Convener Court. On craving pardon, however, he was reinstated in office.

In 1641, Charles I., who was on his first visit to Scotland, granted a special charter to the craftsmen of Aberdeen confirming the privileges granted by his noble progenitors, and especially the charters granted by " our dear, good dame of worthy memorie, Queen Mary," in 1556, and by King James in 1581 (see Appendix). The latter portion of this charter granted by King Charles contains an important clause referring to " decreits, statutes, or proclamations made, or to be made," which was generally regarded as abrogating the Common Indenture so far as it contained anything at variance with the charters which were being confirmed.

It may safely be assumed that Dr. Guild, who was one of the Chaplains in Ordinary to Charles, and had obtained a charter eight years previously in connection with the founding of the Trades Hospital, had urged the craftsmen to secure this charter. The privileges it confirms are much more favourable to the craftsmen than the liberties granted under the Common Indenture, and the reference to decreets plainly shows that it was the intention to get out of some of the more restrictive provisions of that agreement. The Council, however, declined to recognise this charter, and, in subsequent disputes between the Guildry and the craftsmen, little or no reference is made to its existence.

THE constitution of the Town Council, confirmed by the Common Indenture, remained unaltered until the Burgh Reform Acts. For over three centuries the craftsmen elected two of their number to be constituent members of the Council, while six of the deacons had power to vote at the election of magistrates and office-bearers. The six trades who exercised this privilege were the Hammermen, Bakers, Wrights and Coopers, Tailors, Shoemakers, and Weavers, the Fleshers not being incorporated with the others until after the "sett" of the burgh was fixed. Although there were continual bickerings between the Town Council, the Guildry, and the craftsmen, notwithstanding the Common Indenture, it was not until 1801 that a serious dispute occurred, when a litigation took place that was carried to the House of Lords. This litigation deserves special notice because of its bearing upon the position of the Trades in regard to their private funds.

The Town Council appointed a committee to consider "the amount of the compositions at present paid by craftsmen belonging to the different corporations upon their being admitted freemen thereof, and the propriety of augmenting such compositions." This committee's report, which was given in on 21st September, 1801, narrates that in October, 1641, the Council ordained and appointed that every person, an extranean, admitted a free craftsman should pay for his composition £100 Scots, and apprentices within the town £50 Scots each, besides appearing at the time of their admission completely armed with musket and sword, to be sworn as their own property. By another Act of Council in 1643, it was statute and ordained that each craftsman should pay for his composition 200 merks, and apprentices 100 merks, and that craftsmen marrying a burgess of Guild or free craftsman's daughter should pay only 80 merks, all of them furnishing arms as already described. In 1665 it was reported that former acts and resolutions respecting the admission of craftsmen and the amount of their compositions had not been duly observed and attended to, and it was of new appointed and ordained " that each craftsman extranean, at his entry, should pay 200 merks of composition, with a pick or £4 Scots therefore, for the use of the town's magazine, and apprentices as formerly; and that the acts relating to the sons of free craftsmen, and also those who had married the daughters of burgesses of Guild or crafts-men, shall remain the same." From an examination of the Guildry accounts from 1641 to 1681, it was found that the com-position payable by the craftsmen at their entry, notwithstand-ing these Acts of Council, had been " various and arbitrary." The amount paid was sometimes 200 merks, sometimes 100 merks each; and that without any cause being assigned for such variation or reduction. From 1681 down to 1801 the composition payable by extranean craftsmen appears to have been reduced to £40 Scots, and by apprentices £24 Scots, with five shillings each for arms money. The Town Council's com-mittee, therefore, resolved to recommend, " after deliberately considering the result of their whole examination, as well as the great decrease in the value of money since the compositions payable by craftsmen at their entry were last established, and particularly that the whole of the corporations in place of 20 merks specified in the said Indenture have for many years past exacted from each entrant a much larger sum, as high as £10 or £12 sterling, without ever accounting for or paying to the Dean of Guild any more than two-thirds parts of the said 20 merks, the committee were unanimously of opinion, except Deacons Smith and Henderson, that the compositions at present payable to the Guildry for the Common Good by entrant craftsmen are considerably too small, and that they ought to be augmented or at least restored to what they were settled at in the year 1643, with ten shillings sterling in name of arms money as an equivalent for what arms they for-merly were obliged to furnish at their own expense. The committee therefore recommended—(1) That all the deacons should be ordained to lodge annually a statement with the

Dean of Guild or Town Clerk of the compositions actually paid to the trades by each entrant, and to pay over two-thirds part of every composition in terms of the obligation incumbent on them by the Common Indenture ; (2) That the second or younger sons either of burgesses or craftsmen shall be admitted freemen of the craft which they profess for payment to the Dean of Guild of 20s. sterling of composition, besides the said sum of 10s. for arms money, and that the eldest sons should only pay arms money but no composition ; (3) That all apprentices who shall have served and completed a regular apprenticeship to free craftsmen within the burgh, and whose indentures have been recorded in the town's books within twelve months after the date thereof should be entitled to be admitted free of their respective crafts for payment of one-half of the composition above stated, besides arms money, and two-thirds part of the composition actually paid by them to the craft to which they belonged ; (4) That all craftsmen who have married the daughters either of another free craftsman or of a burgess of Guild should be entitled to be free of the respective crafts to which they enter for payment also of one-half of the sum payable by extraneans, and that such persons who enjoy both the above privileges of apprenticeship and marriage shall be entitled to be admitted for payment of one-fourth part of the composition."

This report was approved by the Town Council, and they appointed that the deacons of the several crafts should lodge a particular account and statement of such persons as had been admitted and received members of their respective corporations for the year preceding, and of the compositions actually paid to the trade by such entrants ; and they also appointed the deacons to account for and pay over two-thirds part of every such composition in terms of the Common Indenture.

It was this Act of Council which led to the litigation that was carried to the House of Lords, and which lasted for a period of fourteen years. Several serious issues were involved. By this time the Trades had instituted a widows' and other benevolent funds for the benefit of their own members, and the additional sums received from entrants over and above the compositions to the town were paid into these funds. The Trades were willing to pay the composition, but they denied the right of the town to any share of the entry money which was voluntarily paid by entrants into the benevolent funds of the Trade. A memorial presented to the Town Council by the Trades sets forth their case as follows :—

These compositions are exactly of the same nature as a price or feu-duty paid by the craftsmen in consideration of certain privileges of trade at that time conferred on them by the decreet arbitral, and thereby secured to be enjoyed by them ever afterwards.   It is therefore clear that the Town Council have no better right to raise these dues on account of the decrease of the value of money than they would have right to increase the feu-duties of such estates as were feued off by their predecessors at that ancient period.   And it is equally clear that these compositions cannot consistently with their rights as a legal body be augmented without at the same time proportionally enlarging their privileges.

From the whole tenor of the submission and decreet arbitral it may be seen that these compositions are exactly of the same nature as that above described, and that the craftsmen had no other object in view, nor obligation incumbent on them, in paying these compositions than solely the privileges of trade thereby conferred on them.

In the next place, the memorialists may observe that it is not in the memory of any person alive that any of the trades which the memorialists represent have of themselves increased the present compositions properly so called paid into their funds ; any increase of entry money which they have made is allotted and paid into particular funds destined for charitable purposes, for which the members derive an equivalent advantage ; for instance, entrants pay to a fund lately established from £15 3s. to £6 6s. each, according to their classes, for which their widows receive an annuity for life.   But surely it would be remote from your honours' views to lay any claim to a share of such funds as these, as if they were compositions, or to maintain that, because the entry money payable to the funds of the corporations is augmented to answer charitable purposes, it should follow as a consequence that a sum which is paid as a fair price for certain privileges should also for that reason be augmented.   This decreet arbitral has fixed and settled the principle that these compositions could not be altered without the consent of both parties, and with their consent it must therefore be presumed that any alteration of these compositions was made.

It will be seen that this was a matter of vital importance to the Trades.   It involved the future prosperity of their respective benevolent funds, and they accordingly raised an action in the Court of Session to have it declared that the Town Council had no power or authority at their own hands to

augment or increase, vary or alter, the fees or dues payable
on the admission of craftsmen to the exercise of their respective
Trades ; that the augmentation or increase of the fees or dues
is extravagant, and if there is any ground for alteration or
variation thereof in any respect, or any power for that purpose
but an Act of the British Legislature, the same ought to and
should be modified and restricted, and a regular table of such
fees established upon just principles of law and equity.

A cross action was raised by the Town Council to have it
declared that in virtue of the Charters and Acts of Parliament in favour of the burgh, the Town Council had full power
and authority to augment or increase, vary and alter, the fees
or dues payable to the town on the admission of craftsmen to
the exercise of their respective Trades; and, in particular, that
it should be declared that the Act of Council of the 21st
September, 1801, is valid and effectual, and that in virtue
thereof the Town Council and their successors in office have
full power and authority to exact and levy the whole dues and
fees thereby established, and to insist for implement of the
other conditions and regulations contained in the said Act of
Council.

Both actions were heard before Lord Newton, who had
previously suggested the propriety of a counter declaration
being brought at the instance of the magistrates with a
view to enable them to vary the rate of dues.   As the
papers in these two actions cover over five hundred pages of
foolscap it is impossible to do more than give the decisions.
It may be here explained that the craftsmen regarded the
action of the Town Council as an attempt to obtain a " grip "
over their funds such as they possessed, and still possess,
over the Guildry funds.   The Council, it is true, repudiated
any such intention ; but the instructions to counsel that were
prepared on behalf of the Trades leave no doubt that such was
the impression among the craftsmen at this time.   On July
4th, 1807, Lord Newton pronounced the following interlocutor :—

> The Lord Ordinary of consent of parties allows a Summons of Declara-
> tor at the instance of the Magistrates and Council of Aberdeen against
> the Incorporated Trades of Aberdeen, to be repealed *incidentor* in this

process ; conjoins the two actions ; and in respect it is not denied that the exigencies of the burgh require the increase of dues complained of by the Incorporated Trades, assoilizes the Magistrates and Town Council from the declarator at their instance, in so far as regards the dues payable to the Guildry of the town in name of composition for entry ; but finds that the Magistrates have no right to claim from the Trades any further part of the composition paid by intrants to the Trades than the sums specially fixed in the Common Indenture, and which the town have been in use to receive past memory ; therefore decerns and declares in terms of the declarator at the instance of the Trades, in so far as respects the composition paid by the intrants to the Trades ; and decerns and declares in terms of the declarator at the instance of the Magistrates, in so far as respects the sums paid by the intrants to the Guildry in name of entry ; superseding extract till the first sederunt day in November next.

Against this interlocutor both parties gave in representations, and on 11th March, 1808, the following interlocutor was pronounced:—

The Lord Ordinary, having considered the representation for the Incorporated Trades of Aberdeen with the answers thereto for the Magistrates and Town Council of Aberdeen together with the counter representation for the Magistrates and Town Council with the answers thereto for the Incorporated Trades ; in respect the power of the Magistrates of Aberdeen to augment the dues of entry of Guild burgesses has been recognised by a solemn judgment of this court in the case of Duncan against the Magistrates, finds that, upon the same ground, they are entitled to raise the dues of admission upon Craftsmen burgesses when, as is admitted in the present case, the exigencies of the burgh require such augmentation, as the same is not to be considered of the nature of a custom or tax, but as a reasonable price or compensation for the advantage which the Guild burgesses or craftsmen burgesses are to derive from their admission into the incorporation ; therefore adheres to the former interlocutor, assoilizing the Magistrates and Town Council from the action of declarator and reduction brought at the instance of the Incorporated Trades against them, in so far as regards the dues payable to the Guildry in name of composition for the entry of craftsmen burgesses : 2nd—Finds that, upon a just construction of the decreet arbitral of 7th July, 1587, which usually passes by the name of the Common Indenture, the Dean of Guild or Magistrates of Aberdeen are entitled to demand from the Deacons of the incorporations two-thirds of the sum which is exacted by them on the admission of intrants into their incorporation, and that the sum acclaimable by the Dean of Guild or Magistrates is not to be limited to two-thirds of the sum of 20 merks, which at that time was in use to be exacted for said admissions ; and in so far varies the former interlocutor as to decern and declare in the declarator at the instance of the Trades that the Magistrates and Dean of Guild are

entitled to demand two-thirds of the sum actually paid for the admission
of craftsmen into the incorporations ; and with this variation adheres to
the interlocutor brought under review, and refuses the desire of both
representations. And, as the case has now and formerly been very
deliberately considered, dispenses with any representation against this
interlocutor. But supersedes extract till the third sederunt day in May
next.

The Trades were not satisfied with this decision, although
it defined their position more satisfactorily than ever it had
been, and an appeal was carried to the House of Lords. Their
lordships, however, confirmed the judgment of the Court
of Session, giving the Town Council power to increase and
vary the amount of the composition. The Trades, however,
now knew how they stood. Whatever rate was fixed by
way of composition to the Common Good could not interfere
with any sums they might choose to levy on entrants as contributions to their benevolent funds. Their right to possess
such funds was recognised, and, so long as they paid the
composition demanded, the Town Council could not interfere
in any way with them.

Fourteen years after the dispute began—and a costly dispute it proved to both parties—the following arrangement
was arrived at between the Town and the Trades in regard to
this vexed question :—

At Aberdeen, the twenty-sixth day of September, Eighteen hundred and fifteen years, in presence of the Town Council.

Which day the Provost stated to the Council that several meetings had
lately taken place between the Magistrates and the delegates appointed by
the Incorporated Trades with the view of bringing about an amicable settlement of the claim of the Dean of Guild for his proportion of compositions
payable to the Trades on the admission of intrant members agreeably to
the decreet arbitral in 1587 (usually called the Common Indenture) and
the decreet of the Court of Session, afterwards affirmed by the House of
Lords ; that he had now the satisfaction to inform the Council that an
arrangement had been concluded between the parties whereby it was proposed that the Dean of Guild should receive two hundred pounds in full of
all claims for bygone compositions, and that in future the compositions
(whereof two-thirds to be paid to the Dean of Guild) should not be less
than what is contained in the resolutions of the delegates after engrossed.

That a minute agreeable to this arrangement had been drawn up and
agreed to by the delegates for the Trades, and it was the opinion of the
Magistrates that the terms therein stated are fair and reasonable for both

parties and should be acceded to by the Council. Which having been considered by the Council they unanimously approved of the Magistrates' procedure in this business and the arrangement recommended by them in the terms of the minute now laid before them, and they authorise the Dean of Guild on payment of two hundred pounds to discharge the incorporations of all claims he might have for his proportion of bygone compositions paid to the Trades preceding the date hereof, and appointed the said minute to be recorded in the Council Register for preservation, of which the tenor follows, viz. :—"Trinity Hall, the twenty-third day of September, Eighteen hundred and fifteen. At a meeting of the delegates appointed by the seven Incorporated Trades of Aberdeen for endeavouring to settle with the Magistrates respecting the Dean of Guild's proportion of compositions payable to the Trades on the admission of intrant members in terms of the Common Indenture. Convener Nicol in the chair. Having resumed consideration of the subject of said composition, and the terms of the Common Indenture, 1587, and decreet of the Court of Session dated 4th July, 1807, 11th March, 1808, and 10th February, 1809, afterwards affirmed by the House of Lords, and having communicated with the Magistrates relative thereto, the said delegates unanimously resolved—

"That the seven Trades shall pay to the Dean of Guild two hundred pounds sterling in full of all demands for his proportion of bygone compositions paid to the Trades on the admission of intrant members preceding the twenty-sixth day of September current.

"Unanimously resolved that from the date hereof and until the thirty-first day of December next, every extranear intrant shall upon his admission pay to the Boxmaster two pounds sterling and each apprentice one pound sterling in name of composition.

"Unanimously resolved that from and after the said thirty-first day of December next all intrants shall be obliged upon their admission to pay to the Boxmaster in name of composition sums of money not less than the following, viz. :—Extranears ten pounds sterling ; apprentices five pounds sterling ; and all freeman's sons-in-law two pounds sterling each—and that two third parts of all the said compositions be paid by the Deacon or Boxmaster to the Dean of Guild agreeably to the Common Indenture.

"Unanimously resolved that a minute to the above effect be entered in the Sederunt Book of each of the said Trades. (Signed) William Nicol, Convener ; William Milne, Hammermen ; Alex. Barron, Baker ; George Gibb, Wright and Coopers ; Geo. Anderson, Jun., Tailors ; William Marr, Shoemakers ; Jas. Henderson, Weavers ; Alex. Neilson, Fleshers."

CHAPTER VI.

CONSTITUTION OF THE ABERDEEN CRAFTS.

ABOUT 1520 it became common in the leading burghs in Scotland for the Magistrates to grant Seals of Cause to the different bodies of craftsmen. The power to form associations and elect deacons had already been conferred on the craftsmen by Act of Parliament and Royal Charters, but attached to that power was the condition that the deacons must be elected with consent of the Town Council or chief officer of the town. By this time most of the burghs had, such as it was, a regularly elected municipality or governing body, and, as the deacons were empowered to exercise judicial functions over the members of their own crafts, it became necessary to define their jurisdiction by means of charters granted by the aldermen, baillies, and communities. Under these local charters or Seals of Cause, the deacons were granted " full, plain, and free powers, express jurisdiction and authority to correct, punish, and amend all manner of crimes, trespasses, and faults of the said crafts, or committed by the brethren and servants of the said crafts (blood and debt excepted), with power to onlaw and amerciate the said trespassers and committers of the said crafts, &c." In short, the deacons of the crafts exercised full jurisdiction over all members, journeymen, servants, and apprentices, not only in matters relating to their handicrafts and privileges, but also in all matters affecting their conduct as citizens generally. Many of the criminal offences that are at present tried in the Burgh Police Court, such as breaches of the peace, drunkenness, assault, offensive and abusive language, &c., were all disposed of by the deacons. It was seldom necessary to impose fines. After a warning or first conviction the delinquent was threatened with the loss of his freedom and trading privileges, and this threat appears to have acted with a most wholesome effect. Second convictions, therefore, for any offence are rare; and, on the whole, the deacons seem to have performed their judicial functions with firmness and to some purpose.

In addition to granting Seals of Cause* to individual crafts, the Council passed the following general enactment:—

23rd October, 1536.—The said day ye provost and consale ordains ye deacons of everie craft to serce, vesy, and seik all faltis of their neighbours of thair ain craftis, and whar thair beis ony faltis in thair craftis that thai correct and puniss ye same and cause it be mendit; and failzeing therof ye said deacons to be punished be ye bailyies therefra themselffs.—*Council Register, vol.* xv., *p.* 235.

Under these Seals of Cause the craftsmen were better able to guard and protect their special trading privileges, and to prevent encroachments by unfreemen and others who had not qualified themselves by becoming freemen and members of the crafts. So strictly were these monopolies maintained that it was impossible for a craftsman to carry on business on his own account within the burgh until he had become a freeman or free burgess. While merchants had to give evidence of their fitness to carry on business by showing that they were possessed of a certain amount of money or land, the craftsmen had to furnish satisfactory evidence of their "habilitie" to exercise their craft. In the first instance, therefore, a craftsman applied to the deacon of his own craft to be taken on trial of his qualifications, and if his fellow-craftsmen were satisfied that he was a proper person to be taken on trial, a petition was presented to the Magistrates and Town Council to the effect "that the petitioner, having learned the art and trade of a ——, is desirous of being admitted a Freeman of Craft of the —— Trade of Aberdeen, and for that purpose is willing to be bound to actual residence, and to pay Scot and Lot, Watch and Ward, in common with the other inhabitants, according to his rank and station, but before being admitted it is necessary that his qualification be tried. May it therefore please your honours to remit to the —— Trade of Aberdeen to take trial of the petitioner's qualifications to be reported." This petition having been attested by the deacon, the magistrates remitted "to the —— Trade of Aberdeen to take trial

* For Seals of Cause, see chapters devoted to each Trade.

of the petitioners qualifications to be reported." The Trade
thereupon took him on trial, instructed him to make an essay
or masterstick, which consisted of one or more articles according to the custom of the particular Trade, and, if found satisfactory, the applicant was again presented to the Magistrates
and Town Council, when, after taking the oath of allegiance,
he was "admitted and received a Free Burgess of the Burgh
of Aberdeen, of his own craft only, with all the liberties and
privileges thereto competent in virtue of the Decreet or Indenture passed between the Brethren of Guild and Craftsmen of
the said Burgh, dated in July, one thousand five hundred and
eighty-seven, for payment to the Common Good of said Burgh
of —— and of five shillings Scots, to the Lord Provost, in a
white purse, as use is; declaring always that by acceptance of
said admission, the said —— becomes solemnly bound to
discharge every civil duty incumbent by law on a true and
faithful Burgess of the said Burgh. At which time he found
caution in common form." The following is an example of
how the admission of craftsmen was usually recorded :—

15th September, 1616.—The quhilk day George Pyiper and Alexander
Andersone, wrichtis, compurand sufficientlie in armour, ilkane with an hagbute and bandeleire and sword, wes ressauit and admittit friemen of thair
said craft and burgesses of this burght, ilk ane of tham for the soume of
twentie merkis Scottis money, peyit be thame to the deane of gild, with
this allwayis restrictioun and conditioun that they shall use and exerce
thair said craft proffessit be them allanerlie, and clame nor pretend no
forder libertie, preuilege nor freedome nor is sett doun and prescryuit to
craftismen be the contract and indenture past betwixt the brethern of gild
and thaim, in the yeir of God 1587 yearis ; and incais they or any of tham
do in the contrare, being convict thairoff, to be depryuit aud dischargit of
his friedom, and all libertie and preuilege they may joise and bruik thairby
in any tyme thaireftir, and gaive thair aytheis judiciallie on the premissis
and remanent poyntis of the aythe given be burgesses of this burght the
tyme of thair admission ; lykas ilk ane of thame payit fyive schillings in a
quhyte purs according to the forme vsit and wount.—*Council Register*,
vol. xl., *p.* 718.

As will be seen from the following entry in the Council
Register, the Magistrates occasionally exercised their discretion of refusing to grant a remit, if they considered the
character of the applicants unsatisfactory :—

27th February, 1729.—The Magistrates declined to grant a remit to an applicant until he had produced a certificate of his good behaviour from Glasgow whence he came last, but that they would grant the remit desired upon producing to them the said certificate.—*Trades Hall Papers.*

The following was the oath taken at the beginning of last century by merchant and craft burgesses when admitted to the freedom by the Town Council :—

I   Do solemnly swear in the presence of God that I presently own, profess, and shall adhere to and maintain the true reformed *PROTESTANT RELIGION*, denying the Heresies of *Popery* and *Quakerism* ; and if I shall at any time hereafter (as God forbid) Apostatize from the said *PROTESTANT RELIGION*, by owning or professing *Popery* or *Quakerism*, I hereby renounce all Benefits and Priviledge competent to Me as BURGES of ABERDEEN, alike as if I had never been admitted thereto.

I   Do sincerely Promise and Swear that I will be Faithfull and bear true Alledgeance to Her Majesty Queen Anne.

I   Do solemnly swear that I shall be obedient to the just and good Government of the said Burgh of Aberdeen, and shall to the best of my power maintain and preserve the Peace and all the due Priviledges thereof, particularly—

  I. I shall be leall and true to the said Burgh and Freedom.
 II. I shall never skaith their wares.
III. I shall foresee their profit, warn them of their skaith, and stop it to my power.
 IV. I shall obey the Magistrats and their Officers in all things lawfull.
  V. I shall vote no person to be Provost, Baillie, nor Counsellour of this Burgh, except Burgesses and actual indwellers within the same.
 VI. I shall give leall and true counsell and advice when it shall be asked.
VII. I shall conceal the Counsell and Secrets of the said Burgh.
VIII. I shall own no Unfreemen's Goods under Colour of Mine.
 IX. I shall Scot, Lot, Watch, Wake, and Ward with the inhabitants of this Burgh.
  X. I shall purchase no Lordship, Authority, nor Jurisdiction contrair to the Priviledges and Liberties of this Burgh, but shall mantain and defend the same to my Life's End.

So HELP ME GOD.

ADDITION FOR CRAFTSMEN.

I   shall keep my self within the Bounds and Liberties of the Indentur past betwixt the Brethren of Gild and Craftsmen of this Burgh, the Seventh of July, One thousand five hundred and eighty-seven. I shall be lyable to and obey the Town's Statutes.

So HELP ME GOD.

Nota.—That all Chirurgeons, Apothecaries, Litsters, Barbers, and others who are not incorporat among the ordinar Trades, Do at their admission as Burgers, Swear the forsaid oath, except the fifth article thereof, because they are only admitted Burgers in *Sua Arte* allennarly, and are not Burgers of Gild, nor Incorporat as said is.

In addition to subscribing the above oath, every craftsman had to take the following oath to his own craft :—

Be God him selff and as I sall answer to God at ye dreadful day of judgement upoun ye condemnation or salvatioun of my soul I sall perform these conditions ensuing :—

1. I sall be ane trew and loyall subject to ye kyng his majestie and his royal successors whom we acknowledge to be supreme governor over all persons as well ecclesiastical as civil within his majestie's dominions.
2. I sall perform my oath given to ye weill of ye toun of Aberdeen.
3. I salbe obedient to the Deacon-Convener and to ye haill lauchfull ordinances of his court.
4. I salbe obedient in ye lyke maner to ye deacon of my awin craft, and to ye haill actis and ordinances of his court or conventiounes and sall tender ye weill of my craft, and nowyse reveill ye lauchfull secrettis thairof. And furdder, I sall to ye uttermaist of my power, concur to ye weill, standing and plenishing of our convening house and hospital of ye Trusties foundit be Dr. Williame Guild.

Prior to the time when the Common Indenture or " Magna Charta " of the burgesses was entered into, no definite arrangements existed regarding the amount of composition which had to be paid by burgesses of trade to the Common Good. Craft burgesses, as well as the merchant burgesses, were liable to all stents or taxes that were imposed for keeping up "the common warkis of the toune," and for providing gifts to royalty when the town was honoured with their presence. And in addition to being liable for all necessary stents and taxes, the burgesses had also, prior to the reformation, to provide for "upholding decoring, and repairing" an altar in the parish kirk. Under the Common Indenture a definite scale of composition was fixed, the eldest son of a craftsman being made free of the town for the bancate only ; other sons had to pay forty shillings Scots additional ; apprentices ten merks, and extraneans twenty merks, two-thirds of which was to be "wared and bestowed upon the aid, support, and common help of the town," and the other third "with the bancate to be bestowed at the pleasure of the deacon of the crafts and their brethren forsaid freemen of the craft." The bancate money, it may be explained, was a small sum exacted to provide "a common meal" on the occasion of an entrant being received into his craft. This is an ancient custom which has not yet died out.

Patrimony, it will be observed, has been a prominent characteristic in the constitution of the crafts. In becoming a freeman of his craft, a father not only acquired rights and privileges for himself, but his family were admitted to the same privileges at merely nominal rates, and, in many cases, under less strict conditions. The eldest son had always the preference, then the remaining sons; sons-in-law were also placed on the same level as sons. It is worthy of note that, in some of the Trades, a craftsman, on marrying the heiress of a burgess, was placed in the same favourable position as an eldest son—a remarkable proof of the value that was attached to this patrimonial element, and also affording a striking illustration of how the Guilds were based on the simple family compact. There can be no reasonable doubt that the Guilds took over this patrimonal characteristic from the family, the same principle that obtained in the family being adopted as far as possible in the wider and more extended combination of the Guild.

Alterations were frequently made on the rate of composition paid to the Common Good. In 1641 the Town Council ordained that every extranean should pay for his composition £100 Scots, and apprentices within the burgh £50 Scots each, besides appearing at the time of their admission completely armed with musket and sword, to be sworn to as their own property. In 1643 the amount was fixed at 200 merks for extraneans, and 100 merks for apprentices; and again in 1665 it was ordained that each extranean should pay 200 merks "with a pike, or £4 Scots therefor, for the use of the town's magazine." It is evident, however, from what appears in the Council Records, that the craftsmen not only demurred paying, but actually refused to pay, those increased compositions, and from 1681 down to 1815, when a compromise was effected, the composition actually paid by an extranean was about £40 Scots, and £24 Scots by apprentices, besides five shillings Scots for arms money.* On 23rd September, 1815, the rates of composition were fixed as follows :—

Extraneans	£10	0 0
Apprentices	5	0 0
Sons and sons-in-law	2	0 0

These rates were subsequently raised on 25th March, 1839, to the following :—

Extraneans	£15	0 0
Apprentices	8	6 8
Sons-in-law	6	6 8
Younger sons	3	6 8
Eldest sons	2	8 0

besides £1 3s. 0½d. for stamp, diploma, and remit. When special trading privileges were abolished in 1846, these high rates continued to be exacted in consideration that craft burgesses had still certain privileges remaining which were not enjoyed by ordinary citizens, such as a preferential right to the benefits of Robert Gordon's Hospital, exemption from the Bell and Petty Customs, &c. But gradually these disappeared or became of less value, and in 1872 the Trades appointed a committee to inquire into the subject and endeavour to obtain a reduction of the fees on account of the loss of the trading and other privileges. After a good deal of negotiation the rates were reduced to the following uniform rate :—

Extraneans	£6	0 6
Sons (whether eldest or younger) . . .	4	3 6

When the Bell and Petty Customs were abolished, and the preferential claim which burgesses of trade possessed to Robert Gordon's Hospital was reduced under the new Provisional Order, a claim was again made in 1882 for a further reduction of the burgess dues, and on the 10th March of that year a

---

* This payment of arms money is still made in accordance with ancient custom. When a burgess appears before the Lord Provost and Town Council to receive his diploma or burgess ticket, he presents his lordship with a small white purse containing five ordinary pennies, five pennies of the present day being the equivalent of five shillings Scots. The arms money went to a fund for providing the town with weapons, ammunition, &c.

committee of the Incorporated Trades effected an arrangement under which the payment should be reduced to a uniform sum of a guinea, to include all fees.*

In early times the dues payable by a craftsman to his own craft were insignificant. It was only when the crafts began to accumulate funds for the benefit of widows and decayed members that the entry moneys were raised. For long the chief payments consisted of "quarter pennies," and dues paid by the members for every journeyman and apprentice they employed; but for some time previous to the abolition of trading privileges the quarter penny system was dropped, and a slump sum at entry substituted. The entry money has varied in the different Trades according to the benefits they were able to afford.

The office-bearers of a craft association have, since the earliest period of their history, consisted of a deacon, a box-master or treasurer, and several masters, usually four. These

* The report of the final settlement was in the following terms :—" Your committee, having been requested to attend a Conference at the Town House upon Tuesday, the 18th day of April current, met with the Law Committee of the Town Council, who were represented by Lord Provost Easlemont, Baillie Ross, Baillie Duffus, Mr. Paterson, and Mr. George Walker. The Lord Provost, having introduced the subject, stated at the outset that he did not want to lay stress upon the legal aspect of the question as he feared the members of the conference might not be able to agree on that score, both sides having doubtless considerable confidence in their own views, and, therefore, he would rather put it as a matter of loyalty and policy, or perhaps of sentiment, whether the connection which had so long existed between the Magistrates and Town Council on the one part and the Incorporated Trades on the other part should now be severed. His lordship frankly admitted that a substantial reduction of the amount presently exigible might be made with propriety, and he asked your committee whether, all things considered, we were prepared to agree to a uniform payment of £2 2s. for each entrant, this payment to include all fees which are presently exacted from entrants. Your convener, in reply, explained what was the position of your committee in this matter, and that we had attended more to learn on what grounds any payment by them should be continued than to consider the amount of such payment, but that, at the same time, we were prepared to report to the general body of the incorporations any suggestion which the Law Committee had to offer. He might, however, take it upon himself to say that there was not the least chance of a payment of £2 2s. being agreed to. The Lord Provost, having explained that neither party was expected at this Conference to bind their constituents but only to recommend what in their opinion might be a fair basis of compromise, a general conversation ensued, in which most of the members of the Conference took part, and ultimately, on the suggestion of the Lord Provost, it was unanimously agreed that both parties should recommend to their constituents that the payment should be reduced to the uniform sum of £1 1s., to include all fees ; it being understood that the subject should not be again brought forward, but that upon this arrangement receiving the sanction of the Town Council and of the Incorporated Trades, the same shall become final and absolute, and be received as a permanent and lasting settlement of a long-vexed question. It being further understood that, when agreed to, this new arrangement shall date back to the 26th of October last, the date of the convener's letter to the Town Council, and that the guinea would be paid for all the craftsmen who have since that time joined the incorporations.—P. Raeburn, Convener ; Ebenezer Bain, Jun., Master of Hospital; Andrew Robb; John Croll; James Mitchell ; W Graham.—Trinity Hall, Aberdeen, 21st April, 1882."

office-bearers are elected annually, and, as a rule, hold office for two years. The deacon has always been entrusted with a large amount of power. Every entrant has to render obedience to him and to "all the haill acts and ordinances of his court or convention;" and the records of the Trades contain numerous instances where deacons resorted to the extreme measure of committing recalcitrant members to the tolbooth for defying their authority; and also where the deacon in turn has been punished for non-fulfilment of or failure to perform his duties. The office-bearers are elected annually, and from time immemorial the election day has always closed with " a common meal." Previous to Dr. Guild's gift of the Trinities, the meetings of the crafts in Aberdeen were held in the houses of the deacons, or a public inn, the expenses incurred about an election time appearing in the accounts after the following fashion :—" At Deacon Currie's at dinner and to the fiddlers, £6 13s. 4d. Scots " (about 11s. sterling); " ane gallon of ale to the lads that day, £1 1s. 4d. " (1s. 9d.); "opening the box, 10s. 8d." (10¾d.); " to the clerk for ale and other expenses, £1 3s. 4d." (1s. 11½d.). The boxmaster was, as a rule, restricted to a fixed sum annually for general expenses; and at times when there was dearth in the town the members were ordered to pay the expenses of the " common meal" out of their own pockets.

All journeymen and apprentices, although not members of the societies, were enrolled in the books of their own craft, while apprentices were entered in the books of the town as well as their craft, to enable them to claim the rights of an apprentice when they came to apply for their freedom. This registration of craftsmen has been useful in many ways. The books of the various Trades have been found valuable registers for tracing pedigrees,* the patrimonial element having had

---

* In tracing historic family names, the Trades Records have also been found useful. The following note was recently received from Mr. W. E. Gladstone in reply to a communication stating that a George Gladstaines, pewterer, had joined the Hammermen Trade in 1656, and gifted 300 merks to the Trades Hospital in 1698 :—

" Dollis Hill, N.W., July 13, 1897.

" Dear Sir,—I thank you very much for the information so kindly given.

" It is the first time that I have heard of the name of Gladstaines so far north. He was probably one planted out ; but he seems to have been a man of substance.

" Your very faithful Servant,
" W. E. GLADSTONE.

" E. Bain, Esq."

the effect of inducing sons to follow the same occupation as
their fathers. There is more than one citizen at present living
who can trace his pedigree in the Trades Books to his great-
great-great-grandfather, and from the minutes he can ascertain
something about their position and standing in the town.

When we come to deal with the crafts separately, a description of the different kinds of essays or mastersticks which
were prescribed for entrant craftsmen to test their ability to
work will be given. After an essay has been prescribed, two
essay masters and an oversman are appointed to visit the
entrant and see him working at his essay, and if they have
any suspicion that he is being assisted, they have power to
lock him into a workshop while he is at work. An entrant is
now frequently permitted to make some special article as his
essay, which could be preserved as a memento of his entry into
his craft. There are at least three of these in the Trades Hall
at present, one a unique piece of weaver work by James
Wilson, weaver; another, the arms of the Hammermen Trade,
chased in brass by Mr. Robert Rettie; and a third, a beauti-
fully finished and hooped quarter cask made by Mr. George
Gorrod, and which is looked after by the Boxmaster of the
Wright and Cooper Trade.

CHAPTER VII.

THE CRAFTSMEN AS CITIZEN SOLDIERS.

THE obligations imposed upon craftsmen under their burgess oath, " to watch and ward the town," was no empty meaningless phrase—at least in Aberdeen. Few towns in Scotland passed through so many troublous epochs, and none suffered more from the ravages of war than this very town which boasts for its motto the peaceful sentiment of " Bon-Accord." From the days of King William the Lion, when he established his palace in the Green, to the Rebellion of '45, Aberdeen was an important centre of action during the many troublous periods of Scotland's history. In 1179 it was a town of such size as to be considered worthy of being pillaged by Esteyn, one of the kings of Norway; its castle was seized by the English in 1292; when Sir William Wallace marched his army of relief from Dunnottar to Aberdeen in 1297, the enemy plundered and set fire to the town, and at a later stage Aberdeen had to suffer at the hands of the English for the support and shelter it gave to the Scottish champion. In the days of Robert Bruce, Aberdeen was the scene of many a bloody conflict; the castle was retaken from the English, and King Robert rewarded the citizens by bestowing on them a number of charters. Then came the historic battle of Harlaw, in which the citizens of Aberdeen, under Sir Robert Davidson, offered a determined resistance to Donald, Lord of the Isles; but it would take us out of our way to recount even the leading disturbances that occurred in Aberdeen during several centuries. It was favoured with many a royal visit, from the Jameses, Queen Mary, Charles II., and the leading notables in the country, and these marks of royal favour brought the town into a prominence that was not without its disadvantages. Then again, during the Covenanting days, and the rebellious periods of 1715 and 1745, Aberdeen bore the brunt of many a sanguinary conflict.

At all these eventful epochs the craftsmen, in their capacity of citizen soldiers, had to play their part. Down to the time of the second rebellion it was imperative that every free craftsman should be fully equipped with the weapons of war. On being admitted a free burgess he had to appear before the Magistrates clad "sufficentlie in armour, with an hagbute, bandaleire [wooden powder case], and sword," as a guarantee that he was able to "watch and ward;" besides having to contribute arms money towards the maintenance of the town's magazine. In token of their prowess at the battle of Harlaw in 1411, tradition says that each of the deacons brought back as a trophy a sword taken from the enemy. Three of the crafts—the Hammermen, the Tailors, and the Weavers—have still in their possession swords which are said to be the veritable weapons brought back from Harlaw, and their make and appearance do not belie the tradition.

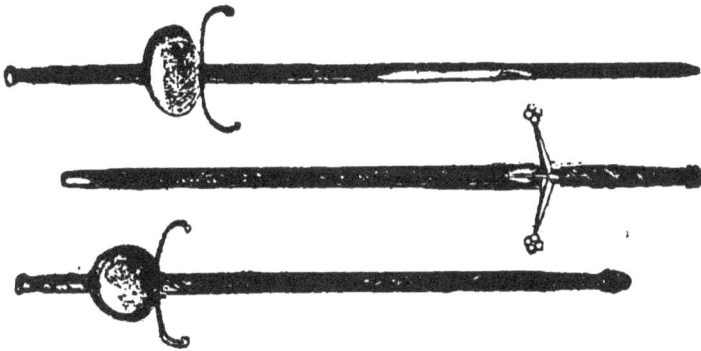

The following Act of Parliament, passed on 6th March, 1457, and copies of which are to be found carefully preserved among the papers of several of the Trades, will give an indication of how the citizens were trained to the arts of war at this period:—

Item.—It is decrtyt and ordainyt that wapin-shawing be halden be the lords and baronys spirituall and temporall four tymis in the year, and that the fut ball and golf be utterly cryed down and not to be used, and that bow marks be maide at ilk paroch kirk, a pair of butts and schuting be used ilk Saturday, and that ilk man shoot sex shotts att the least under the pain to be raised upon them that come not, att the least two pennies to be given to them that comes to the bow marks to drink. And this to be used

frae pasch to allowmass efter, and be the next mydsummer to be reddy
with all their greath without faizie.   And that there be a bower and
fleg in every head town of the shire, and that the town furnish him of
stuff and gaithe aftor as needs him thereto that they may serve the
country with.   And as toichande the fut ball and the golf to be punished
by the barrons unlaw.   And if the pariochine be meikle that there be three
or four or five bow marks in such places as gauys therefor, and that all men
that is within fifty and past twelve years shall use shooting.   And that
men that is outwith and past three scoir yeirs sal use honest gamys as
effers.—*Acts of the Parliaments of Scotland, vol.* ii.

Occasionally the craftsmen made use of their arms for
other than defensive purposes.   In 1638, the deacon-convener
and deacons were accused of " convocating the haill frieman of
thair saidis craftis with all thair servantis and prentissis vpon
Monday last, the twenty-ane day of Maii instant, be fyve houris
in the morning at the craftis hospital, and thairefter convening
thaim all at the mercat croce in armes be eight houris, and in the
meintyme when as a number of seckis of meill, to the number
of fourescoir seckis or thairby, that wer brocht in that day frome
Skeine to hawe beine embarked in Martin Schankis schips, wes
stayed and laid doune at the mercat place, the saidis craftis, with
thair servantis and prentisses, being convenit at the mercat croce
in armes, as said is, with swords, pistollis, and lang wapynnes,
thay mellit and intromittit with the said victuall violentlie
and at thair awn handis compellit the men that brocht in the
same to carie it on thair awin horssis fra the mercat place to
the said hospitall, and conveyit the same the haill way in
armes, as said is, notwithstanding that thay wer commandit
and chairgit be the Magistrattes."   For this offence the Magistrates fined the convener £80 and the deacons £40, and committed them to prison until the fines were paid.   They were
also ordered to pay the owners of the meal for the skaith
done them, and to afterwards appear in the tolbooth " in ane
fencit court, and thair in presens of the Magistrats and Counsal humblie to crawe God and thame pardone for the said riott
and disobedience, and promisis openlie newir to commit the
lyk in tym coming."—*Council Register, vol.* lii., *p.* 380.

During the troublous covenanting times, the craftsmen
suffered severely both in person and property.   At the battle
of Justice Mills on 13th September, 1644, when Montrose with

his three Irish regiments played such fearful havoc in the town, a number of leading craftsmen were slain, including Thomas Robertsone, deacon of the cordiners. In the same encounter Matthew Lumsden, baillie; Thomas Buck, master of kirk works; Robert Leslie, master of hospital (town's hospital); Alexander and Robert Reid, advocates; and about a hundred and sixty other citizens were killed.

When the Rebellion of 1715 broke out most of the craftsmen joined with the Magistrates, but they were not by any means all of one mind. The records of the different Trades tell a curious tale of divided feeling. With the view, apparently, of ascertaining which side each craftsman favoured, all the Trades passed a resolution to the effect that the whole members should again take the oath of allegiance, and those who refused to undergo this shibboleth process, were for the time debarred from the meetings of the craft. Judging from the numbers in the Shoemaker's Trade who subscribed the oath a considerable time after the rebellion had died down, it is evident that a considerable proportion of them were in sympathy with the Pretender; while the Hammermen, a number of whom were armourers and gunsmiths, were almost to a man sturdy Loyalists. Joseph Robertson's "Short Memorandum of quhat heath occurred in Aberdeen since XX. September, MDCCXV.," which, he says, was written by a gentleman in Aberdeen, contains the following interesting account of the part which the Trades in Aberdeen took in the proceedings :—

20th September, 1715.—Said day the Earl Marchall entered the toun with severall gentelmen and inhabitants with ther swords drawn, and went to the Cross, where he, with severall others, went up, and the Chireff deput read, and Jo. Duff proclaimed the pretender and then dranck his health. The names of some of them ye have herewith on the other syde. At night the bells was rung and illuminations ordered, and those that waild not obey, rabbled.

21st.—Patrick Gray, conviner, with all his diacons and boxmasters, entertened Earl Marchall with severall of his company in their Treads hall, and drunck King James' health, and suckses to his armes, &c. In the afternoon the Earl went towards Inverugie, and was attended out of toun by most of thos who came in with him, besides the Convinner and his treads in a seperate body, and as they went threw the old toun they proclaimed the pretender there.

22d.—The Magistrates having mett in the Counsel houss about the toune's affaires, they were insulted by a mobb, who first mett in Mistres Hebbrun's and then came to the counsel house and requyered the armes and amunitions belonging to the toun with the Keys of the Block house, seeing they wer not to regard the majestrates any longer as majestrates : for Earl Marchall had given the command of the toun to Capt. Jo. Bennarman. Accordingly they seazed all, and ever since keep the command of the toun : the neams of most of them you have herewith.

26th.—The Earl Marchal returned, and there haveing been severall metteing amongst the Rebells ffor the chosing a new majestrace, upon the 28th they maid intimatione by beat of drum, that all the Burgers should mett at the new church nixt day in order to chose new Magistrates and Counsell—Notta.—This 28th was the Legall day that the Magistrates and Counsell should be chosen, but the Treads, who are a pairt of the Electors, being in rebelione, there could no Legall Election be.

29th.—The Earl Marchal, attended by some few besides the members of the Colledge and Treads, went to the new church, where the Earl caused Alex^r Charles calle the neams, and then give him a list of those he designed for Magistrats and Counsell, quhilk being read was approven : the names of the Magistrats and Counsell, with a few Electors, you have herewith.

P^{ro} Oct^r.—The Earl Marchal went out of toun towards the camp, and was conveyed by the new Magistrates and Convener, with his treads, having all their swords drawn. . . .

3to.—This day the Marques of Huntly came here with abut 70 horsemen, who was taken to the Counsel house with my Lord Pitsligo, and intertened by the Majestrats. In the mean tym, Capt. Mideltoune brought ffrom a French Veshell in the Road the Laird of Boyn, who was in disguise : he had the Earl of Marchal's Commission, &c, which occasioned great rejoicing, and amongst the rest of the Royall healths, they drunck the D. Orleans, &c.

4to.—Lord Pitsligo and severall others went for the camp at Pearth as did the Laird of Boyne.

5to.—The Marques of Huntly being interteaned by the convener and his treads in there hall, where all the loyall healths wer drunck,—he mounted at the crosse with all his retinue, and was waited upon by the Magistrats and treads, as also by my Lord Frasser and my Lord Aboyn : the Standard carried by Sir Robert Gordon, the whole about 230.

Owing to the commotion in the town, no elections took place among the Trades for that year, and after order had been restored each of the Trades made a special application to the Magistrates for power to hold an election.

The annual elections were again interrupted in 1745, when the second attempt was made to restore the Stuart dynasty, and several pages of the Trades' records for this period are quite blank, no business of any kind having apparently been transacted for several months. In the month of July, 1746, the Magistrates granted special warrants to hold meetings for the election of office-bearers, and, as was the case in 1715, the members had again to take the oath of allegiance. Some of the members protested against taking the oath a second time, and only did so after the Convener Court had passed the following enactment :—

17th December, 1748.—The Convener Court having heard and considered ane act of the Hammermen Trade, dated 30th September, 1748, they approve of the same, and statute and ordain the same to be here insert, of which the tenor follows :—" The Hammermen Trade taking to their serious consideration that when the rebellion in August and September, 1745, broke out, they were then interrupted in their then usual election by the violence of the rebels, but were in 1746 rejoined to the privileges of electing the annual officers for the Corporation by His Majesty's most gracious order in Privy Council, whereas it is undeniable nottour that many in this town and neighbouring county did join the said rebels, and many more were known to be secret abettors of this cause, who yet did not take arms in rebellion, which brought our country under the imputation of disaffection, therefore (and notwithstanding of ane interlocutor of the Lords of Session finding that any tradesman who should take the oaths by law directed once in a reign was not obliged to repeat them previous to any election thereafter during that reign, nor to be debarred from being ane elector for not repeating the said oath) it was advised and fand reasonable to avoid the imputation of disaffection, and to show as much as possible that we were entirely free of any accession to the rebellion, that every member should take the usual oaths as in the case of the commencement of a new reign, and which all the members of this trade who voted at the two preceding elections have done. But some of the corporations, for reasons best known to themselves, have not required any vote in the two preceding elections, and for what is known have not taken the usual oaths to His Majesty since the rebellion in seventeen forty-five broke out. Therefore the trade hereby statute and ordain that no member of this corporation who has not been qualified to His Majesty since the first of March, 1745, shall be allowed to vote in any election of deacon, boxmaster, or masters of this corporation until he first show an attestation of his having taken the oath to His Majesty before two or more of His Majesty's Justices of the Peace since the said first of March, 1746. And the trade further statute and ordain that the deacon of the trade shall be hereby warranted by this corporation in refusing to receive such member's vote until he show attestation as aforesaid. And if any deacon shall receive the vote of any member who refuses to produce such attestation, any two or more members of this corporation are hereby empowered to prosecute such deacon, and the unqualified member so voting before any competent court, on the expense of this corporation, the boxmaster whereof is hereby empowered to issue forth the necessary money for that effect. And the trade hereby further statute that in respect the names of those in the corporation who have since the rebellion in 1745 qualified to His Majesty are recorded previous to this being allowed to vote, that every member who shall hereafter produce ane attestation of his having taken the oaths to His Majesty as law directs shall be recorded as qualified, so that he be not obliged to produce his attestation anew, and that a roll of such as are qualified and have produced attestations thereof, or shall hereafter produce attestation, be annually made out, and be the election roll, and all such as are not so recorded be debarred voting, and held as not quali- fied and incapable of electing or being elected into any office in this corporation whatever." And the Convener Court appoint and empower the convener for the time being to see this act put in due execution among the several corporations.

At various other periods the Trades manifested their readi- ness to perform their duties as citizen soldiers. In 1797 a vol- unteer corps was formed in connection with the Trades, "for internal defence and opposing invasion," the Trinity Gardens being set apart as a drilling ground, and a stand of colours supplied by the Convener Court. During the American war the Craftsmen subscribed £400 "to assist in subduing the rebellion in the colonies," and again, in 1798, a sum of £50 was subscribed to the Government on account of the crisis then existing in the country.

PART III.

THE SEVEN INCORPORATED TRADES.

CHAPTER I.

INTRODUCTORY.

By what may be termed a natural process of selection, the craftsmen in Aberdeen came to be divided into seven separate guilds, Hammermen, Bakers, Wrights and Coopers, Tailors, Shoemakers, Weavers, and Fleshers, each with its own deacon and office-bearers, and having at their head a deacon-convener and head court, consisting of the office-bearers of the individual Trades. These seven societies, however, embraced a number of separate and, to some extent, distinctive handicrafts. The Hammermen, for instance, have at one time or other included cutlers, pewterers, glovers, goldsmiths, blacksmiths, gunsmiths, saddlers, armourers, hookmakers, glaziers, watchmakers, white-ironsmiths, and engineers; the Wrights and Coopers, cabinetmakers and wheelwrights; and the Tailors, upholsterers.

But the classes of craftsmen that associated under one deacon had always something in common. The Hammermen were craftsmen with whom the use of the hammer was a leading feature, glovers in the olden times being makers of much more substantial articles than are used nowadays, while saddlers made the iron as well as the leather parts of harness; the Wrights and Coopers dealt in the same material; and the upholsterers were classed along with the Tailors, because they used the needle and thread.

In addition to these seven, however, separate societies were formed by the Litsters or Dyers, the Masons, and the Leechers (barber-surgeons), all of which elected their deacons, and possessed a constitution similar to the Seven Incorporated

Trades. The litsters formed themselves into a society about as early as any other body of craftsmen in the town. In 1501 their deacon was presented to the Council to be sworn, and to have his election confirmed ; but it does not appear that they ever applied for a Seal of Cause, as was done by the other crafts about this period. On the contrary, the dyers seem to have held aloof from the rest of the craftsmen, and at times claimed an equality with the merchant burgesses—an equality, however, which was never acknowledged either by the merchants or craftsmen. When the question of precedence was rife at the time of the religious pageants, the litsters frequently claimed a superior place, but in 1546 they were definitely instructed to furnish their banner and take part in the Corpus Christi and Candlemas processions along with the rest of the craftsmen :—

25th June, 1546.—The said day, the haill litstaris of this burgh chesit Alexander Fresser, litstar, thair dekyne of the said craft for this instant yeir ; quhilk accepit the said office on him, and is sworne the grit ayth to exerce the same lelie and treuelie, dureing the said yeir : and the bailyeis interponit their auctoritie tharto, and ordanit thame to haue thar banar and Pagane, as uther crafteis of the said burgh hes, ilk yeir, on Corpis Christi day and Candilmess dais processiounis, under the paines contenit in the statut maid tharupon.—*Council Register*, vol. xix., p. 143.

At the beginning of the seventeenth century the question of precedence was brought before the Court of Session, when a decreet was pronounced finding that the litsters could not exercise their own trade and the trade of Guild burgesses at the same time, notwithstanding the Acts of the Convention of Burghs, the custom of the burgh of Aberdeen being different in this respect from that of other burghs.

The claim to be classed before the craftsmen was revived in 1759, when the litsters endeavoured to obtain precedence, or at least equality, for their sons at Robert Gordon's Hospital over the Incorporated Trades. The barbers and bookbinders* also endeavoured to establish a like privilege, but the

---

* The mention of bookbinders in a petition by the convener and deacons of the Incorporated Trades against the claim of the Litsters suggests that they had been associated in a corporate capacity, but this is the only mention of them we have been able to discover in the Burgh Records.

Governors, as the following minute bears, declined to recognise their claim :—

3rd April, 1759.—The said day the Governors being about to proceed to the election of boys to be received into the Hospital betwixt this date and the first day of June next, in terms of the Deed of Mortification, a representation was offered to them in name and behalf of the Convener and Deacons of Incorporated Trades or crafts of Aberdeen, complaining of a resolution and act made by the governors upon the 3rd day of April last, 1758, "finding that in terms of the mortification litsters burgesses had an equal title with any other burgesses tradesmen of the Seven Incorporated Trades or crafts to have their children received into the Hospital," and the said representation being read and considered by the governors, and they having at great length reasoned on the affair, and the question being put, it carried by a great majority that the sons and grandsons of the incorporate tradesmen of the burgh of Aberdeen are to have the preference immediately after the sons and grandsons of burgesses of guild in terms of the deed of mortification in all time coming, and therefore the governors did decree and determine accordingly.—*Hospital Records.*

About the middle of the seventeenth century Archibald Bean, a member of the Litsters Society, left several properties to provide funds for the benefit of decayed members of that craft, and down to April of last year (1886) the funds belonging to the society were administered for that purpose. But the last of the members has now passed away. On 30th April, 1886, John Bannerman, the only surviving member and officebearer, died at the advanced age of 95 ; and the funds that remained after his death, and several old houses, have been claimed by the Queen's Remembrancer on behalf of the Crown. Mr. David Mitchell, advocate, the agent for the Society, is at present engaged in winding up the affairs of this venerable association.

The Barbers, who down to the end of the seventeenth century were designated as chirurgeons* and periwig makers, obtained a Seal of Cause from the Town Council in 1537, authorising them to elect a deacon, make rules, prescribe an examination for entrants, &c., in the same manner as the other crafts. In 1674, when they had established a benevolent fund, they obtained a confirmation of their privileges under the title of

---

* An antique oak chair, which bears the inscription--"H. G., Chirurgie" with the Guthrie arms, is preserved in the Trades Hall, and is said to have been the chair used by the deacon of the Barber's Society.

barbers, surgeons, and periwig makers, but ultimately the association consisted solely of barbers and periwig makers. On 22nd January, 1729, a petition was presented to the Town Council by "Francis Massie, barber and periwig maker, present boxmaster, for himself, and in name of the haill incorporation," for power to raise the entry money from £6 to £12 Scots, on account of the increased benefits that were being given from accumulated funds. The prayer of the petition was granted, the incorporation being ordained to "call the Dean of Guild to their meetings to oversee and inspect their accounts, and to take the Dean's advice in stocking and lending their money." Up to about 1840 there were over thirty members, but gradually the membership fell off, and several years ago the remanent members and beneficiaries entered into a private arrangement for dividing the stock of the society among themselves. There is only one surviving member at the date of writing (1887).

The masons obtained a Seal of Cause in 1532 along with the wrights and coopers, but beyond being coupled with them in the same Seal of Cause the masons never became part of the society formed by the wrights and coopers. When the Seal of Cause was obtained, the masons elected their own deacon, formed a society for themselves, passed bye-laws, and accumulated funds in the same manner as the other associations. But about the middle of the seventeenth century their society underwent a curious metamorphosis. Free or "speculative" masonry was introduced into Aberdeen shortly after the mason craftsmen obtained their Seal of Cause, but little was heard of the mysteries of masonry until some time after the reformation, when a regular lodge was formed in connection with the Masons' Craft Society about 1670. At the outset, freemasonry was simply an adjunct of the original association of craft masons ; but gradually it became its leading feature, and the incorporation of mason artificers eventually became what is now known as the Aberdeen Mason Lodge. The "olde book" of the Aberdeen Lodge contains the "lawes and statutes for measones gathered out of thir old wreatings by us, who ar the authoires and subscriberis of this booke," and the great bulk of these ordinances have reference to the affairs of the incorporation, and are drawn up in similar terms to those enacted by the other craft incorporations in the town. They have nothing whatever to do with speculative masonry, which did not obtain prominence until a charter was obtained from Grand Lodge of Scotland in 1743.

These separate societies having as it were swarmed off by themselves, the seven remained as a compact body, and have acted together for over two hundred and fifty years, aiding and assisting each other in preserving their rights and privileges, and amalgamating for the purpose of instituting various general funds for the benefit of their members and dependants.

Down to the beginning of the eighteenth century the craftsmen rigidly excluded burgesses of guild from their societies; but as the differences between the two classes of burgesses became more amicably adjusted, several of the crafts relaxed their constitution to the extent of declaring that the fact of an applicant being a burgess of guild should not be a bar to his becoming a member of one of the crafts should he be found otherwise qualified. In 1738 the Baker Trade passed an enactment that all members who should become burgesses of guild should still enjoy the same privileges as the other members of the trade, and from that date down to the year 1801, burgesses of guild were called to all the meetings and voted at the elections of the Baker Trade, with the exception of voting for the election of deacon. But in that year the right of burgesses of guild to vote at the election of deacons and other office-bearers was called in question. At this election five burgesses of guild were present. They gave no vote for the office of deacon, but, on his election being completed, they all voted for the masters of the trade and for the boxmaster. A complaint was presented to the Magistrates complaining, *inter alia*, of the interference of the burgesses of guild in the election. The burgesses of guild grounded their defence principally on the Act of the Trade, passed in 1738. After hearing both parties the Magistrates, on the 14th December, 1802, found that " the Act of the Baker Trade of Aberdeen, dated the 11th May, 1738, founded on by the defenders, was contrary to law and *ultra vires* of the corporation, and therefore ordained Robert Spring, the deacon of the trade, to expunge it from their books at the sight of the private complainer. Found that the defenders — William Strachan, Adam Watt, John Wallace, Alexander Hall, and George Henderson—by obtaining themselves admitted burgesses of guild virtually renounced their craft as bakers, and were disqualified from voting in the election in question." The decree then contains the following prohibition :—" And further prohibits and discharges the said William Strachan, Adam Watt, John Wallace, Alexander Hall, and George Henderson from attending or voting in the election of deacon, masters, or boxmaster of the Baker Trade of Aberdeen in future, so long as they remain burgesses of guild of this burgh, under the penalty of £20 sterling each, *toties quoties*." This sentence was ultimately complied with, the minute of 11th May, 1738, was erased from the minute book, and a small fine and the expense of process were paid by the burgesses of guild. In 1803 William Strachan and several other burgesses of guild who were then members of the Baker Trade, raised an action of reduction and declarator. The action of reduction had reference to certain minutes of the trade, at the meetings of which the votes of the members of the guildry had been refused. The business before the court related to the lending of a large sum of money, and after the foregoing sentence of the Magistrates, the burgesses of guild had not been called to the meetings of the trade. The action of declarator was to have it found that the burgesses of guild " were entitled to be called to the meetings of the trade, and particularly in every question regarding the disposal of these funds to which they have contributed."   In this action the trade was assoilzied both by Lord Armadale and Lord Hermand, both Lord Ordinaries finding that the pursuers (the burgesses of guild) were not entitled to vote in the disposal of the funds of the trade. The next case occurred in the year 1815. Three tailors, named Torrie, Spence, and Smith, having become members of the guildry, the trade gave orders that they should no longer be called to the usual meetings of the tailor trade. The tailor burgesses of guild brought a complaint before the Sheriff against the office-bearers of the trade, and craved that the Sheriff should find that they were entitled to be called to the meetings of the trade, and to vote in the election o all the office-bearers with the exception of the deacon, and that they were entitled to vote in all questions regarding the administration of the funds of the trade. In the course of the process the pursuers gave up their claim to vote for office-bearers, and restricted their claim to voting in any matter connected with the funds of the trade. Dr. Dauney, the Sheriff-Substitute, gave judgment in favour of the pursuers, thereby giving them a right to be called to the meetings and voting in the administration of the funds. Against this judgment the trades appealed to Sheriff Moir, who reversed the sentence and assoilzied the corporation by finding that the pursuers, the members of guildry, were not entitled to vote or to be called to the meetings of the Tailor Trade. In this case the names of all the members of guildry belonging to the other trades were mentioned, and it was alleged that in the other trades these members were called to all meetings, and voted in every case, with the exception of the election of deacon, but the Sheriff (Moir), notwithstanding, gave the sentence against the complainers. After the abolition of trading privileges in 1846, the Trades became less strict, and guild brethren who were also craftsmen have been freely admitted.

CHAPTER II.

THE CONVENER COURT.

THE convenery or convention of deacons came into existence in Aberdeen about the end of the sixteenth century. In its original form this body consisted of the deacons only, one of whom was chosen to convene them when any question arose affecting the common or general interests of the craftsmen in the town. The first convener of deacons of whom there is any mention is George Elphinstone, saddler, who held office in the year 1587, when the Common Indenture was drawn up; and shortly after that date a regular court was formed, which held stated meetings, and enacted bye-laws and regulations, for the management of the funds under their charge. When Dr. Guild gifted the Trinity Monastery as a meeting-house and hospital to the Trades, he nominated six of the deacons of the crafts to act along with a patron and convener in the management of the hospital, these six being the deacons who were selected among the crafts to vote at the election of magistrates. In 1657 the Flesher Trade was admitted to the benefits of the hospital in terms of an agreement sanctioned by Dr. Guild; and their deacon being at the same time admitted a member of the Convener Court, the number of trades represented in that body was increased to its present number of seven. In addition to the deacons, the Master of Hospital, the boxmasters, late deacons, and first master of each Trade are also members of the Convener Court.

Although recognised from the outset as a superior court by the craftsmen, the Convener Court has seldom exercised any jurisdiction over the affairs of the individual Trades. When disputes or difficulties arose, it has acted more as a consultative than as an administrative board. On several occasions when the Trades considered that the Convener

Banner (upper left): VIS UNITA

Banner (upper right): FORTIOR

Banner (lower): CONCORDIA CÆLI TRANQUILLITAS.

CONVENER COURT.—Gules, issuing from the dexter flank a dexter hand proper grasping six arrows paleways, points upwards, or; from the sinister flank a sinister hand proper grasping a broken arrow or. Mottoes: *Vis unita fortior* and *Concordia cœli tranquillitas.*

.

Court had overstepped its functions, an appeal was made to the Magistrates or Court of Session, and the decision was invariably in favour of the individual Trades having full control of their own affairs. The last case of this kind occurred in 1711-2, when the Court of Session ruled that a judgment given by the Convener Court regarding one of the office-bearers of the Baker Incorporation was *ultra vires*, and had to be expunged from the minutes of the Convener Court. In 1881 a code of rules and regulations was drawn up for the " guidance of the members in the discharge of the duties of the court," but no departure of any consequence was made from the established " use and want."

Considerable doubt exists as to the period when the Convener Court, or in fact any of the craft associations, commenced to keep records of their transactions. The oldest minute books extant are dated about the time that the Trades began to hold their meetings in the " Trinities " or meeting house gifted to them by Dr. Guild in 1633, but, fortunately, into these books have been copied all the old acts and ordinances of the different corporations extracted, as the fly leaves tell us, " out of the old Registers." These old Registers seem to have been more of the nature of roll books and election records than of minute books for recording business ; and after the old Acts and list of deacons had been copied out of them, they appear to have been held of little account, as all of them have disappeared. The Convener Court alone seems to have made an effort to preserve their old Register, as the following minute bears, but it also has long since disappeared :—

21st August, 1677.—The said day the new Register was accepted by the haill Deacon-Convener Court, and approved by them, and the old Register to be kept within ane ambrie in the Trinities, and the present deacon-convener to keep the key thereof, to the effect that present access may be had thereto as may be needful.—*Convener Court Book.*

We may take it for granted, however, that everything of importance had been copied out of the old Registers into the set of new books that were obtained when the Trinity Monastry was turned into a Trades Hall ; and previous to that date, it has to be borne in mind that written records could have been of little use to the craftsmen themselves. Even as late as 1587, when the Common Indenture was drawn up, none of the three commissioners appointed by the craftsmen could sign their names, the tell-tale explanation at the end of the deed being given—" With our hands at the pen, led by the notors underwritten at our command, because we cannot write ourselffs." And for many years after minute books began to be kept, it was the clerk and not the deacon that signed the minute. It is not until well through the eighteenth century that the deacon's signature appears, and even then there is abundant evidence of the struggle it must have been to put their names in writing. In some cases a deacon seemed to think he was doing well when he put down the initials of his name in capitals, and very original looking capitals some of them are.* Condensation and abbreviation, both in composition and writing, were also enforced virtues. The early Acts and Ordinances, which were penned by scribes and notaries, are remarkably brief, concise, and pithily expressed documents. Half a dozen lines are made to suffice where dozens of pages of foolscap would be required nowadays ; while some of the deeds of gift made about the end of the fourteenth and beginning of the fifteenth centuries are models of brevity and condensation, and remain valid titles

---

* Annexed is a fac-simile of a page of the Convener Court Book of date 17th November, 1711, of which the following is a transcript :—

The which day the wholl Deacon-Convener Court unanimously appoynt and ordain a declarator of their privileges to be entered before the Lords of Counsell and Session upon the expenses of the respective Incorporations. And they hereby oblidge them to advance thairanent what money shall be necessarilly called for. For which this is warrand :—

William Watson.

             David Speidiman, Convener.

Andrew Duckison.   Alex. Hutchon.
John Souttar.
Alex. Jamieson.
George Gordon.
David Gray.
G. C.—George Chalmers (?)
A. S.—Alexander Smith (?)
William Spence.

G. B.—George Bruce (?)
Alex. Duff.
Patrick Gray.
William Anderson.
John Smith.
Al. Duncan.
Alexander Brans.

The which day received by David Speidiman
Charter K. Ja. 6th, dated 22nd July, 1582 ;
Charter Q. Mary, dated 1st March, 1564 ; Gift
K. Ja. 6th, dated 22nd July, 1631, being a
double ; Coppie Gift Char. 1st, dated 1641,
with the principall Gift of the same ; Protest
against Magistrates anent privileges ; old
summons of declarator—Which I bind and
oblidge me to return inteir unlacerat on demand. Copy of a Gift to the town of Pearth :
receipt James Simpson, Convener, for the
Charter under the Great Seall. The principal
Common Indenture written on parchment
with the Seall, with coppie articles of agreement with Wm. Carglie and Wm. Gray,
baylie.—David Speidlman.

Jo. Findlay.
Gilbert More.
James Simpson.
James Hardie.
John Craig.
Thomas Aldjo.
James Clark.
Will. Walker.
Robert Cruickshank.
John Watson.

         Wm. Smith, Clerk.
         17th November, 1711.

The Maies: Say The Wood Owarms for time fail unanimously —
appoynt and Owain a Declarator of their priviledges, to be allowed to
... the Lords of Council and Session upon the ... by their ... for ...
corporations Authority ... Please advise to be done of ... subscribed
... shall be in ... fitly ... for for ... this is warrand

An O: ... Praelegendum orator

... by alsone

Andrew Dickison
John Lowther
Alex Cannidson
George Gordon
Patrick Clay
William Ogiverton
John Smith

Mr ... 1682

and burdens on property to this day. Even some of the more modern minutes are delightful specimens of laconic brevity, as instance the following—" The said day the Convener Court ordained the Master of Hospital never to sell the yaird at Gallowgett Heid, nor yet to hear ony mair thereanent."

Some indication is also given of the fate of the old books in a minute in the Convener Court Book to the effect that " a very old account book of the accounts under the charge of the Convener Court from 1700 to 1739 was sometime ago purchased by John Leslie, when about to be used for snuff paper, and he did so in order to preserve so valuable a book. Convener Leslie has now given it as a present to the Convener Court to be deposited among the records." On the whole, however, the Trades are to be congratulated upon the care with which their records and papers have been preserved. So far as we have been able to learn there are few towns in Scotland where the early records of the craft associations have been so well taken care of, and it is satisfactory to note that an equally careful disposition is being manifested by the present generation, a commodious fire-proof strong room for the better preservation of the books, title-deeds, and papers of the incorporations having recently been constructed in the new buildings. In olden times each craft had its small oak chest (a drawing of one of which is given) with three distinct locks, the keys of which were entrusted to three office-bearers, who had all to be present before the box could be opened; now each Trade has commodious repositories in the strong room for the preservation of their books and papers.

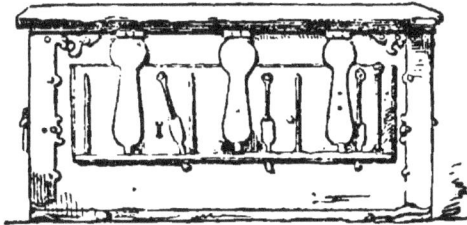

WRIGHT AND COOPER CHARTER CHEST.

The old Convener Court Book, like all the other early records of the Trades, opens with a statute about Sabbath observance, and on the fly leaves are inscribed quotations from Scripture and quaint, old " saws," and scraps of moral and religious rhyme.   Acts were also passed for imposing fines on those found guilty of swearing " or giving the lie," for absence from funerals, and for refusing to be dressed appropriately on all such occasions.   The following pious reminders are copied from the fly-leaves :—

O man call to REMEMBRANCE that worldly glory is but variance.
Memento Mori.

Might thou in witt with Soloman compare ;
    And should thy strength strong Samson's force excel,
In beauty syne pass Absolom the faire ;
    With Enoch years, and Cresus gold might tell,
What shall all help when death shall end the strife ?
Doe than to live, by death to conquer life.

Our life is but a winter's day,
Some only breakfast and away ;
Others, to dinner stay, and are full fed ;
The oldest but sup and go to bed.
Long is the life that lingers out the day,
Who goes the soonest has the least to pay.

All mortal men of death are sure,
    But houre or tyme they cannot tell ;
To watch and pray we should take care,
    And with no wrongeous matters mell.

IN DOMINO CONFIDO, 1677.

This booke belongs to the whole Traids of Aberdeine, and appointed for the use of the Deacon-Conveener Court wherein are contained several Acts and Ordinances to be observed in futur ages by the saidis traids, exactly extracted out of the old Registry from the year of God 1599 to the year 1677.
Soli Deo Gloria.

Then follow the Acts and Ordinances.   It will be observed that a number of them are undated, these having been copied from the old Register, dated 1599 :—

ANENT KEEPING THE SABBATH.

Item, it is statute and ordained that every Deacon convene his own craft and set doun ane ordinance for the glory of God and keeping of his

Sabbath and repairing to the church timeously upon that day, and that no master nor servant should be found absent from divine service under penalties following—to witt, each master, thirteen shillings four pennies ; and the servant, six shillings and eight pennies, for the first fault, and doubling the same *toties quoties ;* and that said servants convey their masters to and from the church in decency as becomes, and that no master shall go to sitt or stand in the fields, but shall punctually attend the reading and preaching of God's Word in good behaviour and decency until the sermon be ended, and the blessing said ; and it shall be lesome to everyone who desires the glory of God to give real information anent the persons who shall contravene and be guilty in the premises.

ANENT SWEARING AND GIVING THE LIE.

Item, it is statute, appointed, and ordained that whatsoever member of the Deacon-Conveener Court shall take the name of God in vain, sitting in ane fenced court or meeting, shall pay for his first fault sixteen shillings four pennies, and for each fault of that nature thereafter the like sum, *toties quoties,* by and attour what other censure the meeting shall propose upon him. And further it is enacted that whatsoever person shall speak rudely or uncivilie in ane fenced court or villipend [vilify] the Deacon-Conveener either publicly or privately, or give ane other the lie either in fenced court or in presence of the Deacon-Conveener to pay for said fault of this nature forty shillings Scots *toties quoties* to be taken up unmitigat or unforgiven.

ANENT ATTENDANCE AT MEETINGS AND BURIALS.

Item, it is strictly statute and ordained that whenever the Deacon-Conveener shall please to call ane quarter court or any other extraordinary meeting the haill members thereof being lawfully warned and called thereto by the Deacon-Conveener his officer, and any of them staying away therefrom without ane relevant ground or excuse shall be liable to pay to the Deacon-Conveener's box thirteen shillings four pennies, and if any of the said members shall remain and come in after the court is fenced, shall consign before they sit down six Shillings Scots in the hands of the Deacon-Conveener before he gives in his excuse for his not timeous coming ; and further, that whatsomever person or persons shall deforce the Deacon-Conveener his officer, in going about his duty in poinding of the absents either from courts or burials, he being lawfully ordained and appointed to about the same, shall pay for the first fault forty shillings Scots, and thereafter each fault to be doubled *toties quoties* by and attour whatever censure the court shall impose upon him, and this Act to stand unalterable in all tyme coming.

28th July, 1685.—The said day the Deacon-Conveener, Deacon, and remanent masters and members of the Deacon-Conveener Court taking to their consideration the ancient Act anent burials to be omitted and not well observed in some time by past, which was made upon the fourth day of March, 1655, in presence of Dr. William Guild, of worthy memory, and William Anderson, Cooper, Deacon-Conveener for the time, they voiced the same should be observed in time coming, whereof the tenor follows :— The said fourth March, 1655, it is statute and ordained by the Deacon-Conveener Court, Deacons of Crafts, and members of the Deacon-Conveener Court, that whatsomever burials within this burgh shall occur hereafter to the whilk the Deacon-Conveener is desired that upon his advertisement be his officer to ilk of the traids within this burgh, the said Deacons of Trades respectively shall give lawful warning to their respective traids to attend him at his own stair foot, the appointed time, in ane decent order, with hats, at least those who are in use to wear hats, and therefra, the said Trade, to convoy the Deacon to the Deacon-Conveener for the time to the effect the haill Trades may go to the burial orderlie, and in ane decent way. And whatsomever tradesman shall contravene this present statute and ordinance shall pay six shillings eight pennies for ilk day's absence, *toties quoties*.

ANENT ATTIRE TO BE WORN AT MEETINGS, BURIALS, &c.

Item, it is statute and ordained that whatsomever Deacon, master, or member of the Deacon-Conveener Court shall come to the Deacon-Conveener Court, or meetings, or to burials, or going about any public affair, wherein the traids are connected, with capes, blue, black, or grey bonnets, and not having hatts on their heids, shall pay thirteen shillings four pennies Scots money *toties quoties* by and attour what other censure the Court shall impose upon him ; and if any Deacon absent himself frae frieman's burials, their wives' or children's, he being in town, and in health of body, he is to be poyndit, and the point to be keepit until he redeem the same by payment of six shillings eight pennies Scots *toties quoties*.

ANENT OPENING MEETINGS WITH PRAYER.

27th May, 1650.—In presence of Doctor William Guild, foundator, the haill Deacon-Conveener Court being convenit, the said day it was strictly statute (the said patron being present) that at all meetings of Deacon, or Deacon-Conveener Courts, ane blessing shall be sought from God, and a right direction of their affairs to his glory, the good of the crafts, and that they may be approvid in their awin consciences in the day of their accounts and this to be done by the Deacon-Conveener, and Deacons of their several Courts respectfully, dutifully, and in a godly manner.

ANENT HOLDING MEETINGS IN THE TRINITIES.

Item, it is statute and ordained that whatsoever Deacon-Conveener, or Deacons of the said traids shall convene with their haill craft or haill masters to their courts or meetings anent any of the affairs belonging to the traids in any other place than the ordinary conveening house in the Trinities, the said Deacon-Conveener and Deacons of traids who shall transgress shall pay to the Deacon-Conveener's box six pounds Scots within forty-eight hours thereafter under the failzie of doubling the sum, and to be poinded precisely for the same, although the said meetings should be held in their own houses.

ANENT APPEALING TO THE MAGISTRATES.

The haill Deacon-Conveener Court statute and ordains that whatsoever traidsmen within the Incorporations of the said burgh shall go to the Magistrates anent any divisions, strifes, or debates (blood and blae excepted), the said traidsman is judged be the said Deacon-Conveener Court to have walked contrair to his oath at his admission of being freiman, and therefore strictly ordains that whatsomever animosities, contraversies, strifes and debates whilk may arise among the said traids betwixt neighbour and neighbour that they shall have redress first to the Deacon of his awin craft, and his Court, and if the matter be not decided there, to have redress sent to the Deacon-Conveener's Court, and who shall contravene therein shall pay to the Deacon-Conveener's box the sum of ten pounds Scots, *toties quoties* ; and that the party offended, and the party offending, when they shall desire the Deacon-Conveener to grant them ane court for deciding of the said contravening, that they shall consign forty shillings Scots, and shall stand and abyd at the Court's determination and sentence as they shall enjoyn in reason and equitie.

ANENT ASSISTING UNFREEMEN.

Item, it is statute and ordained that if any of the freimen of the said Crafts shall assist or maintain any unfreimen in their house or elsewhere, they that have contravened thereof (whatever he be) shall pay into the Deacon-Conveener's box the sum of five pounds Scots *toties quoties* without mitigation.

ANENT THE CONVENER KEEPING WATCH AND WARD.

20th January, 1696.—The said day the Conveener Court did unanimuslie ordain that the present Conveener nor none of his successors in his said office should keep watch and ward as ane single sentinall, but should uphold and maintain their ancient privileges conform to the laudable custom and former use and custom. And the traids to be his warrand, and the boxmasters to have seven parts of expenses, and the hospital the eighth part.

ANENT PAPISTS AND HERETICS.

Item, it is strictly statute and ordained that there shall be none who shall have power to carry place or office among any of the Traids but only those who are of the sound Protestant religion, and do publicly profess the same ; and it is hereby ordained that no papist, quaker, or other heretic shall nowise have power to carry any office or charge among the Traids ; and any of the deacons whatsoever that shall suffer or permit the same to be done, to be fined in the sum of three pounds Scots *toties quoties*, to come to the Deacon-Conveener's box.

K

ANENT "WASHING HEADS."

22nd October, 1695.—The said day the Conveener Court statutes and ordains that the Conveener for the tyme advance all law affairs that concerns the Conveener Court, and that the Conveener uplift the half of the money payed in by the new members, and that the same be applied for the said law affairs, and that the other half be applyed for washing the heids, and in case his intromission be more or less, they are to count conform as the hospital does thereanent at ilk election.*

ANENT BRIBERY.

30th November, 1675.—The said day the haill Deacon-Conveener Court in presence of Mr. John Menzies, their patron, all in ane voice, without ony contradiction, did by thir presents renew, ratify, homologate, and approve ane former act of the Deacon-Conveener Court made by aduice of the deceased Dr. William Guild, foundator, of the date the fifth day of October, 1656, and subscribed by the said Dr. William Guild and the haill members of the Deacon-Conveener Court for the time, hearing for the onerous cause therein contained ; and it is strictly statute and ordained that whatsoever traidsman beis found to be ane finer or preoccupier of votes of whatsoever traid he be of (and being sufficiently proven) that such ane person shall in nowise have liberty to carry any public charge either as Deacon-Conveener, Deacon, Master, or Boxmaster for that ensuing year, neither to be elected nor have voice in any election. And in case any person or persons be found to fine for another he shall be held in the same condition, and ordains the foresaid act to stand inviolable to all future generatoins. And empowers the present Deacon-Conveener and his successors in the said office to call and convene the haill several Incorporations of the Trades about the Lammas time or thereby to make search and inquiry if any person or persons be about to violate or break the foresaid act in any manner of way, and if there be found any strong presumption by excess, or drinking, or night walking with any person or persons that have violate or broken the said act, that it shall be lawful for the Deacon-Conveener and his Court, with advice of the patron, to put such persons to declare upon oath whether they be guilty in that matter or not. And for the faithful performance thereof the said master John Menzies, patron, and the said Deacon-Conveener, with the haill remanent Deacons, have subscribed this present act with their hands for themselves and their successors in name of their respective traids.

ANENT APPRENTICES.

Item, it is statute and ordained that no freiman of the said traids whatsomever that shall conduce and indent with prentiss ane or more, shall

---

* This practice of "washing heids" was very prevalent at one time throughout Scotland. All entrants had to go through the process, and of course there was the usual social entertainment afterwards. Among the Aberdeen craftsmen this custom gave place to the more rational, if not more graceful, ceremony which was wont to take place at the annual riding of the marches.

accept of them by way of indenture or otherwise, under no less years than is agreeable, conform to the custom and practice of the traid, and the master shall in no wise directly nor indirectly, under whatsomever colour or pretext, give his prentiss any backband or discharge of any of the years contained in his indenture ; And if it shall happen that any master be found to transgress herein, to pay into the Deacon-Conveener's box the sum of six pounds Scots *toties quoties.* And further that the prentice so receiving the said backband or discharge, he shall lose all benefit he may have or obtained by his indenture and prentisship. And also that at the expiry of ilk prentice his prentisship, if there be any controversy or debate betwixt him and his master, that the Deacon and masters of the traid shall be the only judges competent thereto, and both master and prentice to be holden to stand to their determination thereanent, as they shall ordain in all points. And this to stand firm and stable in all time coming.

7th February, 1641.—It is statute and ordained by the Deacon-Conveener Court, conform to an act of Council dated the 29th of Sept., 1632, that all indentures that be made betwixt master and prentice shall be presented before the town clerk of this burgh within twenty days thereafter, to the effect he may take ane note thereof in his registry appointed for that effect, and mark the same on the back thereof, and whatsoever craftisman shall fail herentil his prentice not to receive the benefit of ane prentice, but shall come in as ane extraordinar to the council. And ordains every Deacon and his successor in his said office to make due and lawful intimation to his trade of this foresaid Act, and none to pretend ignorance, and who has any indentures mak as said is that, they present the same to the effect thereof.

ANENT FREEWILL OFFERINGS.

19th December, 1632.—Forasmuch as the haill incorporations of the craftsmen within the burgh at that time having contributed liberally towards building and repairing of our church and conveening house founded by that reverend pastor, Dr. William Guild, minister of Aberdeen, to the effect decayed craftsmen (when overtaken with age) may be the better entertained in the hospital of the Trinities ; Therefore the haill Deacon-Conveener Court with ane consent and assent have statute and ordained for them and their successors in all time coming that ilk new admitted freiman that shall be made hereafter shall pay and give in to the master of the hospital, for the time, as much money as they can goodly spare according to their ability, and to give order thereupon conform as the master of hospital, and they shall agree thereupon ; and if any shall refuse (according to their abilities foresaid) to offer to the said house and hospital, they are to be excluded from any part or portion of the said hospital, although poverty should seize never so sore upon them ; and be ordained not to carry office in their respective traids if any shall refuse their help thereto as said is.

22nd July, 1677.—The said day in presence of the said patron, it is appointed that against the Lammas Court next precisely the haill traids to be called for in presence of the said Mr. John Menzies, patron, anent their giving their friewill offerings to the house and hospit d. And the Master of Hospital to do all diligence whilk he can, or may thereanent.

28th July, 1685.—The said day it is statute and ordained with unanimous consent that whatsomever persone or persones in the respective traids that refuses to pay their friewill offerings to the hospital within twa years after they promise the same, the same being required by the Master of Hospital for that effect, that the same persons shall be depryved of any voyce in the Deacon-Conveener's Court or in their own traid court at elections or otherwise, aye and until they pay ; by and attour any other censure the Conveener-Court shall impose upon them. And this act to be insert in ilk respective traids books.

ANENT THE DEACON-CONVENER.

Item, it is statute and ordained with advice of the haill Deacon-Conveener Court *una voce* that whatsomever person he be that is elected Deacon-Conveener shall not continue but for the space of one year except it be unanimously resolved by the haill traids in one voice, and humbly therefore desires that none may pretend ignorance thereof. And this Act to be observed in all time coming.*

Item, it is statute and ordained that upon the day of the election of the Deacon-Conveener every present Deacon shall lift out of his own mouth ane member of his own traid to be Deacon-Conveener, and they to be removed as use is until the voices pass in the election. And this Act to stand firm and stable in all time coming without any contravening whatsomever.

20th September, 1673.—The said day the haill Court statute and ordains that every late Deacon-Conveener (in respect he is acquaint best with the traids affairs for the time) be continued ane year after his outgoing from his said office to be ane adviser and informer to the Court anent their affairs ; providing he remain a master of his own trade, otherwise to be but ane single member of the said Court as formerly, and thereby shall not add any further number of voices upon the said Court as late Deacon-Conveener, and that he shall not remain but for one year only upon the said Court upon the said account conform to the act made anent the late Deacons. This to be observed strictly in all time cuming for the reasons aforesaid.

20th November, 1722.—The said day the Conveener Court put it to ane vote whether or not one Convener or Deacon in this place should continue in their offices more than two years, and was carried *nem con*, to continue two years only.

ANENT WASTING THE CRAFTS COMMON GOOD.

Item, it is statute and ordained that whatsomever person shall happen

---

* This Act was ratified in 1684 " In presence of Alexander Gordon and Andrew Mitchell, and James Shand, Deacon-Convener."

to be Deacon-Conveener for the time, he shall not, upon any pretext whatever, spend or waste any of the Crafts Common Good without the advice or consent of the Deacon-Conveener Court, or at least of the present Deacons ; and further, that he is obliged to take all the pains he can for ingathering of all convictions and fines which shall fall in his time.

ANENT THE CONVENER BEING PRESENT AT ELECTIONS.

26th September, 1648.—It is strictly statute and ordained that at the choosing of ilk deacon and of his boxmaster their accounts before their outgoing thereof this place, that the present Deacon-Conveener for the time, with one or two whom he shall bring with him, shall be present at the laying of the said accounts, and to see that all things be done in due order and moderation ; and whatsomever Deacon and Boxmaster shall proceed to their election without doing of the same, shall be amerciate and fined six pounds Scots by and attour what other censure the Deacon-Conveener Court shall impose upon them. And this to be observed in all time coming, and also at the time to present their register to be signed by them to the effect foresaid as is appointed by Mr. John Menzies, our patron, and his predecessors in the said office.

ANENT THE CONSTITUTION OF THE CONVENER COURT.

20th October, 1670.—The said day the haill Deacon-Conveener Court for the maist part statutes and ordains that it shall be observed in all time hereafter that no old Deacon-Conveener of the said traids shall have any voice in the electing and choosing of the new Deacon-Conveener yearly except he be ane master of his ain traid and be lifted, but that always the two present councillors yearly and Master of Hospital for the time, to be still members of the Deacon-Conveener Court, and to have ane voice therein in everything.

30th April, 1677.—The said day it is unanimously statute and ordained that in all time hereafter that at the next election in this present year every respective deacon of traids shall bring with him three of the ablest of his masters (the boxmaster being always one of them) to be members of the said Deacon-Conveener Court, and the rest of the members thereof to stand as before conform to the acts made or to be made thereanent, and this to be observed in all time coming in respect of several good and serious considerations.

20th September, 1675.—The said day the haill Conveener Court statutes and ordains for good considerations moving them that no person whatsomever in the respective traids shall carry charge as Deacon of their ain traid until first he be one year ane member of the Deacon-Conveener Court, and if any traid shall prevaricate therein the said Deacon so to be chosen not to be holden nor accepted upon the said Deacon-Conveener Court.

ANENT THE MASTER OF HOSPITAL.

1632.—Dr. William Guild, pastor of Aberdeen, and patron to the Traids of the said burgh, did mortify and bestow several annuities and casualties, and in particular did bestow somewhat freely in assisting of the foresaid traids to build and repair their meeting-house and chappel, and for y' effect did appoint that a faithful, Christian, honest man, one of the said traids, shall be chosen yearlie by advice of the patron and his successors, as patrons, with consent of the members of the Deacon-Conveener Court, to collect the whole rents and casualties belonging thereto, as he shall be appointed by the Acts made or to be made thereanent.

25th October, 1656.—It is statute and ordained that whatsoever craftsman shall be elected and chosen to be master of their Hospital, in all time coming, he shall be ane member of the Deacon-Conveener Court, and shall always vote as ane member thereof, and this Act to stand in all ages to come.

10th January, 1659.—It is statute and ordained that no Master of Hospital whatsomever shall have power or libertie of himself to build or repair any house or considerable work belonging to the traids, which shall amount or extend above the sum of twenty pounds Scots, without special leave, order, or warrant from the Deacon-Conveener Court, and ane warrant under the Clerk's hand for that effect ; and in case he do in the contrair, the same to be null, and the traids not to allow the same except the haill Deacon-Conveener Court and members thereof assembled for the time shall give ane complete and full voice therein. And ordains this Act to stand in all time coming.

28th February, 1678.—The said day the haill Deacon-Conveener Court statutes and ordains, in all time coming hereafter, that the Master of Hospital shall be chosen yearly at Hallowmas, after the election of the Deacon-Conveener Court, and to continue yearly only to Hallowmas thereafter, and to have his accounts punctually in readiness before the said time, under the failure of ane hundred merks Scots, and his charge and discharge to be divided into three several parts of his books, with the first anent the affairs of the House and Hospital and rents thereof ; the second anent the Catechist's rent ; and the third anent the Bursars' House and rents thereof. And the Master of Hospital to charge himself with the haill rents and emoluments belonging to the respective charges, and to discharge himself only of what he shall receive, diligence being used by him for receiving the same.

31st October, 1684.—It is statute and appointed that the master of said Traids Hospital, present and to come, shall not give out upon bond or profit any of the Hospital means or moneys without consent of the patron, Deacon-Conveener, and haill deacons. And if he does, in the contrair, he is to charge himself thereof as debtor to the Hospital.

8th May, 1599.—The said day it was strictly statute and ordained that no person be elected and nominate Master of the said Traids Hospital except he be of ane good report, and that he have ane visible fortune in good credit ; and that none voice to give such person or persons that are not *bona fama*, or have a visible fortune, that place although he be lifted.

19th November, 1702.—In presence of Dr. William Blair, Patron, and Patrick Whyt, Deacon-Conveener, it was by voice of Court statute and ordained that notwithstanding of the Act upon the other side made anent the election of the Master of the Hospital, that in case any respective traid lift at the election of the Hospital ane honest man of good report, although he want heritage, and in case he carry to the Hospital, the Traid who lift him, in case he wants heritage, shall be cautioner *ipso facto* by lifting him for his fidelity and due performance of his said office of the Hospital.

23rd October, 1712.—The said day the whole Court with consent of their patron statute and ordained and declared that in all time coming no Master of the Traids Hospital shall presume to give out landward or bestow any money not exceeding four pounds Scots without consent of the Deacon-Conveener and the Deacons or major part of them, which are hereby declared to be a quorum with certification that if any Master of the Hospital do in contrair hereof that the same shall not be allowed to him at counting, but shall lose the same himself. This present Act to stand unalterable, notwithstanding all prior Acts.*

12th November, 1735.—The Court statute and appoint that in all time to come the Master of the Trades Hospital shall have only a yearly allowance of forty shillings sterling in name of all debursements and charges for managing the Hospital funds, providing the lands of Dumbreck continue under the Master of Hospital's management.

ANENT THE PRICE OF COFFINS.

16th October, 1693.—The said day the Conveener Court, taking to their serious considerations the exhorbitant prices taken for deid chists for beidmen within the said Hospital, for remeid thereof hereby ordains that in all time coming ilk beidman's deid chist made of thicke clefts shall be of price three pounds; ilk deid chist having syds and gavills of haill wood, four pounds; and ilk deid chist thereof of haill deals, five pounds of Scots money. And that the said deid chists shall be all coloured at the foresaid price, but in case any of them be required by the Master of Hospital to be picked, then and in that case the wricht to get ten shillings, Scots money, more for the chist picked, and this to be ane standard for the price of the deid chists to be made for the beidmen and poor of the said Hospital in time coming.†

ANENT THE ACCOUNTS OF THE HOSPITAL.

9th December, 1684.—The said day the haill Conveener Court present for the time, taking into their consideration the great loss the mortifications belonging to the said traids sustained, partly by the liberal and excessive spending, and partly by omitting to take particular inspection of ilk mortification by itself; for remeid whereof in time to come, it is strictly statute and ordained by the said Court, with consent of Doctor Patrick Sibbald, Professor of Divinity in Aberdeen, their chosen patron, that the Deacon-

---

* On 3rd May, 1704, the Master of Hospital was fined £6 Scots for employing workmen without the consent of the Court.

† "Picked" evidently means pitched. It may be mentioned that in those days the common class of coffins were V shaped; the better class had "syds and gavills" as above mentioned.

Conveener, Deacons, and remanent masters and members of the Deacon-Conveener Court and their successors in office stand to and observe the conditions and ordinances under specified, viz.:—(1) That there be no monies be cause restand to the Master of the said Hospital be uplifted or transacted without the special advice or consent of their patron for the time ; (2) That there be no houses bought or sold by the said Master of the said Hospital and his colleagues, without the said patron's consent ; (3) That no houses be repaired belonging to the said Hospital which will cost sixteen merks of reparation, without the said patron's consent ; (4) That the said patron have a special voice, advice, and be ane eye witness to the election of ilk Master of the said Hospital, and subscribe the discharge and see every particular of his accounts, otherwise the same discharge not to be valid or sufficient ; (5) That the Master of the said Hospital be chosen yearly by the old Deacons, and in their turn before Michaelmas yearly, as persons best known to the affairs throughout the year, especially conform to the will of the mortifier set down in the said Trades in their *Magna Charta.* And that no persons that joined for the said place get the same at that season. Likewise for the better flourishing of mortifications belonging to the said Traids and the encouragement of good men to add thereto, it is strictly statute and ordained that the free rent of ilk mortification be improven *per se*, and particularly the bursars and castlegate mortification ; and that such money as the bursars have given bond for shall, after the same is uplifted, be secured upon land, bond, or annual rent, where best security may be had for making up that mortification ; (6) That every mortification be kept in retentis ; (7) That no charges and expenses at visitation of houses or public meetings burden the Hospital, but be out of the respective Deacons or others, members then present, their own pockets. And in case any do in the contrair, the Deacon-Conveener and Master of the Hospital for the time shall be answerable to the patron and other judges competent therefor, and shall be liable for cost, skaith, and damage, and, at the patron's pleasure, declared answerable by the haill Traids to carry the like thing again. Likewise compeared the said Alexander Patersone, Deacon-Conveener for the time, and James Smith, gunsmith, Deacon of the Hammermen for the time, for themselves and the remanent persons adherents, and protested that they nor the Master of the Hospital for the time should not be liable for any bye past mismanagement of the said Traids, their mortifications, in respect they had no accession thereto, but that the person or persons in charge for the time be liable for the reparation thereof as their own proper faults and deeds. And that this Act should stand in all time coming.

7th January, 1688.—The said day the said Conveener Court, with consent of the said patron, statutes and ordains that ilk representative Deacon shall charge himself with so much money as any friemen who are now entered shall offer to the house at their entry, and that the said Deacon conform to their respective Trades make thankful payment thereof whomsoever the Deacon-Conveener and Master of Hospital shall call therefor.   As also that the Master of the Hospital charge himself yearly with the haill maills of the houses belonging to the Hospital, at the least show diligence therefor, or then take them in his own hand, and that sicklike that the Hospital rents be nowise burdened with any contribution or money to the poor in the respective traids, but that ilk traid maintain their poor out of their respective boxes ; and sicklike that bursar's bonds be registered to the effect that none may be lost, and this to be observed in time coming and whatsoever Deacons contravenes and goes against these premises shall have no voice in the Conveener Court until he gives satisfaction.

ANENT ELECTION OF DEACONS.

26th September, 1649.—It is statute and ordained that no traid shall go on in an election of a new Deacon except the haill traid be lawfully warned to come to the meeting house and place appointed for that effect. And also it is thought fit and convenient that after the election the late deacon to be ane member of the Deacon-Conveener Court for that year ; and if any Deacon shall act or do in contrair, to pay for the use of the said poor, to the Deacon-Conveener's box, the sum of twenty pounds Scots, and also whatever censure the Conveener Court shall impose upon him.

ANENT THE ADMISSION OF SONS.

10th May, 1662.—It is statute and ordained that in all time coming every freiman's son who shall happen to be admitted freiman in any of the seven traids shall be received and admitted in as easy a way as if his father had been freiman of that self same traid, and this to be observed in all time coming.

ANENT ENTERING CRAFTSMEN.

25th October, 1662.—It is statute be the haill Deacon-Conveener Court in ane voice that ilk entering freimen amongst the haill traids shall be tried by his traid to see if he be qualified in his traid or able to pay what the traid shall impose upon him, and that he may have something considerable to begin him in his traid and employment for serving of the leiges. And that none of the respective traids suffer or allow the entrant either at the giving in of his bill, or at the making of his essay, or at the payment of his composition to drink or spend with any of them, but all the money that wis in use to be superfluously spent to be put into the Traids boxes for the use of the poor. And in case any of the said traids shall break or contravene this present act, after due trial and examination, shall be censured according to the will of the Deacon-Conveener Court.

10th December, 1707.—The said day the Convener Court taking into serious consideration the act anent entering freimen, dated 25th October, 1662, against them drinking and spending at entry, do now of new again not only homologate and approve of the said act, but also hereby statutes and ordaines that in all tyme coming no deacon within this burgh shall suffer or allow either he himself, his masters, or members to cause any new entrant to be put to any expenses of drinking as in former tymes, but that the money so due by any entrant either for drink money or dinner shall be paid into the boxmaster of the traid for the tyme in cash, which is to be made use of for the use of the poor, and this to stand unalterable in all tyme coming under the failzie of ten pounds Scots money, to be paid by any Deacon, Boxmaster, or other member whatsomever that shall be found to contravene thir premises.

ANENT EACH TRADE'S CHAMBERS.

19th November, 1702.—It is statute and ordained that ilk respective traid [have] their own chamber in the Trinities, doors, bands, beds, locks, keys, and shelves, and that the master of the Hospital be nowise affected therewith in any time coming.   And this to be observed in all time hereafter.

ANENT THE DEACON-CONVENER'S BOX.

It is statute and ordained that every entering freiman upon the several incorporations, his sey being passed and accepted by their calling, that the Deacon of the said traid for the time shall punctually exact twenty shillings Scots from the said entering freiman to be given in to the Deacon-Conveener's box upon the day of election conform to our ancient custom ; otherwise ilk entrant Deacon who neglects to exact the said twenty shillings Scots to pay the same himself to the outgoing Deacon-Conveener, or those not to have vote in the said election until the said be paid.

29th October, 1674.—The said day the haill Deacon-Conveener Court do unanimously strictly statute and ordain that in all time coming hereafter ilk member of the Deacon-Conveener Court shall pay in quarterly to the Deacon-Conveener's box precisely six shillings Scots, for prosecuting or defending the actions and pursuits of law concerning the traids affairs, and to be strictly paid quarterly before they have any vote in the said Court, the first quarter's payment thereof beginning at the Hallow Court, 1674, and so to continue quarterly to all future ages, and the person or persons who shall happen deficient in payment thereof as said is, not to be called to meetings and courts of their ain respective traids until they pay the same.   As also that no Deacon of whatsoever traid shall bring any master with him upon the said Court but those who are sufficiently able to pay their said quarterly courts.   And ilk Deacon to be liable for paying the same themselves (in case their masters fail) before ever they get a vote in chosing of a new Deacon, or yet has any vote in chosing of their ain Deacon.   And likewise the haill Deacon-Conveener Court una voce statutes and ordains that in all time coming hereafter the half of each particular sum which is exacted off every new entrant member of the foresaid Court, at and upon the day of election of the new Deacon-Conveener Court, shall exactly come in to the Deacon-Conveener's box the very self-same day before the election, ilk person proportionally as follows—namely, ilk new Deacon-Conveener, immediately after he is elected, to pay in the half of six pounds Scots ; Item, ilk new Deacon who has not been upon the said

Deacon-Conveener's Court before, the half of four pounds ten shillings Scots, ilk Deacon that has been upon the said Court before the half of three pounds Scots ; Item, ilk new boxmaster being a member of the said Court the half of forty-eight shillings Scots ; Item, ilk new boxmaster although not upon the said Court the half of twenty-four shillings Scots ; Item, ilk new single member of the said Court the half of thirty shillings Scots ; Item, ilk new entrant freiman who shall come in amongst any of the said trades to pay in his twenty shillings Scots to the said box conform to ane former act made thereanent. And further that ilk new councillor who has never been upon the Town Council of the said burgh before, the half of two pounds Scots. And ordains all the foresaid particular sums of money to be punctually ingathered by the Deacon-Conveener in place for the time, or any other who shall be appointed for that effect, and the same to be recorded in the public register or any other book that shall be appointed for that use. And whosoever he be that shall collect the same to make just count, reckoning, and payment of the same before his outgoing, and that all shall be furthcoming to the weal, stability, and profit of the said traids, and for maintaining and defending their ancient righteous privileges, offensive and defensive. And that no bill or any other public burden affect the same in any manner of way. And strictly statutes and ordains that the haill premises shall be exactly condynlie observed and fulfilled to all succeeding generations. And whatever person or persons who shall happen to contravene and fail in the premises of any part thereof that they shall be debarred and secluded both as members of the Deacon-Conveener Court and as members of their own traid's courts or meetings, and not to carry charge nor have vote therein. And likewise to be debarred and excluded from all benefit they may have or pretend to the traids house and hospital of the Trinities in any manner of way, and for the faithful performance of the haill premises, and every payment thereof the Deacon-Conveener and haill remanent deacons of their traids for themselves and in name of their respective crafts and their successors has subscribed this present act and ordinance with their ain hands individually.

ANENT BOXMASTERS' ACCOUNTS.

1st December, 1730.—The Court statute and ordain in all time coming, every boxmaster of the respective incorporations shall give in their accounts and boxmaster's book to the conveners and deacons to be by them inspected, and that upon the day of giving the master of hospital his charge the said convener and deacon are to have a competent time for inspecting the said accounts, and making their observes thereupon, and they are to return the said accounts and books within six month after receiving the same.

ANENT FUNERAL EXPENSES.

24th November, 1728.—The Court hereby statute and ordain that in all times coming, when any of the beedmen in the Trades Hospital shall happen to decease, that the master of hospital for the time being shall pay into the boxmaster of the trade to whom such beedman belongs, allenary the sum of £12 Scots, in order to defray the charge of their funeralls, and that thereupon the said trade to whom such beedman belongs shall be obliged to burrie the said beedman without any further charge on the hospital, and appoint no goods, gear, or others belonging to such beedman to be taken out by any person from the hospital, but that the samen shall be disposed of by the master of the hospital in the public account.

ANENT THE FUNCTIONS OF THE PATRON.

27th May, 1728.—The Court taking to their consideration some former acts of this court granting privileges and authority to their patron beyond which is contained in the will of the mortification appointing their patron doe for remeid thereof restrict the powers of their patron to the will of the mortification allenarly, and hereby rescind and declare null all former acts to the contrairy.

The following extracts will serve to illustrate the nature and mode of dealing with breaches of the acts and statutes:—

ASSAULTING THE DEACON-CONVENER.

20th July, 1683.—The said day [before Alexander Idle, judge-substitute for the time] the haill Court present for the tyme having heard, seen, and considered ane bill given in by Wm. Scott, goldsmith, burgess of Aberdeen, against Alexander Annand, younger, wricht, burgess of the said burgh, anent the said Alexander, his injurious speeches, indecent behaviour, and mal-pairt striking of the said William Scott—present deacon-convener of the traids of the said burgh ; and, also having heard, seen, and considered the deposition of certain famous witnesses thereanent, the masters and members of said Court present for the tyme, ordained that the said Alexander Annand should have no voyce in any meetings or court, either of the wright and coupars or of the Deacon-Conveneer Court, nor have no charge among the traids until such tyme that he supplicate the court and give satisfaction for his transgression to the said Alexander Scott, convener, as the said Court shall ordain, and that the haill masters and members of the Conveneer Court should concur and assist to their power to the said convener for his satisfaction ; and that the said Alexander Annand should pay any fyne the Conveener Court should impose upon him for his misdemeanour, before he hath power to voyce, and this to be acted in the convener's books as example to others to do the lyke in tyme to cum.

GIVING THE LIE IN A FENCED COURT.

12th August, 1699.—The said daye George Gordon, tailzeour, was amerciat in fourty shillings Scots for giving his neighbour the lie in ane fenced Court, and for his misbehaviour to the convener, and the Court unanimously ordained that he have no voyce, and be extruded the Conveener Court until he paye and crave the injured's pardon.

A COMPLAINER TO THE MAGISTRATES PUNISHED.

12th May, 1702—The said day John Craig did enact himself not to complain to the magistrates before he complained to the Convener Court conform to the act of the Convener Court under faylzie therein contained, and the court ordained him to crave pardon for complaining against William Donald to the magistrates before he complained to the Convener Court.

AN UNRULY MEMBER.

19th March, 1705.—The said day, considering all the extraordinary enormities committed by William Lorimer, baxter, ane member of this court, and particularlie in his being often drunk, swearing and profaning God's great name, and his probation thereof, and his own confession, they, the said Conveener Court, amerciates him in four pounds Scots, to be immediately paid into the hospital for the public use, and in the meantime debarrs him as a member, aye and until he give such suitable satisfaction to the court as shall please them, and pay the said fyne.

The said day it is also found~(the said William Lorimer's habitual drunkenness and swearing) by the said Court, that they ordain John Craig to possess the chair as late Deacon notwithstanding of use and wont, declaring thereby that these presents shall no wise infer ane statute or ordinance, nor take of the laudable customs of the said trades, and debarrs the said William Lorimer therefrom until his satisfaction of the fyne be paid as use is.

25th July, 1705.—The said day compeared William Lorimer, baxter, and in obedience to the Court, acknowledged his former faults and craved pardon, and upon which the Court received him as a member of their society.

MEMBERS OF THE CONVENER COURT, 1886-7.

Patron—Rev. Alexander Spence, D.D.

Convener . . .	Andrew Robb, Gunsmith.
Master of Trades Hospital	George Rose, Flesher.

HAMMERMEN.

Deacon	Samuel Fyfe, Glazier.
Boxmaster . .	John Scorgie, Engineer.
Late Deacon . .	Marshall Watt, Glazier.
Master	Thomas Gage, Engineer.

BAKERS.

Deacon	Peter Raeburn.
Boxmaster	John Flett.
Late Deacon	Robert Meff.
Master	James Wood.

WRIGHTS AND COOPERS.

Deacon	John Robertson, Cooper.
Boxmaster	James Forbes, Wright.
Late Deacon	George Howie, Wright.
Master	James Thomson, Wright.

TAILORS.

Deacon	James Ogilvie, Upholsterer.
Boxmaster	James Garden, Upholsterer.
Late Deacon	George Rezin, Tailor.
Master	James Macdonald, Tailor.

SHOEMAKERS.

Deacon	James F. Gordon.
Boxmaster	William Henderson.
Late Deacon	Alexander Forsyth.
Master	Andrew Monro.

WEAVERS.

Deacon	Peter Beveridge.
Boxmaster	James Ducat.
Late Deacon	A. M. Byres.
Master	Robert Whyte Mackay.

FLESHERS.

Deacon	George Rose.
Boxmaster	David Milne.
Late Deacon	Charles Mackie.
Master	Robert Sangster.

Factor of Widow's Fund,   Alex. Nicolson, Baker.

Factor of Supplementary do., James Berry, Optician.

Assessors, { John Thomson, Advocate. / David Stewart, Advocate.

CHAPTER III.

DR. WILLIAM GUILD AND THE ABERDEEN TRADES.

DR. WILLIAM GUILD was brought into close contact with the craftsmen of Aberdeen through his father being a prominent member of the Hammermen Trade, and took an active and practical interest in the welfare and prosperity of the craftsmen and their associations during the last twenty years of his life. He gifted to them in 1633 the old Trinity Monastery and chapel to be an hospital and meeting house; founded a bursary fund that has proved a most valuable addition to the educational schemes of the Aberdeen Trades, and these benefactions alone entitle him to prominent mention in a history of the craft guilds of his native city.

William was the second son of Matthew Guild, a well-known armourer or "sweird slipper," who, as a "worthy deacon" of his own craft, gave frequent evidence that he was endowed with remarkable energy and considerable force of character. About the time that William was born (1586) the town was in the midst of serious civil and ecclesiastical troubles, and the public records furnish abundant evidence of the active part that the armourer took in the public affairs of the town. As recorded in a previous chapter, Matthew was one of a number of craftsmen who openly defied the ordinances of the town by "cumyng throw the toune" on a Sunday afternoon "with ane minstrall playand befor thaim throch the Gallowgett," for which they were punished by losing their freedom for a time. Matthew subsequently filled the office of deacon of his craft on six successive occasions, a post of no small importance and influence at that period. William was the second son of the same name, his elder brother having met a violent death at the hands of a son of John Leslie, burgess. There were also three daughters—Jean, who was married to David Anderson of Finzeauch, "an ingenius and virtuous citizen," whose skill in mechanics earned for him the name of "Davie do a'thing;" and Margaret and Christina, who survived their brother, and succeeded to a portion of his estate. Jean left two bequests to the town—one for the maintenance and education of poor orphans (present annual revenue about £75); and another for the maintenance of poor widows of merchant and craft burgesses and of aged virgins born in Aberdeen (present annual revenue about £2 5s.). Margaret married a glazier named Cushnie, and she, along with Christina, were the heirs under Dr. Guild's will who had the option of paying out of the doctor's estate five thousand merks or handing over the Bursars' House in Castle Street for the support of craftsmen's sons at Marischal College. Matthew Guild, being a man of considerable means, and carrying on what at that time was the most lucrative handicraft of the day, was able to give his family the best education attainable. William was sent to Marischal College, which had just been opened for the reception of students, where he made rapid progress in his divinity studies.

At the age of twenty-two Guild published his first treatise, entitled, "The new Sacrifice of Christian Incense; or, The True Entry to the Tree of Life, and Gracious Gate of Glorious Paradise," which was published in London in 1608, and dedicated "to the amiable Prince Henry, to Charles Duke of York, and to the Princess Elizabeth," the family of James I. Next came a small work entitled "The Only Way to Salvation; or, the Life and Soul of True Religion," also published in London. In the same year that he published his first treatise (1608) Guild was appointed minister of King-Edward, in the Presbytery of Turriff. Two years afterwards he married Catherine,* daughter of James Rolland† of Disblair, but they

---

* Catherine Rolland or Guild, who died in 1659, left several bequests to the town to provide bursaries at the University and Grammar School (present annual revenue, £214); for the help and maintenance of widows of decayed burgesses of Guild (present annual revenue, £52); and for the poor of the burgh of Aberdeen, and to the Minister and Kirk-Session of King-Edward, for the poor of the parish (present annual revenue, £93).

† In 1682 the Convener Court bought a tenement belonging to James Rolland of Disblair, "lying on the south side of Castlegate, for 1600 merks, and possessed by Robert Mackie, skipper, for the use of the common good of the said traids." The following minute would indicate that the Convener Court was satisfied with their bargain :—"February 22nd, 1683.—The said day the deacons and remanent masters and members of the said court ordaines that James Rolland of Disblair get ane silver dish worth seven or eight dollars."

had no family. Although living in comparative retirement in the parish of King-Edward, Guild was drawn into notice by his association with Dr. Andrews, Bishop of Ely, who was selected by King James to carry out his scheme for bringing the Scottish clergy into conformity with the English Church. Although it is not exactly known what share Guild had in this movement, which did not meet with much success, it may be inferred from the fact that Guild dedicated his next work, "Moses Unveiled," to Bishop Andrews, that he had consider- able sympathy with the project of the king. It was also through his association with Bishop Andrews that Guild obtained his appointment as one of the chaplains to Charles I.

Through Bishop Andrews, Guild was introduced to Dr. Young, Dean of Winchester, who was in high favour at the court, and who in turn introduced him to the king ; and Guild's next work, "The Harmony of all the Prophets," was dedicated to Dr. Young, to whom he acknowledges his many obligations. Into the reformation controversies, Guild, now a doctor of divinity, entered with great zest. In 1625, he wrote "Ignis Fatuus ; or, The Elf-fire of Purgatory," and an annex on the same subject, dedicated to the Earl and Countess of Lauderdale. In 1626 he published a treatise on the pre- tensions of the Romish Church to antiquity, entitled "Popish Glorying in Antiquitie turned to their Shame," which he dedicated to Sir Alexander Gordon of Cluny, and in 1627 " A Compend of the Controversies of Religion," both works having been printed by Edward Raban, in Aberdeen. Raban printed no fewer than thirteen works for Dr. Guild. In 1631, Dr. Guild was appointed successor to Mr. James Ross, one of the ministers of Aberdeen, after, as the Council Register bears, "having preached in the pulpits of the town, several times, to the con- tentment and general applause of the whole congregation, and withal knowing him to be a man of learning, good life, and conversation."

The peculiar circumstances under which Dr. Guild sub- scribed the covenant have laid him open to very severe strictures by some of his contemporaries. In 1638, when he declined to sign the covenant except under certain limitations,

L

he was not by any means singular in so acting, and little notice would have been taken of his reservation, but for the fact that two years after, when the Principalship of King's College was vacant through the resignation of Dr. William Leslie, who was deprived of office because he would not sign the covenant in accordance with the Act of 1640, which commanded " the confession covenant to be subscribed by all his Majesty's subjects of what rank and quality soever, *under all civil pains*," Dr. Guild agreed to sign it unreservedly. The reservations or limitations which Dr. Guild stood out for in 1638 are fully set forth in the following interesting certificate granted by the Commissioners of the Covenanters— the Marquis of Montrose, Lord Couper, the Master of Forbes, Sir Thomas Burnett of Leys, Laird of Morphie ; Mr. Alexander Henderson, minister of Leuchars in Fife ; Mr. David Dickson, minister of Irwin ; and Mr. Andrew Cant, minister of Pitsligo :—

Doctor William Guild and Mr. Robert Reid have subscribed the Covenant made by the Noblemen, Barons, Gentry, and Ministers, anent the maintenance of religion, his Majesty's authority and laws, with these express *Conditions*, to wit ; That we acknowledge not, nor yet condemn, the Articles of Perth, to be unlawful or heads of Popery, but only promise (for the peace of the church, and other reasons) to forbear the practice thereof for a time.

Secondly, That we condemn not episcopal government, secluding the personal abuse thereof.

Thirdly, That we still retain, and shall retain, all loyal and dutiful obedience, unto our dread Sovereign the King's Majesty ; and that in this sense, and no otherwise, we have put our hands to the foresaid Covenant, those Noblemen, Barons, and Ministers, commissioners, under subscribing, do testify at Aberdeen, the 30th July, 1638.

(Signed)   WILLIAM GUILD.
             ROBERT REID.

Likeas we under subscribers, do declare, that they neither had, nor have any intention but of loyalty to his Majesty, as the said Covenant bears.

(Signed)   MONTROSE.
             COUPER, &c.

In the same year that he signed the covenant, Dr. Guild was appointed a Commissioner to the memorable General

Assembly which met in Glasgow and abolished the hierarchy of the Church of Scotland. Dr. Guild does not seem to have been a silent member of the Assembly, for on his return to Aberdeen he found the feeling against him so strong that he deemed it advisable to leave the country for a short time.* After residing in Holland for a few months he returned and published a tract on the covenant entitled "To the Nobilitie, Gentrie, and Others, a Friendly and Faithful Advice," in which the doctor argues with great earnestness in support of the doctrine of passive obedience and non-resistance.

Dr. Guild was chosen Principal in 1640, but it is said he accepted office with great reluctance. And the fact that he did not consent to the fixing of a day for his installation till about a year after his election, gives colour to the statement that he "accepted the office of Principal rather in compliance with the wishes of others than to gratify any desire of his own."

After holding office for about ten years Dr. Guild got into trouble in consequence of his too pronounced adhesion to the royal cause. A Commission of Inquiry visited King's College in 1649 by whose orders the Principal, Sub-principal, and two of the professors were deposed, but the order was not carried into effect; and it was not until two years after, that Dr. Guild was finally deposed from office by a body of five commissioners from the army of General Monk. On the appointment of Rev. Mr. Row, one of the ministers of Aberdeen to the Principalship in 1652, Dr. Guild applied to be restored in his old pastoral charge, but was unsuccessful; and he then retired into private life. During his retirement he wrote a number of works, including "An Explication and Application of the Song of Solomon," "The Sealed Book Opened: or an Explanation of the Gospel of St. John," "An Answer to a Popish Pamphlet, called the Touchstone of the Reformed Gospel made specially out of themselves," and "The

---

* The following entry in the Kirk-Session Records is significant of the state of feeling at the time:—"10 Nov., 1639.—Doctore Gul. Guild, moderator—This day, James Davidson, servant to Alexander Gordoun, wobster, being convict be the depositions of sindrie famous witnesses admitted, sworne, and examined for speiking some injurious disdainfnl words againis Doctor Williame Guild, and saying ' dirt in Doctor Guilde's teith,' wes therefor ordainit to be put in the jogges the morrow, and thairefter to be qubeipet at the staik in the correction hous."

Novelty of Popery discovered by Romanists out of themselves."
Guild died in 1657, and was buried in the north-west portion of
St. Nicholas Churchyard, where a handsome monument, bearing the following inscription, was erected by his wife. The
monument was recently renovated by the Incorporated Trades.

SANCTISS. ET INDIVID. TRINITATI
S.
ET PIÆ MEMORIÆ GULIELMI GUILD,
QUI IN HAC URBE NATÛS ET INSTITUTUS,
SACRISQUE STUDIIS A TENERIS INNUTRITUS,
PRIMUM CURÆ ECCLESIÆ DE KINEDWARD ADMOTUS,
EAQUE PER XXIII ANNOS ADMINISTRATA,
A MUNICIPIBUS SUIS IN HANC URBEM VOCATUS.
JAM SS. THEOLOGIÆ D. ET CAROLO REGI A SACRIS,
PER DECENNIUM HIC ECCLESIASTIS MUNERE FUNCTUS ;
UNDE TRANSLATUS AD COLLEGIUM REGALE,
UBI PRIMARII ONUS AD DECENNIUM SUSTINUIT ;
DONEC REBUS APUD NOS TURBATIS,
INTEGRITAS EJUS LIVOREM TEMPORUM NON EFFUGIT ;
INDE IGITUR DIGRESSUS,
HIC, UBI CUNABULA, NIDUM SENECTUTIS POSUIT :
NON TAMEN INERTI OTIO DEDITUS,
SED VOCE, CALAMO, ET INCULPATA VITA,
ALIIS EXEMPLO FUIT.
AMPLUM ET INNOCENTER PARTUM PATRIMONIUM,
MULTO MAXIMAM PARTEM PIIS USIBUS LEGAVIT.
CONJUNX QUOQUE,
QUÆ SUA ERANT IISDEM USIBUS ADDIXIT.
VIXIT ANNOS LXXI,
ET
AD VII KALENDAS AUGUSTI, ANNI MDCLVII,
IN SPEM OPTATISSIMÆ RESURRECTIONIS,
MORTALITATUM EXPLEVIT.
CATHARINA ROLLAND, SUPERSTES VIDUA,
DILECTISS. MARITO,
CUM QUO CONCORDITER XLVII PLENOS ANNOS VIXIT,
H. M. L. M. F. C.
NEC CŒPISSE, NEC FECISSE VIRTUTIS EST,
SED PERFECISSE.

It is beyond our function here to discuss the different
estimates of the character of Dr. Guild. A strong polemic and
ecclesiastical controversialist himself, he did not fail to have
his detractors as well as his admirers. Spalding indulges in
some specially severe strictures upon him in his "Journal of the
Troubles and Memorable Transactions of Scotland, from 1624
to 1645," making a number of grave charges against him, more
especially with regard to the demolition of the Bishop's house

in Old Aberdeen, which, however, was the doctor's own property, having been gifted to him by Charles I. in 1641. Alluding to this and other acts of Dr. Guild which he strongly condemned, Spalding says :—" John Forbes and Thomas Mercer, by the tolerance of Dr. Guild, principal, caused masons to throw down to the ground the bishop's dove cot (whilk indeed was ruinous and unprofitable), to be stones to the bigging of a song-school, whilk by some was not thought to be sacriligious, but yet was evil done as others thought. . . . In the same manner, he (Dr. Guild), dang down the walls of the Snow Kirk to big the college dykes. . . . Now he is demolishing the Bishop's house, pitiful and lamentable to behold; kirks and stately buildings first casten down by ruffians and rascals, and next by churchmen under colour of religion. . . . Dr. Guild at his own hand cause break down the great oaken joists within the bishop's house, and transported them there-frae for reparation of the college. Pitiful to see so glorious a building thus thrown down by dispiteful soldiers, and then demolished by Doctors of Divinity." And, finally, Spalding adds :—" Dr. Guild goes on most maliciously and causes cast down the stately wall standing within the Bishop's close, curiously builded with hewn stones, and took the stones down to the college for such vain uses as he thought most expedient (such was the iniquity of the times), and break down the ashler work about the turrets, raised the pavement of the hall and caused laid them down to lay the floor of the common school."

All this may be highly objectionable in the eyes of many, but this at least can be said for Dr. Guild, that he was not using the old buildings for his own private ends, but for the benefit of the college ; and it is only right to state that, after all his bitter denunciation, Spalding himself makes the apologetic admission—"It is true this house, yards, and precincts were given to him by the estates whereof he might have made a more godly use by upholding rather than demolishing the same."

Our business here, however, is not so much with what Dr. Guild " dang down " as with what he built up. In 1631 he purchased the Trinity Monastery and Chapel, for the purpose

of founding an hospital and providing a meeting-house for the
Incorporated Trades, and it may truly be said that to this
benefaction the remarkable financial prosperity of the
Aberdeen Trades is largely due.   Up to that time they
had existed as detached bodies; their meetings were held
in the deacons' houses, or public ale-houses; they did not
possess any common bond of union.   The Convener Court
existed more in name than in reality.   It had no functions
recognised by law; the Deacon-Convener's office was honorary,
not administrative, and his services were only sought on the
occasion of public demonstrations and festivals, or to convene
the craftsmen to take common action with regard to their
trading privileges.   The funds of the individual Trades were
also at this time but trifling.   All the money that was collected during the year barely met law expenses and the
pressing necessities of the poor.   A very small sum indeed
would represent the total wealth of the Trades when they
became linked together under the charter obtained by Dr
Guild from Charles I. for the administration of their common
hospital.

Viewed from a mere money point of view, Dr. Guild's
benefaction was not so very large, but looked at as the
main factor in establishing a visible bond of unity among the
craftsmen, and taking into account the spirit of mutual help-
fulness which he encouraged during the twenty years that he
continued to take an active part in the affairs of the Trades
and the hospital, the influence of Dr. Guild's gift upon the
Trades of Aberdeen cannot be over-estimated.   He was, as his
contemporaries well knew, and were always ready to acknowledge, a sagacious man of business as well as an able ecclesiastic.   He was quick to perceive what the craftsmen were
most in need of ; and he helped them to supply that need in a
manner that reflected credit on his sagacity and foresight; in
short, he made the motto of the craftsmen—"*vis unita fortior*"
—a living reality, and to him more than to any other man was
due that concord and unity which have enabled the craft
burgesses in Aberdeen to hold their own against their more
wealthy brethren, and to accumulate funds for assisting the
aged, the widowed, and the fatherless.   Dr. Guild was also

instrumental in inducing a number of other generous citizens to assist in establishing the Hospital.*

The history of the venerable Monastery and Chapel which Dr. Guild gifted to the Trades—for they were in a sadly dilapidated condition when he bought them in 1631—carry us back to a very primitive and ancient Aberdeen—to a period when very little is accurately known regarding the inhabitants and institutions of the town. Like other religious institutions elsewhere, the Trinity Monastery passed through many vicissitudes. It twice reverted to the crown; was sacked and set on fire by religious mobs, and otherwise abused and ill-treated during the days of the reformation. But, notwithstanding all these ups and downs, the titles and charters, dating from 1381, have been carefully preserved, and are at present in the custody of the Master of Trades Hospital.

King William the Lyon, who established in 1211 a branch of the Order of the Holy Trinity, called the Red Friars, which had been instituted by Pope Innocent III. in 1200, gifted to this branch of the Order his palace which he had erected in 1181 "on the south side of the Green," to be used by them as a convent or monastery. This order of friars, says Kennedy, "was sometimes distinguished by the name of Mathurines, after their house at Paris, which was dedicated to Saint Mathurine. Their principal occupation was soliciting money from the benevolent for the redemption of Christian captives taken by the Turks or the piratical states of Barbary. They pretended to be canon regulars, their houses were denominated hospitals or convents, and their superiors ministers. . . . The habit of the Order was white, with a red and blue cross patté upon the scapular."

From the deeds and papers in the possession of the Trades pertaining to the Monastery it appears that on 29th September, 1381, William de Daulton, predicant or Black Friar, gave a donation of 13 shillings 4 pennies Scots to the Trinity Convent to be paid annually from his house and land in the Shiprow for the weal of his soul, the souls of his father and mother, and all the faithful departed. This charter of donation has appended to it the seal (Fig. I.) of the Dominican

* A list of donations and bequests to the Incorporated Trades will be found in the appendix.

Friars. The following note descriptive of this seal (which is in a good state of preservation) is given by Laing in his well-known work on seals :—

A full-length figure of St. John the Baptist, holding in his left hand a circular disc, on which is the Agnes Dei, to which the right hand is pointing. In the background are two trees and foliage. The inscription appears to be, " Sigillum commune fratrum ordinis predic de Abyrden." Appended to a charter by William de Daulton, brother of the Order, granting to the minister and Trinity Friars of Aberdeen an annual rent of 13s 4d. out of his lands at Aberdeen, 30th September, 1381.

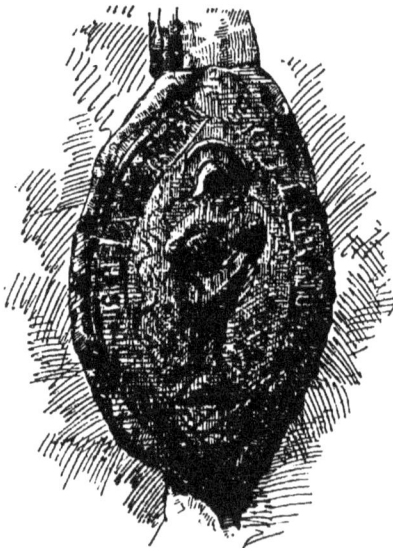

FIG. I.

The next document is a precept of sasine on ten merks Scots, granted annually by Isabella de Douglas, Countess of Mar and Garioch, to the Trinity Convent, from the lands of Westin, Kyncragg, and Terlayn, for the support and maintenance of a priest of their order, to celebrate a daily mass for her and her friends' souls, dated 8th June, 1405. A charter confirming this donation was granted by the Earl of Mar and Garioch at Kildrummy Castle on 5th December, 1406, in presence of the Bishop of Ross.

Then follows a charter of donation by Andrew Straton, burgess of Aberdeen, of 8 shillings 4 pennies Scots, to the Trinity Convent, to be paid annually from his house on the north side of the Netherkirkgate for the celebration of an anniversary service, viz., a placebo and dirige on the Sunday after Corpus Christi day, or on the day of his burial, with a trental of masses the following, for his soul, the souls of his wife and children, and the faithful departed in the pains of purgatory.—Dated June 20th, 1522.

William Blinshell, cooper, and burgess of Aberdeen, left 13s.

Scots to the Trinity Convent in 1522, to be paid annually from his house on the south side of the Shiprow, for celebrating an anniversary service on the second Sunday after his decease in the following manner:—The Friars, on that day, were to give the Town's Crier two pence to perambulate the town and summon the people to pray for his soul, afterwards to toll the bells and place six lighted tapers before the altar of the Virgin Mary, and then sing a solemn mass and dirige for his soul, and the souls of Margaret Chalmers and Annabell Scroggie, his wives, the souls of his father, mother, brothers, sisters, benefactors, friends, and all the faithful departed, and particularly for the souls of those persons whose goods he had unjustly obtained without making restitution or recompense to them for the same, and a trental of masses to be said during the following week.

We have next a charter of donation by John, Earl of Caithness, of 10 merks Scots to the minister and friars of the Trinity Convent, to be paid annually from the rents of the Island of Stroma, for founding a trental of masses to be continually celebrated by them, viz., five masses every week of the year, two of which to be sung, one on Friday for his father William's soul, and the other on Wednesday for himself; the other three to be sung on Monday, Tuesday, and Thursday for his friends ; and besides these, also four other solemn masses with placebo and dirige to be sung at the quarters of the year, one to be for his father William, another for himself, to be celebrated on the day of his decease, and the remaining two for his friends, successors, etc., etc., making the whole number to be annually performed amount to 264. This charter is dated at Wick, Caithness, 19th October, 1523.—(Scotch parchment). A sasine on the above was delivered in the Earl's name by "John o' Grot, of Duncansbay, baillie to the Earl in these pairts." An additional grant was made by George, Earl of Caithness, of 10 merks, upon condition that at all times of public worship in Trinity Chapel, the officiating curate, preacher, or minister, and the poor or beadsmen of the said hospital shall offer up the suffrages of their prayers to God for all heavenly and earthly blessings, prosperity, honour, and happiness to the said George, his successors, and honourable family.   This second grant is dated 20th December, 1673.

The Monastery remained in the possession of the Trinity Friars until about 1589, when the whole property passed into the hands of the Crown.   In that year a charter was granted under the broad seal of James VI., giving a life-rent of the place and monastery of the Trinity Friars, with all the revenues, privileges, &c., thereof, in feu-farm to Thomas Nicolson (brother of John Nicolson, advocate and commissary, &c., Edinburgh), he paying to the Crown, as annual feu-duty for the same, of 40 shillings Scots, and an augmentation of 40 pennies above the former feu-duty.   About thirty years after this charter was granted by James VI., Thomas Nicolson disposed of the place and monastery, with all the buildings, lands, revenues, and privileges, to James Mowat of Ardo for the annual payment of a feu-duty of £2 Scots and 40 pennies of augmentation during his lifetime, and thereafter paying the same to the Crown.   By a second charter under the broad seal of Charles I. the place and monastery was granted to Thomas Mowat, son of James Mowat of Ardo, "the said place and monastery having reverted to the Crown upon the decease of Thomas Nicolson of Cold-brandspeth, who had a life-rent under the charter from James VI."   This second charter is dated at Whitehall, May 10th, 1628.   Three years after, the Monastery was purchased by Dr Guild, with all the lands, houses, rents, revenues, rights, and privileges belonging thereto, on payment of the annual feu-duty of 40 shillings and 40 pennies Scots, during the lifetime of the said Thomas Mowat.

At this time the property appears to have been in a very ruinous condition.   In 1559, when a general attack was made upon all the religious houses in the town, the Trinity Convent suffered to a greater extent than any of the others.   The reformers not only set fire to the buildings and tore down the walls, but one of the monks, named Friar Francis, was stabbed, and his body thrown into the fire and burned.

The following is a "trew double of the annuities and fewes due to the said Hospital trew subscribed aff the principal coppie, collationed and attested be Alex. Cruickshank, and whairof this is ane double, he being clerk to the Trades":—

Ferryhill payes 20 lib. yeirlie of few dewtie, . . .	lib.	20 00	0
Craibstone in the Garrioch payes 2 libs. yeirlie of few dewtie, ...		2 00	0
West toune in Cromar payes yeirlie 10 marks of annual, .		6 13	4
Lethentie in the Garrioch payes yeirlie 2 lib. annual, . .		2 00	0
Milne of Forbie payes yeirlie 5 marks payable by the Earle of Erroll, ...		3 6	8
Earle of Caithness for the Isle or Lands of Stroma payes 10 marks, ...		6 13	4
Alexander Sinclair in Cathnes for sd. lands of ——, . .		2 00	0
		42 13	4

Alexander Donaldsones house besyd the shoar payes yeirlie 20s., ...	lib.	1 00	0
The Catte polls foir land laitlie belonging to Wm. Gray, 6s. 8d. ex., ...		0 6	8
The Treasurer of Aberdeen for half nett of the ovlt water 10s., ...		0 10	0
Mathew Donaldsons house 24s., ...		1 4	0
Duncan Donaldsones airs for his lands a rig at the Crabstane and the butts at futtie 42s., ...		2 2	0
Walter Cochran for his lands that wer Charles Keillos 6s. 8d.,		0 6	8
James Robertsone for his house at the shipp raw port 3s. 4d.,		0 3	4
Johnn Findlay, cordiner, for his house in the braid gaitt, 6s. 8d., ...		0 6	8
The lands of Umqˡ Wm. in the Nether kirk gaitt 30s., .		1 10	0
The place of Carmelit freirs which the principal of the College payes 6s. 8d., ...		0 6	8
Mr. Thomas Blackhalls house in the Grein 6s. 8d., . .		0 6	8
Umqˡ Ion Berrihills in the Grein 4s., . . .		0 4	0
Umqˡ Alexr. Hills land in the Grein 6s. 8d., . . .		0 6	8
Umqˡ Ion Ros in Wreights land in the Grein 2s. 6d. ex.,		0 2	6
David Cohoz land in the shippraw 5s., ...		0 5	0
Andrew Lousone in the shippraw 3s. 4d., ...		0 3	4
Alexr. Jaffray in the shippraw 26s., ...		1 6	0
Alexr. George in the Shiprow 6s. 8d., ...		0 6	8
Umqˡ Thomas James Cowie in the ——— . .		0 13	4
Do. Thomas Cullens land in the Gallowgait 6s. 8d., .		0 6	8
Do. Galloways house in the Nether kirk gaitt 8s. 4d. .		0 8	4
Do. Wm. Youngs house in the gallowgaitt 21s., . .		1 1	0
Do. Alexr. Blenschells west land in the gallowgaitt 5s.,		0 5	0
Do. Thomas Paips house in the castlegaitt 21s., .		1 1	0
Do. Thomas Mortimers house in the castlegait 5s., .		0 5	0

Mr. Thomas Jonstounes sister for the house and yaird
    besyd the Trinities, ... lib. 1 1 0
Umqᴸ William Clarks land 5s., ... 0 5 0
  Do. Alexander Litsters 5s., ... 0 5 0
  Do. Alexander Foulertounes land, Baxter, 8s. 4d., . 0 8 4
Archibald Boyds land in the Guestrow 6s. 8d., . . . 0 6 8
David Rennies land in the Guestrow 6s. 8d., . . . 0 6 8
William Caddenheads land som tym in futtie 7s., . . 0 7 0

                                                    lib. 17 16 10

          Without the toune, . . . lib. 42 13 4
          Within the toune, . . . 17 16 10

                   lib. 60 10 2

From the following entry in the Council Register it would
appear as if the town had offered to buy the convent in 1597,
but there is no record of the transaction having been carried
through:—

    25th April, 1597.—The said day the haill toune being convenit as said
is consentit to the buying of the Trinitie Freris place within this burght,
yardis and kirk theirof, and willit and desyrit the prouest and baillies to
deal with the heretabill propritaris of the said place, and to gif the sowme
of sax hundrath merks therefor, of the reddiest of the patrimonie and
yeirlie rent of this burght, gif the same may be had of that price, and na
taxation to be stentit nor imposit upon the inhabitants for bying thereof,
upon quhilk lykvayes the said Alexander Rutherfurd, prouest, cravit act
of court and instrument.—*Council Register, vol. xxxvi., p. 715.*

It is worthy of note that one of the first ships built at
Aberdeen was constructed in the gardens adjoining the Monas-
tery, the south wall of which overlooked the upper part of the
then harbour, or rather part of the estuary of the Dee.
Authority to build a bark was granted to a "tymber man" from
St. Andrews, by the magistrates, in the following terms:—

    20th February, 1606.—The samyn day, anent the bill geivin in by
Alexander Davidsoun, tymber man in Sanct Androis, mackand mention
that he hes agreet with the honest men that hes bocht the Wod of Drum
for als mekill tymber as will big ane bark, quhilk bark he intendis, God
willing, to big within this towne, and becauss the kirkyard of the Trinitie
Freris, quhilk is filthilie abusit be middingis, is the maist meit and convenient place for bigging of the said bark, he humblie desyred for sic
service as he micht do to the towne, that he may have licence and guid-

will of that rowme for bigging of the said bark, seing the tymber is redie in ane flott to cum to this burght as at mair lenth was contenit in his said bill; quhairanent the prouest, baillies, and counsall advysing, they fund the desire thairof verie reasonable, aud grantit and gaive licence to the said Alexr. Davidsoun to big his schip in the pairt foresaid, viz. : in the said Trinity Freris Kirkyaird, conform to the desyre of his said supplication, and for that effort ordanis all those qho has laid middingis in the said kirkyaird or thairabout, to remove and tak avay the same within aucht dayes next efter the dait heirof vnder pain of ane unlaw of fyve merkis to be upliftet of the persone failzeand, and ordanis intimation to be maid heirof to those quho has the saidis middingis at the pairt forsaid. —*Council Register, vol* xlii., *p.* 582.

When Dr. Guild acquired the buildings in 1631, he obtained subscriptions from the different Trades to assist in reconstructing them, the contributions he received being entered as follows in the Convener Court Book:—

15th June, 1632.—The said day the haill traids according to their abilities, did enter in to Doctor William Guild for building aud repairing their meeting house and chappell, everie traid proportionallie as follows, but since that tyme everie particular man's offering is notted in ane book whilk is keepit always in the custody of the present master of the Traids Hospital.

HAMERMEN.—Imprimis—William Udny, Deacone of the Hamermen, payit in that day in name of his craft to the said foundator, in part of payment of their offerings, the sum of fyve hundred thirty-three pounds six shillings eight pennies Scots.

BAKERS.—Item, George Leslie, Deacon of the Bakers, payit the said day in name of his craft to the foundator, in pairt of payment of their offerings, the sum of two hundred pounds Scots.

WRIGHTS AND COOPERS.—Item, Robert Irvine, Deacon of the Wrights and Coopers, payt the said day in name of his traid to the foundator, in part of payment of their offerings, the sum of five hundred and forty merks.

TAILZEOURS.—Item, Thomas Gardin, Deacon-Conveener for the tymn, in name of the Tailyeour Craft, payt in the said day to the foundator, in pairt of payment of their offerings the sum of three hundred merks, by and at'our ane hundred thirty nyne pounds, which the said Thomas Gardin had debursed upon the said work, as his particular compt given in by him did bear.

CORDINERS.—Item, Thomas Robertson, Deacon of the Cordiners, did pay in name of his craft to the said foundator, in pairt of payment of their offerands, the sum of three hundred and fifty merks money with ane bond of John Mercles, containing ane hundred and fifty merks payable at Martinmas next to come.

WEAVERS.—Item, Thomas Clark, Deacon of the Weavers, did pay in the said day in name of the said craft to the said foundator, in pairt of payment of their offering, the sum of three hundred merks.

FLESHERS.—Item, It is to be remembered that at the tyme the fleshers was not as yet received with the traids, but at the time of their admission, which was in the year 1657, Andrew Watson, their present deacon, did give in for the use of the hospital funds in name of the said traid two hundred and forty pounds Scots.

Notwithstanding these contributions, amounting in all to about £2200 Scots, the following appeal had to be made to the Town Council, a petition which reveals that, at that time, the Trades had very little funds at their command :—

19th September, 1632.—The said day anent ane supplicatioune given in to the Prouest, Bailies, and Counsell, be Thomas Gairdyne, tailzeour, deacone convenir of the haill craftis of this burghe, for himself and in name and behalf of the remnant deacones and bretherne of the said craftis, makand mentioune that they hed causit build and repair the Trinitie Frieris Plais of this burghe, quhilk Mr. William Guild, ane of the towne's ordinar ministers, hed laitlie conqueist and mortifiet to be ane hospitall for decayet craftismene within the samen ; upon the bigin quharof thay had bestowit the best pairt of thair monies quhilk thay hade to the fore in thair comon boxis, sua that thair stock and rent for the present will be verra meane, and seeing that poore decayed craftismene hes no plais in the gild bretherene's hospitall, and the nichtbouris of the craftis are most willing to contribute to the worke according to thair power, quhairby thair brethren may be supplyit, and the toune and sessioune easit of ane burdeine : Thairfor they humblie desyrit thair Wisdomes of the Counsell to put to thair helping hand to the furtherance of the worke, and in regard that they ar memberis of this commoun wealthe, to grant unto thame thair charitabill help and support thair unto, for the quhilk they sall endeavour to approve thame selffis thankfull, and both redie and forward in anything concerning the guid and weil of the toune, according to thair power, as in the saids supplicatioune at lengthe wes conteuit. Quhair-anent the saidis Prouest, Bailies, and Counsell, advysing and considdering the necessitie and gudness of the wark, thay gave and grant to the deacones and maisteris of the craftis of this burghe the composition of ane Gild Burgess sic as thay sall present to the Counsell (except the wyne siluer), quhilk will be twa hundreth markis, yeyrlie, and ilk yeir for the space of fyve yeirs nixt efter the dait heirof, to be employit on profite, and maid furthcumand be thame in al tyme cuming, to the behoof of the decayit craftismen quho sall happen to be admitit in the said Hospitall as bedalls thairoff : with conditione alwayis that the decones, maisteris, and friemen of the said craftis, and thair successouris, carie and behave thame selffis dewtifullie in al thingis to the counsell, which sall tend to the comon

GATEWAY OF OLD TRADES HALL.

weil and benefite of the toune, and beare burdeine thairin with the gild
bretherne thairof, according to thair power. And at the expyring of the
saidis fyve yieris that they mak just compt and rekoning to the counsall
waring of the saidis moneyes, quhilk sall acquire be the saidis compositiounes, togedder with the yeirlie annual rent that sall accrue thairupon.
Council Register, vol. lii., *p.* 73.

Some time after the buildings were restored, a fine gateway was erected, bearing the following inscription :—

Fundavit Gulielm' Scot 1181.

[The Imperial Crown and ensigns armorial of the kingdom.]

To ye glorie of God
And comfort of the Poore
This Hows was given
To the crafts by Mr. William
Guild, Doctour of Divinitie
minister of Abd : 1633.

Underneath are the family arms of Dr. Guild with the
letters D. W. G. Foundator, and the words

*He - That - Pitieth - The - Poore - Lendeth - To - The - Lord - And -
That - Which - He - Hath - Given - He - Repay - Prov.* 19.17.

This gateway was removed entire when the new hall in
Union Street was erected, and was built into the wall on the
Denburn-side where it can still be seen.

The chapel which was attached to the Monastery has
entirely disappeared, having been taken down in 1794 and a
new kirk erected by the Established Church. The old chapel
was long used by the craftsmen as a place of worship; but as
they had also seats in the church of St. Nicholas and in old
St. Paul's Church, it was subsequently let to different religious
sects at a rental of from five to seven pounds a year, the
Crafts reserving the right to a certain number of seats and
lofts for their own use. The following interesting minutes
about the Trinity kirk appear in the Convener Court Book:—

6th December, 1688.—At Aberdeen at ane meeting of the Deacon-
Conveener, Deacons, and remanant masters and members of the Deacon-
Conveener Court of the traids in Aberdeen, holden within the Trinity
Hall of the said burgh upon the 18th December, 1688, in presence of John
Leslie, Deacon-Conveener, the maisters and members of the said Con-

veener Court having taken to their consideration the great profit and advantage that would redound, not only to the spiritual good of the haill traidsmen within the said burgh, and to their emendation to have ane good and faithful minister to preach in this Trinity Church, but also that it would be very useful and advatageous to the spiritual good of the number of old and decayed persons who lived adjacent thereto ; and the haill Conveener Court present for the tyme having agreed to and pitched upon Mr. William Mitchell, last preacher of the gospel at Aberdeen, to serve thereat the said kirk, it was desyred by the said Deacon-Conveener that the members of the said Conveener Court should have ane voyce whether or not the traids in the said burgh should give the said Mr. William ane call for that effect, and trye if he would accept thereof ; lykas by voice of the masters and members of Court convened for the time, it was voyced and ordained *nemine contradicente* that the traids in the said burgh grant bond such ane manner as they shall after discern upon. And the said Mr. William Mitchell did give his oath anent the premises whereupon the said conveener in name of the said traids asked and required act and instrument.

21st February, 1704.—The said day the Conveener, Deacons, and remanent masters and members of the said Conveener Court statutes, appoints, and ordains that all persons who shall be permitted to build seats or dasks in the Trinity Church of Aberdeen that they first apply themselves to the Conveener and Deacons, and they, or knowing wrichts at their order, shall appoint places in the said church for the petitioner, and that the said dasks or seats be of good work, and that they be built regular for avoiding confusion, and also ordains that none shall put their arms on their seats or dasks built by them, but allenarly their names or marks ; and also that no person building seats shall have liberty to lift, demolish, or take down the same, but that they shall remain in the said church as mortified thereto in all tyme coming.

8th January, 1723.—The said day the Court ordained David Cruickshank, officer of the Traids Hospital, to ring the Trinity Bell each Sabbath day hereafter at the second and third bells in Sanct Nicholas for the better warning the inhabitants, for which cause the Court allows him six shillings of addition off of each traid, which makes now three shillings off of each traid. And this to be observed from and after date of their presents.

In 1793 the chapel and grounds were feued to William Michie, wright, at an annual rent of £14, the Trades taking him bound to build a church or place of worship, and reserving to themselves the bell, clock, arms, hearses (chandeliers), and any other antiquities they might wish to preserve. The bell, which was subsequently erected over the school-house attached to the hospital, was twice recast—once in 1763, when, says an entry in the Convener Court Book, it was "sent to London and cast of new with the same inscription, and done with the addition of being recast—James Noris, Convener, in the year 1763, the bell to be sett with the same tune and bigness." In 1811 it was again recast, but this time there was no direction as to preserving the old inscription, and it came from the hands of the founders with the bald record— "Recast by the Trades of Aberdeen, 1811. John Webster, Convener; John Chalmers, Hospital." It is to be regretted that the old inscription was not preserved. It may be of interest to be informed that John Webster (who, by the way, was the grandfather of Mr. John Webster, LL.D., for some years M.P. for the city of Aberdeen) and John Chalmers were in office at that period, but it would have been a thousandfold more interesting to have had the old inscription preserved. The bell now hangs in a side vestibule in the new Trinity Hall, and its deep and sonorous tones must be familiar to those who have happened to be present at any of the annual election dinners.

In 1794, when a division occurred in the East Church congregation on account of a minister being presented to the charge who was distasteful to them, an application was made to the Presbytery for permission to erect a Chapel of Ease. This permission having been granted, a new church was erected on the site of the old Trinity Chapel, which was demolished. A manse was also erected adjoining the new church; but neither church nor manse was long devoted to the purposes for which they were erected. They were fated to undergo even greater changes than the friars' monastery and chapel, for the Chapel of Ease is now a Variety Music Hall, and the manse forms part of an adjoining public-house!

CHAPTER IV.

THE BURSARS HOUSE.

By a deed, dated 15th September, 1655, Dr. Guild left five thousand merks to the Master of Hospital, Deacon-Convener of the crafts of Aberdeen for the time, and remanent deacons, for "ye intertaining of thrie poore boyes yt ar craftsmen's sounes, as bursers in the new colledge of Aberdeine, yt ar of good ingynes, and able for ye said colledge ;" but under a proviso in the will he gave his heirs the option of giving, instead of five thousand merks, "his fore house in ye Castellgate, wherein I dwell, and brew house, with rowmes above, in ye other syd of ye close." When the doctor died his heirs elected to hand over the property which, by the way, was at one time supposed to have been given to Dr. Guild by Charles II., in return for a basin filled with gold, which he presented to His Majesty on his visit to the burgh. The title deeds of the property, however, effectually dispose of this pretty legend. It originally belonged to the well-known Rolland family. William Rolland fell heir to it on the death of his father William in 1567 ; then it descended to a brother named James, was next owned by Alexander, son of James, and was then sold by "the said Alexander, and Bessie Tullidaff, his wife, to Dr. Guild, in 1628, for the sum of 2500 merks Scots, with free passage to and from the same by the foregate thereof and turnpike in the close." The "brew house, with the rowmes above, on the other syd of the close," had been sold by James Rolland to Thomas Nicolson, son of Provost George Nicolson (1622), but these properties also returned to the Rolland family. Dr. Guild became proprietor in 1636, the sasine bearing that it followed upon "a disposition and resignation thereof by John Moir, collector of the kirk-session, and his patrons, and also of Richard Paip, William Scott, and the above-mentioned William Rolland, the former possessor thereof, and Jane Stewart, his spouse."

In this deed Dr. Guild stipulated that " in caise any variance be concerning ye bestowing of any of these burses upon any of ye forespecified, I ordain yat ye eldest minister in Aberdeen (as most conscientious to see the mortification goe right) decide in ye matter, and yat impartiallie ye said benefit be bestowed out of ye maills of ye said houses upon ye unablest in means and best qualified in gifts as they shall answer to God, which house, likewise in all tym coming (yat it, nor ye maills thereof be not perverted to any other use) I ordain to be called ye Bursers House, and that when any of them are laureat they by writ oblige themselves for the benefit received when God enables them to add to ye mortification and that yis yeir writ be carefullie keiped in the Master of Hospitals Box, either by itselfe or rather in a book made for the purpose, and who shall sett the said house by advice of ye said Deacon-Conveener and Deacons, and uptake the maills thereof and be conjunct with them in the patronage and election of ye said bursers."

Under an authority from the Court of Session, obtained in 1884, the Trades disposed of the Bursars House and other property which had been subsequently purchased in the same locality, and the money is now otherwise invested.

For the first hundred years or so the rents or maills of the houses thus bequeathed were fully required to support the stipulated number of bursars. About 1710, however, there seems to have been a scarcity of bursars, and as the bursaries were then paid in the shape of fees direct to the professors, these gentlemen, not unnaturally, took steps to have the terms of the will duly carried out. In 1710 the principal and professors of Marischal College raised an action in the Court of Session against the Master of Trades Hospital, Deacon-Convener, and Deacons of the Crafts, to have it declared that in terms of Dr. Guild's Mortification, they shall present and maintain three bursars at the College, and pay the fees of the bursars at the rate of 20 merks Scots each yearly to the professors of the College ; that in the event of no craftsmen's sons in the town of Aberdeen being found qualified to enter the College, then to declare that the Master of Hospital, Convener, and Deacons, be bound to find duly qualified bursars from some other part of Scotland, and have them presented; and also to ordain them to count and reckon for the rents of the property mortified for the period up to the raising of the action. The professors maintained that in case of a bursar giving up his presentation before his time was finished, or if he died, or when his time was finished, the Trades were bound at once to fill up the vacancy by presenting a craftsman's son; and that in case of their being unable to find a tradesman's son qualified for the presentation, then the patrons were obliged " to present any poor boy that is qualified and unable to maintain himself," a bond being taken from them or some of their friends binding them to refund the amount of the benefit got by them from the mortification.

The case having been duly heard, the Lords of Session found that the mortifier (Dr. Guild) determined no preference as to the persons to be presented bursars, but allowed the Master of Hospital, Convener, and Trades of Aberdeen to prefer the craftsmen's sons within the town of Aberdeen to be bursars in the first place, when they can be found qualified; and failing them they must present any other craftsmen's sons in Scotland. They also decided that there must be three bursars always presented. They refused the claims of the professors for 20 merks for each of the bursars, but ordained the craftsmen to fill up the vacancies at once, in terms of the Mortification. The Trades were also ordained to produce their books and count and reckon for the rents of the Bursars' House during the period when bursars were not presented. After this date the fund seems to have prospered considerably. In 1837 the managers prepared a report for a Royal Commission, in which they state that " the whole funds are not distributed, though the whole free income might be so if there should be claimants entitled to it. A certain fixed sum, above the average of college bursaries, has been set apart for each bursar for these many years, and since 1825 no applicant has been denied or refused a bursary. The balance of income, if any, after paying bursaries has been employed at current interest to form a fund for rebuilding the property, and that by authority of the managers. It may be proper to state here, however, that in addition to the bursaries enjoyed by tradesmen's sons, the managers have been in the way of giving premiums for merit to bursars, varying in value from one to five pounds, and that such has been included as part of the annual expenditure."

From a table prepared a few years ago by the present writer, it appears that since 1858, £3350 has been paid in bursaries. At present the value of bursaries is £25, tenable for four years, and should a student qualify at the bursary competition to take one of the college bursaries he gets as an addition to his Trades bursary a sum equal to one-half of the bursary he proves himself able to take. Thus a student qualifying for, say, a £20 bursary would receive in all £35 as his Trades bursary. The stock of the fund which has been carefully "nursed" for a number of years, considerable sums having been lent out of the other funds for the purchase of additional property without any interest being charged, now amounts to over £5000. A portion of the surplus revenue is devoted to paying the fees and books of sons of members of the Trades who choose to attend the evening classes at Robert Gordon's College.

CHAPTER V.

TRADES HOSPITAL.

PRIOR to 1609 aged and decayed craftsmen were admitted into St. Thomas' Hospital, an institution founded by Canon Clatt for the reception and maintenance of indigent and decayed burgesses, merchant and craft alike ; but by the following Act of Council the craftsmen were excluded, and its entire benefits monopolised by the merchant class of burgesses or guild brethren :—

1st March, 1609.—The said day the provost, baillies, new and auld counsall, considering that divers persons his been admitted and received to the hospital of this burght in tymes bygane wha hes not been burgess of gild, express against the terms of the foundation of the hospital, be the whilk it is specially provided that none sall be admitted thereto except decayed brither of gild of this burght allenarlie. Therefore to avoid the said abuse hereafter, and in respect that the rent of the said hospital is given and mortified thereto be the brither of gild of this burght, and be nane others, they enact and ordain that nane sall be admittet nor received to the said hospital in tyme cuming unless that they be burgesses of gild of this burght according to the tenor of the foundation thereof. excluding hereby all craftsmen of this burght, extranears or utheris whatsomever from having ony place in the said hospital in tyme cuming except burgesses of gild allenarlie unless the foundation thereof be altered, and that livings be deited and mortifiet thereto be craftismen.—*Council Register, vol.* xliii, *p.* 884.

This procedure on the part of the Magistrates and Council —at that time almost exclusively composed of merchant burgesses or guild brethren—of excluding the craftsmen from the benefits of St. Thomas' Hospital, although resented at the time, proved a blessing in disguise to the craftsmen, for it was this exclusion from the town's hospital that induced Dr. Guild to found an hospital for the craftsmen, an institution that in many ways proved of great service and utility to the Trades. Originally only six Trades were admitted to the benefit of the hospital—the Hammermen, Bakers, Wrights and Coopers, Tailors, Shoemakers, and Weavers—the six Trades which had the privilege of sending their deacons to vote at the election of Magistrates. In 1657, however, a few months before Dr. Guild's death, an agreement was entered into between the Convener Court, and "Andrew Watson, deacon of the Fleshers, and John Craighead, late deacon of the said traid, for themselves, and in name and behalf of the rest of the freimen of the Flesher traid," whereby the Flesher trade was incorporated along with the other six, and admitted to all the benefits of the hospital on payment of four hundred merks Scots. This turned out to be an exceedingly wise action on the part of the Flesher craft, for it is a somewhat striking fact that the other crafts, who were not embraced in Dr. Guild's foundation, including the Masons, Litstars, Barbers, &c., who all had deacons at one time or other, have dropped out of existence, while the Seven have thriven and prospered under this visible bond of unity.

Under his deed of gift and charter of administration, Dr. Guild reserved during his lifetime "the power and patronage and direction in all things as shall seem most expedient to be done," and, as appears from the Convener Court Books, he presided at a number of meetings where additional regulations were drawn up for the better administration of the hospital. In one of these regulations it was made incumbent on every craftsman to make a freewill offering to the hospital funds— freewill so far as the amount was concerned, but compulsory in respect that no craftsman could reap any benefit from the hospital unless he had made such offering. The funds of the hospital were also augmented by a number of bequests and donations by the more wealthy craftsmen, and in a very short time the institution became thoroughly established and well supplied with funds.

In course of time, the severe and monastic life imposed upon the inmates became very irksome, and very few of the aged craftsmen were willing to submit themselves to its rigorous discipline. The nature of the life that was led in this hospital may be gathered from the following extracts from the deed of foundation :—

"I WILL also, that they be always present at the Sunday and weekly sermons (unless they be confined to their beds by sickness), as also at the public morning and evening prayers (especially in summer). ALSO, I ordain that in their own chapel a portion of the Word of God be read twice daily, and prayers offered up by a suitable reader (who shall have fifty merks paid him therefor yearly), to be properly chosen by the patron, which service shall be between nine and ten in the morning or forenoon, and between three and four in the evening or afternoon : and whoever (except through sickness) shall be once absent, let him be admonished ; if twice, punished by the director ; and if thrice, removed from the hospital.

"I WILL also, that no woman dwell in the said hospital (although the wife of one that is admitted), or stay therein for a moment ; and that no one who is admitted wander in any way forth thereof through the town or streets ; and that they all be always clothed with gowns of a single and decent colour ; MOREOVER, that the said beadmen be subject and obedient to the commands and admonitions of the foresaid director, and that they be an honest, godly, and peaceable conversation. And if any of them wander without, or be troublesome within to any of their comrades, or commit any other fault, or be found disobedient, or a breaker of the rules of this mortification, he shall be punished in his person, or removed from the hospital, by the said director, who, however, in this case shall take the advice and consent of the foresaid minister of the Word of God and deacon-convener, who have, and by these presents shall have power, one poor man dying or removing from the said hospital or being otherwise withdrawn, to choose and put in another poor man in his place, in form aforesaid.

"I WILL also, that one of the foresaid poor men be janitor of the said hospital weekly, having the keys of the doors and gates thereof (except the keys of the private rooms) ; and keep this order—First, in the morning, he shall open the outer gate and the door of the house and chapel at half-past seven hours, that they may go to public prayers in the church, or to hear a discourse, and at that same hour shall ring the bell a little, that by ringing thereof the rest being awakened may make themselves ready for the foresaid exercises : Next, the same janitor shall ring the bell regularly about the ninth hour in the morning, and the third hour in the evening, to summon the rest to hear prayers and the reading of the Scriptures in the chapel : And from thence they are to go to their own private rooms, and use their trade till the eleventh hour in the forenoon, and the sixth in the evening, and then they shall assemble in the common hall, and under a common president dine and sup together, the hebdomadar always publicly giving thanks."

About the beginning of the present century the hospital became tenantless, and a Decreet of Declarator was obtained from the Court of Session, authorising the Master of Hospital to give grants of money to those who objected to living in the hospital. Eventually the hospital system was abandoned, and for many years the funds have been administered in accordance with the Decreet of Declarator obtained in 1803. (See appendix.)

The office of patron to the Incorporated Trades was established under the hospital charter, which lays down that he must be "a preacher of the Word of God at Aberdeen." The appointment is for life, unless the patron chooses to resign, one of the few instances of which occurred when Rev. Dr. Murray resigned at the Disruption because he considered it incumbent on him to give up the post when he left the Established Church. A change of opinion, however, has taken place on this point, as the present patron, Rev. Dr. Spence, is a minister of the Free Church.

The duties of the Master of Hospital are defined in the statutes passed by the Convener Court (see Chap. II.), the charter simply stating that he must be "a diligent and godly man, able to exercise the office, and who shall give an account of his diligence, care, and faithful administration to the said minister, deacon-convener, and other deacons of the trades the week preceding the election of the deacon-convener or deacons yearly." The Master of Hospital was frequently entrusted by the whole Trades to organise their charitable work in times of dearth, and when distress was more than usually prevalent. Before the poor law system was established, the Trades extended their charity to all connected with them, journeymen as well as their own regular members ; and as the great bulk of the benefit was given in food and clothes, the Master of Hospital bought in all the supplies, making purchases of meal to the extent of eighteen hundred bolls at a time. Each trade got its proportionate share for distribution, the box-masters having charge of the " girnals " in which the meal was stored.

There was also in connection with the hospital a reader to conduct morning and evening prayers, and to visit the aged craftsmen in their own houses. Lists of the Patrons, Masters of Hospital, Legal Advisers, Catechists, and Housekeepers are subjoined :—

LIST OF PATRONS.

1632. Rev. Dr. William Guild, Principal of King's College.
1657. Rev. John Menzies, Professor of Divinity, Marischal College.
1684. Dr. Patrick Sibbald, Professor of Divinity, Marischal College.
1698. Rev. William Blair, minister of St. Nicholas.
1716. Rev. Thomas Blackwell, Principal of Marischal College.
1728. Rev. Mr. John Osborn, Principal of Marischal College.
1749. Rev. Mr. John Bisset, minister of St. Nicholas.
1757. Rev. Mr. James Ogilvie, minister of St. Nicholas.
1776. Rev. Mr. Thomas Forbes, minister of St. Nicholas.
1783. Rev. Dr. George Campbell, Principal of Marischal College.
1795. Rev. Dr. James Sherriffs, minister of St. Nicholas.
1814. Rev. Dr. James Ross, minister of St. Nicholas.
1824. Rev. Dr. William Lawrence Brown, Principal of Marischal College.
1828. Rev. Dr. George Glennie, Professor of Moral Philosophy, Marischal College.
1836. Rev. John Murray, minister of the North Parish Church.
1843. Rev. Simon M'Intosh, minister of the East Parish Church.
1853. Rev. Dr. James Forsyth, minister West Parish Church.
1879. Rev. Dr. Alexander Spence, minister of Free St. Clements.

LIST OF MASTERS OF HOSPITAL.

Thomas Gardine,	taliour,	1632	Patrick Murray,	baker,	1658
Thomas Robertson,	shoemaker,	1633	Alex. Ettershank,	couper,	1659
Hew Anderson,	goldsmith,	1634	Do.	do.	1660
William Ord,	wright,	1635	Do.	do.	1661
Hew Anderson,	goldsmith,	1636	John Craighead,	flesher,	1662
Thomas Robertson,	shoemaker,	1637	Do.	do.	1663
Do.	do.	1638	Do.	do.	1664
Do.	do.	1639	Do.	do.	1665
Do.	do.	1640	Do.	do.	1666
William Ord,	wricht,	1640	John Kennie,	baker,	1667
Do.	do.	1642	Do.	do.	1668
Alexander George,	smith,	1642	Wm. Thomson,	couper,	1669
Do.	do.	1643	Alex. Charles,	wright,	1670
Do.	do.	1644	Do.	do.	1671
Alex. Williamson,	baker,	1645	George Rose,	pewterer,	1672
Do.	do.	1646	Do.	do.	1673
Do.	do.	1647	Alex. Galloway,	goldsmith,	1674
Alexander George,	smith,	1648	James Blinshell,	weaver,	1675
Do.	do.	1649	Alexander Still,	taylour,	1677
Do.	do.	1650	William Mayne,	wright,	1678
Alex. Cruickshank,	cooper,	1651	William Scott,	goldsmith,	1680
Alex. Williamson,	baker,	1652	James Thomson,	tayleior,	1682
Robert Lindsay,	gunsmith,	1653	Alexander Idle,	shoemaker,	1683
Do.	do.	1654	William Chapman,	baker,	1684
Patrick Murray,	baker,	1655	George Gordon,	weaver,	1685
Walter Melvill,	goldsmith,	1656	John Wobster,	couper,	1686
Do.	do.	1657	John Leslie,	weaver,	1688

Patrick Whyt,	hookmaker,	1688	James Smith,	sadaler,	1744
Do.	do.	1689	Do.	do.	1745
Thomas Ritchie,	weaver,	1690	Do.	do.	1746
William Couts,	wright,	1691	John Sim,	cooper,	1746
Do.	do.	1692	Do.	do.	1747
Do.	do.	1693	John Morice,	baker,	1748
George Gordon,	tayleior,	1694	John Thom,	blacksmith,	1749
Do.	do.	1695	Do.	do.	1750
Do.	do.	1696	James Norie,	tailor,	1751
William Couts,	wricht,	1697	Do.	do.	1752
Do.	do.	1698	George Donaldson,	weaver,	1753
Charles Sangster,	weaver,	1699	Do.	do.	1754
Do.	do.	1700	William Green,	wright,	1755
Do.	do.	1701	Do.	do.	1756
Wm. Duckieson,	shoemaker,	1702	George Forbes,	baker,	1757
Do.	do.	1703	Do.	do.	1758
John Findlay,	couper,	1704	John Milne,	tailor,	1759
Do.	do.	1705	Do.	do.	1760
Gilbert Duff,	couper,	1706	Alexander Ross,	flesher,	1761
Do.	do.	1707	Do.	do.	1762
Do.	do.	1708	Patrick Durward,	baker,	1763
John Gray,	baxter,	1709	Do.	do.	1764
Do.	do.	1710	Patrick Gordon,	saddler,	1765
Do.	do.	1711	Do.	do.	1766
Wm. Duckieson,	shoemaker,	1712	Alex. Ross,	flesher,	1767
William Spence,	hookmaker,	1713	John Morice,	baker,	1768
Wm. Anderson,	tayliour,	1714	Do.	do.	1769
Do.	do.	1715	John Forbes,	baker,	1770
Alex. Smith,	shoemaker,	1716	Do.	do.	1771
Do.	do.	1716	Wm. Leonard,	tailor,	1772
Do.	do.	1717	Do.	do.	1773
Robert Law,	wright,	1718	James Hacket,	shoemaker,	1774
Do.	do.	1719	Do.	do.	1775
Do.	do.	1720	Alex. Scott,	wright,	1776
Robert Lamb,	weaver,	1721	Do.	do.	1777
Do.	do.	1722	Do.	do.	1778
Do.	do.	1723	Do.	do.	1779
Do.	do.	1724	Do.	do.	1780
Do.	do.	1725	James Lamb,	tailor,	1781
Do.	do.	1726	James Gordon,	goldsmith,	1782
David Speediman,	glover,	1727	Do.	do.	1783
Do.	do.	1728	James Meldrum,	shoemaker,	1784
Do.	do.	1729	Alex. Martin,	flesher,	1785
Do.	do.	1730	Do.	do.	1786
John Stratton,	taylor,	1731	Alex. Hutcheon,	shoemaker,	1787
Do.	do.	1732	James Ramsay,	tailor,	1788
Do.	do.	1733	Charles Cooper,	blacksmith,	1789
Wm. Chrystall,	wright,	1734	Charles Gordon,	cooper,	1790
Do.	do.	1735	George Craig,	shoemaker,	1791
Do.	do.	1736	Do.	do.	1792
Patrick Barron,	wricht,	1737	Do.	do.	1793
John Auldjo,	baker,	1738	James Couts,	weaver,	1794
Do.	do.	1739	John Leslie,	goldsmith,	1795
John Sim,	cooper,	1740	Do.	do.	1796
Do.	do.	1741	George Smith,	glazier,	1797
James Smith,	sadaler,	1742	Do.	do.	1798
Do.	do.	1743	William Cowie,	saddler,	1799

William Cowie,	saddler,	1800	Charles Playfair,	gunsmith,	1844
John Barron,	watchmaker,	1801	Wm. Murray,	wright,	1845
Do.	do.	1802	Do.	do.	1846
John Fraser,	shoemaker,	1803	Hugh Sutherland,	glazier,	1847
Do.	do.	1804	Do.	do.	1848
John Webster,	weaver,	1805	Robert Watson,	wright,	1849
David Reid,	wright,	1806	Do.	do.	1850
Do.	do.	1807	John Fraser,	shoemaker,	1851
William Douglas,	shoemaker,	1808	Do.	do.	1852
Do.	do.	1809	John Fyfe,	tailor,	1853
John Chalmers,	wright,	1810	Do.	do.	1854
Do.	do.	1811	George Donald,	glazier,	1855
William Smith,	glazier,	1812	Do.	do.	1856
Do.	do.	1813	James M'Kenzie,	baker,	1857
James Matthews,	shoemaker,	1814	Do.	do.	1858
Do.	do.	1815	Robert Beveridge,	weaver,	1859
George Anderson,	tailor,	1816	Do.	do.	1860
Do.	do.	1817	Robert Thomson,	tailor,	1861
Do.	do.	1818	Do.	do.	1862
Do.	do.	1819	James Berry,	watchmaker,	1863
Do.	do.	1820	Do.	do.	1864
Do.	do.	1821	James Mitchell,	baker,	1865
Do.	do.	1822	Do.	do.	1866
Do.	do.	1823	Wm. Allan,	wright,	1867
George Watson,	shoemaker,	1824	Do.	do.	1868
Do.	do.	1825	Daniel Laird,	tailor,	1869
James Cobban,	wright,	1826	Do.	do.	1870
Do.	do.	1827	Alexander Adam,	cooper,	1871
Do.	do.	1828	Do.	do.	1872
Wm. Smith,	glazier,	1829	James Abel,	baker,	1873
Do.	do.	1830	Do.	do.	1874
Alex. M'Kenzie,	weaver,	1831	John Mitchell,	weaver,	1875
Alex. Cooper,	saddler,	1832	Do.	do.	1876
Do.	do.	1833	Alex. Robertson,	plumber,	1877
David M'Hardy,	smith,	1834	Do.	do.	1878
Do.	do.	1835	Peter Raeburn,	baker,	1879
James Topp,	baker,	1836	Do.	do.	1880
Do.	do.	1837	Ebenezer Bain,	wright,	1881
Eric Finlayson,	tailor,	1838	Do.	do.	1882
Do.	do.	1839	Andrew Robb,	gunsmith,	1883
Robert Williams,	cooper,	1840	Do.	do.	1884
James Clyne,	shoemaker,	1841	George Rose,	flesher,	1885
John Leslie,	weaver,	1842	Do.	do.	1886
Charles Playfair,	gunsmith,	1843			

LIST OF LEGAL ADVISERS.

William Smith, N.P.,	.	1677	Alex. Sherrifs, advocate,	1795
J. Anderson, N.P.,	.	1679	James M'Cook, do.,	
Alex. Irvine, N.P.,	.	1679	David Hutcheon, do.,	1801
William Fraser, N.P.,		1681	Adam Coutts, do.,	
Alex. Mitchell, N.P.,	.	1682	Alexander Allan, do., .	1815
Thomas Shand, N.P.,	.	1704	James Nicol, do., .	1840
John Deans, N.P.,	.	1713	Marianus Massie, do., .	1843
John Taylor, N.P.,	.	1724	Alex. Henderson, do., .	1852
James Taylor, N.P.,	.	1756	John Thomson, do., .	1868
Thomas Duncan, advocate,	1768	David Stewart, do., .	1877
David Morrice, jun., do.,				

LIST OF CATECHISTS.

1727. Alexander Lyell, shoemaker, was, by the Convener Court, with consent of the patron, nominated and admitted to wait upon the Beidmen, and to pray with them at the ordinary hours, and to instruct them in the points of faith, professed in this National Church, and necessary to salvation. Salary, as appointed by the mortification, 50 merks Scots, during his continuance in said office and good behaviour thereintill.

1740. John Youngson, wright, in place of Alexander Lyell, deceased. Same salary and conditions.

1750. Alexander Dawson, shoemaker, in place of J. Youngson, deceased.

1762. Thomas Murray, tailor, in place of Alex. Dawson, deceased. Same salary as before.

1766. James Bruce, tailor. The salary was raised from 50 merks Scots to £5 sterling, and the allowance to the Beidmen from 1s. 2d. to 1s. 6d. weekly, upon the representation of Anne Brown, mistress of the house, that she could not give them a sufficient dyet for the former sum.

LIST OF HOUSEKEEPERS.

——. Mrs. Jean Chessor.

1714. Mrs. Sim (Marjorie Wright), widow of George Sim, cooper. On 3rd March, 1715, the Master of Hospital was ordained to pay the "Goodwife" of the Hospital weekly, as was formerly in use by other Masters.

1722. Mrs. Fraser (Margaret M'Kay), widow of James Fraser; resigned in 1742 on account of old age. Pensions, 8s. Scots weekly, in respect of her long services.

1742. Mrs. Smith (Christian Clark), widow of Robert Smith, saddler; died in the Hospital, 1750. "Paid expenss of Funeralls of Mrs. Smith, £33 ,, 8 ,, 2 ,, Scots.

1750. Mrs. Margaret Grub, who resigned in 1765 on account of sickness, and received a pension of twenty-six pounds Scots yearly.

1765. Mrs. Main (Ann Brown), widow of Andrew Main, shoemaker. Died January, 1799.

1799. Miss Main; resigned in 1814.

1814. Mrs. Strachan, widow of George Strachan, shoemaker. Died January, 1821.

1821. Mrs. Neilson, widow of Alexander Neilson, flesher. Died 1st March, 1851, after 30 years' service.

1851. Mrs. Hannay, daughter of Convener Wm. Murray, wright.

1868. Miss Wilson; resigned 1880.

1880. Miss Barbara Macpherson.

THE extension of the railway system to Aberdeen sealed the fate of the old Trades Hall. When the Aberdeen Railway was projected in 1844, the hall and site, which extended from the foot of the Shiprow to near the present line of railway, were scheduled, and although not required for railway purposes, the buildings had to come down when Guild Street and Exchange Street were constructed. The last of the buildings was taken down in 1857, and while the excavating operations were in progress a careful watch was kept for relics and antiquities, the following notes being taken by a local antiquarian at the time:—"A great number of human bones were found when the digging for Guild Street commenced, which had probably been the site of the ancient burial grounds of the Trinity Friars. It had extended to the south end of the convent, and ran east from the side of the church for some space. The bones were generally in a very great state of decay, the skulls dropping to pieces when lifted. The remains of a coffin in one instance were found, which fell to dust on exposure. About the middle of this part of the ground were found a bit of iron resembling a key, and the bowl of a small spoon curiously ribbed on the back. The foundation walls of the hall, which were probably those of the old convent, were built with lime on the outside and with clay between the stones. The walls were several feet in thickness. At the east end of the hall, twelve or thirteen feet below the surface, were found the remains of a more ancient building, composed of rude stones cemented with clay. Below some of the lowest were found oaken boards which seem to have formed part of some ancient vessel, and near the same place five or six oaken beams were found, which had probably supported rafters in the old building (King William the Lion's

OLD TRADES HALL

palace). They had holes in the side as for the ends of posts being morticed into them. The ground here was very moist, puddled with clay and small stones. On excavating westward, the old wall was found continued along the side of the more modern one at the distance of about fourteen inches. About the middle of this part of the building a silver tablespoon was found, much corroded as if by the action of fire. A portion of what looked like a buff jerkin, and some remains of old shoes with very large hobnails in the heels, were also found."

Many interesting relics were transferred from the old hall to the new buildings in Union Street. The collection of antique oak chairs, presented from time to time for the use of the deacons of the different Trades, has been long looked upon as the most complete of its kind in Scotland. Some of them date from the time that the craftsmen held their meetings in the deacons' houses, while it is tolerably certain that one of the largest chairs belonged to the old monastery. This chair is mentioned in an "inventory of the plenishings belonging to the Trinity Hall, taken in presence of Patrick Whyt, Deacon Conveener, 1696," as " King William's Cheer," and although some of the framework has evidently been renewed, the panels (showing carved heads of monks and warriors) evidently belong to the early monkish period. The Convener's chair, which stands about six feet high, has finely-carved Gothic panels ; and some of the other chairs of smaller size exhibit no small amount of originality of design and finish. The inventory taken in 1696 gives the following list of chairs, &c., all of which are in the new hall, and in an excellent state of preservation :—

King William's cheer and pictur.

Hammermen—Ane cheer, gifted by Lawrence Mersar for the use of said Traid ; ane cheer, gifted by Matthew Guild, armourer ; ane cheer, gifted by George Anderson, goldsmith, Deacon Conveener in 1609 ; ane cheer, gifted by William Anderson, goldsmith, Deacon Conveener, 1654 ; ane cheer, gifted by Alexander Paterson, armourer, Deacon Conveener, with his pictur, 1685 ; ane cheer, gifted by Patrick Whyt, hookmaker, Deacon Conveener, with his pictur, 1690 ; ane cheer, gifted by James Anderson, glazier, 1692.

Bakers—Ane cheer, gifted by John Middleton, baxter, Deacon Convener, 1634 ; ane cheer, gifted by Christian Mitchell, daughter to William Chapman, sometime Deacon of the Baxters, 1668, and another on Januar, 1704.

Wrights and Coopers—Ane cheer, gifted by Jerome Blak, couper, 1574 ; ane cheer, gifted by William Ord, wright, Deacon Conveener, 1635.

Taylziours—Ane cheer, gifted by Thomson Cordyn, taylyer, Deacon Convener, 1627 ; ane cheer or round table, gifted by Alexander Cocnie, taylyer ; ane cheer gifted by John Forbes, tailyeur, 1694.

Shoemakers—Ane cheer, gifted by Thomas Robertson, shoemaker, Deacon Convener, 1633 ; ane cheer, gifted by Alexander Idle, shoemaker, Deacon Convener, 1679 ; ane cheer, gifted by William Dickson, late Deacon, 1686.

Weavers—Ane public cheer for their Deacon, 1684.

Fleshers—Ane cheer, gifted by Andrew Watson, Deacon ; ane cheer, gifted by John Craighead, Deacon.

Ane cheer marked W. P. coft (bought) to the Hospital ; ane cheer, gifted by John Archibald.

Of the five chairs belonging to the Hammermen Trade the oldest (Fig. II.) is that supposed to have been gifted by

FIG. II.

Laurens Mercer, a contemporary of Matthew Guild. The chair bears no date, but simply the initials "L. M.," with the arms of the Mercer family (on a fess, three bezants; a mullet in base and three crosses, potent in chief) and underneath the motto—*Crux Christi mea corona.* Laurens Mercer was several times deacon of his craft from 1572 to 1596, and although others of the same name joined the trade some time after, the chair, from its appearance and construction, bears evidence of having been presented by the Mercer who figured so prominently in Matthew Guild's time, and who also shared the same punishment as Guild for "cumyng throch the Gallowgett on a Sunday with ane menstrall playand befor thaim."

A chair presented by Jerome Blak in 1574 is ornamented with a carving of the Black arms (a saltire, between a crescent in base, a mullet, in chief; for crest a hand holding a cooper's adze, in dexter proper). The chairs presented about the middle of the seventeenth century are all of superior design and better construction, the chair presented by Andrew Watson, flesher, in 1661 (Fig. III.),

FIG. III.

being about the most elaborate. The arms of his trade are carved and coloured on the upper part of the back, and on the centre are the arms of the Watson family (an oak tree eradicated in base, surmounted by a fess, charged with crescent, between two mullets). Watson was deacon when the Flesher Trade was joined to the other six under Dr. Guild's

N

deed of mortification for the administration of the Trades Hospital.   The chair presented by Alexander Idle, shoemaker, in 1679 (Fig. IV.), has the crown and cutting knife of his craft

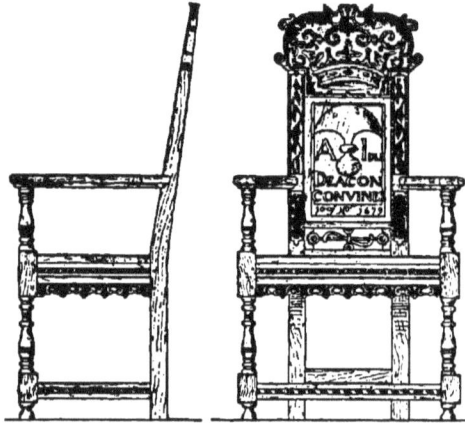

FIG. IV.

carved in the back, with his name, " A. Idle, Deacon-conviner, 30th November, 1679."   Idle had a somewhat chequered career.   The books of his trade show that at one time he must have carried on a fairly extensive business, but in the end of his days he entered the hospital as a beadman.   It is uncertain who the " W. P." refers to on the chair (Fig. V.), which,

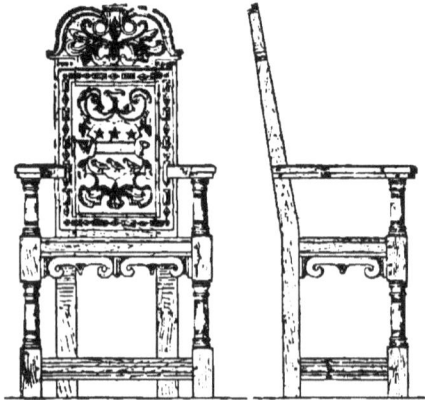

FIG. V.

according to the inventory was bought by the Master of Hospital prior to 1696.   It bears the Paterson arms (a fess ; in base, three pelicans vulning; three mullets in chief). Patrick Whyt, hookmaker, presented a portrait of himself, as well as a chair (Fig. VI.). He was several times deacon of the

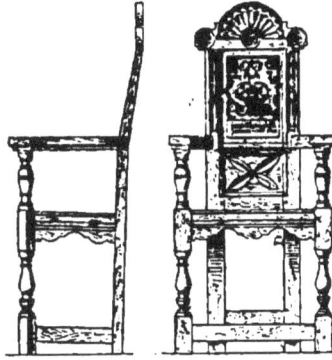

FIG. VI.

Hammermen Trade, with which the hookmakers were associated, and was also elected Deacon-Convener in 1690.

FIG. VII.

At that time hookmaking seems to have been somewhat extensively carried on, as numbers of apprentices appear on records as having been indentured to the calling, which, by the way, included reedmaking and all working in wire generally. Wire windows are frequently mentioned as essays prescribed for this class of tradesmen during the sixteenth century. Whyt's chair, besides bearing his name and designation in full, has a shield charged with the Hammermen arms, and also two fishing hooks in saltire, and one in pale with the initials "P. W." in monogram.

A chair (Fig. VII.) bearing the Guthrie arms (1 and 4 three garbs; 2 and 3, a lion rampant) and the initials "H. G.," with the word "Chirurgie" underneath, is evidently a relic of the Leechers or Barbers Society, now extinct. The weavers provided a chair (Fig. VIII.) for their deacon in 1684. It bears

FIG. VIII.

the arms of the trade, with their motto, *Spero in Deo et ipse facit*. An odd looking chair (Fig. IX.) was presented by Alexander Cockie in 1617, who embellished it with his arms —"a cock; on a chief the sun in its splendour, and a crescent between two mullets," and his initials " A. C." The back folds down upon the arms, and forms a most convenient card table. On one of the chairs belonging to the Bakers is a portion of the Bakers arms, and also the Middleton arms, with the inscription, " My soul prais thou the Lord. I. M. John Midleton, deacon, 1634." Thomas Robertsone, who presented a chair to the Shoemakers in 1633 bearing the inscription "Thomas Robertsone, Deacon-Conviner, Grace me God, 1633," was killed

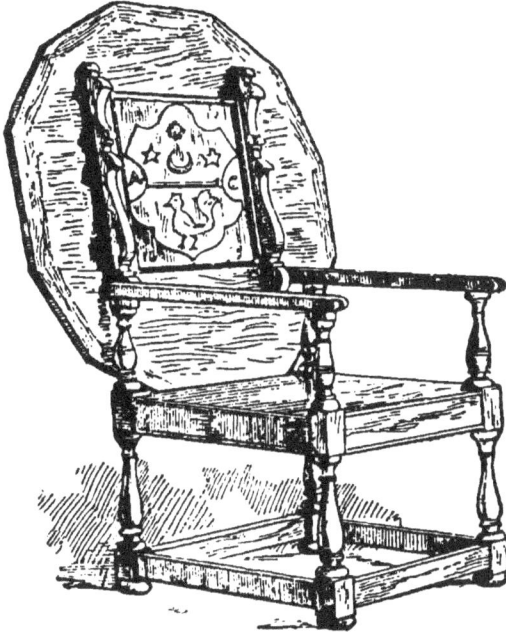

FIG. IX.

on the 13th September, 1644, at the battle of Justice Mills or Craibstane during the covenanting troubles. Three other cordiners were killed in the same affray.

There are also two massive oak tables* in the hall, at one

* On 10th November, 1699, "the Convener Court ordained Charles Sangster, Master of Traids Hospital, to employ and pay William Coutts, Deacon Convener, for repairing the great table in the Trinities. Lykwise the said William Coutts accepted of the said employment and promised to project the work betwixt the Pasch next, under the failzie of ten dollars, and thereupon has subscribed these presents." And, again, on 18th January, 1703, "the Convener Court ordains the Master of Hospital to cause mak up the red marble table, and to mak use of the great wainscot table in their church for that effect."

of which it is said the Lion King was wont to preside. Both tables have stone tops about six inches in thickness. On the ends of one of the tables are shields, one being the Guild family badge, and the other the initials "D. W. G." We give side and end elevations of the principal table.

The collection of portraits removed from the old hall to the new building has been considerably augmented of late years, and now forms a highly interesting collection both as works of art and as memorials of worthy citizens well known in their day and generation. When we mention that there are examples by Jamesone, Dyce, R.A.; Alexander, Archibald Robertson, Joseph Nisbet, G. Reid, R.S.A.; William Niddrie, James Cassie, A.R.S.A.; J. Giles, R.S.A.; J. Stirling, J. Mitchell, and G. W. Wilson, it will be seen that the collection is fairly representative of the works of local artists.

The curious production representative of William the Lion is one of the few relics of the Trinity Monastery. When and by whom it was originally painted are matters apparently now beyond human ken, and not a little of its artistic value has been lost on account of a "repairing" which it underwent in 1715. In that year the Convener Court "granted warrant to William Anderson, present Master of Hospital, to agree with

ST. WILLIAM, KING OF SCOTS, SURNAMED THE LYON, THE FIRST FOUNDER OF THE TRINITIE FRIERS AT ABERDEEN, WHER HE HAD HIS CHAPPELL, THE CHIEF PLACE OF HIS RETIREMENT FOR HIS DEVOTIONS. HE REIGNED 49 YEERS, BEGINNING 1165; DYED AT STRIVILING, 1214, AND WAS BURIED AT ABERBROTHICK.

From Original Painting in Trades Hall.

■

Charles Whyt, painter, anent renewing King William the Lyon, his pictur, as cheap as possible, always not exceeding fifty shillings sterling." Fortunately the "renewing" did not go the length of any interference with the face. We have it on the authority of an artist who took a drawing of the work in 1821 for Lieutenant-General Hutton* that the face had been left untouched. The king is represented wearing a curiously-formed helmet, and holding a book in one hand and a rod in the other. There is a chain round his waist—indicative, it is said, of penance for the part which history says he had in the murder of Thomas-à-Becket.

The portrait of Dr. William Guild, which gets the place of honour in the new hall, bears no artist's name, but has been generally ascribed to Jamesone. Guild was a contemporary of Jamesone's, is said to have been at school and college with him, and was, moreover, a close relation ;† so that nothing is more probable than that Jamesone had painted a portrait of one who as Principal of King's College, a chaplain to Charles I., a leading ecclesiastic, and as a generous benefactor to the town, must have held a prominent position among his fellow-citizens. That the picture was touched up by a later hand there is no doubt. In 1741, the Convener Court granted warrant to the Master of Hospital to pay to William Mossman, a guinea "for his pains and trouble in repairing Dr. William Guild's picture ;" and in the Master of Hospital's accounts for

---

* An engraving from a drawing taken about 1820 appears in Volume III., page 298, of the "Transactions of the Antiquarian Society of Scotland," along with the following letter from Lieutenant-General Hutton to the secretary of the Society :—

"London, 34 Southampton Row,
"Russell Square, 22nd Oct., 1821.

"Dear Sir,—I request the favour of you to present from me to the Society the picture of King William the Lyon, which I took the liberty of sending to your care lately, and I shall be much honoured if it should be deemed worthy of a place in the Society's museum. It is a copy made by an artist a few years ago from the original painting, which is supposed to have belonged to the Monastery of the Trinity Friars of Aberdeen, of which the King was the founder, and is now preserved in Trinity Hall there. It appears from the records of the Incorporated Trades of Aberdeen that in the year 1715, it having become much defaced in consequence of its great age, an agreement was made with Charles White, a painter, to repair it for a sum not exceeding fifty shillings sterling, which was accordingly done, with the exception of the face, which, the artist who copied the picture informed me, has been fortunately left untouched. It is painted in fresco, and its dimensions are about four feet in height by about two feet nine inches in breadth.—I remain, yours &c., "H. HUTTON.

"John Dillon, Esq., Secretary."

† David Anderson of Finzeauch, the artist's uncle, was married to Jean, sister to Dr. Guild.

the following year there appears—" By cash to William Mossman, painter, for mending Dr. Guild's picture, £12 12s. Scots." This sum is equivalent to twenty-one shillings sterling.* On the 18th May, 1731, the Convener Court granted warrant "to their Master of Hospital, at the sight of the deacons, to satisfie and pay William Mossman, painter, for drawing Dr. William Guild, their foundator, his picture, for which this is warrand." This seems to have been an order for a drawing taken from the original, which there are good reasons for believing is the picture now in the hall, and for mending which Mossman was paid a guinea ten years after. It is hardly probable that his own drawing could have required " mending " so soon after it was executed. It is much more likely that, in 1731, Jamesone's original had been showing signs of decay, that Mossman had been ordered to make a copy of it; and that then ten years after he had been employed to " mend " the original itself. The picture, as it stands, notwithstanding its renovation, is an excellent one. An admirable engraving was taken from it some years ago by R. M. Hodgson, who also ascribes the original to Jamesone.

With regard to the portrait of Matthew Guild, father of Dr. Guild, there is less doubt of its being a genuine Jamesone. It bears the inscription, which Jamesone put upon nearly all his portraits—the date of the birth and age of the subject; and we have also the familiar broad hat which appears in not a few of Jamesone's male figures.

There also hang in the new hall several examples by Cosmo John Alexander, a grandson of Jamesone's, all very fair specimens of portraiture. The portrait of Alexander Webster, advocate, by Dyce, is justly regarded as one of the finest bits of portraiture in the collection, and has on more than one occasion been exhibited in collections of old Scottish masters in the south. Alexander Webster had no direct connection with the Trades, but he took a warm interest in the Trades School, which was instituted in 1808, about the time his father held the office of Deacon-Convener.

---

* At the same time the Convener Court expended about £500 Scots in decorating the hall, the Master of Hospital having been authorised " to employ Robert Norrie, of Edinburgh, painter, to paint and colour the Trinitie Hall in the best and genteelest manner."

Subjoined is a complete catalogue of the pictures, with short biographical notes :—

1. Rev. WILLIAM GUILD, D.D.   *George Jamesone.*

(See pp. 143 to 151.)

2. ALEXANDER PATERSONE, Armourer.   *Artist unknown.*

Elected Convener of the Trades in 1684.

3. ROBERT MACKIE.   *J. B. Graham.*

Elected Convener, 1775. His gravestone, in St. Machar Churchyard, states that he was "sometime skinner, and Convener to
the Incorporations."

4. JOHN LESLIE, Goldsmith.   *Artist unknown.*

Elected Convener of the Trades, 1802. He was the chief promoter
of the Trades' Widows' Supplementary Fund in 1816. In 1822
a volume was published, entitled, "Interesting Anecdotes,
Memoirs, Allegories, Essays, and Poetical Fragments tending
to amuse the Fancy, with many other Curious Things," which
had been prepared by Leslie, the profits on which were to be
devoted to the Shipwrecked Seamen's Fund. As an evidence
of Leslie's own character, this collection of fragments, some
of them evidently original, is very instructive. On the
subject of charity we find the following :—"Under the Gospel,
God is pleased with a living sacrifice ; but the offerings of the
dead, such as testamentary characters, which are intended
to have no effect so long as we live, are no better than dead
sacrifices ; and it may be questioned whether they will be
brought into the account of our lives if we do no good while we
are living. These death-bed charities are too like a death-bed
repentance ; men seem to give their estates to God and the
poor just as they part with their sins—when they can keep
them no longer." Leslie was a liberal giver in his own lifetime. He not only founded the Supplementary Widows' Fund,
but he gave a handsome donation towards the foundation of
its stock.

5. GILBERT MOIR, Cooper.   *Artist unknown.*

Elected Convener of Trades, 1710.

6. Rev. WILLIAM BLAIR, D.D.   *Charles Whyt (?).*

Elected fourth Patron of the Trades, 1698. Was appointed Minister
of St. Nicholas in 1680.

7. Rev. THOMAS BLACKWELL.   *Artist unknown.*

Elected fifth Patron of the Trades, 1716. He was born in Aberdeen and took his degree of M.A. in his seventeenth year. Was appointed Professor of Greek in Marischal College in 1723, and elected Principal in 1748. He was author of a "Life of Homer," the "Court of Augustus," and was recognised as the "restorer of Greek Literature in the North of Scotland," and one of the best Greek Professors in Europe. His widow founded the Professorship of Chemistry in Marischal College, and left an annual prize—now amounting to £25—for the best English essay on a prescribed subject.

8. Rev. JOHN OSBORN.   *Cosmo John Alexander.*

Elected sixth Patron of the Trades, 1728. Was Minister of St. Nicholas Church from 1716 to 1748; and Principal of Marischal College from 1727 to 1748.

9. Rev. JAMES SHIRREFS, D.D.   *Artist unknown.*

Elected eleventh Patron of the Trades, 1795. Was Minister of St. Nicholas Church from 1778 to 1814. Author of "An Enquiry into the Life, Writings, and Character of Rev. Dr. William Guild."

10. JOHN MERCER, Saddler.   *Artist unknown.*

Elected Convener of the Trades in 1618, 1619, 1620, 1630. (See No. 19.)

11. Mrs. JOHN MERCER.   *Artist unknown.*

(See No. 19.)

12. Rev. GEORGE CAMPBELL, D.D.   *Archibald Robertson.*

Elected tenth Patron of the Trades, 1783. Was appointed Minister of St. Nicholas Church in 1756, and three years afterwards was elected Principal of Marischal College. He was one of the most eminent divines of the Scottish Church, and published a number of valuable treatises, the best known being his "Philosophy of Rhetoric," "A New Translation of the Gospels," and "A Dissertation on Miracles." He was one of the founders of the Aberdeen Philosophical Society. Died 1796.

13. Rev. JAMES OGILVIE.·   *James Nisbet.*

Elected eighth Patron of the Trades, 1757. Was translated from Inchture to St. Nicholas Church in 1729. He was a descendant of the noble family of Findlater, through the Ogilvies of Birdsbank, near Cullen.

14. Rev. JOHN MOIR.   *Cosmo John Alexander.*

Rector of West Tinfield, Yorkshire. He mortified 1000 merks Scots for the support of a Philosophy Bursar at Marischal College; and in the event of no Tradesman's son applying for the said Bursary, the money was to be devoted to the maintenance of decayed Tradesmen, preference always being given to the name of Moir.

15. THOMAS CLERKE, Weaver.   *Artist Unknown.*

Elected Convener of the Trades, 1642. He was the first Weaver who attained to the office of Deacon-Convener.

16. Rev. THOMAS FORBES.   *Artist Unknown.*

Elected ninth Patron of the Trades, 1776. Was translated from Slains to St. Nicholas Church in 1748.

17. Dr. PATERSON.   *Artist Unknown.*

18. THOMAS MITCHELL.   *Cosmo John Alexander.*

Provost of Aberdeen from 1698 to 1700, and from 1702 to 1704. (See No. 19.)

19. Mrs. JANE MERCER or MITCHELL.   *Cosmo J. Alexander.*

In 1726, Mrs. Mitchell mortified to the Trades 1000 merks Scots; and on the 9th August, 1737, she presented the pictures of her father and mother (10 and 11), her husband (18), and herself, along with 100 merks Scots "for a further increase of the stock for the support of the fabrick of the Trades' Hospital," upon condition that the Trades preserve the pictures in their Hall in all time coming.

20. Rev. ALEXANDER SPENCE, D.D.   *George Reid, R.S.A.*

Elected eighteenth Patron of the Trades, 1880. Born at Glenbucket Manse in 1804; was ordained Minister of St. Clements, Aberdeen, in 1837. At the Disruption Dr. Spence left the Established Church, and was appointed Minister of Free St. Clements. Dr. Spence is the first Minister of the Gospel elected Patron of the Trades who was not at the time a Minister of the Church of Scotland.

21. MATTHEW GUILD.   *George Jamesone.*

Born 1542. Father of Dr. William Guild, founder of Trades' Hospital. Elected Deacon of the Hammermen Incorporation in 1587 and subsequent years. He was one of the leading tradesmen of the city; and while Deacon of his Craft, took an active part in the settlement of the disputes existing at the time between the Guildry and the craftsmen. Died 1603.

22. ALEXANDER WEBSTER.   *W. Dyce, R.A., R.H.S.A.*

Son of Convener John Webster. Was a member of the Aberdeen Society of Advocates. While his father held the office of Convener, he took a great interest in the Trades' School, which was instituted in 1808.

23. ALEXANDER ROBB.   *William Niddrie.*

A Deacon of the Tailor Incorporation. Author of a volume of "Poems and Songs," including "Laddies at the Squeel," and a number of other well-known local rhymes. Died 1859.

24. JOHN FRASER.   *J. Giles, R.S.A.*

A Deacon of the Shoemaker Incorporation. Elected Convener, 1853. Was also a member of the Town Council, and was several times elected a magistrate. He prepared a Roll Book of Trinity Hall, from 1587 to 1873.

25. JAMES TOPP.   *W. Niddrie.*

A Deacon of the Baker Incorporation. Elected Convener of the Trades, 1838. Was for several years factor of the Widows' Fund. Died 1859, aged 82.

26. Rev. JAMES FORSYTH, D.D.   *James Cassie, A.R.S.A.*

Elected seventeenth Patron of the Trades, 1853. Was Minister of West Parish Church from 1843 till his death in 1880.

27. ALEXANDER MACKENZIE.   *James Cassie, A.R.S.A.*

A Deacon of the Weaver Incorporation. Elected Convener of the Trades on six occasions, viz., 1832, 1833, 1836, 1837, 1840, 1841.

28. Rev. JOHN MURRAY, D.D.   *James Cassie, A.R.S.A.*

Elected fifteenth Patron of the Trades, 1836, but resigned his office in 1843, when he left the Established Church at the Disruption. Died, 1st March, 1861.

29. Rev. SIMON MACKINTOSH.   *G. Washington Wilson.*

Elected sixteenth Patron of the Trades, September, 1843, on the resignation of Dr. Murray. Was Minister of the East Parish Church. Died, 23rd January, 1853, aged 37.

30. Sir ALEXANDER BANNERMAN.   *Artist unknown.*

Born, 7th October, 1788. Was elected M.P. for Aberdeen in 1833, being the first Member that sat for the City on the passing of the Reform Bill. On resigning his seat in 1847, he was appointed Lieutenant-Governor of Prince Edward Island, and thereafter Governor of the Bahamas and Newfoundland. Died in 1865. His portrait was presented to the Hall by the Astronomer-Royal in 1880.

31. GEORGE WATSON. *J. Stirling.*

A Member of the Shoemaker Incorporation. Sat for a number of years in the Town Council, and held the office of Baillie.

32. GEORGE HENRY. *J. Mitchell.*

Lord Provost of Aberdeen from 1850 to 1853. He was elected an Honorary Member of the Weaver Incorporation, his portrait being also painted at their request. He was the last in Aberdeen to wear his hair powdered.

33. Rev. JAMES ROSS, D.D. *Artist unknown.*

Elected twelfth Patron of the Trades, 1814. He was appointed Minister of St. Nicholas Church in 1794.

34. KING WILLIAM THE LION.
(See Page 182.)

35. PATRICK WHYT. *Charles Whyt (?).*

Was elected Convener of the Trades seven times—from 1690 to 1705. Joined the Hammermen Incorporation as a hookmaker. The portrait was presented by himself in 1690, along with a chair which is also preserved in the Hall.

36. W. PHANES. *Artist unknown.*

A Deacon of the Tailor Incorporation. Elected Convener of the Trades, 1693. He was the grandfather of William Cruden, Provost from 1784 to 1786, and from 1789 to 1791.

37. Rev. ANDREW CANT. *Artist unknown.*

Succeeded Dr. William Guild as one of the Ministers of Aberdeen in 1641. Was one of the most popular preachers of his day, and the person from whom it is said the "Spectator" derived the word "cant."

38. WILLIAM CHRISTIE. *Artist unknown.*

A Deacon of the Tailor Incorporation. Elected Convener of the Trades, 1657.

39. JOHN LOW. *Artist unknown.*

A Deacon of the Tailor Incorporation. Elected Convener, 1784.

40. INTERIOR OF OLD TRINITY HALL. *John Russell.*

Contains portraits of Deacon John Macdonald, tailor; Deacon Robb, tailor; Convener Sutherland, glazier; Deacon Stewart, flesher; Convener William Murray, wright; Convener C. Playfair, gunsmith; Convener Topp, baker; Deacon Tough, shoemaker; Deacon Stephen, baker; Deacon Greig, shoemaker; Convener Berry, optician; Convener Mackenzie, weaver;

Deacon Riddell, wright; Donaldson Riddell, officer. One of
the heads is painted out, because, says the artist, "the individual was not satisfied with his likeness and scratched it
out."

41. DAVID McHARDY.   *George Reid, R.S.A.*

    A Deacon of the Hammermen Incorporation. Was a member of the
    Town Council for a number of years, and was several times
    elected to the Magistracy.

42. JAMES HENDERSON.   *Archibald Reid.*

    A Deacon of the Wright and Cooper Incorporation. Was presented
    with his picture on the celebration of his fiftieth year as an
    acting member of the Incorporation.

Among other relics transferred from the old to the new hall
were three swords (see p. 109) belonging to the Hammermen,
Tailors, and Weavers, and several remnants of banners said to
have been used at the pageants in the pre-Reformation days.
The punch bowls (Fig. X.) belonging to the Convener Court,

FIG. X.

the Hammermen, the Wrights and Coopers, and the Tailors,
have also been preserved. The largest bowl was presented
to the Hammermen by Convener Affleck, who, although a
shoemaker himself, presented the bowl to the Hammermen
because he considered "they were the best brewers and
drinkers of punch among the whole of the craftsmen." This
bowl is about two feet in diameter, and stands fully twelve
inches high. The two large Bibles that were wont to be
used in the Hospital are also in the Master of Hospital's press.
One of them is a 1578 Bible, but has been allowed to fall

into a very tattered condition ; the other, dated 1672, is in a better state of preservation.

It can well be believed that the craftsmen quitted their old hall, so full of interesting historical associations, with feelings of deep regret. It was a veritable breaking away from the past ; and coming as it did about the time that the special privileges of the craftsmen were abolished, their regret was rendered all the more sincere. When a proposal was made to erect a new hall, a veteran craftsman was heard to declare that before he would quit the old building he would rather subscribe " to have every stone of it clasped together with silver " than give a penny to build a new place of meeting. Another member, Deacon Alexander Robb, a local poet with no mean talent for versification, sang the following lines at one of the last convivial gatherings held in the old hall, to the tune of "Happy are we a' thegither " :—

O banish, Muse, a' thoughts o' sadness,
   Soun' your notes baith clear and bright,
Be naething heard but strains o' gladness
   On this happy festive night.
The Muse reply'd, in deep dejection,
   How can I my chanter blaw
In notes o' joy—the last election
   That tak's place within this ha'.

When reminiscent mem'ry traces
   A' the scenes that here hae been,
The kindly hearts, the happy faces
   That aroun' this board I've seen :
Then comes the sick'ning, sad reflection,
   When I look aroun' you a'—
This is, alas ! the last election
   E'er we'll see within this ha'.

Nae mair at sovereign's coronation
   Will the festive board be spread ;
Nae mair we'll hear the grand oration
   When a king or queen is wed ;
Nae mair, wi' shouts o' satisfaction,
   Raise the loud hip, hip, hurra !
For, oh ! this is the last election
   E'er will happen in this ha'.

Nae mair will lords or earls be treated,
    Whan they come to visit here;
Nae mair Lord Chancellors* be seated
    Close to our Convener's chair.
These glorious scenes o' retrospection
    Soon will fade like melting snaw,
For, oh ! this is the last election
    In our famous ancient ha'.

Nae mair the cheerfu' sang amusin'
    Will re-echo through those wa's ;
Nae mair the bursts of elocution
    Bring down thunders o' applause.
My heart is sad when I consider,
    Ere anither year or twa,
That nae ae stane upon anither
    Will be left o' a' this ha'.

But whare's the use o' waefu' skirlin',
    Lat us a' be happy yet,
Altho' rail trains will soon be dirlin'
    O'er the spot whare now we sit.

---

* Deacon Robb was not indulging in imaginative flights when he alluded to Lords and Earls and Lord Chancellors having honoured the Auld Tarrnty Ha' with their presence. The Earls Marischal and Huntly, and in later times Lord Brougham and Mr. Joseph Hume, are mentioned in the Trades' records as having partaken of the hospitality of the craftsmen. When Lord Brougham visited Aberdeen in 1834 he was presented with an address in Trinity Hall, to which he replied :—" Gentlemen, I beg leave to return my warmest thanks for the kind manner in which you have received me, and I will never forget, so long as I live, the reception I have received from all classes—from the Incorporations and the inhabitants, civil and religious, in the great, the ancient, the loyal, and the flourishing city of Aberdeen. This is the first time I have been in any large meeting of my fellow-countrymen since great changes have been effected in the representation of the people of Scotland ; and as I will shortly return to London I shall have the satisfaction to assure my Sovereign and my colleagues of the excellent working of the system of which they were the authors, and of which I, amongst others, had a humble share." Some years previous (in 1820), Mr. Joseph Hume also visited Aberdeen, and the craftsmen took occasion to offer their thanks to the eminent economist for his "patriotic, able, and independent conduct, and particularly for his unwearied exertions in behalf of the burgh of Aberdeen." Mr Hume, we are informed by the minute in the Convener Court Books, "gave a speech of considerable length on Scotch Burgh Reform, and assured the meeting that if he were again returned a member for this district of burghs he should still persevere in the same independent and upright line of conduct he had hitherto pursued. Whereupon the meeting having been so much gratified and honoured by Mr. Hume's company, requested him to drink a glass of wine with them, which he most readily accepted, and after loyal and patriotic toasts, Mr. Hume's health was drunk with three times three and loud applause. Mr. Hume returned them thanks, and expressed himself in the most handsome and flattering terms, and Mr. Hume being under pressing engagements to leave this place, drank the health of the Corporations and retired. The whole proceedings were conducted in the most gratifying manner, and the evening was spent with the utmost hilarity and good humour." The Convener's signature to this minute is conspicuously absent !

O, never lat us be down-hearted,
"Let us drive dull care awa,"
Nor think our glory is departed
Whan we leave our ancient ha'.

Anither ha' will soon be finished
Whare the sang o' joy shall rise,
Our comforts a' be undiminished—
A Corporation never dies.
Then why su'd we be now unhappy,
Sorrow disna' set's ava;
Push about the enlivenin' drappie—
Soon we'll get anither ha'.

The new Trades Hall, situated at the south-east end of
Union Bridge, was erected in 1846 after plans by Mr. John
Smith, architect (see frontispiece). The main entrance is
from Union Street, and on the first floor are the hall, measuring sixty feet by thirty feet, with open ornamental roof ; two
committee rooms, a common room, and retiring room. From
the Denburnside, entrance is obtained to the school rooms,
used as a Trades School down to 1878. In the upper portion
of the building are the kitchen and housekeeper's apartments ;
and immediately above the school is the strong room, in which
are stored the books and papers belonging to the different
Incorporations.

CHAPTER VII.

THE HAMMERMEN TRADE.

UNDER the general designation of Hammermen or Smiths, various, and to some extent distinct, crafts were associated under one organisation. The use of the hammer, and generally, tools for working iron and other metals, appears to have been the main requisite for craftsmen who came within the jurisdiction of the Trade. The fact that skinners, glovers, and saddlers were members of this craft would appear to favour a wider qualification, but it has to be borne in mind that the gloves of the fifteenth and sixteenth centuries bore little likeness to the dainty articles in use nowadays ; while originally the saddlers made the iron as well as the leather parts of the harness. In the days of the pageants and religious processions on church festival days, the number of crafts embraced under the name of Hammermen varied considerably, and the frequent mention of disputes about their exact position in the processions, would indicate that they had no fixed number of crafts in their society. As time wore on, and as new branches of industry were established, such as watchmakers, coppersmiths, white-iron smiths, and others, where the use of iron tools was a leading characteristic, these new branches of industry were placed by the Magistrates under the supervision of the deacon of the Hammermen Trade. It is not quite certain that the tinsmiths or white-iron workers were ever fully admitted into the craft ; so far as appears from the records they were simply granted " a tolerance" in order to bring them within the jurisdiction of the deacon, and render them amenable to the ordinances of the craft.

The title-page of the oldest existing minute-book of the Hammermen Trade bears that it belongs to the " Hamermen Craft, freimen burgesses of Aberdeen, namely—Goldsmyths,

HAMMERMEN [15th May, 1682].— Gules, a dexter arm issuing from the sinister flank fessways, the hand bearing a smith's hammer proper hafted argent, and over it a crown or ; in the dexter nombril a smith's anvil of the second, and above the same in chief a tower of Aberdeen [triple-towered argent].   Motto : *Finis coronat opus.*

blacksmyths, skynaris, pewteraris, glasiers, wrichtis, potteris, armeraris, and saidlers," a classification that existed about 1590, although it is difficult to discover how the wrights came to be mentioned, as there is no evidence in the records that any members of that craft were at any time associated with the Hammermen. In course of time the area was extended until there were at least a dozen distinct branches, viz.—Cutlers, pewterers, glovers, goldsmiths, blacksmiths, gunsmiths, saddlers, armourers, braziers, hookmakers, glaziers, and engineers.

Armourers, pewterers, and glovers bulked largely in the Hammermen Trade in early times, but by the end of the seventeenth century they disappeared almost entirely as working craftsmen. The gunsmiths of the present day cannot be looked upon as the descendants of the old armourers, as they were admitted under a distinct essay at the same time that armourers were being admitted. Hookmaking was also an important branch of industry, but this handicraft has also disappeared, although not until about half a century ago. The hookmakers, as appears from their essay, were also general wire workers, and made the wire windows and guards that were common while glass was a luxury enjoyed by the few. From the frequent mention of glovers in the records it is evident that the manufacture of leather gloves must have been carried on to a very considerable extent. In early times gloves were much used as pledges of friendship, as tokens of loyalty and devotion, and as tenures by which estates were held. An instance of this is recorded in the case of the lands of Balnacraig, in the parish of Lumphanan, "which were to be held by Robert de Camera or Chalmers of the Earl of Moray, for a pair of white gloves, to be rendered yearly at the manor of Caskieben, the residence of Garvieaugh." The presentation of white gloves at maiden circuits is a survival of the ancient custom of using gloves for gifts and presentations.

Although watchmakers were not admitted to full membership until the beginning of the present century, the Hammermen as far back as 1699 claimed jurisdiction over them. In that year the Town Council had accepted Charles Anderson, watchmaker, as a burgess *sua arte*, entitling him to carry on business without joining any of the regular incorporations. The Hammermen protested on the ground that he "made use of hammer and forge," and their deacon was instructed "to pursue for damage and for remeid of law and justice." They do not appear to have been successful, as Anderson's name does not appear in the minutes or in any list of members.

It was not until 1805 that full control over watchmakers was obtained. In that year an Edinburgh lawyer was consulted as to the general practice, and he informed the Aberdeen Hammermen that "although the invention of watches was much later and was originally an art, yet the watch and clockmaking business has long ago become a trade by the makers taking apprentices and employing journeymen, and in almost every town has been joined to the Hammermen craft as not being exempt by any law in favour of manufacturers and artists." Accompanying this opinion was a somewhat characteristic communication from John Begg, an Edinburgh watchmaker, who held that his trade, being an art, should be above the jurisdiction of any trade, and not be shackled by any incorporated body. As to the question in dispute, Mr. Begg confidently asserted—"I believe there are few living that is better acquainted with the issue of the already trade monopoly of the Hammermen Incorporation, arrogating to themselves a right of hypothec in consequence of their charter to force and compel watchmakers to join them, or prohibit such from following their business as watchmakers within burghs, than I am." He then goes on to point out how the watchmaking business was kept out of the country in consequence of the heavy dues exacted by the incorporations, and how the business was driven into the hands of those who were not trained to the business. "There is," he adds, "scarcely a cloth shop, hardware shop, jeweller's shop, pedlar, taylor, cobbler, but sells and takes watches to repair, although they know no more about a watch than—to make use of a homely fraise—a cow does of a new coined shilling."* Fortified with a knowledge of the custom elsewhere, the

---

* This "homely fraise" of the Edinburgh watchmaker has a somewhat different rendering in Aberdeen. "He kens nae mair aboot it than a coo kens aboot chemistry," is the more alliterative local rendering.

Aberdeen Hammermen Trade was ultimately successful in bringing watchmakers within its jurisdiction.

From 1595 skinners came to be classed among the Hammermen, although the shoemakers also claimed to exercise a certain amount of jurisdiction over them. By the following minute of Council, however, it will be seen that the Town Council recognised the claim of the Deacon of the Hammermen to look after them :—

15th April, 1595.—The said day the prouest, baillies, and counsall with consent of George Elphingstoun, saidler, dekyn of the Hammermen, grantit ane licence and onsicht to Willeam Gardin, skynner, to work within the burght and vse his said craft and occupation quhill Witsonday in the year of God 1597 yeiris, quhill thay have a pruiff of his workmanship and worthiness, and that be reason of the necessitie of the said craft within this burght.—*Council Register, vol.* xxxii., *p.* 175.

The only explicit reference to tinsmiths, or "white iron men," occurs in a minute of the trade dated 30th January, 1694, which states that "the traid having considered Patrik Morgan, whyt iron man, his supplication, they did accept him as ane journeyman for payment of eight shillings Scots money of quarterly penny, and to bear and maintain him in the pairt possession of his trade upon his own expenses, he always making himself freeman when he is able to pay the traid their banquet siller, and both parties to abide at their promises and required act and instrument."

The records of this Trade afford interesting illustrations of how handicrafts arise, flourish for a time, and then die out, or become transferred to other parts of the country. It is almost certain that the art of sword making was introduced into Aberdeen from the Continent at an early period in the town's history, and reached its highest prosperity during the troubled periods of the seventeenth and eighteenth centuries, when masters and workmen alike had to furnish themselves with weapons of one kind or other. The extensive orders given by the Town Council from time to time also show that an extensive armoury was kept up; and the frequency with which we find armourers mentioned as office-bearers in the Hammermen craft adds another evidence that the "sweird slippers" were men of substance and standing in the town.

Then, again, there is a curious illustration of displacement in the case of the pewterers. At one time pewter and "timmer" utensils were in almost universal use, but gradually "white iron men" and silversmiths arose and the pewterers disappeared. The manufacture of cutlery by machinery has also left few of that craft in Scotch towns; and as for those interesting classes of craftsmen—the glovers and the hookmakers —they have entirely disappeared from our midst. It is interesting to mark how handicrafts come and go in a community, and still the means of livelihood develop and multiply as the needs of the population increase.

Two Seals of Cause were granted to the Hammermen, one in 1519, and another of a more extensive character in 1532. The following are the full texts of both :—

17th September, 1519.—The said day the provost, bailzies, and conseill, being present for the tyme, with aviss, conseill, assent and consent of the nytbours being present for the tyme, gaf grantiet and concedit to yar evil belouit nytbours and servands David Bruce, William Wallace, William Loremer, and Andrew Smith, deckinss of the hamirmen craft for this instant yeir, and to utheriss quhatsomever yair successours, deckinss of the said craft, yar full pouer and licence to resaif, uptak, and inbring of everie brother of the said craft yat uptakis or haldis of new bouthe or forge to wyrk within this burgh for his entry siller half ane mark at his first beginyn. Secondly, of ilk master yat takis an prenteis at his begining half a mark. Thirdly, of every feit man yat wirkis for mait and fee ane pound of wax yeirly. Fordly, of ilk master man of the craft every ouk a d. of offerand to yar patroune Sanct Elen ; and attour, the saids prouest, bailzies, and consail hes gevin, grantit, and assignit, and, be thir presents, gevis, grants and assignis to yar said deckins and yar successours yar full, plain, and express auctorite and pouer to amend, puniss, and correct all manner of trespassours and failtars of yar said craft, for all trespasses and faltis committit be yam, concerning yar said craft, and all uther small faltis doune amang yamself, outakiug bluid, weck and dait. The quhilkis deweties, yat is to say entry siller, prenteiss siller offerand of masters lb. of wax of feit servandis, togidder with the correctionis of the falts forsaid, salbe applyit all the mest proffect it may be to the honour, utilitie, and profeit of yar said patroness alter and uphald of the chaplain of the samen as yai will answer to God and yar said patron, be the aviss, sycht and consideration of all the maisters of the said craft ; quilk masters, and ilk ane of yam sall zeirlie uphald and finde ane honest candill of ane pund of wax of yar awne expenss, and sua yai sall God willene decore and dote yar said altar with vestments, bukis, touellis, chandelairs, ymages, and all

other ornaments according to the honour of God and yar said patroue.—
Council Register, vol. x., *p.* 112.

6th February, 1632.—Be it kend till all men be thir present lettres us
provest, bailzies, counsale, and communitie of Aberdene, our commond
weill of ye same, in yat part, hard sem considerit, and understand be us
to have gevin, grantit, and committit, and be ye tenor herof, gevis, grantis,
and committis to our lovit nytbours Walter Hay, goldsmyth, deacon of ye
craft of ye smyths and hammermen of ye said burgh, and to his successors
deaconis of ye same, for us and our successors, in all tymes to cum, our
full, fre, and plane pouar and auchoritie upon all and sundry occupears
and exercers of ye said craft within ye fredome, to correct and puneiss
ye trespassers thir unlaw amerciaments and mendis devisit be ye
said deacone and his successors to uptak and inbring to the commond
weill of ye said craft, blind and blay being exceptit to us and
our punicioun. Secondlie, we ratifie and affirmes yat na freman
sal be maid of ye said craft until he be exeminit be ye said decane
and his successors of ye said craft, and yat yai be fundin be yame,
sufficient craftsmen, and made his masterstick of wark, and yat he
be proven worthy, be his wark, to be ane maister, and admittit be
yame, and presentit to us as ane abill person to be maid freman of
ye said craft : and yat nane be sufferit to hald nor uptak with nor
forge of his awin until he be freman and admittit be us and ye said
decane, as said is. Thirdlie, yat it sal be liesume to ye said decane and
his successors, with the aviss and consale of ye principale nytbours of ye
said craft to mak statutes and ordinances to the honor of God, and ye
patrounn Sanct Elene, and commond weill of ye guid town and craft forsaid. And to be observing and keeping of all thir premissis in form and
effect, as said is gevin and grantit to the said Walter Hay and his successors, decanis of the said craft, present and to cum, for ever, all pouar
and privilege afore grantit to yis writ, for us and our successors, to yam,
thir decanis, and craft, present and to cum ; the said decanis and his
successors being obligit to answere to us and our successors for all and
sundry thair nytbours, maisters, servandis, and prentisses of ye said craft
for all falts yat lyis under thair correctioun, gif he or his successors levis
ony sic faltis unpunishit ; and to do justice to all the occupears of the said
craft at all tymes when thay are requirit, but feid or favour. And gif
ony occupear of the said craft disobeiss and contempiris ye said decane or
his successors, yat thay complain to us or our successors, and we sall caues
be obeitt conform to thir pouar. Providine alwais yat ye said craft cheis
not ane decane in tymes cumine bot he yat be responsable to answer ye
toun, conform to yis pouar. And we ye saidis provest, bailzies, consale,
and communitie, and our successors, sall varrane, keep, and defend all and
sundry ye premisses to ye said decane and his successors be yis writ gevin
under our commond seill at Aberdene, ye saxt day of Februar, ye yeir of
God ane hundret and thretty and two yeirs.—*Council Register, vol.* xiv.,
p. 109.

In the year 1556 the deacon James Huntar exceeded his powers by deciding in some cases of debt that came before him, all such cases having been expressly excluded by the second Seal of Cause from his jurisdiction. The deacon was tried before the magistrates [12th June] who pronounced the following judgment:—

Yat ye said James [Huntar] had wrangit in holding of ye saidis courtis in maner forsaid quharfor he was in amerciament of court to forbeir in time cuming.—*Council Register, vol.* xxii., *p.* 339.

There does not appear to have ever been a sufficient number of goldsmiths in Aberdeen to form a separate incorporation, to enable them to take advantage of the Act of 1457, which provided that "there shall be ordained in each burgh where goldsmiths work ane understanding and cunning man of good conscience who shall be deacon of the craft; and when work is brought to the goldsmith and it be gold, he shall give it forth again in work no more than twenty grains and silver eleven grains fine, and he shall take his work to the deacon of his craft that he may examine that it may be fine as above written, and the said deacon shall set his mark and token thereto together with the said goldsmiths; and when there is no goldsmith but one in the town he shall show that work tokened with his own mark to the head officers of the town, which shall have a mark in like manner ordained therefore, and shall be set to the said work." And, again, in 1483 it was enacted "that henceforth there be in each burgh of the realm where goldsmiths are, one deacon and one searcher of the craft, and that each goldsmith's work be marked with his own mark, the deacon's mark, and the mark of the town, silver of the pureness of eleven penny fine, and gold of twenty-two carats fine."

The appointment of a "tryar of gold and silver" seems, however, to have been found requisite in Aberdeen, for we find that in 1649 the Town Council passed the following ordinance, selecting a goldsmith who was evidently a man of some standing, as he had been elected deacon of the Hammermen craft no fewer than five times between 1636 to 1655 :—

7th November, 1649.—The said day, the counsall, taking to thair consideratioun the insufficiencie of silver work maid within this burghe, have nominat and appointit, and be the tennour heirof nominatis and appointis William Andersone, goldsmyth, to be tryar of all gold and silver wark to be maid within the said burghe for the yeir to cum, and being sufficient and markit with the prob to put on the towne's mark, and for that effect nominatis and appointis the said William Andersone keeper of the towne's mark for this present yeir ; the said William Andersone being personallie present, acceptit the said office, and gave aith *de fideli administratione*, and obliest him that all wark that sowld pass his mark and the towne's mark sall be elewin pennie fyne ; and if thair be ony wark fund of less walew markit as said is, he sall be lyable for the samen according to the ordinar rait. *Sic. sub*ʳ· William Andersone.—*Council Register, vol.* liii., *p.* 243.

The oldest minute book of the Hammermen Trade opens with the following preface :—

This buik pertenis to ye hamermen craft frieman burgesses of the Burghe of Aberdeen, namely, Goldsmyths, Blacksmyths, Skynaris, Pewteraris, Glasiers, Wrichtis, Potteris, Armoraris, and Saidleris, according to the privilege granted to the saidis crafts the sext Februar, ane thousand six hundred thirty and twa years ; Walter Hay, Goldsmyth, then Deacon for the tyme.

Quharin is contained certain auld and new actis and ordinances made obefoir be ye deacon and maisters of the said crafts, extracted and drawn furth of thair Couirt buiks be ane notar publick, Conveener-Court Clerk, to be in all tyme coming observet and keepit be the haill members of the said calling, as their lawes and constitution amongst them, grounded upon reason and conscience.

Whilk the haill crafts above written are all bound and incorporate in ane fraternity, and has given their gryt solemn aiths to maintaiu the liberties of saidis crafts, and to observe and keep the haill Acts, statutes, and ordinances, insert in this present book at their utter power, during all the days of their life tymes.

In addition to the old Acts, a list of deacons from 1568 has been preserved, and also the names and signatures of members who could write, from the year that this book was commenced (1633). Among the members is an offshoot of the Gladstone family—George Gladstaines. (See page 106.)

It is impossible to say how many members there might have been at a given period, as the names of new members were simply added to the roll, while no indication is given, except in a few instances, when members died. Among the Acts and statutes which follow, a number are undated, these having evidently been copied from the old register :—

ANENT KEEPING THE SABBATH.

Imprimis, it is statute and ordained for the glorie of God and the weall of the said craft, that the haill friemen thereof, with their prentisses and servants, under thair charge, keep the hollie Sabbath Day in tyme of divine service both forenoon and afternoon at their awin kirks, and that nane of them wilfully absent themselves thairfra under the pains following, namely, ilk maister six and eightpence *toties quoties;* ilk servant three and fourpence ; and ilk prentiss twa shillings *toties quoties* all to be collected to the poore ; and gif the prentiss hes not money, to be punishit in his person at the discretion of the court and maisters of the saids craft.

Item, it is statute and ordained that it sall not be liesum to no servant nor prentiss to absent thamselves from the kirk on Sabbath Day at divine service, and to come with their maisters orderlie, and that they be not out of the kirk at nyne hours and eleven ilk Sabbath, and wha beis absent sallpay four shillings *toties quoties.*

4th February, 1677.—This said day, it is statute and ordained unanimously be the haill traid that no journeyman, prentiss, nor servant to any of the incorporation, presume to sit nor enter the hammermen's loft at sermons and preachings, and if the officer suffer them, to be fynd for the samen *toties quoties,* according to the will of the craft.*

ANENT OBEDIENCE TO THE DEACON.

Item, it is statute and ordained that na occupear of the said craft sall contemn nor disobey the Deacon of the saidis craft and his successors in office nor commands ; and whasomever does contrair the same sall pay to the common box fourty shillings money, or ane greater sum, according to the evidence, to be modefeit and sett down be the deacon and maisters, and to mak ane publick amends by and attour the said unlaw.†

ANENT APPRENTICES DRINKING AT NIGHT.

Item, it is statute that forsameikle as the gryt abuse among the prentisses of the saidis crafts, and anent the many complaints given in obefoir in presence of the deacons and maisters, declaring that they debore at nicht be visiting and drinking, neglecting their due tym to cum to thair wark, and to ryse early in the morning for entering thereto, intollerabill to be sufferit in ane civil burgh : For remeid thereof, it is condescendit that ilk servant and prentiss of the saidis craftis keep their ordinar dyet of

* In the loft set apart for the freemen of the craft the deacon and office-bearers occupied the front form. The journeymen and prentices had to seat themselves in another part of the church.

† The following instance is recorded of a member being punished for a breach of the above statute :—

26th August, 1693.—The said day William Cook, being desired be the deacon to call ane young boy to compear before him, it being only so far as the Trinity door, he not only contrair to the Act of the book denied obedience to the said deacon, but did in ane fenced court swear, "God damn him if he would go down staires either for deacon or maisters," and did speak other indecenit speeches in ane fencit court ; in respect whereof the Court ordained him to be removed from their Court, and not to be received at Court or meeting untill he pay fourty intermediate, and go to their beyds at ten hours at night (except otherwise they be employed in thair maister's business), and wha bees drinking or waigering in other men's houses or on the streets of the get aifter ten hours at night, the contraveners sall pay to the crafts box the pains following, namely :—The servants six shillings and eightpence *toties quoties*, and prentises three shillings and fourpence, and if he have not monies to be punishit at the will of the deacon and maisters.*

ANENT AMUSEMENTS ON THE SABBATH DAY.

Item, it is statute and ordained that no servant nor prentiss of the saidis crafts be found at ony tyme hereafter playing on the Sabbath day in the tyme of divine service at golff, fute ball, kyills, bowllis, cairts, or dyce, or other pastimes whatsomever ; but that thay and everie ane of tham keep precislie sermons with thair maisters under the pains above written, and that thair maisters sall reveal upon the contravener to the deacon to the effect ordour may be taken therewith as effeirs.

ANENT MASTERS PLAYING WITH THEIR SERVANTS.

Item, it is statute and ordained that it sall not be liesum to no maister of the saidis calling to play at no pastyme upon any work day with no servant of any of the saidis craftis, and what maister happens to contravene herentill sall pay to the common box the sum of fourtie shillings *toties quoties ;* and gif it happens the servants be found playing on the work day, in that case he sall tyne his half-year's fee, except he get good-will of his maister.

ANENT ADMISSION OF MEMBERS.

Item, it is statute and ordained that nane occupear of the saidis craftis sall keip to work therein as ane maister until the tyme he be examined be the deacon and principals of the saidis craftis and founden worthy thereto, mackand ane maisterstick of work of his awin occupation to be set down to hym be the deacon and maisters of the saidis craftis ; and gif the intrant

shillings Scots, conform to the Act of the book ; as also that he bill the Court, and crave the deacon and members' pardon for his uncivil carriage.

9th September, 1693.—Be it knowu to all men, be thir presents, me, William Cook, blacksmith, burgess of Aberdeen, forsamukle as I am attached and incarcerate in the burgh tolbooth of Aberdeen, at the order of Patrick Whyt, deacon of the Hammermen Trade, and his assessors for my misdemeanours, and cursing and swearing in ane fencit Court in the Trinities, and now being sensible of my trausgression, and willing to submit to the traid for my misdemeanours, and being resolved (by the grace of God) to carry more decentlie amongst my brethren and neighbours in tym cuming, conform to the laudable acts and ordinances made anent our court and convention as the same are booked and recorded in our court books, and my oath judicially given for that effect, therefore I bind and oblige me not only to carry and behave as becomes at meetings and conventions of the said traid in tym cuming, but also to pay and deliver to the present boxmaster and his successors in his said office, for the use, utility, and behoof of the said incorporation, the sum of a hundred pounds Scots money as ane penaltie imposed upon me be the said deacon and maisters for my bypast transgressions, and that at what tym and whensomever the boxmaster sall require the same. Item, there is ane cautioner for William Cook his performance and registration.

* It is worthy of note that in many of the Acts all apprentices who are unable to pay the fine are to receive corporal punishment at the hands or will of the deacon.

beis fund qualifiet to be admitted frieman for sik composition to be paid
be hym to the common box according to the crafts ordinance, providing
always the intrant give content to the towne of his composition to thame
accordingly.

ANENT MASTERSTICKS OR ESSAYS.

Item, it is statute and ordained that whasomever myndes to come in
amongst the saidis craft to be frieman amongst them sall mak and present two pieces of work for his maisterstick sufficiently made and wrocht
according to that calling he myndis to lyve be. To witt, the saidleirs ane
man's stock and ane woman's stock of ane saiddell ; the armourers, ane
mounted buckler sword, together with ane rapier mounted ; the gunaris,
ane pistol with ane hagbute ; the smythis sall mak twa pieces of wark of
sik as is wrocht in the toune ; the pewterraris, ane bassin with ane stoup,
and so furth ; the rest of the callings accordinglie according to thair calling, so that every entrant sall keep true with his awin calling, and not
middle with any other man's wark.

Item, it is statute and ordained that all skynneris that beis received
and incorporate hereaifter amongst the saidis craft sall come in orderlie
be form of say and trying of their gratification as becometh, and to pay
thair composition or banquet siller conform to the craftis ordinance, and to
mak ane essay as follows—Ane pair of gluffs for ane man and ane plain
chevring to ane woman.

ANENT SPOILED WORK.

Item, it is statute and ordained that na occupiar of the saidis craftis
sall receive or tak ane uther occupiar's wark out of his boothe except he
spille the samen, and known be the deacon and principals of the saidis
craftis as spilt wark under the onlaw of twentie shillings ; and, furdder,
it sall be leisom to ane other maister gif so he is to work the same wark
on the spilleir's expenses, and that for eschewing of slander to the guid
craft.

ANENT APPRENTICES.

Item, it is statute and ordained that no maister of the saidis craftis
indent nor conduce with ane prentiss himself for less years than six years
as prentiss, and ane year for meat and fee.   And the clerk of the samen
sall make all fit indentures ; and the maisters to present all such indentures publicly in presence of the deacon and maisters for the time thereof,
and wha contravenes hereintill sall pay ane onlaw of fourtie shillings
money to be inbrocht to their awin box.

Item, it is statute and ordained that it sall not be liesum to no freman
of the saidis craftis to fee nor conduce ony servant or prentiss until the
tym he cum to be deacon of the craft and acquaint hym therewith, and of
the form of their agreement under the pain of forty shillings to be paid
be the contravener to the convener box.

ANENT ATTENDING FUNERALS.

Item, it is statute and ordained that whasomever of the said crafts beis warned be the officiar of the said crafts to convoy any man or woman depairted either of thair craft or ony other craft within this burt, the person or persons that beis absent, being in the toune, sall pay six shillings *toties quoties*, and to be poynded therefor, and that all freemen that are in use to weir hatis that thay so address themselves therewith.

ANENT SLANDER.

Item, it is statute and ordained for keeping of concord amongst the saidis crafts in tyme cuming that it sall not be liesom to nane of the members thereof, directly or indirectly, to offend others in word, work, nor deed, tending to their honesty and credit, and wha happens to do the same and lawfully proven, sall be convicit in ane onlaw of four shillings usual money of Scotland, to be uplifted and unforgiven for helping of the poore of the saidis crafts.

ANENT OPENING LOCKS WITH CROOKED IRONS.

19th August, 1699.—The said day the said Hammermen Traid taking to consideration the damage and prejudice that both the said traid, as also the inhabitants, sustain by opening of locks with crooked irons, and the *mala famas* and bad reports raised upon the blacksmiths thereanent, have unanimously strictly statute and ordained, that no person or persons presume, nor take upon hand, to directly or indirectly, of the said traid at any tyme heirafter to open any locks whatsomever with crooked irons or any of the lyke instruments (except with the keys of the said locks).

ANENT BEHAVIOUR IN THE KIRK.

16th December, 1699.—The said day it was strictly statute and ordained that without prejudice of former laudible acts made anent due observance of the Sabbath Day, that in all tyme coming no person or persons of the said Hammermen Traid sall presume in tyme of divine service, and within the loft and desks therein, directly or indirectly to speak audibly, indecently, or about worldly affairs, to molest any of thir neighbours in hearing or attending the word preached, and whoever contravens, after being found guilty, to pay to the boxmaster for the use of the poore, six shillings Scots *toties quoties* by and attour any other censure the court sall please impose upon the transgressors.

ANENT WORKING TO GUILD BRETHREN.

8th October, 1670.—The said day the haill skinners freemen of the incorporation unanimously did enact and oblige themselves that in all tyme hereafter none of themselves nor any of their prentisses, journeymen, or servants, sall directly or indirectly goe and work to any brother of gild as his hyrling or servant in any manner of way, and that under the failzie of ten pounds Scots *toties quoties*, to be precisely uptaken and given in to the boxmaster for the use of the incorporation.

4th January, 1689.—The said day the deacon, maisters, and members of the said Hammermen Traid ordained that no glover nor skynner within the said burgh should work to any burgess of gild within the same upon any pretence whatsoever, nor pluck, peal, nor alme ony skin to ony person or persons, nor work no other manner of work under pain of being deprived of his freedom of the traid.

ANENT RECEIVING BENEFIT.

15th February, 1673.—The said day it is statute and ordained that whatever freman and member of the traid sall supplicat the calling for supplie and charitie and receives support from the craft, that he sall not be charged thereafter to any court or meetings until he refund to the traid all such charitable supplies advanced to him, and to have no vote in court until the same be repayit.

ANENT ELECTION OF DEACONS.

21st August, 1675.—The said day it is statute and ordained unanimously be the haill craft that there sall be no election of ane deacon in all tyme hereafter upon that week that Cowan fair stands, or any other great public mercat about that tyme whilk the skinners are necessitat to be absent and thereby wanting their voyces in the election, but when there sall be ane compleet meeting of the haill incorporation.

ANENT THE CONDUCT OF JOURNEYMEN AND APPRENTICES.

24th December, 1681.—The said day it is statute and strictly ordained be the deacon and maisters of the said calling that in all tym cuming the journeymen and prentisses of the said calling is to compear before the deacon of the Hallow Court for receiving their respective injunctions from the said deacon, conform to the compleents that sall happen to be given in against them.

5th September, 1691.—The said day it is statute and ordained that all prentisses and fialls sall compear at their master's command or at command of the deacon, and enter themselves and pay their entry money, as also give their oath of fidelity when required; and in case they do in the contrair it is unanimously statute and ordained that the person or persons contravenirs sall not be repute or holden prentiss or journeyman until they give satisfaction, and in case they offer to bill [apply] as freemen, to be rejected until they give satisfaction.

ANENT WHITE IRON SMITHS.

6th November, 1694.—The said day the traid strictly statutes and ordained that in all tyme heirafter, in case any person or persons sall happen to supplicate the Hammermen Traid to be incorporate as ane white iron worker, as Peter Murisone hath done laitly, that they nor either of them sall not be received unless they pay the full composition that other friemen of the said Hammermen Traid is in use to pay for the tyme; and whatsoever frieman of the said traid sall take the supplicant's pairt in prejudice of the traid and of this present act, sall pay fourty shillings Scots money by and attour what other amerciament the deacon and maisters sall impose upon him.

ANENT SMITHS AND THEIR COAL.

Item, it is statute and ordained that no frieman of the said craft sall take upon his hand to sell himself or gif to any unfrieman, or outlandishman ony smiddie coll under the pain of forty shillings the first fault, the second fault doubill onlaw, and so furth accordingly as the samen beis proven.

13th July, 1695.—The said day it is statute and ordained be voice of court that no frieman of the blacksmith art buy smiddie coal out of shippes or boattes, but that only the present deacon for the tyme buy the same, and make pryce thereupon, for the common good of that arte.

ANENT BRASIERS.

22nd January, 1696.—The said day it is statute and ordained that in all tyme coming no frieman of the brasier traid be admitted frieman of the said Hammermen Traid except he pay the full composition to the traid, conform to the act of the book as other friemen in the said traid ordinarlie pay at their entry, conform to the act in the book.

ANENT CUTLERS AND ARMOURERS.

Item, it is statute and ordained for good order in tyme cuming betwixt armourers and cutlers, to wit, that ilk ane of the saidis calling sall hauld thamselves content with thair awn calling, and that nane of thame mix with others calling, nor mak use thereof to no persone or persones neither to burgh nor landward under the pain of fourty shillings Scots.

ANENT SKINNERS.

Item, it is statute and ordained that it sall not be liesum to the skynneris incorporat to buy any sheep skynes, or any other sort of skins whatsomever, on the mercat day until it be strucken nine hours in the day, and wha contravenes hereuntill sall pay fourty shillings money *toties quoties* to the common box.

ANENT BLACKSMITHS AND GUNSMITHS.

25th May, 1692.—The said day the haill blacksmiths of the incorporation enacts and obliges them noways to work any wark belonging to the gunsmith traid, but to keep themselves at their awin wark conform to the old act.

ANENT JOURNEYMEN JOINING THE CRAFT.

27th February, 1729.—The court hereby statute and ordain that in all tyme coming no man shall be admitted as a frieman in this corporation until two years after expiring of his apprenticeship, and serving for that space as journeyman either in this burgh or somewhere else.

ANENT FOUNDERS.

14th February, 1704.—The said day the court ordained that no man sall enter as founder, but sall pay the full banqueting money as ane extranean for the said traid, whereupon William Aberdour, founder, with consent of the traid, took instruments in the traids hands.

On account of the similarity of the handicrafts embraced in the Hammermen Trade, there was continual overlapping among the different classes of craftsmen, and numerous convictions are recorded for contravening the ordinance compelling each man to confine himself to his own craft. With the view of more strictly defining the work of each craftsman, the essays were in some cases made very specific, and strict injunctions were imposed that only certain kinds of work were to be performed. The following are the essays that were usually prescribed :—

Blacksmiths.—Ane bigg lock with pipe and six cross marks, and ane pair of bands (hinges) with five joints.

Hookmakers.—Fish hooks, hooks and eyes of several sizes, with three tinning heats, and ane wire window.

Skinners and Glovers.—First, ane pair of men's gloves, doe leather, prick drawen three seams about the thumb, four seams, each point to be coloured both collours and topped ; second, ane pair women's gloves, kid or lamb leather, the thumb seemed round drawn with two prick seams about it, the points to be round seams in the middle, and two prick seams without the two round seams, the rest of the seams to be single prick seam coloured a light cloath collour, evenly ; third, ane purse of haill leather with two welted lugs and two dyce knaps about the lugs, and twelve single knaps about the mouth, two bye purses with twenty drawers of three platts ; two single knaps and ane dyced knap on each drawer, the drawers to be dyed reed, the purse to be purple (?), and all the knaps to be mounted with gilded leather, and the hinger to have ane knap.

Plumbers.—A sheet of lead twelve feet long and three feet broad equally wrocht, half a stone of shot, and ane eln of burnt pipe to be wrocht with his ain hand.

Coppersmiths. — Ane brass tee kettle and broath pott tinned.

Watchmakers.—Ane eight day clock to be made and perfected be himself and wrocht with his own hand.

Card or Reedmakers.—Ane pair of stock cards, ane pair of wool cards, and ane pair of tow cards.

Pewterers.—Ane posset can of pewter with two stoups, and two handles, and ane church cup of pewter.

Armourers.—Furbishing ane flahilt for a broad sword, and a broad blade, rough ground, and furbished with ane small sword blade, also rough ground and furbished and both points broken off and the broad sword ground on buff point, and both mounted with fashionable scabbards, to be perfected with his own hand.

Goldsmiths.—A tea pot and stone ring to be wrocht by him with his own hand.

Saddlers.—Ane man's stock, and ane woman's stock of ane saiddell.

The Town Council does not appear to have regulated the price of goods manufactured by members of the Hammermen Trade to any great extent. On the 16th October, 1580, the Magistrates "statut and ordainit that the blak smyth sall tak and receive for the gang of the grytest horss schone six s. viiid. ; smaller horss and neggis four s. ; and the contravenir heirof to pay fourtie s. unforgiven." The skinners were also interdicted in 1507 from washing "clethis, hidis, skynnis, nor vyther stuf, in the comon riuolis, loche, nor watteris ; and that nay red fische, quhit fische, claythis, nor vyther stuff that may infect the watter, be cassin nor weschin in it."

In 1852 the Hammerman Trade obtained an Act of Parliament "to confirm, amend, and regulate the administration of the estates and affairs of the said Society ; and for other purposes relating to the Society." This Act confirms the titles of the properties acquired by the Trade since 1694 ; and also confirms the regulations which had been adopted in 1714 for establishing a Mortification, and subsequent alterations made in 1811. This Mortification, which was instituted by William Lindsay, goldsmith, and which is in the nature of a capital accumulating fund, has proved of great advantage to the Trade, and been one of the chief instruments in their financial prosperity.

P

The chief properties acquired by the Hammermen Trade since 1694 are the Craibstone rig, on the north side of the Bow Bridge; the baulk rig of Hammerfield; the lands of Hammerfield; the croft of Futtiesmyre, near the Links; Tolmie's Croft, "in the territories of Footie;" the Sow Croft, near the Heading Hill; the Dean's Croft, Old Aberdeen; Longland's Croft, "on the King's highway leading to the Bridge of Dee;" Dunn's Croft, "near the Crabestone;" Windmill Croft; Greathead Croft, Dee Street; part of Clayhills; piece of ground on the west side of Union Terrace; part of Poynernook, &c.

On the emblazoned panel belonging to this Trade are given the arms (patent 15th May, 1682) a list of acting members, and the following eulogy in verse of the different branches of the craft :—

> Our Art over all Mechanics hath renown,
> Our Arms the Hammer and the Royal Crown.
> Around this shield ten ovals you behold,
> Wherein ten several emblems stand in gold,
> Deceiphering ten distinct trades to be
> All comprehended in our Deaconrie.
> And yet the ten have but one general name—
> The generous, ingenious HAMMER-MEN,
> Whose profound skill in their renouned Art,
> Doeth to each corner of the worlde impart
> Profite and pleasure both ; for every man,
> From the greatest monarch to the country swaine,
> Is to their art obleged lesse or more :
> By them, crowns doe the heads of kings decore
> By them, each warlick instrument is made ;
> By them, the ploughman labure for our bread ;
> It's by their art we calculat our tyme ;
> By them, vast armies in their armor shine.
> Without their art, no comonwealth could stand—
> Without them traffic fails by sea and land,
> All handicrafts, no doubt, acknouledge will
> Their livelyhoods depends upon their skill.
> There's non but knows from whence they had their spring—
> Their art did with the infant world begin ;
> That every age hath bettered ever since ;
> It first with Tubal Cain did commence,
> Which cunning men designed in Scripture phrase,
> That doth import a high and lofty praise.

The anvill and the hammer you behold,
Above the which is plact a crown of gold,
The badges of their honour let's us see,
All other traids to their's are pedantrie :
But in the least on no trade to reflect,
Let every on to them pay that respect
They doe deserve, since their ingenious art
By words can never have its due deseart,
And so let God, who doeth infuse all skill,
Within men's breasts protect them ever still.

CHAPTER VIII.

THE BAKER TRADE.

TRADITION gives the weavers and bakers priority among all handicrafts, and not without some show of reason. In the natural order of things, food and clothing are the two first requisites of man, in whatever condition he is found, and so it has happened that in newly-formed communities weavers and bakers came to be established earlier than the other crafts less necessary to civilised life. In Scotland this has been the case with the bakers more so than in many other countries, notably in England, where the baking of bread was carried on more in the household than in the bakehouse. In Aberdeen down to the middle of the last century the baking of oat cakes was far more common among the males than the females, the special privilege of baking " ait kakis " being as jealously guarded by the craftsmen bakers in Aberdeen as any other branch of their business. It is a curious fact that this branch of baking is rapidly returning again to ordinary bakehouses; while, unfortunately, the knowledge of the art is rapidly dying out among modern housewives. In Scotland, too, the baking of loaves and biscuits has been more strictly confined to the male sex than in other countries. In England, for instance, almost every housewife bakes a considerable proportion of the loaf bread required for the household ; but in Scotland, and notably in Aberdeen, the baking of loaf and biscuit bread has been preserved as a strict monopoly for the men bakers. According to the acts and ordinances of the Baker craft in Aberdeen, women were not allowed to bake any bread, pastry, or pies to be sold in the streets or in shops, a restriction which was maintained until the abolition of trading privileges in 1846.

The Magistrates in Aberdeen began at an early date—as soon, in fact, as we have any mention of Magistrates in the

BAKERS [15th May, 1682].—Or, two baker's peels in saltire gules, each charged with three loaves in pale argent, between a tower of Aberdeen in chief, and a millrind in base of the third [!] Motto : *Floreant Pistores.*

public records—to take cognisance of the Baker craft. In 1398 the bakers are dealt with in their collective capacity, and for the better regulation of the Trade a system of marks was instituted for the different makers of bread in the town The following is the minute in the Council Register for the year 1457, vol. v., p. 337, the different marks being rudely drawn opposite each name :—

This ar ye baxteris of bred whilkis sal visit the craft and na oythers in the first :—

Andrew Baxter, with his mark.................................... ✶

William Club... ⊙

William Atkynson... ⌒

Thom of Spens... ✚

William Buchane... ∴

Thom. Imlach... ✚

William Catnea... ⊙

Robert Ranyson.. ⊙

John Whyt and }
  Will. Baxter } .... ⊙

Thom. Gladi.. θ

Andrew Mair.. /---

The price and weight of bread seem to have been matters as carefully looked after in the early history of the town as it is to-day. On 8th October, 1507, the Council ordained that "all baxteris sall have breid of quheit sufficient, gud and clene stuff, penny breid and tua penny breid," and on 21st October, 1544, the "bailyeis commandit and ordinit all four the officiaris, in jugment, to pas throcht all the rewis and streitis of the toune, als oft as neid beis, and vesy and seik all caik baxteris that bakis ony cakis to sell, and tak all thair girdilis thai apprehend baikand siklik cakis, and present the said girdilis to thame, and verefy that thai tuik the same fray caik baxteris, baikand caikis to sell, and thai sall haue the said

escheit to thaim for thair travell; and causit the officiaris
suer the gryt aith to exerce the same lelilie and trewlie, without feid or fauour, and to present the saidis girdilis as oft as
thai culd apprehend thame."

On 8th April of the following year "Sandi Kemp," baxter,
was "convictit be the counsale for the offering of the France
capitane of tene dosoun of iij d. braid of quhit, for the boll of
quhit, contrair the commond weill of the town, and hindering
the proffeit thairof, and he and all wther baxteris of the guid
toun ordinit to decest fra doyng of sic thingis in tymes
cumyng, vnder the pane of expelling of thame of thair craft
within the said burgh, for yeir and day, and paying of xl s. to
Sanct Nicholace wark vnforgevin. And als ordinit the said
Sanderes to pay viij s. to the sustentatioune of the seik folkis,
for the falt bigand unforgevin."*

The following extracts from the Council Register furnish
interesting information as to the price of wheat and bread,
and also the kind of bread that was baked at the different
periods :—

9th August, 1549.—The said day, it is statut and ordinit be the prouest,
bailzies, and counsale, present for the tyme, in presens of the maist pairt
of the baxsteris of this guid tovnn, havand respect to the prices that the
quhit gevis for the tyme in this tovnn, viz., xxxij s., or xxxiiij s. at the
maist, that thair be na manner of iiij d. breid bakin within this tovnn
frathinfurth, vnder the pane of eschaeting of the same, but allanerly tua
penny breid and penny breid, that be guid stuf, frosche, veill bouttit, and
without mixtiour, and ueill bakin ; the prise of the tua penny breid xiij
vnce, and penny breid vij vnces ; and gif ony breid beis fundin incontrar
heirof quhen it is weyt be the bailzie, thane and in that caise it salbe
lesum to the said bailzeis that apprehendit it to eschait and daill the same
to the purale for thair contentioun, without ony forder calling, accusing,

---

* It would appear from the following entry in the Council Register that there had been
several other unruly members among the craft :—

"15th April, 1484.—In the court haldin be the ballies of Abirdene, in the tolbuithe, the xv
day of Aprile forsaid, it was ordanit be ane assise, a d forbiddin that, in tyme comming, Johne
the Rosse, baxter, sall bere na wauppynis vnder nicht, sic as ane swerd, or vthir fensabil
wauppynnis, for certain causes considerit be thaim, vndir the pain of tynsale of his fredom, bot
gif he be chargit be the officlars. And for the said John the Rosse, William Futhes is becumin
law burgh that William Vmfray salbe vnscathit in tym cumin, vtherwayes than as law will.
And the said William Vmfray gas fundin Thom. Sympson law bergh for him, that the said
Johne the Rosse salbe scathles in likewise. Attour the assise hes ordanit that gif it happynnis
the said Johne the Rosse, in tyme tocum, to forfaute aganis William Vmfra, or his broudre
Malstre William, like as he has done of before, that he sall pay v. merkis to Sanct Nicholace
wark, and that he sall do alsmekil sted and serulce to thani, as he done them grevans, &c."
—Council Register, vol. vi., p. 839.

or connuikit of thame ; and als tha statut and ordinit that all manner of flower, quhit, ry, and ry meill that hapnis to cum to the tovn frathinfurth one of the avin auentour, that the baxsteris of this guid tovne sall haue the same, of the same price the towne hapnis to by the same, sa far as tha ma loise amangis thame, and pay the fremmit men thankfully, and na wther man to haue ony part tharof quhill the said baxsteris refuise it.— *Council Register, vol. xx., p. 274.*

16th December, 1549.—The said day, Alexr. Jaffray, John Foullis, Charle Dauesoun, Duncane Colle, George Anderson, and Jonat Ancroft, baxstaris, tha and ilk ane of thame is conuikit be the sorne assise aboun writin for the brakin of commond ordinance and statutis of this guid tovne, in selling of breid of quhit of less prise thane the statutis maid thairwpoun, and of insufficient stuf, quherfor ilk ane of them is in ane amerciament of the court, and that is gevin for dovme. And the bailzies ordinit the officiaris to pas incontinent and pund every ane of theme therfor, and cals thame all in iugment to keip the said statutis, and to baik and sell xiiij vnce of guid, clein, dry, and veill bakin fresche stuf for ij d., and to haue breid rady at all tyme to serue the tovne sa lang as tha haue stuf, vnder the pane of eschaeting of the haill braid fundin with thame for the tyme.—*Council Register, vol. xx., p. 330.*

12th August, 1555.—The said day, Alexr. Jeffray, Duncane Fraser, Williame Congiltoun, Dauid Saidlar, Johnne Fowlis, Charles Dauidsone, Reche Myln, Alexr. Kemp elder, Alexr. Kemp youngar, Alexr. Kay, and Duncane Colly, baxteris, and ilkane of thame were conuickit in judgement, and put in amerciament of court, for the braking of the commound ordinance and statutis of this guid toune of selling of quhyt breid of less messour and price nor wes gewin and dewisit be the counsell to thame of befoir to obserf and fulfill ; quhairfor thai war in amerciament of court to forbeir in tyme cumyng and amend as law vill, and that wes gewin for dome, and the baillies continewit thair vnlawis to be modiffit be thame eftirwart.

The said day, the haill counsell statut and ordanit that the baxteris of this guid toune sall balk and sell twenty tua vnce of quhyt breid, sufficient stuf, and weill bakin, for four penneis, and tuenty-aucht vnce of ry breid, sufficient stuf, and weill bakin, for four d. ; and that na breid be sauld be thame quhill thai be considderit and vestit be ane of the baillies ; and quhowsone the breid beis takin out of the owne, that ane of the baillies salbe aduertist and requirit to do the same ; and that na baxter sall baik ony breid vpone Settirday befoir tua eftir none; and quha beis fundin cumand in the contrar heirof, the hail baikin stuf beand fundin and gottin in his possessioune to be escheit and delt ; and gyf ony baxter hawand stuf beis fundin wantand baikin breid, and nocht vsand his craft to serf the toune and nightbouris therof in contemptioune of this ordinance, the same beand knawin and vnderstand, the haill victuall and stuf beand fundin in his possessioune to be escheit and delt to the puir folkis. And this statut to induir and haf stryntht quhill the fest of Michaelmes nixt cumis, and further induiring the counsellis will.—*Council Register, vol.* xxii., *p.* 124.

4th October, 1555.—Item, it is statut and ordanit, with consent of the haill baxteris, beand convenit, that nane of thame pass in the contray to by quhit, of darrer prices bot as tha ma keip and obserf the statut and by ordinance gewin thame be the counsale for this present yeir ; and alse that nane of the saidis baxsteris by quhit attour his nychtbouris heyd : that is to say, where his nychtbour hes bene to mak ony bying or bergane of quhyt, and biddeu ony money thairfor, that his nychtbour bid na mair nor is offerit, nor mak him to by thair, wnder the pane of fourty s. for the first falt, and tynsell of fredome for yeir and day for the secund falt, gif he beis convickit for the same.—*Council Register, vol.* xxii., *p.* 165.

The Bakers were granted a Seal of Cause* in 1534, but for a considerable time prior to that date they were in the habit of electing deacons, and reporting their election to the Magistrates and Town Council. Although briefer than some of the others, the Bakers' Seal of Cause is more comprehensive and explicit than the most of these local charters. It is as follows :—

Be it kend till all men be thir presents, We, the Provost, Baillies, Counsell, and communitie of the burght of Aberdeen, the commonweall of the same in that pairt having seen, considered, and understood be advyce, and we being rightly advysit thairupon, to have grantit, given, and committit, and be the tenor hereof grants, gives, and commits to our lovittits neigbouris, John Bannerman, and Alexander Marr, baxteris, deconis of the craftis of baxteris of the said burght for the tyme, and to their successors in all tyme to come, ane full, free, and plane power, and authoritie upon all and sundrie occupiaris and exerciseres of the said craft, within the said burght, and freedom of the samen : To correct and punish the trespassers thair unlaws, amerciaments, and escheats to be advysit and modified be the saidis deacons and their successors ; to uptak and inbring to the commonweall and utilitie of the said craft (blood and blae being excepted) to the punitioun of us and our successors. Also we ratify that no freeman sall be maid of the same craft until he be examined be the saidis deacons or their successors—deacons of the saidis Craft for the time—and that he be found be them ane sufficient craftsman and mak his maisterstick of work, and that he be proven worthie be his work to be ane maister and admittit be the said deacons for the tyme and presented to us as ane able

---

* The Bakers have for a long time been under the impression that they had no formal Seal of Cause. Kennedy (Annals, vol. II., p. 225) says he was unable to discover it in the registers of the Town Council ; but the present writer fortunately discovered an authenticated copy in the Records of the Trade.

person to be made freeman. Sicklik it sall be liesum to the saidis deacons and their successors with the advice and counsell of the principal neighbouris of the said Craft to mak statutes and ordinances for the commonweall of the said Craft and honour of the said burght; give and granted to the saidis deacons and their successors, deacons of the saidis craft fra us and our foresaids all power and privileges obefoir written for us, the said deacons and their successors answering to us and our successors for all and sundrie, the neighbouris, maisters, servants, prentisses, and occuparis of the said Craft for all faults that lies under their correction, gif they leave any such faults unpunishit, or punish thame otherwise nor they ought to do of law and good conscience, and that they do justice to all occuparis of the said Craft at all tymes when they are required without fear or favour, and gif any occupier of the said Craft disobeys or contemns the saidis deacons or their successors deacons for the tyme that they complain to us and our successors, and we cause them be obeyed conform to their power; providing always that saidis craft choose no deacon in tyme coming but them that be responsible to the town, conform to their power, and that they answer to us and our successors for the haill craft, and all things concerning them and their craft whatsomever they be requirit thereto. And we, the saidis provost, baillies, counsell, and communtie, sall warrant, keep, and defend all and sundrie the promisses to the saidis deacons and their successors as said is be this writ, and attour we will and ordain that it sall not be liesum to the one deacon of the deacons above written to do or statute any thing above written concerning the weal of the saidis craft, particularlie by himself, but that they sall both agree and concur togidder in all tymes they have to do, touching the said craft, and siklyke their successors in tyme coming; in witnessing those present powers and privileges, we causit appense our common seal, the twenty-fifth day of April, the year of God ane thousand fyve hundreth thretee and four years.

The old Acts and Ordinances of the craft were carefully copied from the old registers into a minute book, commenced in 1632, which also contains a list of deacons from 1572. The preface runs—"Thir followes the good and laudabill actes and statutes of the Baxter craft of Aberdeen, being ye second craft within ye samyn, to be keipit and observit in all tymn cuming." The mention here of the Bakers being the second craft recalls the fact that when the Wrights and Coopers claimed possession of the second window in the old Trinity Chapel the Bakers raised an action at law to have it declared that they were the second craft in the order of precedence, and being successful, no further attempt was made to disturb the existing arrangement.

On the fly leaves of the oldest minute book—which, by the

way, is ornamented here and there with red capitals—are a number of moral and pious extracts such as—

> Wealth may take wings and riches flee away,
> But God's a rock that ne'er will decay.

———

> Behold the staitt of all the sones of men
> That live to die, but knowis not how nor quhen,
> How grass like they do whither and decay,
> How soone death doeth mawe them down lyk hay ;
> How vain a thing of all things is man,
> For, loe, his lyf is measured by a span ;
> How he is borne with plentis, brocht with pain,
> And how with grief he gois to grave againe.

Then follow the acts and statutes, a number of which, as in the case of the other Trades, are undated :—

ANENT SABBATH OBSERVANCE.

Item, it is statute and ordained at Aberdeen the twentie-ane day of February, 1634 years, George Leslie, baxter, being deacon, that ilk free-men hereof, baith servants and prentices sall keep the holy Sabbath Day precisely at sermone beforenone and afternoone, and sall nowayse absent thaim selffis thairfra (health of bodie servin) under the pain of six shillings Scots ilk person *toties quoties*, as they happen to contravene thir present ordinance ; And ilk servant and prentices of the said craft [that] is vagaboundis on ye Sabbath and strayer heir and there be playing at lynks, kyillies, bou'lls, and other unlawful games, so that they neglect their dewtie towards God and their masters.   Thairfor it is strictly statute and ordainit that gif ony of them beis found brakeries of the said Sabbath Day at any tyme hereafter, ye contravenaris hereof shall pay to the collec-tour for helping of the poore of their craft four shillings Scots *toties quoties* for thair absence from the service ; and if they be found playing at the forsaids pastymes on the said Sabbath Day sall pay six shillings and eightpence *toties quoties*, and to be punished in thair person otherwise ; or otherwise reported to the session that they may tak ordour there-with as appertenis.

ANENT "SCHEILLING" WHEAT.

Item, it is statute and ordainit that ilk freeman hereintill sall have no power to scheill quheat at the flour mill within this burgh, but twa birne quheat at ane scheilling, and everie ane to have his rowme about, and ony quantitie ground as neid requires, and wha does in the contrair hereof sall pay six shillings *toties quoties*.

ANENT DRINKING AND DEBAUCHING.

Item, it is statute and ordainit that gif ony servants or preutisses beis found drinking and debauching in hous on the Sabbath night, or drinking in tyme of divine service, the contravener thereof sall pay to the collectour for helping of the poore six shillings *toties quoties*.

ANENT CARRYING WEAPONS.

Item, it is statute and ordainit that it sall not be leasom to no servant nor prentiss to wear upon him either whinger or durk or dagger, but ane big knyff for eating of his meat, laiking a poynt, or either he be going to landward in his master's service, and wha contravenes hereintill sall pay six shillings *toties quoties*.

ANENT PRENTICES BAKING BUNS AND PIES.

Item, it is statute and ordainit that no prentiss nor servant sall baik any buns or pyes to sell in tyme cumying under the pain of confiscation thereof beside and attour ane unlaw to the poore of the craft.

ANENT APPRENTICES MARRYING.

Item, it is statute and ordainit that it sall not be leasom to no prentiss within his prentissship to marie nor spouse hym to ane wyff, nayer to commit fornication nor adulterie within their prentissship, and wha contravenis hereintill to begin of new agaiu and serve over the whole years contained in his indenture. Otherwyse, in case of refusal, naways to receive the benefit of ane freeman.

ANENT WEARING HATS AT FUNERALS.

Item, it is statute and ordanit that ilk freeman hereof that has hattes, or in use to wear any, sall come with thair hattes on thair heads to all burials they happen to be warned unto, and that nane absent thameselffs theirfra. And wha contravenes hereinn sall pay six shillings *toties quoties* for helping of the poor of the craft. And nane appoint in the contrair.

10th August, 1636.—The day and dait of the Act within written, ane Act and ordinance is ratified and approven as all freemen of the said craft that wears hattes on their heids on the Sabbthe day, sall come lykewise decentlie on Tysday and Thursday at sermones as occasion offers, and wha contravenes hereintill sall pay to the poore of the craft six shillings and eightpence *toties quoties*.

ANENT JURNAY-BOYES.

Item, it is statute and ordainit that no freeman hereof sall have jurnay-boyes in thair baikhous ; but that everie maister have them either feed prenties or servant with thame, and wha contravenes hereintill sall pay six shillings *toties quoties* to the collectour for helping the poore.

ANENT APPRENTICES.

Item, it is statute and ordained that no freeman sall be maid at no tyme hereafter without he serve lawfully prentice within the samyn be the space of six years fullie togidder as prentice and servant, aud gif the master depart this present lyff withiu the years of his prenticeship, it is considered and concluded be the saidis deacon and maisters that he shall serve aue other maister of this craft the rest of the years that are not out-run, so that it sall nowyse be leisom to the said prentice to attain to the benefit as ane freeman hereof while unto the time he obtemper this present ordinance.

Item, it is statute and ordained that no freeman hereof presume nor tak upon hand to accept or receive either prentice or boyes iu thair service unto the time they come duly to the court and pay their entry to the collectour in presence of the deacon and maisters, and wha contravenes hereintill sall pay six shillings *toties quoties* for helping of the poor.

Item, it is statute and ordaint that no freeman hereof sall have two prentises servin him at one tyme, and who contravenes hereintill sall pay to the collectour of the craft for helping of their poor ten merks *toties quoties*. And nane appoint in ye contrair.

Item, it is statute and ordained that na indenture betwixt maister and prentiss sall be presented before the deacon and maisters except it be under the subscription of the clerk of our own court under the pain of six shillings to be paid to the collectour be the breaker of this ordinance.

Item, it is statute and ordained that ilk maister sall present and exhibit before the haill calling their prentisses indentures sic as they happen to conduce with, to the effect the same may be tryed whether or not thay be orderlie accepted, and wha contravenes hereintill sall pay six shillings *toties quoties* to the collectour of the craft.

Item, it is statute that na new admittit frieman hereof sall accept nor conduce with ane prentiss untill he be past three yeirs as ane frieman, and wha contravines herintill sall pay ten pounds money.

Item, that no frieman sall take ane other callauts aff off their hand until he give satisfaction for bygone rests.

ANENT PAYMENT OF DUES.

Item, it is statute and ordained that ilk master of this craft admitted freeman sall put and deliver at ilk quarter court their quarter stage [penny] with their servants and prentices, and that for helping of the poor of the craft, and everie dues astrictit furth thereof. And the maister to answer for their prentices and servants, and pay conform but [without] ony post-ponis or firstings, under the pain of 13 shillings *toties quoties* by and attour thair quarter stages for disobedience.

ANENT BUYING WHEAT.

Item, it is statute and ordanit that it sall nowyse be leasome to no free-man hereof to buy any quheat or buy he himselff frae ane extraniar, or any other merchant within this burgh arriviug thereat. Bot ye same stuff sall be coft [bought] be the Deacon of this craft iu name, and to the utilitie of the hail bretheren hereof. And quha contravenes herintill sall pay to the collectour in name of the craft twentie shillings Scots for ilk brak thereof.

Forsaemikle as the bretherne being informed that certain of the brither of gild of this burgh frequents to landward south and north and buys without to their ain selves, thinking thereby that the baxters will buy the same aff of thair hands to the great prejudice of the craft for remeid, whereof it is statute and ordained that whasomever of the said craft buys any of the said quheat so coft in smalls in landward sall pay four pounds money *toties quoties* as they happen to contraven.

15th August, 1637.—The said day it is statute and ordained be the deacon and maisters of the said calling (for exchewing of scandal to the said craft) that it sall not be lesum to no freeman of the said calling to buy ony quheat meall on mercat dayes that happen to come into the mercat to be sauld, neither in smalls nor greats, and wha contravenes hereintill shall pay fortie shillings on ilk boll thereof *toties quoties* for helping of the poore of the craft, and this act and statute to be intimate to the whole craft that they pretend no ignorance thereof, with special provision always that they that buys quheat small aforehand to be in-brocht to this burgh on mercat days then always to be free of this ordinance and no otherwise.

ANENT BUYING NEW WHEAT.

8th August, 1636.—The said day it is statute and ordained that gif ony frieman of the said calling buy ony new quheat be himselff at ony tym hereafter the same being about four bolls, in that case the buyer sall distribute two bolls thereof to the nicbbours gif they require the same for mixing of old quheat therewith.

ANENT KEEPING LATE HOURS.

Item, it is statute and ordaint that whatever frieman, prentice, or servant, beis found out of thair ain house at ten hours at night, or found in any unlawful place, sall pay six shillings and eightpennies *toties quoties* for helping of the poore of ye same.

ANENT SELLING FLOUR TO UNFREEMEN.

Item, it is statute and ordained that whatsomever person or persons of this calling sall be found to sell any flour, in greaties or smallies to unfriemen, or sall happen to gif flour to their servants for thair service sall in that case pay six shillings money of this realm *toties quoties* how oft the same be tryit be witness or aith of pairties. As also that no frieman permit nor suffer any unfree person to bake buns in their baik hous in tyme cuming under the lyke pains.

ANENT ENTRY MONEY.

Item, it is statute and ordained forsameikill as the great leniency that entered freemen here had anent their composition or banquet either, whereas other crafts within the same taks twies als mutch, to remedy whereof the deacon and maisters have ane statute and ordinance that whatsomever sall enter in amongst them as friemen sall pay forty pounds of composition to the craft for their part by and attour sic devotie as belongs to the toun, so that the entrant sall save the craft thereanent at the toun's hands, and nane appoint to the contrair.

ANENT THE TRADES HOSPITAL.

Item, it is statute and ordained, forsameikill as the most pairt of the freemen within this burgh having given in thair several contributions be thamselves to the Trinitie Hospital founded by the Rev. pastor Doctor William Guild, and to the effect the said hospital and convening house thereof may be the better maintinit, therefor it is statute and ordanit be advice of deacon and maisters and whole craft convenit that ilk new admittit frieman that be received hereafter in this incorporation sall give in their talent to the said use within yeir and day after their admission and this according to thair descrition and habilitie.

Item, it is statute and ordained that whosoever of this craft withholding his help from the hospital of the said crafts sall have no pairt nor portion of the mortifiet moneys dedicat to that use ; neither to have vote in choosing of the deacon and masters of their craft or admission of the said hous of any frieman.

ANENT BRIBERY AND CANVASSING.

Item, it is statute and ordained that whosoever of this craft convocates themselves for choising of the deacon obefoir the day of election or subornes any others to chois any man before the said day, the doer, whasoever he be, sall be convict in six pounds money to be paid into the deacon-convener's box, and gif he have no monies to be debared of all vote in any meeting whatsomever and sicklike wha pays not their quarter stages, either prentice or servant, entries, unlaws, and convictions given in against them sall have no vote in choosing of the deacon in tyme cuming.

ANENT MEETING IN THE TRINITIES.

Item, it is statute and ordained that whasomever deacon convenes in their ain house either with his haill craft or with their haill maisters to hold court or meetings anent any affairs of the craft and convene not formally in their convening hous of the Trinities the deacon sall pay to the Deacon-Conveener's box six pounds money *toties quoties*, and that he sall pay the same within forty-aucht houris thereafter under the pain of doubling thereof and poinding therefor.

ANENT BEHAVIOUR AT MEETINGS.

Item, it is statute and ordained that whasomever court beis holden either general or particular within the said convening hous, the court ance being fencit, and whosoever thereafter speikes without leve askit and given sall pay six shillings *toties quoties*, and if he refuse sall be presently poinded therefor.   And gif ony be refracter to be defraudit of thair vote or any benefit of court till the same be obeyit.

ANENT SLANDER AND SCANDAL.

Item, it is statute and ordained that whatsomever frieman hereof that slanders and villipendes the actis and ordinances of their present buik and disobeys the same sall not bruik office as deacon or master thereof in no tyme cuming without he make ane lawful satisfaction to the haill craft and to exact from him five pounds without any mitigation for his ignorance.

Item, forsameikill as certaine nichtbouries of this craft, at lawings and other societies, and offendis thair nichbours be offensive speeches against all civil ordour or Christainitie and to the effect there may be ane solid ordour in tyme cuming and such matteris and wrongs suppressed thairfor and ordained that whosoever of the saidis craft offendis ane other publicly or privately in any pairt whatsomever be offensive and scandalous speeches the doer sall be convictit and unlawed for four pounds *toties quoties* as the same beis proven either be witness or aith of parties and that to be inbrocht to the weall of the craft and nane appoynt in the contrair.

ANENT SECOND SONS.

Item, it is statute and ordained that no man's second soune, frieman of this craft, sall be maide frie nor injoy the benefit hereof except he be ane prentiss and indenture made thereon according to the form.

ANENT BUYING FOREIGN FLOUR.

Item, it is statute and ordained that no forrin flour be coft be no nichtbour of this craft fra any whatsomever, under the pain of forty shillings to the craft; and forder, that no flour be baiken chaiper nor four shillings the peck, under the pain of six shillings and eight pennies ilk peck that beis baiken better chaip.

ANENT PRICES FOR BAKING.

Item, it is statute and ordained that no master of the craft tak upon hand to baik any burges' flour in burges' ovens, nor to baik better chaip the burges man's flour nor four shillings the peck, conform to the above written act, and wha contravenes hereintill sall pay eight shillings to the collectour for helping of the poore.

ANENT SERVANTS SKAITHING THEIR MASTERS.

Item, forsameikle as the servants and prentisses of their incorporation hes the whole credit of thair maister's stuff and everie guid and gear, and thereby may harm thaim many wayis behind thair backs to thair hurt and prejudice, thairfor it is statute and ordained gif ony of the said servants and prentisses wrangs or skaithes thair maisters directly or indirectly at ony tyme hereafter be away taken of thair stuff, moneys, or thair guids, the doer thereof sall be expelled out of all service and baik-houses, and never to receive the benefit of the craft as friemen in ony tyme thereafter, and to be punishit in his person at the will of the maisters.

ANENT BUYING OATMEAL.

Item, it is statute and ordained that it shall not be leasom to no free-man to buy, receive, or intak in thar house or baikhous ony aittmeal on Setterday or Weddinsday mercat dayss till the same be put in the common mercat of this burght under the pain of twentie shillings money *toties quoties*, and gif it happens the magistrates attache any of the said freemen hereof for buying of meal unlawfullie the transgressor to free the whole of the craft of the toun's unlaws.

ANENT QUARRELLING.

Item, it is statute and ordained that it sall not be leasum to prentiss nor servant to put violent hands in others be way of deuty, but that everie servant and prentiss complain to the maister to the effect he may tak ordour therewith as appertains, and wha lifts his hands or feet to his nichtbour in baikhous or elsewhere sall pay to the collectour for helping of the poor of the craft twenty-nine shillings money *toties quoties* by and attour amends to the pairty at the will and discretioun of the Deacon and maisters.

ANENT THE WEIGHT AND STAMPING OF BREAD.

6th November, 1634.—The said day it is ordained that ilk twelf penny quheat loaf sall contain ten ounces of sufficient weall bakin bread and the twa shilling loaf to be conform, and in the meantime ordains every neigh-bour of the calling to have his stamp on his bread, and that the sufficiency or insufficiency of the said bread or lacking of the stamp be tried by the deacon or ony of his maisters whom he pleases with him until Candlemas next 1635, and who contravenes this present ordnance sall pay six shillings money *toties quoties* to the craft.*

ANENT CRYING PIES IN THE STREET.

23rd February, 1665.—The said day it is statute and ordainit be unanimous consent of the haill trade, that Alexander Innes, baxter, shall not goe through the street crying with pyes, nor no other of the said traid, and if they be found to do in the contrair, the contraveneer sall pay to the boxmaster four pounds Scots for the use of the poor of the said traid.†

ANENT NON-PAYING CUSTOMERS.

8th December, 1676.—The said day it is strictly statute and ordainit that no neighbour of the traid sall in any ways, directly or indirectly, baik nor work to any neighbour's customer, until first he have payt his former

---

* Numerous instances are recorded of members being punished for breach of this statute.

† Alexander Innes, being the youngest member of the trade, was officer at the time he committed this offence.

baiker of all bygane rests [debts], and who sall contravene herein to pay into the box the summe of four pounds Scots money for the use of the poore *toties quoties;* and also that the contravenirs sall pay to the former baxter such compt as sall be restand to him be his former customer, and this to be observed in all time coming.

ANENT PAYING THE TOWN'S DUES.

15th August, 1683.—The said day it is statute and ordained of unanimous consent of the haill baxter traid that whosomever of whatsomever rank or quality shall be admittit frieman of the said traid and received in their incorporations shall liberat and free the deacon, boxmaster, and remanent members of the said vocation at the hands of the Dean of Gild and counsell, as also at the hands of the Deacon-Conveener and members of his court anent all wyne arms and other public dues, due and payable upon the said entrant his accompt; and this act to be observed for all tyme coming without any opposition or contradiction.

ANENT HOURS OF APPRENTICES.

9th June, 1663.—The said day it is statute and ordained be the deacon with unanimous consent of the haill maisters and friemen of the baxter traid within this burgh that none of their prentisses nor servants be absent from their maister's service be the space of ane full hour together without leave askit and given unless they can instruct ane reasonabill cause for their absence which shall be allowed be the deacon and traid, and sic lyke that none of their prentisses and servants be out of their maister's house after nine hours at night without leave of their said maisters or ane reasonabill excuse to be shown to the said deacon and traid as said is, and if any of the saidis prentisses and servants contravene and come in the contrair of this present ordinance, it is statute and ordained that the persons so transgressing shall pay into the boxmaster of the said traid threttie shillings Scots money for the use of the poore, *toties quoties,* so oft as they or any of them shall be found absent from his service, or absent from his maister's house at nine hours at nyght as said is.

ANENT THE WEIGHT OF BREAD.

15th October, 1666.—This said day the haill trade and all in ane vo·ce declares and ordains that everie twa shilling loaf of white bread to be baikin hereafter shall be of weight twenty-seven ounces of raw douche and leaven, and the contravener to be censured at the discretion of the trade. The said day ordains that everie aucht penny loaffe of oat bread shall be of weight nynteen ounces of leaven, the contravener to be at the discretion of the traid.

ANENT BISCUIT BAKING.

21st May, 1667.—The said day it is enacted, statute, and ordained be the deacon and haill traid that no frieman of the traid baik nor sell any

Q

biskit bread at any time hereafter under the pain of forty shillings *toties quoties* to be paid be the delinquent to the boxmaster for use of the poore of the traid ; and siclyk statute and ordain be the deacon and traid that no servant or unfrieman baik nor sell ony bread neither in private nor in public in prejudice of the freiman and maisters with certification that any servant or unfrieman that contravenes this statute shall be utterlie debarred from any service or societie amongst the bakeris in this burgh in all time thereafter.

ANENT THE WEIGHT OF LOAVES.

23rd November, 1669.—Item, it is statute and ordained that ilk wheat halfpenny loaff sall weigh fifteen ounces, and ilk eight penny oat loaff twentie ounces, and ilk two shillings wheat loaff to weigh thirty ounces.

ANENT FINDING SECURITY.

14th January, 1669.—The said day it is enacted and ordained be the haill traid that none who sall hereafter enter friemen of the traid sall come in friemen thereof unless he first give and find a sufficient cautioner for his composition and other things incumbent to him to doe, and that before he supplicate the trade for the said effect, or then to pay and deliver ready money for his said composition.

ANENT LIGHT BREAD.

14th January, 1669.—The said day it is statute and ordained that in all tyme cuming there sall tuo of the traid go through the haill traid weeklie, visiting time about, and notiss and tak inspection of the un-sufficince of bread, and if any of the traid be found guilty theirin to report the same to the deacon and maisters of the traid.

ANENT BANQUETS AND FEASTS.

21st February, 1671.—The said day the haill trade unanimously statute and ordained that in all tyme hereafter there sall be no banquets nor feasts exacted off of ony entrant frieman, but the said feast to be con-verted into money according to the modification of the traid, and to be given into the boxmaster for the use of the craft and the poore thereof. And this to be observit in all tyme to cum without alteration.*

ANENT ALLOWING BOYS TO BAKE SMALL BREAD.

1st August, 1672.—The said day it is statute and ordained that no frieman of the calling give to any of their prentisses or boys any flour of their wheat baiking nor give them libertie to baik any rolls, biskettis, or wastalls for their awin use to sell through the toun, and that under the pain of forty shillings Scots to be paid to the boxmaster be ilk contravener hereof *toties quoties*, for the use of the poore.

* This act soon fell into desuetude.

ANENT BUYING WHEAT FROM STRANGERS.

12th February, 1691.—The said day, by pluralitie of voyces, it is statute and ordained that it sall be noways leasome nor lawful to any frieman of the said traid to buy any wheat or rye be himselff from any extraniner or any other merchant within the said burgh arriving thereat, but the same stuff shall be bocht be the deacon of the craft for the tyme in name and to the utilitie of the haill brethren thereof except the deacon refuse, and that under the failzie of twenty shillings Scots for ilk boll that shall be bocht to be paid to the boxmaster of the said baxter traid for the tym for his contravention without exemption, and this to stand unalterable in all tyme cuming.

ANENT THE BAKING OF BANNOCKS.

25th November, 1678.—The said day the traid statute and ordained that none of the craft baik plack bannaks of oatmeal or pairings under the failzie of four pounds *toties quoties*, and that none suffer the same to be baikin within their baikhouses under the said failzie.

ANENT HAVING MORE THAN ONE SHOP.

24th November, 1685.—The said day it is strictly statute and ordained that whatsomever frieman of the baxter traid that has more stocks or shops than ane, and that sells breed in ane place more than what by the calling sall be called ane stock or shop, the person guilty sall pay to the boxmaster of the craft four pounds Scots for the first fault, and so to be double the *toties quoties*, and this to stand unalterable in all tyme cuming.*

ANENT BAKING PIES.

18th July, 1694.—The traid ordains that no frieman sall baik pyes or taarts or pudens for less than forty pennies or three shillings, and wha contravenes to pay into ther box fortie shillings Scots *toties quoties*, and this to stand unalterable.

ANENT SELLING BISCUITS ON THE STREETS.

4th April, 1716.—The said day the baxter traid by ane voice *nem. con.* enacted and ordained that in all tyme cuming no members of this incorporation, either by themselves, servants, or others whomsoever in their or either of their names, presume to sell ony bisckit through the town, or any other sort of bread whatsomever in tyme cuming under the failzie *toties quoties* of four pounds Scots besides confiscation of the bread so offered to be sold, and this to remain unalterable in all tyme cuming.

ANENT EXTRAORDINARY DRINKING.

5th February, 1717.—The said day the traid taking to serious consideration the great abuses that hath been committed many years bygane

---

* This act was repeatedly re-enacted for the purpose evidently of providing openings for new members

by extraordinary drinking on entrants, for the remeede of which in tyme cuming doe hereby statute and ordain that no say maister chosen by the said traid shall have liberty to drink upon any entrant in any tyme thereafter under the penalty of ten merks Scots money.

ANENT FEMALE PASTRY BAKERS.

12th April, 1726.—The said day the baxter traid taking to their consideration the great loss sustained by this traid through several women within this town thus working in their own houses plum cake, seid cake, sugar biscuit, and other pastry, and bringing the same to the several bakehouses of the freemen of this traid to be by them fired, and which pastry they thereafter sell and vend through the town, for remeid whereof for the future, the said traid hereby statutes and ordains that no freeman of this traid in time coming shall give the use of his oven for firing the above pastrie so wrocht as aforesaid being for sale, and that under the penalty of ten merks Scots.

ANENT THE NUMBER OF APPRENTICES.

17th July, 1732.—Abstract—That no master have serving him more than three apprentices at one and the same time ; no member to take a second until three years of the former apprentice's time be expired ; that no member take in an apprentice until he (the master) has been five years a freeman.

ANENT ADMISSION OF BURGESSES OF GUILD.

11th May, 1738.—Abstract—It was statute and ordained that in all time to cum any member or members of the corporation who shall be admitted burgesses of Guild shall notwithstanding their being so admitted Burgesses of Guild be entitled to, and have the full exercise of their trade and employment without the least molestation.*

ANENT THE BAKER'S DOZEN.

27th October, 1772.—The said day the traid taking under their consideration a practice which has of late prevailed among the members thereof in regard to the way and manner practised by them in disposing upon and selling of bread, by allowing to their customers and others who purchased from them at the rate of thirteen for the dozen of small bread, and so on in proportion, it is hereby statute and ordained that any member doing so shall be declared incapable of holding office, &c.

ANENT GIFTS OF SWEETIE LOAVES.

18th August, 1777.—Abstract—It is ordained that all members of the craft charge their customers and others who may employ them one penny sterling for each roast, tart, pudding, and pye that shall be roasted, fired,

* This Act was cancelled by order of the Magistrates.

and prepared in their oven ; one penny halfpenny sterling the dozen for dry bread, and four pennies sterling for casting and firing the pound weight of seed cake, and the one half of the said sum when only fired, and they do hereby abolish their former practice of complimenting their customers with sweetie loaves or any kind of loaves whatsoever at Christmas or at any other time of the year.*

From an entry in the Council Register in 1674, it would appear as if the Aberdeen bakers had not been giving satisfaction to the inhabitants. In that year "Alexander Bruce, baker in Edinburgh, was allowed to supply the inhabitants with bread, and admitted a burgess on account of the bakers of the town being deficient in making good bread."

The price of wheat and flour was fixed by the Trade at intervals when a change was deemed necessary, and the deacon had also power to regulate the quantities that were to be allocated to each master baker. In 1634, the Trade assumed the function of ordering each baker to have a separate mark for his bread, and two of the members were appointed to "go through the town to tak imposition of insufficient bread." The following are a number of entries as to the prices :—

6th May, 1665.—No flour to be sold under auchteen shillings the peck.

18th September, 1666.—No wheat to be bought higher than ten merks the boll, " unless that the pryce rise."

12th September, 1667.—No wheat to be bought above seven pounds the boll.

23rd November, 1669.—No wheat to be purchased above ten merks the boll, and no flour to be sold under sixteen shillings ilk peck.

13th December, 1670.—No wheat to be purchased above seven pounds Scots the boll, and no flour to be sold under eighteen shillings ilk peck.

7th November, 1671.—No wheat to be sold above seven pounds ilk boll.

4th February, 1673.—No flour to be sold under sixteen shillings ilk peck.

20th November, 1673.—No wheat to be bought above six pounds the boll, and rye four pounds ten shillings the boll.

12th May, 1674.—Flour not to be sold under twenty shillings Scots ilk peck.

11th September, 1719.—No wheat to be bought above six pounds Scots each boll, and rye four pounds and ha'f a merk per boll.

* All the members present—eighteen in number—signed this Act.

An arrangement was entered into in 1711 under which a monthly inspection was to take place, the bakers agreeing to it in the following minute :—

6th February, 1711.—The deacon gave in ane act of the Town Council anent the weight of bread, and appointing him to survey the sufficiencie of the baxters' bread monthly, and to report to the magistrates under the respective failizie therein contained as the said extract of the said act under the hand of the town-clerk, dated the 16th day of May, 1705, and the traid considering the benefit and justice of the said they hereby ratify and homologat and confirm the same in the whole circumstances thereof.

The essays which were prescribed at different periods for entrant bakers give a good indication of the various kinds of work performed by bakers. Previous to 1669 it is merely stated that the entrant shall "mak ane sufficient essay," but after that date the articles to be made were, as will be seen from the following extracts, specifically described :—

14th January, 1669.—The said day it is statute and ordained that all those who sall enter frieman of the said traid hereafter sall have for his say, first to peit the oven, and his say to be ane ait bakin, and a wheat baikin, with ane pye with six corners, and ane coffine of ane wheat pye with six houssis with ane bannack of six two shilling quheat bread.

10th February, 1714.—Appoints the petitioner to peet the oven the night before working, his say is to be to take ane boll of wheat of the growth of the shire of Aberdeen, and to mill the same, and that for taking off the heit of the oven, to baik ane batch of oat loaves, as also ane batch of white loaves, consisting of half ane boll of flour with ane ry consisting of half ane peck of flour formally wrocht, and ane dish of minced pyes consisting of nynteen in number ; and that he sall tak an exact course of the oven so that the bread baiken may be baised ; and that he sall tak up so much watter to each batch as may fully serve without addition ; all this to be performed in the deacon's baikhous.

14th September, 1719.—Appoints the say to be as follows :—Ane boll of wheat of the growth of the shire of Aberdeen to be milled and dressed be himself : half ane boll of flour thereof to be boutted and baiken be him in white loaves well baken, baised, and crusted with ane bannock of six two shilling loaves ; and also ane batch of oat loaves consisting of half ane boll of meal, and ane pye, consisting of eight houses, containing six or eight fowls ; and ane large pudding to fill ane six pound plate ; all to be formally wrocht, and to peet the oven before working the same.

17th July, 1781.—Appoints the essay to be ane boll of wheat to be dressed by himself, ane half thereof to be baked in loaves well baked, and crusted with a bannock of nine two penny loaves ; six pecks of meal in oat loaves ; a florentine of fowls ; a florentine of beef ; and a dish of tarts, seventeen in the dish of preserves and prunes, two feet diameter, the whole to be formally wrocht, well baked, and seasoned with his own hand the liquor and seasoning to be taken up at once without any addition, which essay to be wrocht in the deacon's bakehouse, the meat to be seasoned and the oven peated the night before working.

8th March, 1796.—The essay appointed to be a bannock of eighteen two penny loaves from a batch to be well crusted and the seasoning and liquor to be taken up at once ; to make a dish of seventeen tarts prunes and preserves two feet diameter ; two florentines of eight hens in two plates ; two apple pies and two florentines of mutton ; two dozen of cheese cakes, to be wrocht in the deacon's bakehouse.

9th November, 1808.—Essay appointed be six two penny loaves from a batch to be well crusted and the seasoning and liquor to be taken at once, which he obliges himself to execute with his own hands.

It was the custom in the Baker Trade to make a meal of the essay after it had been duly inspected and found sufficient. The essay at present prescribed is similar to the one last mentioned.

If the number of convictions recorded in the books of this Trade is to be taken as a criterion of the general conduct of the bakers, it must be acknowledged that strict adherence to the letter of the law could not have been a cardinal virtue among them in olden days. The craft met for the transaction of business far more frequently than any of the others—once or twice a week as a rule, the principal business being to fix the price of bread and to punish offenders. Their meetings appear to have been of a statutory character, as not unfrequently the minute runs—" The said day the court met and adjourned." The following are a few out of the numerous convictions recorded :—

12th February, 1691.—The said day the boys and prentisses under subscribend enacted themselves not to play at dyce nor cards, nor to keep uncivil and begarly company in tyme hereafter, under the failzie of forty shillings, *toties quoties*. [Follow the names of a number of boys.]

4th April, 1694.—The said John Marishall, prentiss to James Douglass, was amerciat in twentie shillings, to be payt to the boxmaster, for his playing at the cairts, and was ordained to pay other fortie shillings in case he be found in the like transgression which he hereby adheres to.

28th January, 1697.—The said day John Buchan and William Donald was amerciat ilk ane of them in twentie shillings Scots for abusing ane another in presence of the deacon, and both of them oblige themselves not to abuse ane anither either be word or deed under the failzie of four pounds Scots, to be payt for the use of the poore in case any contravene their presents by and attour what other censure the craft shall put on them.

17th September, 1634.—The said day Andrew Thomson, prentiss to Alexander Williamsone, baxter, is convicit in ane unlaw of ane rex dollar, to be payt by him to the craft, for nicht walking, shouting, and debording on the nicht when people wess in their beddes, as was clearly proven, and whilk he could not deny, and gif he be found doing the like hereafter sall doubill unlaw.

17th October, 1717.—The said day George Watson, servant to John Kelly, enacted himself to attend upon the public worship profest be the Protestant religion upon the Lord's day when able to goe thereto, and noe ways to be found vaging or straying either alone or in company on the Sabbath dayes in tym hereafter in tyme of divine service, and that under what penalty the baxter traid of this place for the tyme shall be pleased to impose.—(Signed) GEORGE WATSON.

18th February, 1729.—The same day David Lindsay, gave in a complaint to the traid that David Moncrieff, contrary to the oath taken at his admission, had revealed some of the secrets of this trade ; as also that the said David Moncrieff has aspersed the said David Lindsay by saying that when any meal was given in to him to be bakin the said David Lindsay took by two pecks thereof for his own use, upon which the said David Moncrieff being examined, he absolutely refused that ever he uttered any such expression. In testimony whereof he hath signed hereto.—(Signed) DAVID MONCRIEFF.

19th December, 1766.—The traide having met and taken into their serious consideration the dangerous and audacious riot and tumult which happened in this burgh upon the night betwixt Thursday last and this morning, which tends not only to the subversion of all good order and the danger and hurt of all the inhabitants, but also threatens this burgh with a real scarcity of provisions by deterring the farmers and others dealing in victual from bringing meal into the mercat, which has hitherto, by the great care and vigilance of the magistrates and corporations, been more plentifully supplied, and at a lower price than most other parts in Britain, and though some of those who are present at these lawless insurrections may not be active therein, yet by their presence they increase the disorder, therefore, they unanimously resolved that such of their apprentices, journeymen, or servants as shall be found in any mob or tumult within this burgh or neighbourhood shall be deprived of the libertie of entering freemen, and they further resolved that no person so offending shall at any time hereafter be employed by any freeman of Aberdeen, and that each of the masters will do their utmost to discover and inform upon such of their servants as shall be concerned in any riots or tumults hereafter, that they may be convicted and punished according to the law.

In addition to maintaining a " dask " or loft in one of the

city churches, as well as in the Trinity Chapel, the bakers, as will be seen from the following minute, erected a seat in the old St. Paul's Chapel (Episcopalian):—

17th February, 1725.—The said day the baxter traid taking to their consideration that this traid mostly are hearers of the Word of God in St. Paul's Chappell in Aberdeen, and that the said traid have no place for their accommodation in the said chappell, they hereby authorise and empower their present-deacon and masters to agree with a sufficient workman for building a seat for the said traid in the said chappell upon the public charge of the baxter traid, for which this shall be warrant.

The estate of Kincorth, Nellfield Cemetery, Garden Neuk, Gilcomston; Butts of Footdee, and feu-duties in Tannery Street are the principal properties belonging to this Incorporation.

Underneath the emblazoned arms of the Baker Trade painted on their "brod," in the Hall, is the following panegyric on the craft:—

> When from the shades of Night and Chaos came,
> This vast round Globe, and Heav'n's all beauteous frame,
> The same dread Word that stretch'd the ample sky,
> And bad bright Orbs in myriads rowl on high,
> Commanded from the fertile womb of Earth,
> The vegetable kinds to take their Birth;
> Each various fruit: and chief the gen'rous grain,
> The favour'd race of Mankind to sustain.
> Obedient at his call each springing field,
> Verdant with Life abundant Harvests yield,
> Which, ev'n tho' ripe, were crude in some degree,
> For Heav'n provides, but man the cook must be:
> By careful art, and all-correcting fire,
> Refin'd and Bak'd, they answer'd each desire;
> Diffusing strength thro' all the human frame,
> And aiding, with glad-warmth, the vital flame.
> Hence comes the swain's brisk mein and healthful air,
> And that gay bloom that crowns the sprightly fair;
> Then, let the BAKER with due praise be crown'd,
> And Floreant Pistores echo round—
> So old, so universal is our Trade,
> So useful, that the staff of life is Bread;
> And, what immediately does life sustain,
> Of ev'ry art the precedence should gain.
> In various forms we work the yielding paste,
> To strength adapt it, and to curious taste:

And while we rev'rence Heav'n's Omnific Pow'r,
We imitate His works in miniature ;
As from the formless chaos of the paste,
Which, with fermenting fluids we conjest,
Loves rise, like worlds, from our creating hand,
And various figures rise at our command.
O'er our fair Labours, artful we diffuse,
Choice cordial sweets, and rich ambrosial dews,
Consign'd to the deep oven's glowing cell,
They, in their mimic Purgatory, dwell,
Till time suffice, then forth they come releas'd,
Fragrant to smell and grateful to the taste.
In mathematick form the pye we rear,
Which, like some sumptuous castle does appear,
Beasts, fowls, and fruits, the Magazines supply,
Which round the crusted walls we fortify.
Magnificently roof'd it stands in state,
Till scal'd and plunder'd by some potentate.
Without our aid, what regal table's spread ?
What Hero fights without the strength of Bread ?
Round the wide world, our labour still is dear,
To soldier, sailer, peasant, prince, and peer.
The priest and lawyer's vocal lungs we aid,
And help the merchant to pursue his trade.
What Nymph so lovely, or of birth so high,
But will to pastry her soft hands apply ;
And who the occupation shall despise,
Which ev'n the fair disdain not to practise.
But higher yet, our honours we pursue,
Angels ate bread, and angels bak'd it too ;
Abra'm, the friend of God, in Mamre's plain,
Three angels once did kindly entertain.
Fine flour his princely spouse did knead and bake,
And social they, of human food partake.
And once Elijah, wand'ring in the wild,
By haughty Iezebel's proud threats exil'd,
As stretch'd beneath a juniper he lay,
Slumbring and faint, and far from human way,
An angel, Heav'n-descended, form'd a cake,
And to divine refreshment bid him wake.
Tho' we have angel's sanction, yet our cause
Fresh lawrels from the prince of angels draws ;
When, here on earth, he taught us how to pray,
Give us our daily Bread he bid us say ;
Nor is it foreign to our honour'd trade,
That with five loaves, five thousand souls He fed.

He too, the mystick presence did consign
Of his own flesh and blood, to bread and wine,
Ev'n He, by whom the numerous worlds were made,
Partook on Earth the sustenance of Bread ;
And after his ascention from the grave ;
When to the twelve He his third presence gave,
Them fishing on Tiberian waves, He call'd,
And to the shore, their loaded netts they haul'd ;
When to a fire, and bread thereon prepar'd
By His own hands, which He amongst them shar'd.
While thus with noblest Trades we boast our part,
Nor yield to any in the sphere of Art,
May He, the Sun of Righteousness, display,
On all our actions his celestial ray ;
May we in peace our daily bread possess,
And smiling Providence our labours bless ;
Contented may we live, and die resign'd,
And, in the skies, a crown of glory find.

CHAPTER IX.

THE WRIGHT AND COOPER TRADE.

WORKING the same material, and using very much the same class of tools, it was natural that the Wrights and Coopers should club together into one association. It has generally been supposed that Masons were at one time associated with the Wrights and Coopers, but there is no evidence that this was the case farther than that the Masons are mentioned in the Seal of Cause granted in 1532 to the "Couparis, Wrichts, and Measones." This does not imply that these crafts formed one association. At that time each craft had its separate deacon, and it was not until nearly a century after that date that the Wrights and Coopers came to act under one deacon and one set of office-bearers. The Masons appear to have kept by themselves, and there are good grounds for believing that their Incorporation or Trade was the nucleus of what ultimately became the Aberdeen Mason Lodge. In the oldest minute-book belonging to the Aberdeen Lodge there are inscribed the "Laws and statutes for Measones, gathered out thir old wreatings by us, who ar the authoires and subscribeiers of this booke," and these laws and statutes bear such a close resemblance to those enacted by the other crafts in the town, that there is little room for doubt that the original organization was constituted in a manner similar to the other craft associations.

The coopering trade was very early established in Aberdeen in connection with the curing of fish, at one time the staple industry in Aberdeen. About the year 1280 large quantities of salmon and salt fish were sent to different parts of England in barrels, and the Aberdeen coopers seemed to have been famed for the quality of the casks they produced. This was an opinion which the coopers themselves held down to quite a recent period. In 1740 they enacted that no coopers were to be

WRIGHTS AND COOPERS [168].—Quarterly. First: Gules, a tower of Aberdeen. Second: Gules, a compass or. Third: Azure, a square or. Fourth: Azure, a wright's axe argent, slassed or. Motto: *Our Redeemer liveth for ever.*

WRIGHTS AND COOPERS [6th April, 1696. *New Grant*]. — Quarterly. First: Gules, a wright's compass or. Second: Azure, a cooper's axe argent. Third: Azure, a square or. Fourth: Gules, a cooper's compass or. Over all, on an escutcheon, the Coat of the Royal Burgh of Aberdeen [Gules, three towers triple-towered, within a double tressure flowered and counter-flowered argent]. Above the shield, on a suitable helmet with a mantle gules doubled argent, and wreath or, gules, argent and azure, is set for crest an adder in circle proper, with this motto in an escroll above: *Our Redeemer liveth for ever.*

■

employed except they served their apprenticeship in the town, "as the coupars of Aberdeen have been long famous for the best work all over the kingdom, so they could not be so much answerable for a journeyman's work who had not been bred with some of themselves." Like the bakers, each cooper had his own special mark, and their work was supervised by the magistrates, for the purpose of seeing that all barrels were of sufficient measure. On 8th October, 1507, it was enacted by the Council "that all couparis mak sufficient barrelis of mesour, efter the law of the realme, and consuetud of this burghe, and ilkan man set his avne merk to his avne werk; and quhay failzeis hereintill, to be punisit efter the tenour and rigour of the law." Previous to the practice of preserving salmon in ice, all the salmon exported either to England or the Continent, were packed in barrels or kits and pickled with salt and vinegar, as many as 1500 barrels of salmon being exported in the course of a year. The price of salmon barrels was fixed from time to time by the magistrates, in accordance with the price of staves. On 17th April, 1729, the magistrates appointed that the coopers "shall for the year following have for each salmond barrell, and for packing, ticketing, and double girding of the same, three pound Scots, and no more, the price of the staves fitt for salmond barrells being presently forty-two pounds Scots the thousand; and they appoint the coupers of the burgh to observe this Act under the failzie of five pounds Scots, to be paid to the Dean of Guild for each transgression."

A couple of centuries ago the coopers were extensive importers of timber, and in so doing they frequently came into collision with the Burgesses of Guild. On 15th June, 1641, "William Andersone and John Makie, coupers, friemen of the burgh, were convict of thair awne confessioun for frauchting of William Walker, skiper, his ship laitlie to Norroway, contrair to the priviledgis and liberties of craftismen, and bringing of the said ship to the burghe loadenit with timber and dailles contrair to the privileges and liberties of the said burge as said is, and thereby usurping the libertie of gild burgessis whairanent they referrit themselffis in the counsillis will, be thair supplication subscruit with their hand. For the quhilk the said Wm. Andersone and Johne Makie wer unlawit in the soume of ane hundrethe poundis to be payit equallie betwixt tham to the deane of gild ; and ordains the said dean of gild to buy the said loadening frae the sadis couparis for the use of the toun as he buyes the lyk commodities frome strangeris and unfriemen be resone they have no richt to traid with oversea wairis." The fact of a couple of coopers being able to freight a cargo—small though the craft might have been at that period—is a good indication of the extent to which the coopering trade was carried on in the town.

In addition to a Seal of Cause granted in 1527, a second grant of privileges was made to the masons, wrights, carvers, coopers, slaters, and painters, under which each of the crafts mentioned had power to elect its own deacon. The masons, as already mentioned, developed into a free mason lodge, the painters amalgamated with the hammermen in their capacity as glaziers, the carvers remained eligible for membership among the wrights ; but as to the slaters, we have been unable to discover whether they had any corporate existence. That they were looked after by the magistrates is, however apparent from the following entry in the Council Register :—

28th June, 1648.—The said day the Counsell considering the exorbitant pryces taken be the sklaitters from all they work too, of their extortioning of the inhabitants of this burghe, for remeid hereof, and restraining sic exorbitanires in tyme coming, statute and ordaines that every maister sall have 24s. ilk day without meat or drink : and everie man that works with the trewall 12s. daylie, and the carier of the lyme 6s. 8d. daylie, all but meat or drink, except those they work to sall be pleasit of thair owne accord ; and this statute to endure during the Counsellis plesure.—*Council Register, vol.* liii., *p.* 169.

The following are the Seals of Cause granted in 1527 and 1541 :—

Curia Ballivorum burgi de Aberdeen tenta in pretorie ejusdem quinto die Mensis Augusti, Anno Domini Millesimo quingentisimo Vicesimo Septimo.

The said day the Provost, Baillies, and Council of this burgh of Aberdeen with consent and assent of all the neighbours of the town being present for the time representing the haill body of the town, gave, granted and assigned to their lovit neighbours and servitors John Souper, James

Wright, and George Baxter, deacons of the Coopers, Wrights, and Masons crafts for this instant year, and to their successors, deacons of the said crafts for ever and all manner of time to come, their full, free, and plain power and licence to receive, uptake, and inbring of every brother of the said crafts that enters of new to work within the said burgh for his entry silver half a merk at his first beginning; of every master that fees of new an apprentice at the entry of the said apprentice half a merk; of every feed man that works for meat and fee yearly one pound of wax; and likewise of every master man of the said crafts every week one penny of offering, which entry silver, apprentice silver, weekly offering, and yearly pound of wax of the servants shall be well, truly, and faithfully gathered by certain masters of the said crafts, and truly spent in the decoring, upholding, and repairing of St. John, Evangelist's Altar within the parish kirk of Aberdeen, their special patron in Imagerie, vestments and towels, chandeliers, desks, lights, and all other ornaments required to the service of God and of their said patron, and attour the said Provost and Baillies, Council and community give grant and assign to the said deacons and to their successors, their full plain and powers express jurisdiction and authority to correct, punish, and amend all manner of crimes, trespasses, and faults of the said crafts, or committee of the brethren and servants of the same crafts, ontak bluid and ditt; with the power to onlaw and amerciate the said trespassers and committers of the said faults, the unlaws and amerciaments be applied to uptak and inbring: Providing always that the said unlaws and amerciements be applied to the honour and decoration of the said patron, with all the duties above written, shall be put to the greatest profit that may be by the advice of the said crafts to the honour and utility of the said patron as they will to God, their patron and their own consciences, by the advice and consideration of all the masters of the said crafts, whilk masters and each of them shall yearly decorate their said patron with an honest candle of a pound of wax, and uphold the same, and in this way God willing the said patron and chaplainry shall be honestly decorated, and doted with all necessaries effeiring to the honour of God and their said patron.*

Be it kend till all men be thir presents, us provost, baillies, counsill, and communitie of the burgh of Aberdeen, To have given and committed, and be the tenour hereof gives, grants, and commits to our neighbours and craftsmen under written, That is to say, measons, wrights, carvers, coupers, sclaters, painters, and to the deacons of the samen crafts and to their successors or actuall indwellers in our said burgh our full, free, plain power, privilige, and authority upon all and sundry occupiers, users, and exercisers of our said craft, within the freidome of Aberdeen. To correct, punish the tresspassers, their own laws and amerciaments, and to take and unbring

* From a parchment copy written in modern style by William Carnegie, Town Clerk, in 1793.

the utilities and common weal of the said craft; and to do justice to all
parties complainen of the said craftsmen intill their actions (blood and blae
reserved to us and our punition); acts and statutes among themselves to
make and cause to be keepit, to the honour of God and St. John, their
patron, and utilitie of the said craft frae the present the said act as an
statute to us first, and they be admitted to us as consonant to justice and
reason (and not else), with power to choice deacons of the saids crafts,
they being condign and worthy to choyce the said office, and be admitted
by us thereto whilks shall answer to us, to all and sundrie neighbours,
masters, servants, and prentises of the said crafts for their faults and crimes
that lyes under their correction if they leave such faults unpunished whilks
neighbours, masters, servants, and apprentices we shall cause intend and
obey their said deacons and their successors in all time to come in all liesome things concerning their said crafts or any point thereof, and if any of
them disobey and beis contemptuous to the said deacons and to their
statutes made by them and admitted be us as said is they complain to us
thereupon, and we shall cause them be obeyed and the deforcers, desobey-
ers, and contemors really punished theirfor in their persons or goods as we
shall advise for the time; and also we ratefie and approves and confirms
that no freeman shall be made of the said crafts neither be us nor our
successors until he be examined be the deacons of the said crafts and found
sufficient by experience of his work and presented to us be the said
deacons as an convenient and able person to be made freemen of his craft
or he be admitted be us thereto, and that none be sufficient to hold and
uptake an booth of his own to occupie the foresaid crafts to joyse the
privilege of an freeman untill the time that he be made free admitted be
us advice of the deacons of the said crafts as said is. And generally all
and sundry our privileges to joyse and brook and exerce that concerns the
said crafts to the common weal thereof, and of our said burgh, conform to
the old laudable use and consent of privileges grantit be us and our predecessors in tymes bygone to be observed in all times to come, providing
always that this gift of authoritie and privilege make no derogation to the
Act of Parliament made of new anent craftsmen in our Sovereign lords
last Parliament, and we, the said Provost, Council, and communitie, binds
and obliges us and our successors magistrates to keep and defend all and
sundrie the liberties, gifts, and privileges above written to the craftsmen
foresaid, and to defend them and their successors thereintill, but without
revocation or obstacle in all times to come against all deadly. In witness
of the whilk to this our gift of privilege we have appended the common
seal of the said burgh, together with the subscriptions manuall of the
said provost and baillies att Aberdeen, the sixteenth day of April, one
thousand five hundred fourty one years. Sic. Sub. Thomas Menzies,
Provost; Andrew Menzies, David Anderson.

A ratification of this grant of privileges is recorded in
the Council Register (vol. xvi., p. 785) as follows :—

6th May, 1541.—The said day the haill towne present for the tyme consentit and assentit to the giving of the privileges to the wrichts, messownis, cowpers, carvars, and painters, read be the provost in judgment. And affermis the samin and ordains thair commond seill to be affixit to the samin and charges the keeparis of the same to seill the foresaid privilege.—*Council Register, vol.* xvi., *p.* 785.

The wrights complained to the Magistrates in 1565 against unfreemen being allowed to labour and exercise the craft, whereby those who were free of the craft were skaithed and deprived of their means of livelihood, and the Council granted them the following special privilege :—

7th July, 1565.—The said day anent ye supplicatioune presented and exhybit unto ye provost, baillies, and counsell be Androw Bisset and Gilbert Andersone, dekynis of ye wrychtis in name of ye remanint friemen of thair said craft, complenand that yai ar hurt and wrangit in ye libertie of thair craft be unfremen that ar sufferit to labour and use ye exertionne of thair craft within yis burgh quhair throw quhilkis ar friemen of thair craft and scottis and lottis, wachis, walkis, and wards, can skantlie get be thair laubour thair necessar sustentation. And thairof desyrit ye provost, baillies, and counsell to menteynie thair libertie and privilege that na unfriemen be sufferit to use and exerce ye said Wrycht Craft within yis burght bot thai only quhilk ar free of thair craft and thai obleist thame to guarantee ye toune sufficientlie for reasonabill expenss to be modifeit be ye counsell having consideration of thair wyffs, bairns, and familie, and sic thingis as belangis to the sustentatioun thairof ; quhilk supplicatioune and desyir ye provost, baillies, and counsell thocht reasonabill and grantit thairto, and obleist thame to observe ye same, and with consent of ye said dekynis modifeit ye expenss and stipend of thair labour as follows :—That is to say, ilk maister to have for his dais labour aucht penies besyd his ordinar meit and drink, without his ordinar coistis, to have thre schillings for his dais labour, and his feit servant that can labour to have xiid. in ye day besyd his costs, and twa schillings without his costs, and prentisses to have be discretionne as beis appointed betwix ye maister of ye wark and ye warkman, and as ye pris of victuallis and viciaris rysis, or diminissis ye prices and expenses foresaid to be alterat be the counsell in reasonable maner.—*Council Register, vol.* xxv., *p.* 617.

About the end of the sixteenth century the wrights and coopers agreed to act under one deacon, the arrangement being that the wrights and coopers should have the privilege of electing the deacon alternately. This arrangement was "homologat and approven" in 1694 in the following terms :—" In presence of George Leslie and Alexander Gordone, baylyes, it is statute and ordanit unanimously be the haill traid, for holding and keeping peace and concord amongst them as formerly, and also according to antient practique, that ane wright be still deacone to the traid for ane year, and ane couper for ane other year, and so to continue, *vicissim*, tyme about.   And upone the day of election, only the thrie maisters of that traid who falls to be deacone to go downe staires, and not the haill six maisters, and this to be observed in all time coming."

No attempt was made to break through this arrangement until the annual election of 1833, when a motion to discontinue the rotation system was carried by the casting-vote of the deacon.   An election followed under the new arrangement, but an action was immediately raised by the dissentients in the Court of Session to have the minutes of election reduced and annulled.   The minority were successful, the old order was re-established, and the majority were found liable in expenses.   In course of time the number of coopers became greatly reduced, chiefly in consequence of the substitution of boxes instead of barrels for packing salmon and other kinds of fish, and a difficulty often arose in finding a sufficient number of coopers to fill one-half of the offices.   Accordingly, in 1874, an agreement was entered into with consent of the whole members, that the old order should be abolished, and this arrangement has been allowed to remain undisturbed.

Both the wrights and the coopers were in the habit of taking their goods to be sold at the Market Cross when "the Timmer Market" was a weekly, in place of a yearly, institution.   All kinds of furniture were made by the wrights in early times, cabinetmakers not being known until a comparatively recent period.   The wrights frequently complained to the magistrates against the unfreemen of the Old Town coming to the Market Cross to sell their goods, and in consequence of the frequent encroachments the following prohibition was issued :—

22nd April, 1691.—In presence of the Provost, Baillies, and Counsell of the burgh of Aberdeen, the said day anent the petition given in to them by James Colinsone, deacon of the Wright and Cooper Trade of Aberdeen, for himself, and in name and in behalf of the rest of the said calling; mentioning that whereas they had several Acts of Counsell in their favour, approvan of and confirmed by their predecessors, that no wark should come to the public mercatt in the said burgh but what should be revised by the Dean of Guild, and deacon of the said calling to con- sider the sufficiency thereof, in respect that the inhabitants of the same are mightly prejudiced thereby, especially by the unfriemen of the Old Town and others within the town and freedom in bringing in upon mercatt days unsufficient chaires and all other work belonging to the said Wright and Cooper Trade contrary to the privileges and Acts of Counsell concurred in their favours. Therefore desiring the said Provost and Counsell to take the premises to their serious consideration and to homo- logate their former acts concerned in their Trade's favour thereanent for visiting of the mercatts weekly, and to punish the transgressors according as they should find expedient; which petition the said provost, baillies, and counsell having heard, seen, and considered, and being ripely and att length advised therewith, and with the said acts of counsell in their favour, do hereby homologate and approve the same; and hereby ordaines and appoints the said James Colinsone, deacon, aforesaid, to revise and take inspection of all timber work brought to the Mercatt Cross of Aber- deen to be sold, such as chairs, and all other work belonging to the said Trade by any unfreemen ilk mercatt day, and in all time coming after the date of thir presents, the said provost, baillies, and counsell being always judges therein, and to collect and ingather the said fines accordingly for the use of the town.

The oldest minute-book, which is dated 1682, contains, as the preface bears, "the acts and statutes recorded in their former books, and now ratified and homologat and approved, 1684." These are as follows :—

ANENT KEEPING THE SABBATH.

Item, it is statute and ordained for the glory of God and good example of neighbours that ilk freeman with their servants and prentices keep the holy Sabbath at divine service both forenoon and afternoon, and that none wilfully absent themselves therefrom under the pains following, namely—the master shall pay six shillings eight pennies, and the prentice or servant three shillings four pennies scots money *toties quoties*. And that none be playing at links, bowls, or other pastimes, or drinking in taverns or ailhouses in time of divine service under the pain of double unlaws; and that there be ane visitor of the said crafts that shall go throw the town and pairts thereabout to try the breakers and violators of this ordinance; and when they apprehend such persons, masters or prentices, to make declaration thereof to the Deacon-Conveener, or the deacon of their own craft, to the effect they may take such order there- with as appertains, and that by and attour what censure the kirk-session shall put upon them. And this to stand unalterable in all time cuming.

ANENT BITTER AND DESPITEFUL SPEAKING.

It is statute and ordained that none of the said crafts, superior or inferior, shall use any bitter, dispiteful, or litigious language either to molest ane another before the court, or at any man's table where the crafts shall happen to be in companie, but honestly and humbly reason ane with ane other with reverence, and leave askit and given by the company convenit. And whasomever transgresses the same he shall be debarred fra the company till his fault be confessed, and to be in the crafts amerciament, and his unlaw to be fourtie shillings scots *toties quoties*.*

ANENT APPEALING TO OTHER COURTS.

Item, it is statute and ordained be the deacon and masters that none of the occupiers of the said crafts, masters, servants, or prentices shall not gang before no judge, spiritual or temporal, with no wrong nor injurie (except blood or blae) whatever, before the deacon and masters of the craft, and the fault being instructed and made out before them ; and whosoever contravene the same, his unlaw be taken up and unforgiven, as it shall please the craft to modifie.

ANENT THE ELECTION OF DEACONS.

In presence of George Leslie and Alexander Gordon, baillies, it is statute and ordained unanimously by the haill traid for holding and keeping peace and concord amongst them as formerly, and also according to ancient practique, that ane wright be still deacon to the traid for ane year, and ane coupar for ane other year, and so to continue *viccissim* tyme about. And upoune the day of election only the thrie masters of that traid who falls to be deacone to goe down staires, and not the haill six masters, and this to be observed in all tyme coming.

ANENT ATTENDANCE AT MEETINGS.

Item, it is ordained that any disobedient person, warned to the court be the officiar after the hour appoynted, being within the town, shall pay in fines for his absence four shillings scots, and to be poynded therefore except he show ane reasonable excuse. ·

ANENT APPRENTICES.

Item, it is statute and ordained that no prentice be accepted by any of the freemen for fewer years than five, and one year thereafter for meat and fee ; failing to do so he is to lose the benefit of his prentisship and be classed as an extranean.

* Among the few breaches of this act recorded is the following :—

2nd April, 1735.—The court, considering that Adam Baxter called William Moir a brute in presence of the court, they therefor amerciate him, the said Adam Baxter, in fourty shillings Scots, to be paid by him to the trade, for use of the poor, for the said transgression, in terms of the third act of this book ; and debar him from voting in any affair of the trade until satisfaction be made before the court, which being paid by the said Adam Baxter, the trade discharge the above amerciament, and ordered the said sum of forty shillings to be repaid to him.

ANENT SUMMER AND WINTER WORKERS.

The deacons and remanent masters and members of the said traid having taken into their serious consideration the great damage and disadvantage which did redound and befall to them through accepting, hiring, and feeing of unfreemen or journeymen in the winter quarter who spent their time and labours in the country in the summer quarter when the freemen of the said traid hath greatest necessitie of them ; they for remeid thereanent have statute and ordained, and be thir presents with unanimous consent and assent for themselves and their successors in their said offices, statute and ordains that every freemen of the said traid who shall accept of any unfreeman or journeyman, hereafter in winter that uses and frequents to work in the country in the summer, shall pay to the boxmaster of the said traid for the time the sum of six pounds Scots, *toties quoties*, who shall be convictit of the said fault, and found guilty of the said transgression, and this act to stand unalterable in all time coming.

ANENT "DIGHTED" DEALS.

16th April, 1698.—The said day by voyce of court, it is strictlie statute and ordained that no frieman of the wright traid, work ony deals dighted on both syds and sex and greeped for less pryce than four shillings Scots ilk daill ; and ony daills dighted upon the ane syde and sex and greeped for less price than three shillings four pennies for ilk dail, and ilk clift at three shillings four pennies sex and greeped. And also that no cooper mak and pack salmond barrell for less price than four marks for ilk barrell. Likewise it is statute and ordained that whatsomever person or persons, either wright or cooper, shall happen to transgress in the premises, and that the same be proven against them any manner of way, that the person or persons transgressors shall pay to the boxmaster for the time for the use of the poor ten marks Scots money, to be uplifted and unforgiven, and ordains this act to stand in all tyme coming.

ANENT WHEELWRIGHTS.

30th August, 1709.—The whilk day the wright and cooper trade considering that the wheelwrights may several ways encroach upon their trades and airts which may occasion debates in the incorporation, for preventing of all mistakes and encroachments compeared the said Charles Ramsay, wheelwright, and bind and obliged him for himself and in name and behalf of his successors wheelwrights, that he nor they shall not in all tyme coming meddle with nor taking on them to make or mend any wright or coupar whatsomever, or any other airt thereto belonging, but allenarly with wheelwright wark, or what may directly concern the same, under the pain of fourty pounds to be paid to the boxmaster at the time by an attour forfaulture or privileges and benefits in the said traid, that they shall not receive or permit any wright or coupar, servant or journeyman whatsomever, in no tyme coming to work in their shops.

ANENT CARRYING WEAPONS.

3rd October, 1704.—The said day it is statute and ordained by unanimous consent in presence of Patrick Whyt, Deacon Convener, that no member whatsomever of the said incorporation shall come either to court or meeting wherever the same be, with long rules, compasses, gaiges, or any private weapon, and whosoever contravenes the premises, and brings either to meetings or courts, weapons or any working instrument, excepting folding rules, shall pay twenty shillings scots *toties quoties* before he who shall happen to contravene shall have vote or concern in the said traid.

ANENT DRINKING.

17th March, 1707.—The same day the haill traid unanimously statute and ordain that none whatever, servants or prentice, visit, convene, or debauch, and drink together to the scandal of the incorporation, nor shall they be tollarat to take on them the title of deacon, boxmaster, or other members of the traids as they have done heretofore ; and in case the same abuses do continue among servants, the contraveners thereof shall in no time coming have any benefit in the traid, besides further censure as the traid thinks fit to impose.

ANENT COMBINATIONS AMONG WORKMEN.

27th June, 1732.—Abstract—The trade condemning the many and great abuses and evil practices that have lately crept in amongst and prevailed with their journeymen and servants, and their entering into signed associations among themselves whereby they become bound to one another under a penalty not to continue in their master's service or to work after seven o'clock at night contrary to the usual practice.   .   .   . The trade approve the acts made against meetings of servants and apprentices, fixing the hours from 6 a.m. to 8 p.m., and no master to employ journeymen who had been dismissed for breach of this ordinance.

ANENT COOPERS' APPRENTICES.

6th February, 1747.—It is statute and ordained that no freeman of the Coupar Trade shall at any time hereafter employ as a servant or journeyman any stranger or others who hath not served ane apprenticeship to some member of the Trade within their burgh, because as this Trade have great trust from the merchants both in receiving, curing, and packing their fish, pork, and beef, whereof embezzlement could be made without being easily discovered, and that the masters must often entrust their servants by themselves with the doing thereof, so they cannot with the same certainty answer for the fidelity of stranger servants as they can for those who have served apprenticeships in town, and have given testimony of their honesty ; besides it being a piece of justice due to apprentices and an encouragement to others to follow after the business ; and as the coupars of Aberdeen have been long famous for the best work all over the kingdom, so they could not so much answer for a journeyman's work who has not been bred with some of themselves, it not being so easy a matter to take full grown people out of their way as to teach young ones, besides a coupar must necessarily entrust a journeyman to push work as he could not afford to teach and pay him at the same time, whereas their apprentices are not entrusted until they know them capable, so that it clearly appears that there is a hazard in their work being made worse, and the whole trade suffering in their reputation for the best of work. . . . It is therefore enacted that no journeyman be employed who has not served an apprenticeship to some of their trade within the burgh, under the penalty of one shilling sterling for each day he shall employ such person, to be payed to the boxmaster for the use of the poor.

In addition to the foregoing there is a long act prohibiting members from taking on work too cheaply, so that " they are unable to pay for the timber, and keep their families." There is also an act under which a master is liable to a penalty of six pounds Scots if he employs a journeyman who " works after hours on pretence that he is working for his master." The following are a few extracts of sentences passed for breaches of the acts and ordinances of the craft :—

At Aberdeen, 27th February, 1694.—In presence of Adam Mark, deacon, the said traid ordained that George Wright should have no voice amongst the traid until the deacon did get amends for abusing him, when he was going about to furnish a man to their majesties' service at the time, conform to the magistrates order, and denied the deacon assistance when required, and thereupon the deacon required act.

31st December, 1702.—The said day the traid by voyce of court statute and ordained that John Scott, plumer, have no voyce airt nor pairt among the wright and coupar traid in tyme coming until he suplicat the traid, and give satisfaction for taking brybs and connivieng with unfreemen, divulging the traid's secrets contrair to his oath, and thereupon the deacon took instruments.

At Trinity Hall, the thirteenth day of October, 1704, in presence of John Findlay, deacon, compeared John Watson, John Youngson, William Pirie, John Kempt, Patrick Gray, John Mair, and George Gray, and submitted themselves to the court of the Wright and Coupar Trade for their abuse therein in contravening and vilipending the deacon and other misdemeanours. And the trade having considered the circumstances of the matter they ordain John Watson and John Youngson to crave the conveener, deacon, and traid's pardon, and ordains William Pirie, John Kemp, Patrick and George Gray, and John Mair, each of them to pay two pounds scots and to crave pardon also. And that ilk ane of them bind themselves to the paine in all time coming for their peaceable behaviour under the failzie of six pounds scots, by an attour extrusion. And ordains public satisfaction to be given, and the refusers thereof to have no voyce or concern in the traid until this present act be fulfilled.

18th June, 1706.—The said day anent the complaint given in against James Robertson, wright, for his contumecy to the Deacon Convener and his unmannerlyness to the Deacon and Court in contempt of their respective authority, and the court considering the same, they do by thir presents expell and debarr him from the court meetings or concern of the said trade, and fixes and amerciates him in twenty shillings scots *toties quoties* until pardon be sought and granted from the deacon and trade, and ordains this act to stand unalterable.

16th June, 1706.—The said day anent the complaint given in by the whole court against Alexander Anderson, wright, for his disobedience to the deacon's commands as their officer and public servant of the traid, and for his breach of his oath of admission, and several other unchristian faults ; and the court considering the same and being well known to them, they do hereby fine and amerciate him in the sum of ten merks scots for his faults and unchristian behaviour, to be paid to the poor of the traid within terms of law, and also hereby debarrs and excludes him being a member of this court or traid or from voting or sharing in their concerns in all tyme hereafter. And hereby ordains that no member of this court converse with him as their neighbour or a member of his family in respect of his perjury. And ordains this act to stand unalterable until the fine be paid, and the highest of satisfaction given.

1st August, 1701.—The said day Alexander Burnet, coupar, was amerciate in fourty shilling scots conform to the act in the books for saying to the deacon in a fenced court when he civilie socht his poynd, "the divell tak' it from him." And ordains the fine to be paid, and the court's pardon obtained before he get a voyce.

11th August, 1707.—The said day the whole trade excludes and debarrs Alexander Annand, wright, for his robbing and endeavouring to tear in pieces ane bond belonging to the trade in face of court, and in contempt of their authority, from having any voyce or concern in courts or meetings until he make satisfaction to the trade, and undergo whatever they shall inflict upon him for such an intollerable cryme.

The essays prescribed for wrights about the middle of the last century were remarkably severe tests of workmanship ; indeed, it is doubtful if there are many wrights of the present day who could make such an essay as the following :—A spring table, consisting of three folding leaves, every leaf folding above another ; the first leaf, when folded over, is to answer a dining table ; the second leaf to answer a quadvile or whist table ; the third leaf to answer a backgammon table, the said three tops are to hang on one pair of hinges ; out of the body of said table is to arise a writing-desk with nine drawers, and a book-frame on springs, the said frame to have eagle claw feet with a shell or flower on the knees of every foot, the said table is to have close banded and chequer feather bands. A medall case of thirty-six drawers with a carriage below, which is to have eagle claw feet, on the tops of which case to be a scroll pedament with a shield in the centre for a coat of arms ; every drawer to be divided into thirty-six parts in order to hold different kinds of meddals ; every one of these parts is to be round and hollow within, with a hole below in order to take the meddal out and in. A dressing chest of drawers and cabinet, the drawers to have two projections consisting of four drawers in each projection, with a sliding cupboard in the middle, the cupboard to be circular on the back, with ane Esiolloy (?) shell the whole breadth of the cupboard ; above the cupboard there is to be a writing table to draw out with springs supported by itself, every drawer to be divided so as to hold all manner of necessaryies for a lady's toilet, every division of said drawers to have boxes for filling its own place four square every way. There is to be a cabinet on the top of the said drawers with arch-headed doors. In the inside of the cabinet is to be a prospect full of drawers ; below the said prospect there is to be eight drawers, and above it six in the flanks are to be sliding partitions for books, the whole outside to be feather headed. The middle part of the cabinet to be scroll pediment with the two sides of the ingoing circular. A library table consisting of twenty-four drawers, six on every side, with a swinging ball or bowl in the centre of said table to hang plumb at any position, the table and drawers to be cross banded and chequer feather binded. A dining table, six feet long on the top, by five and a half feet in breadth, with two folding leaves, the said leaves to be hung without the help of any kind of metal hinges ; the table to have eagle claw feet, with a moving ball in the centre of the claw to answer instead of brass castors ; the carriage of the table to be made to answer the top by an equal margin below when folded out or folded in, and round the top of the table on the edge is to be a piece of carving commonly called the egg and anchor. The frame of the table is to be chequer feather banded of different kinds of wood. A table twelve feet diameter on one carriage for folding in four corners for a corner table, and to serve when folded out, all hung with hinges, for a large dining table, and the frame to fold together to serve for a corner table.

The cooper's essay was simply " ane salmond salt for holding four barrels of salmond, or ane three boll salt for brewing ; ane firlot and peck, ane salmond barrell conform to bind and measure of Aberdeen, the goadges made for that effect to be given to him be the deacon and masters."

The essay masters were strictly enjoined " to examine the work without speaking to each other, and declare their voices to the clerk and deacon, so that the one could not know what the verdict of the other was." When testing an applicant the essay masters had, and still exercise, the power, when considered necessary, of locking him into a stranger's workshop while he is at work. The fine imposed on an essay master for failure in his duty is four pounds Scots.

Under the following resolution, passed by the Convener Court, Wheelwrights were joined to the Wrights and Coopers in place of the Hammermen :—

11th August, 1709.—The Convener Court ordains and hereby appoints that wheelwrights petitioning to be incorporate shall be joined to the wright and cooper traid in tyme to come, and not to the hammermen traid, and orders the wright and cooper traid to make a report to the Town Council.

In addition to the amount annually set aside for the education of orphans and children, an additional educational fund was established in 1862, by the widow of the late Mr. James Allan, upholsterer. On the death of her husband, Mrs. Allan directed that her annuity from the Trade and from the Widows' Fund should be retained by the boxmaster in a separate account for future disposal by Mrs. Allan or her trustees, as she or they might afterwards direct. A short time after Mrs. Allan's death, the trustees directed that the revenue from the accumulated annuities should be made available to the Trade ; and, as they considered that the sons of members were already well provided for (educationally), they proposed that, as the capital would yield a sum of £10 per annum, two bursaries of £5 each should be given to daughters who had passed school age, and who might wish to continue their studies (preference being given to the most necessitous and deserving). Rules were accordingly drawn out in 1879 to carry this direction into effect, the scholarships being made tenable for two years.

The Wrights and Coopers are superiors or proprietors of a portion of the estate of Garthdee, ground at King Street Road, Princes Street, Canal Terrace, Bon-Accord Street, Crown Street, Loanhead Terrace, Springbank Terrace, Rosebank Terrace, Gallowgate-Head, Banchory Park, Urquhart Road, Mounthooly, Old Aberdeen, &c.

The panel with the emblazoned arms of the Trade, which hangs in the West Committee Room, along with the others, was painted by Charles Whyt, painter, his payment "not to exceed fourscore pounds Scots, and all other dues." On 18th June, the Trade "appointed and ordained that the boxmaster cause made ane square whyt flag of whyt taffitie, and in the midst thereof the arms of the Wright and Cooper Trade, conform to Mr. Lyon's order, as they are painted on the broad in the Trinity Hall; and that the same be painted on fine holland by Charles Whyt, on both syds, and the same to be perfected and ended in all haste." Underneath the arms on the panel are the following lines :—

> Our trade is renown'd by sea & land,
> By timber work compleated by our hand,
> Which trades practised by us, are holden rare,
> As witness our Compass, Adze & Square.

> The Carpenter & Hooper makes one trade,
> In great esteem these men ought to be had,
> Their traid should be the first in place by right,
> For Mary was betrothed to a Wright ;
> And Justin Martyr, he down right awoues,
> That Jesus Christ himself made yokes and plows.
> Great families deryves their pedigree,
> From persons matcht with them, as wee may see,
> Assume their honores, & themselvs sett forth,
> By reckoning   .   .   .   worth.*

* When the "brod" was touched up about thirty years ago the painter seems to have filled in several words at random. In the next line he also altered the word Virgin to Origin !

Shall not the Virgin, who was matcht with one
Of this high trade, Honor reflect thereon?
If Christ, both God & man, this trade did try,
Let none compute with it : let all stand by.
From the first Adam some their trade commence,
The second Adam will speak better sence.
Did not just Noah, at command of God,
Build the life saveng ark of goopher wood, †
Which did hold man, beast, fowl, & creeping thing,
Till the great deluge should asswadge again :
By which, the seed of each kynd sav'd should be
To yield the earth a new posteritie.
God also did Bezaleel's heart inspire, ‡
Who was the son of Uri, the son of Hur,
With Aholiab Ahisamach's son,
The first of Judah's tribe, the last of Dan,
With his ouen sprit in Wisdom & in Art,
And all whom he had blist with a wise heart
To carve in wood, and in all kynd of work,
The tabernacle, the mercy-seat, & ark.
Which they all wrought in gold & shittim wood,
In which were keept God's laws, & holy word.
When Ahab § & his father's hous had gon
From God's commands, & unto Baalim ran,
Did not Elijah, sent by th' word of God,
Convert that people, & their king Ahab?
To do this mighty work, this prophet thought
It needful that four barrells should be brought
Of water fill'd, which, on the sacrifice,
And wood, he ordred to be poured thrice,
Which round the Altar ran, & then he cry'd—
"O Lord God hear me, that your people stray'd,
May turne their hearts again, yea & admire,
The God of Israel : "—then straight down fell fire,
Which did consume all the burnt offering
And wood, & lick't the water up again.
'Twas by our art, you see, the Lord did save
Poor mankynd, & all breathing kynd that live,
Our art should be then honor'd by all men,
Since it hath always helpfull to them been.
Then may all know our art proceeds from none
But the wise, great, & glorious God alone
To whom let us give praises, thanks, & honour
And glorie this day forth for now & ever.   Amen.

† Gen. ch. 6, v. 14.   ‡ Exod. ch. 31,   § 1 Kings, ch. 13.

·

TAILORS [15th May, 1682].—Quarterly. First : Gules, a tower of Aberdeen. Second : Azure, a pair of scissors or. Third : Argent, a smoothing iron azure. Fourth : Gules, a tailor's bodkin proper, hafted or. Motto : *In God is our Trust.*

CHAPTER X.

THE TAILOR TRADE.

THERE is good evidence to show that the tailors were organised before the close of the fifteenth century. In addition to the ordinary causes which induced all craftsmen to combine, the tailors had two special reasons—they had to take special steps to protect themselves against encroachments by the tailors residing in Old Aberdeen and the outskirts of the town, and they had also to combine for the purpose of excluding females from exercising any branch of the craft. The tailors claimed the monopoly of making all kinds of garments, both male and female, and, as will be seen later on, it was only after a keen struggle that the craftsmen granted women even the partial privilege of making certain articles of female attire.

The first recognition of the Tailor Craft by the magistrates appears to have been on 6th February, 1511, when the baillies "consentit and ordainit the dekinys of ye tailzeour craft to call all ye tailzeours of yis burgh befor yame and consider, see, and understand, all poynts of yair craft, and reforme and causs to be reformitt all poynts and falts y' yai fynd amang yair said craft, and quhair yai can not reform thame to present ye said faltis to ye said bailyies.—*Council Register, vol.* ix. *p.* 79.

This power was further extended under the following ordinance, granting to the Tailors the same powers as had been conferred upon the Hammermen* :—

9th June, 1533.—Item, the haill toun being convenit for the maist part in the tolbooth, grantit the same privileges to the tailyours thae haue grantit abefoir to the smythis and sic lik pouar thae chesand and present- and to thame ane sufficient dekin, sicklik as the smythis hes done that sall

---

* See Hammermen Seal of Cause, pp. 198, 199.

answer to the toun for the haill craft, and dicerns them thair commound seill thairupon.

The oldest existing minute-book of the Tailor Trade has the following preface :—" Acts and Ordinances of the Taylzior traid in Aberdeen ordained be John Forbes, present deacon of the said traid, with consent of the maisters and members of the said Incorporation, to be extracted out of the old registers and hereinsert, homologat, and approven under the hands of Alex. Mitchell, clerk to the traids of the said burgh, in ane fenced court, 1694." The following are the acts and ordinances, including those copied out of the old register :—

ANENT SABBATH OBSERVANCE.

Item, it is statute and ordained for the glorie of God that ilk maister, prentiss, and servant keep the holy Sabbath day at prayers and preaching, and that nane wilfully absent themselves therefra under the pains following :—The maisters, six shillings eight pennies; the servant, three shillings six pennies ; and the prentiss to be punished in his person if he has not money to pay the onlaw at the will and discretion of the deacon and maisters.

ANENT OBEDIENCE TO THE DEACON.

Item, it is statute and ordained that no frieman speak irreverantly to the deacon in fenced courts or elsewhaur, neither to tak ony speech upon him except he be asked, or ask the same be licence, under the pain of fourty shillings to the poore's use.

ANENT GENERAL BEHAVIOUR.

Item, it is statute and ordained that if any of the members of the said calling offend ane other be wark, word, or deed, at any tyme hereaifter, the party offending sall pay to the poore of the calling four pounds money *toties quoties*, by and attour satisfaction by the pairty grived, according to the gravity of the fault.

ANENT FEEING SERVANTS.

Item, it is statute and ordained that no freeman shall fee nor conduce with any servant or boy for less than three years, under the pain of fourty shillings, and that they fee them before the deacon for the tyme.

ANENT THE ELECTION OF MASTERS.

Item, it is statute and ordained be the haill craft, be common vott, that ilk new elected deacon to be chosen hereafter shall have absolute power, with consent of the lait deacon, to choyse, nominate, and elect his six maisters, als freely as if they had been chosen be vott of the haill craft.*

---

* This statute was modified to the extent that the deacon "lifted" a certain number of the Trade out of which the boxmaster and maisters were chosen.

ANENT ATTENDANCE AT BURIALS.

28th October, 1631.—Item, the said day forsameikle as the great abuse befoir complained upon be the Magistrates of this burgh and haill deacons of crafts anent the untymeous coming of freemen to burials of freemen, their wives, and children departed, and through not coming with hatts on their heads who are in use to wear them, for remeid whereof the deacon and maisters, with consent of the haill craft, hes ordained and ordains everie freeman that is warnit be the officer to go to burials, that they and every one of them come to their deacon's stair fitt tymously, and convoy their deacon to the burial or burials, and that everie ane have their hatt on their head who has any or in use to wear ; and who contravenes here-untill shall pay to the craft eight shillings *toties quoties.*

ANENT KEEPING THE SECRETS OF THE CRAFT.

18th February, 1678.—In presence of Alexander Milne, deacon, it is strictlie statute and ordained unanimously be the haill traid that whatever entering freeman of the craft, or any other freeman thereof, shall anyways reveal or divulge to the Magistrates or any Burgess of Guild, directly or indirectly, any of the craft's secrets, especially anent their procedure when entering freemen of the traid, anent the composition or other expenses and deburgements, that the person or persons so doing (being made out) shall never carry public charge amongst the said traid as deacon, maister, or boxmaister, until they give to the traid all satisfaction anent the said misdemeanour.

ANENT ENTRY MONEY.

20th August, 1685.—The said traid taking into their consideration the grudging and clamour of some supplicants or entrants to be fremen of the traid upon the account of the present expenses in giving ane dinner or feast when they are incorporat in this society as freiman, as also anent the complant that when there was ane order of counsel to take trial of the supplicants qualifications, the supplicant, by the information of others, was so instructed that what he could do then, could doe so weill thereafter, for remeid whereoff the haill freemen of the said traid by voice of court ordained for the use of the poore and common good of the said incorporation, the following rates should be fixed :—Prentiss, four score ten merks ; journeymen, four score ten pounds ; and extranear, 100 pounds Scots.

ANENT THE ELECTION DINNER.

24th August, 1708.—The which day (for many good and reasonable causes) the traid statute and unalterably ordains that in all tyme coming, the deacon of the said traid shall at his outgoing as deacon pay the whole expenses of the dinner at the election of a new deacon yearly, and that the same dinner be sufficient and after the accustomed manner, and hereby declares that the traids public funds, nor no other private person shall be concerned in payment of the expenses or any part thereof, but allenarly the said off going deacon under the failzie of twenty pounds Scots money to be paid by the contravener for the use of the said traid, and be the said contravener to have no pairt or portion or concern in the said trade until the samen be paid.*

ANENT JOURNEYMEN.

6th March, 1728.—The trade hereby statute and ordain that no person whatever shall be received as journeyman in this trade for the future, except allenarly such as have served as apprentices to freemen of this trade.

ANENT FINES.

22nd January, 1733.—The trade unanimously statute and ordain that in all time coming no fine that shall be paid into the trade be any member thereof, or by any person whatsomever shall be repaid to the party that shall pay the same upon any application or pretence whatsomever.

Previous to 1661, when the art of needlemaking was introduced into this country, the instruments used by tailors were of a very rude description, bone and box skewers and rough pieces of iron and steel being used for needles, while thimbles were not in ordinary use until introduced into this country from Holland by a Dutchman named Lofting, in 1695.

The female labour question appears to have been a very knotty problem to the Tailor Craft in Aberdeen. The craftsmen had a monopoly of making female as well as men's garments, and they resented very keenly the introduction of female labour, while the proposal that women should be allowed to set up in business as mantlemakers filled them with dismay. They resisted long, but ultimately they had to give way, although even to the last it was only a partial concession which was made. The women were granted certain modified privileges, and compelled to come within the jurisdiction of the craft, but they were not admitted to full membership. The women were simply granted "a toleration" to make certain classes of work, and even in granting this privilege the tailors in Aberdeen were, we believe, the only craftsmen in Scotland who allowed females to share in their special privileges.

---

* In 1711 it was ordained that the dinner was not to cost more than fifteen pounds Scots. If the deacon was re-elected the trade defrayed the expenses of the dinner, and the trade also agreed to pay the dinner at the passing of entrants.

When the women first began to encroach on the exclusive privileges of the craftsmen, the Aberdeen tailors sought advice in different quarters. They applied, among others, to the Magistrates, but their honours declined to interfere on the ground that the application by a female for liberty to make mantles was "unprecedented." After several women had been prosecuted for encroaching on the privileges of the tailors, a compromise was effected by which women were to be allowed to make mantles, and, in some instances, petticoats, but on no consideration whatever were they to import or deal in stays and other articles of female attire.

The minutes in the books of the Trade with regard to the granting of "tollerations" to the mantua-makers are very voluminous, and afford unmistakable evidence of the reluctance with which the craftsmen yielded to their demands. On 30th May, 1717, a deputation was appointed to meet with a Rachael Baxter anent a petition she had presented craving liberty for mantle-making; and after consultation the following minute was adopted:—

The trade hereby grants libertie to the said Rachel Baxter for mantua-making allenarly within the said burgh, and admittit, and hereby admits, her free in this incorporation for that effect (with and under the restrictions following) that she shall neither take to be prentiss nor employ in any work either within or without doors as servants but only women, and that these women servants, or prentisses, shall be feed or entered in the same way and manner as the other prentisses or servants in the said tailor trade agreeable to their constant practice and constitution; second, that she shall have only the privilege of mantua-making, and no ways make stays, or import the same to sell from any other place, and that the traid's clerk shall be employed to draw her indentures with her prentisses and agreements with any servants who are to be still subject to the rules of the traid in such cases, for payment of ane certain sum of money for banqueting money to the boxmaster of the tayliour traid of this burgh, which is accepted of by them for her freedom in the tayliour traid, as above expressed, and this besides of her expenses due and quarterly penny as use is in such cases; and it is hereby declared that thir presents to be no precedent to any woman in tyme coming, and the said Rachel Baxter obliged herself to implement the haill premises as above expressed, and for that end subscribed thir presents. (Signed) Rachel Baxter.*

* It is worthy of note that Rachel wrote a much superior signature to the bulk of the craftsmen, a remark which applies to the other females who were subsequently admitted to similar privileges.

In another case the minute runs :—

7th November, 1728.—The said day Janet Pirie, lawful daughter to John Pirie, shipmaster in Aberdeen, gave in a petition to the Trade mentioning that she, having learned mantua-making, and being to exercise the said employment within the burgh with the liberty and toleration of the trade for that effect, and therefore craving that the trade might consider the premises and grant her a toleration and liberty for exercising the said employment upon her payment yearly to their boxmaster such a sum as they should appoint, which petition, being seen and considered by the said trade, they hereby grant liberty and tolleration to the said Janet Pirie to exercise the employment of mantua-making within this burgh, and with and under the restrictions and conditions following, allenarly and no otherwise, namely :—*Primo.*—That she shall take no men apprentices, nor employ men servants in any work whatever relating to her employment directly or indirectly, but allenarly women apprentices and servants. *Secundo.*—That she shall only make gowns and petticoats for women, and shall not make or mend any other kind of women's cloaths, and shall not make or mend any kind of men's cloaths. *Tertio.*—The said Janet Pirie is not to import or sell any stays whatsoever. All which the said Janet Pirie binds and obliges her to stand to, implement, and perform under the penalty of twenty shillings sterling for the first transgression, to be paid by her to the boxmaster for the use of the poor, and double the same penalty *toties quoties* thereafter she shall transgress the premises or any part thereof. And that it shall be lawful for the boxmaster to call and convene the said Janet Pirie at any time he shall think convenient, and crave her oath on her transgressing the premises, and to which proof she hereby subjects herself. And it is further hereby declared that the said Janet Pirie's apprentices shall have no benefit herefrom. And the said Janet Pirie obliges her to pay yearly to the Trade's boxmaster for the said tolleration fifteen shillings sterling money during her exercising the said employment at the term of Martinmas next.

When about half-a-dozen women had been granted this privilege, including Mrs. Catherine Wilson, daughter of Mr George Wilson of Finzean, a grand-nephew of Dr. William Guild, the craftsmen became alarmed at their increasing number, and resolved to increase the dues.

7th November, 1728.—The Trade, taking to their consideration that the number of the women mantua-makers in this burgh is very much increasing, and that the same is a great hurt and prejudice to this Trade, do therefore statute and ordain that every woman who for the future shall be tollerate to work at mantua-making by the Trade, shall pay yearly to the boxmaster of this Trade for such tollerance the sum of twenty-four shillings yearly, without any mitigation or defalcation whatever.

This rate was raised in April, 1734, to thirty pounds Scots for the daughter of a burgess, and four pounds sterling if an unfreeman's daughter. In 1732 the boxmaster was authorised to pursue all mantua-makers "who exercised the said trade, and have no tolleration therefore from the trade," and amongst those who were prosecuted for carrying on the business without having obtained the necessary "tollerance," was Mrs. Ann Forbes, daughter of Lachlan Forbes of Edinglassie. She left the town, however, before the summons could be served. Another instance of the vigilance with which the tailors guarded their privileges is to be found in the following minute instructing a search after skinners who might be suspected of making breeches :—

2nd October, 1772.—The said day the trade granted warrant to the deacon and maisters to search after what power the skinners in this place have for making of breeches, and what expenses may be wared thereanent to be allowed.

A curious case is recorded in the books of the Trade which also illustrates the antipathy that existed with regard to women interfering with the privileges of the craft. On 30th October, 1661, George Watt was charged with having "wilfully and contemptuously questioned the lawful authority and just and good government of the burgh in giving order with his ain hand without the magistrates' permission to tak and apprehend ane piece of stuff, belonging to Isobel Wallace, servant to the Lady Craigievar, from the said Isobel her servant woman who was carrying the same out of the town for behoof of her said mistress, and in detaining and refusing to produce the same before the magistrates according to the council's order made thereanent." Watt raised an action against the Magistrates before the Privy Council ; but for doing this it was complained that he "did all that in him lay to mak ane great rupture and division between the counsell and the tradesmen within the burgh," the result being that he was "deprived of his libertie and freedom of the tailor trade within this burgh in any time hereafter," it being also "ordanit his boothe and chope door to be closed up." In the following year it is recorded that Watt "craved upon his knees the magistrates and counsells pardon," and on doing so was "reponit to his freedom and liberty on payment of 90 merks scots and five shillings of arms money as use is."

The first mention of upholsterers in connection with the Tailor Trade occurs in a minute dated 14th September, 1767, when the Trade "granted warrant to the boxmaster to prosecute before the magistrates, George Bartlett, who had sett up the trade of upholsterer without any manner of freedom or title thereto." From that date all upholsterers had to join the craft, their essay being "to stuff and make ane cover of a sopha." Numerous complaints were also made about this time against tailors who, while qualified to make only one class of work, undertook to make work for which they had not been tested ; and it was declared "contrary to the constitution of all communities that any should work and practice any piece of material work wherein they are not sworn to be qualified by the ordinary course of tryal, and conform the constitution of the communitie, therefore the said traid statute and ordain that no entrant freeman for the future that qualifies himself only for men's work, and refuses, or does not qualify himself for women's clothes by passing a say for both, or either, shall be tolerate or allowed to work either in women's clothes or men's clothes without he pass the say conform, and that his working or practising the said traid shall only be conform to his say passed at his admission."

The tailors had numerous disputes in regard to hours and wages. In 1720 the rate of wages was fixed at four shillings Scots (fourpence sterling) per diem, the working hours to be from 7 a.m. to 9 p.m. On 2nd August, 1734, the hours were fixed from 6 a.m. to 10 p.m., and these hours continued for over thirty years ; but the journeymen ultimately rebelled against both the long hours and miserable pay :—

20th May, 1768.—Whereas ane illegal combination has lately been entered into by the journeymen tailors to oblige the freemen to raise their wages from eightpence to tenpence per day by refusing to work themselves, and detering others by threatening all the country lads from engaging to serve the masters of the trade, whereby great inconvenience has been brought on many of the members of the trade, the meeting having taken the same under serious consideration, and being of opinion that eightpence a day is the highest wages the masters can afford to their journeymen, and that the journeymen have at present no reason to complain of the lowness of their wages, as the price of meal and other necessaries is of late much fallen, have unanimously resolved, and do agree, in order that the young men may not be encouraged in their unjustifiable attempt by the conduct of any particular master or any difference among them, that they shall strictly observe all the former acts and regulations of the trade with respect to the journeymen ; and particularlie that no freeman shall employ any married journeyman at more wages than eightpence a day, and that they shall not employ any journeyman who shall refuse to work at those wages, and shall take upon him to work for himself within the freedom or liberties until they be brought to trial and punished therefor, and that under the penalty of ten pounds Scots, to be paid to the boxmaster, for every breach of this resolution whenever the majority of the trade shall find the same incurred.

The following minutes give particulars of a strike which took place among the journeymen in 1797, when a number of them had been summoned before the Magistrates and sentenced to fines and imprisonment for their conduct :—

19th June, 1797.—It was represented to the trade that their journeymen had entered into an illegal combination for the purpose of raising their wages. The trade unanimously recommended Mr. M'Donald to give in a statement of this matter to the clerk and authorized him to bring a prosecution against the delinquents for redress, and the whole number agreed to this, and not to give any additional wages to their servants, the said wages having been twice raised within a few years.

5th July, 1797.—The magistrates sentence upon the complaint at the instance of the deacon with concurrence of the Procurator Fiscal against certain of the journeymen taylors having been publicly read, the court appoint the same to be put to immediate execution and to be copied into their sederunt book, and of which the tenor follows—"July, 1797.— Assoilizes the defender, James Aliaster, who has been passed from by the complainers and discerns, and having advised the proof brought by the complainers and whole process, Finds, that the complainers have brought sufficient evidence of the combination stated in the complaint, and therefore fines and amerciates each of the defenders, Malcolm Robertson, William Troup, William Sinclair, Robert Torrie, William Anderson, William Mackenzie, Alexander Smith, John Robb, James Beverley, James Ross, David Mackenzie, and John Innes in nine shillings sterling to the private complainer, and in one shilling sterling to the procurator fiscal, and further discerns and ordains them and each of them to be incarcerated in the tolbooth of Aberdeen for eight days and to find sufficient caution, acted in the Burgh Court books that they shall immediately after being set at liberty return to the service of their former masters respectively, and serve them at the rate of seven shillings and sixpence a week, and that they shall not leave their service without giving the masters one months previous warning at least of their intention so to do. And grant warrant to the towns sergeants to commit the said defenders prisoners to the tolbooth of Aberdeen, and to the keeper of said tolbooth to receive and detain them therein for said eight days, and thereafter until they pay the fine awarded against them respectively, and find caution as aforesaid, signed, George More, provost; William Littlejohn, baillie; Charles Farquharson, baillie; Robert Garden, baillie."

The following account, rendered in 1727, will give some indication of the prices charged by master tailors about this period :—

ACCOUNT CONVINER LESLIE TO GEORGE FINLAYSON, TAYLOR.

December 5, 1727.

For cloath, ...	£9	6	8
For three ell of lyning to lyne his vest, . . .	1	0	0
For halfe an ell of hardin for pockets and binding, .	0	2	6
For tuo duson and an halfe of big butans, . .	0	12	6
For tuo duson and an halfe small butons, . . .	0	3	10
For hair, ...	0	6	0
For silk, ...	0	3	0
For threed, ...	0	9	0
For a quarter of buchram, ...	0	9	6
For making a bige coat, ...	1	4	0
For making a vest, ...	0	12	0
For making a cover coat, ...	0	6	0
May 6.			
For making a pair of bricks, ...	0	6	0
	14	10	4

Abd., 7th Decr., 1727, received payt. of the above accot. be me—G. F.

The tenacity with which the special privileges of the craftsmen were maintained was well illustrated by a litigation which was commenced by the Tailor Incorporation in 1817, and lasted for four years, in regard to an infringement of their privileges by Messrs. James Mowat & Company, manufacturers, and James Stott, a servant of the company. It was contended that as the partners of the firm of Mowat and Company were burgesses of Guild, they were protected against the conclusions of summons. The Magistrates took this view of the case, but, on appeal, the Lords of Council and Session found that the Seal of Cause obtained by the Tailors in 1533 necessarily implied the exclusive privilege of exercising their craft within the burgh ; that being a member of the Guildry did not warrant an infringement of any of the privileges of the crafts any more than a member of one craft would therefore be entitled to exercise another craft ; and they therefore found that Mowat & Company were not entitled to employ persons as tailors in the burgh who were not members of the Tailor Incorporation. The defenders were found liable in expenses, amounting to £143 1s. 11d.

There are remarkably few convictions recorded in the books of the Tailor Trade as compared to some of the other crafts, the principal offences being the opening of "slop" shops, working to unfreemen, and working in private houses. Their charity also took some peculiar forms, as, for instance, on 26th May, 1798, the Trade granted warrant to the box-master to lend Alexander Thomson £3 sterling on his bill to enable him to make a voyage to London for the benefit of his health ; and another instance is recorded of a widow being presented with a mangle, " said mangle to remain the property of the Trade."

An additional fund was established in 1756 for increasing the stock of the incorporation, to which a certain proportion of the entry money was allocated ; and in 1785 a daughters' fund was also established, both of which have proved of great benefit. In 1832 Alexander Watson left £100 to establish a mortification for the purpose of educating sons of freeman tailors from eight to eleven years of age.

What is known as Milne's Mortification, founded in 1736 for the education and fitting out of tailors' sons, was originally under the management of the Patron, Convener, Master of Hospital, seven Deacons, and seven members of the Tailor Trade, but in 1765 a decreet arbitral was pronounced, whereby a sum of £300 was paid to the Master of Hospital, to be divided among the other six Trades, as a consideration to them for renouncing and conveying from themselves and their successors, in favour of the Tailor Trade, all right and title to the balance of the mortification.

The Tailor Trade obtained a private Act of Parliament in 1853 " to confirm the titles and conveyances, and to amend and regulate the affairs of the said craft." The ground and

properties purchased from time to time by this Trade include
the Sillyward Croft, near Schoolhill ; Craigmill Croft, Gallow-
hill Croft, Coul's Croft, Summer's Croft, two rigs at Sandy-
lands, northmost half of Symon Croft, pieces of land at
Ferryhill and Cooperstown, six lots of the land at Pitmuxton,
Combs Croft, now called the lands of Newbridge ; ground in
the neighbourhood of the harbour, &c., &c.

Whether it was the case that the tailors of the olden days
were not poetically inclined, or had more practical matters to
attend to, it is hard to say, but their " brod " containing their
coat of arms is not—like those of the other Trades—adorned
with any poetic eulogy of the craft.

SHOEMAKERS [18th November, 1651].—Gules, a shoemaker's shaping knife fesseways, with the edge turned towards the chief, the blade proper and hafted argent; over the same a crown or; and in the dexter canton a tower of Aberdeen. Motto: *Lord crown us with Glory.*

CHAPTER XI.

THE SHOEMAKER TRADE.

THE shoemakers, long known as cordwainers or cordiners (from *cordonnier* [f.], a worker of leather), were early associated under a deacon. They had evidently taken advantage of the Act of 1424 authorising craftsmen to elect " ane wise man of the craft," and the following entry in the Council Register shows that even as early as 1484 the Magistrates had come into conflict with them regarding their deacon :—

27th May, 1484.—The same day the alderman, baillies, and counsall, because thai have fundin grete faute in the craft of the cordinaris, at this tyme thai have put down the deacons of the said craft, annulland all powaris that thai gif to thaim of befor, and will fra hynce furth tak the correction of thaim all in tyme to cum, and to puniss thaim after thair demerits that sal be committit in tyme command.—*Council Register, vol.* vi., *p.* 848.

This arrangement, however, by which the Magistrates were to take the correction of the work of the cordiners into their own hands, does not seem to have worked well, for we find from an entry, a few years after, that two visitors were appointed with the same powers and functions as the deacons of the other crafts. These men were, no doubt, members of the cordiner craft, and the powers conferred on them are similar to those conferred by the formal Seals of Cause granted about thirty years afterwards to most of the craftsmen in Aberdeen :—

31st September, 1495.—The saide day the Alderman and diuerss of the counsall and communitie present for the tyme thought it expedient for ye commone proffit, for the correction of evil werk maid be ye cordinaris and cersing and reforming of it yat William Tamsone and Thomas Meldrum sal vesie, consider, and understand ye craftsmen of thar craft within this burghe, yat yai werk diligentlie, and to correct evil werk, and insufficint stuff as the vyss is of uyiris burrowis, and gif ony dissobeis the saidis William and Thomas, heirintill, in contrar to the common profit, yai sal present ye falt to ye alderman and balzeis, quhilkis sal punis them efter ye laws of ye realme, and consüetude of uyiris burrowis.—*Council Register, vol.* vii. *p.* 663.

In 1501 a more explicit order was issued by the Magistrates, with consent of the cordiners, for the appointment of " tua mene of thar craft to serce ande consider ye wirk of thar craft," a warrant that may be regarded as the first formal Seal of Cause that was granted to this craft, a Seal of Cause being, as has already been pointed out, a recognition or confirmation granted to a particular craft of the right to elect a deacon. The powers of the deacons were more specifically set forth in the Seals of Cause of certain crafts than in others ; but once the right was conferred on a particular body of craftsmen, they considered themselves entitled to make and pass by-laws for carrying on all the affairs of their craft or society. The right to choose a deacon was originally acquired in virtue of Royal Charters and Acts of Parliament ; all that was afterwards required was a recognition of that right by the local Town Council, whose consent had to be obtained.

In 1520 a more formal Seal of Cause was granted to the shoemakers, the original of which was written in Latin, and on that account seems to have escaped notice, and led to the belief that the shoemakers did not possess anything in the nature of a Seal of Cause. The Seals of Cause granted to some of the other Trades about ten years after are more specific, but the recognition by the Council of the powers of the cordiners to elect a deacon and to make by-laws is as legally confirmed as in the case of the other crafts.

The following is a translation of the grant formally constituting the shoemakers into a corporation ;—

13th June, 1520.—Which day all and sundry the artificers and masters of the cordoner craft of the burgh of Aberdeen, viz. :—John Wishart,* William King, Thomas Brodie, John Malcolm, John Cooper, alias Common, Alex. Jullidiff, John Coutts, James Baker, John Green, Alex. Michilson, and Patrick Baxter, burgesses of Aberdeen, being assembled in the

* A son of this John Wishart's met with an untimely end. It is recorded that on 18th March, 1583, "Johne Wyschert, cordonar, was slain be James Paterson, hangman, who was hanged for the crime and his heid fixed on the Justice Port thairfor." The mention of hanging recalls the fact that the last man who paid the full penalty of the law at Gallowhills was a member of the Wright and Cooper Trade named Morrison, who was hung in 1776 for the murder of his wife.

principal chamber of John Wishart, convened for the purpose of electing
new deacons and office-bearers in the said craft, and of rectifying and
amending all and sundry defects existing at the time in the forsaid craft,
and forwith they unanimously continued the said John Wishart in his
office of deacon as before for the ensuing year, and of new elected as deacon
coadjutor and consort an honest and worthy man William King, and
associated him with the said John in the exercise and discharge of the
deacon's office. They also elected Alexander Yulidiff and Patrick Baxter
as overseers in the said craft to examine and inspect the work of all the
cordiners whatever, both intranears and extranears, whether the same be
sufficient or not, and to intimate and make known to the said deacons
defects of workmanship existing at the time in the forenamed craft. They
afterwards appointed James Dow as beadle to the said craft, in which
office he shall have two pence for his trouble from every master of the said
craft ; moreover, thereafter they determined to establish a box into which
they may collect or cause to be collected every week from the several
masters for payment of the just and customary stipend of the chaplain of
the altar, of the martyrs, Crispin and Crispian, one penny in the week
from every master of the said craft, and from each servant, apprentice, and
domestic, one halfpenny only, for the collecting of which they constituted
John Cooper alias Common and Thomas Brodie, honest and trustworthy
men, as collectors, out of which contributions they shall really pay, and
effectually satisfy, to the chaplain for the time being, without any dispute,
delay, strife, or process of law, at the two terms of the year, viz. :—
Martinmas and Whitsunday, the sum of 32 Shillings by equal portions
according to ancient practice, at each term aforenamed 16 Shillings ; and
if the craft aforesaid shall prosper, and the contributions accumulate and
multiply, the chaplain's stipend shall be augmented nearly to the amount
of the contributions, and the accumulating surplus shall be reserved in the
box for the repairs of the altar and other necessary furniture thereof, shall
pass and be applied to the upholding and repairs of the altar as aforesaid,
and this they ordained to be infallibly and inviolably kept and to be preserved by their successors for ever ; moreover, if any one shall fail in the
payment of the said pence and halfpence, and if any shall be found disobedient to their masters, then shall it be lawful to the deacons with the other
masters of the said craft to punish the offenders according to the degree of
his offence, and whosoever shall harbour the rebellious and disobedient
person for the purpose of executing any work pertaining to the cordiners
after notification has been given to the masters, or shall give out to the
rebellious and disobedient person any work to be performed by him with
out his workshop, and receive the same without the consent and assent of
the deacons, shall really pay and effectually satisfy to the box eight
shillings unforgiven towards the repair and upholding of the said altar and
ornaments thereof ; and in the same manner shall be punished whoever
shall act against the craft or the ordinances of the craft ; and a rebellious
person shall not be admitted to any work among the masters of the

cordoner craft, until, having asked and obtained permission from the deacons and masters, he with humility present himself to an assembly of the said craft and penitently confess his fault. And every master shall be answerable for the inmates and servants in his workshop every week on Saturday for the receipt of the said pence and halfpence from his domestics and servants, and shall deduct them from their wages : moreover, Thomas Brodie straightway in presence of the deacons and others promised to the box 32 pence which he had received long since, nearly two years ago from his servants for their delinquencies, and which he was bound to pay in wax to the altar aforesaid, which 32 pence the craft with one consent intended to give, bestow, and apply to the repairing the base of the chalice, and this faithfully by touch of hands of the notary, their chaplain, the deacons, and masters, their hands mutually touched in token of faithful intention, all fraud and guile apart, they decreed and determined respectively to maintain the premises for ever.—*Council Register, vol. x., p. 264.*

In 1523, the Aberdeen shoemakers applied to the Edinburgh craftsmen for a copy of their regulations, and obtained the following document, which is to be found annexed to a Latin copy of the grant of 1820, in possession of the Trade :—

10th June, 1523.—Item, yis is ye wyss maner and constitution ordanit amang ye haile body of ye craift of ye cordonaris of Edinburg, maide be ye haile maisters of ye craift. In ye first as for upsettin of ane buythe tua markis.

Item, suchen yat tak ane prentis yai suld give ane hauff mark to ye repacione of ye altir.

Item, alsua ye haile body of ye craift sall excers yat na mane hald na buythe na zit to sueir (swear) na mane to work, but giff he beis suffycient maister and mak guid sufficient stuyff to serue ye kingis legis, ye quhilk we have actit in oure burt, undir oure seile of causs ; Alsua, al ye maisteris of ye craift, ilk mann giffis ilk oulk ane penny to ye altir, and ye seruandis siklyke sall pey ane excep prenteiss quo salbe frie quhill yair termes be gane.

Alsua, ane certainne of ye maisteris sall excers ye mercatt to se giff it be sufficient stuyff to serue ye Kingis legis, al stuyff yat is not sufficient yat yai sele yair, to be gewin to ye Kirk Wark without remissioune. Thir ar statuts and ordinances sende oute of Edinburt, to ye maisteris of ye Cordonar craift of Abirdein yat yai mai vse sic lyk according to ressoune.

The rigorous supervision which had to be exercised over the cordiners with regard to the price and quality of shoes sold at the "schone mercat" may have been a reason why the Magistrates were chary in delegating too much power to the craft, and this fact may have led to their Seal of Cause being so meagre. The following entry in the Council Register will give an indication of the strictness with which the cordiners were looked after by the Council :—

27th October, 1541.*—The said day John Herkill, Malcolm Herkill, Jno. Germond, Patre Cults, John Donald, James Dowe, James Prestonne, Alexr. Robertsonn, Gawane Wishert, Wm. Ingrm, Hare Robtson, Sande Mechelsonn, and David Reidheid, cordonars, thai and ilk ane of thame war convikit be the sworne assiss aboune wrytine for the braking of commond ordinans and statutis of this gud toun of the warkmaschip, in selling of insufficient schoine and mekill darrar than the statutis maid obefoir propertes, aganes the commond weill, quharfor thai war and ilk ane of thame in amerciament of court to ferbeir in tyme cuming, and amend as law, and that was gewin for dome. And becaus it was considerit be the prowest, ballies, and counsel, that the ledder is darrar nor it hed wont to be, thai haf dispensit with the said craftismen, and hes lycent thaim to sell thair schoine, quhill thai be forther awysit, of the prycis efter following : that is to say, the best dowbill solit schoine thai can mak for men for xxviii. d. at the hiast, uthers for xxvi. d. or twa schillingis, efter the qualite and quantitie of the person that byis, and the

* The following extract from an heirship inventory will give an idea of the plenishing of a cordiner about this period :—

17th Februar., 1541.—Heir followis the airschip gudis that William Ingram, asks at Jonat Bissit the relict of umquhill Cristofer Ingram, my broder freman of this burghe of Abirdeine, and at Robert Barbour, now hir husband, for his entries, as I that is seruit as narrest and lauchful air to hym.

Item, in the first, ane gowne of scottis blak, lynit with blak-gray.

Item, ane sakot, coytt and doublait ; ane sark, a pair of hoiss, a hat, a bonat.

Item, ane swerde and quhanger, ane leyth aix, ane jak, and ane steil bonat.

Item, ane standan bed, ane nop bed, a pair of scheittis, tua blankittis, and ane covering to the bed.

Item, ane press, ane almery, a pot, a pan, a playte, a dische, a salsar, a chandelir of brace, a tangis, a spyt, with ane lanterone, ane brew fatt, ane kymmeoun, ane geil fatt, ane stand and ane buckat.

Item, ane standard buird with trestis buirdclayeth, tua formis, ane cheir, ane quart, ane poynt and ane choppin.

Item, ane schaiping knyff, ane schawing irne, ane pair of buyt treis, ane scherping buird, ane trink aild with the steil to scherp the schawing irne.

Item, ane kyst, lokit fast, ane scherp rak for ledder, ane blunt rak, 'tua settis with feit necessar thairto.

Item, ane blek tub furneyst, ane oil barrel, with ane oil choppin.

Item, ane resp, ane turcas, and fouir cuschin nails of irne.

Item, ane traschor, ane stuffyn slyise with ane yeirning slyise, ane conze, ane camoll with ane obfuse—(currier's tools).

Item, ane kestrel, ane hand-leddar with ane elison, ane pryce with ane turning staf.

· Item, solis examplis (patterns), over ledJar examplis, with a wanpa for a buytt—(vamp for a ·boot).

Item, ane pair of greite lastis, ane myddil pair of lastis, and ane less pair of lastis.

Item, ane stark to work the leddar vpon with thair feitt, ane clock, &c., &c.—and thir guidis following belangis to the kirk-yaird.

Item, ane fiesching buird with ane fuytt and ane flesching irne.

Item, ane cleik, and bramskin of leddar with ane bark pok.

· Item, ane skep, ane schod—schnillis with ane lyme tub.

best singill solit schoine thai can mak for **xx. d.**, and uthers for **xviii. d.** and **xvi. d.** ; the best doubill scholit for women thai can mak for **xx. d.**, **xviii. d.**, or **xvi.**, efter their qualite and quantite that byis, and their singill scholit for **xiii. d.**, **xii. d.**, and uthirs for **x. d.** : item, barnis schone within **xii.** yeir ald for **x. d.**, uthirs for **viii. d.** or **v. d.**, efter the eild and qualitie of the barne.   And this act to remane induring the touns will : and quhat craftisman that braks the samyn, the rest of his wrought ledder to be escheitt, and furthyr to be punyst as law will.—*Council Register, vol.* xvii., *p.* 19.

The price of shoes was fixed at frequent intervals after the following fashion :—

7th October, 1586.—It is statut and ordanit that na cordonar within yis burght, or without the samen, sell ouy schone darrer nor of ye pryces following :—That is to say the best single soillet schone for men, vi. ss. ; secundar, v. ss. ; wemen schone, iiii. ss. ; bairnis schone, **xxx. d.** ; ii. ss. and twenty pennies haueing consideration of ye aige of ye barne and ye best pair of buitis for **xxx. ss.** ; secundar, **xxviii. ss.**, and **xxvi. ss.** viii. d., and sall not be lessum to na cordinar within this burght to sell ony schone or buitis but of thair awin making vnder ye pane escheiting yairof haueing consideratioun the best barket hyd l. ss. ; the secundar, **xlvi. ss.** viii. d., and **xL ss.** ; and yat na cordonar nor saidlar bark ony ledder in tyme cuming or zit by ony roch hydis heirefter, or sell ony barkit ledder to extranearis or onfremen vnder ye pane of confiscation yairof, and and gif yai be thryss convict for ye braking of ye statut the contrauener to be dischargit of his fredome and to bruik na preuilege within yis burght heirefter.—*Council Register, vol.* xxxii. *p.* 119.

In regard to the " schone mercatt " it was enacted, in 1619, that one of the baillies should attend the market and " tak with him ye deacone of ye cordinaris, and sall serche and try ye haill schone presented to ye mercat gif ony of thame be insufficient, and sic as sall be found spilt, rottin, and insufficient, or yet be of hors ledder, sall presentlie be confiscat and dealt to ye poore."

The shoemakers, like the rest of the craftsmen who came to the " mercat " to sell their wares, were exceedingly jealous of their privileges being encroached upon by strangers, and numerous cases are recorded of fines being imposed both by the Magistrates and by the Trade for such offences.   The following may be given as examples :—

9th May, 1695.—I, James Leslie, lawfull sonne to Patrick Leslie, merchant in Auld Meldrum, for saemeikle as I am apprehendit in buying and transporting aboutt twentie five peare of maid shoois from Edinburt to Abirdene to sell and retaill, in prejudice of the Shoomakertraid in Abirdene, quho peyes Scott and Lott within the said Burghe. Thairfoir be order of the Counsall of Abirdene and Robert Davidsone, present deane of gild of the said burghe, and the said James Leslie faithfulie binds and obleidgis me not only to absteine and forbeire from sic ane transgressioune in tyme couming, But als not to buy and sell any maid shoone which I have now or sall hapen to buy within the towne or shyre of Abirdene— except I buy the said shoois from Friemenn Shoomakeris, burgess of the said burghe of Abirdene. And that under the failzie of ane hundreth merkis Scots money, to be peyit to the Boxmaster of the said Shoomaker Traide for the uss of the puir of the said Incorporatione, in caice I be fund to contraveine the premisess; and consents to the registratioune heirof in the bukis of Counsall and Sessioune Sherrif Commiseare or burghe court bukis of Abirdene To have the strength of ane decreit that letters of horning and uytheris may pass heiron.—*Shoemakers' Records.*

Att Aberdein, the 28th November, 1698.—The traid, in presence of William Duckieson, deacone, ordained George Cruickshank in Old Aberdein, to be poynded for selling of shoone in common mercats, contrair to the laws and custome, and this to be ane Warrant.—*Shoemakers' Records.*

As an illustration of how keenly the shoemakers resented encroachments by unfreemen, we give the text of a petition which was presented to the Town Council on 6th September, 1665, by " Archibald Hog, deacone of the cordoneres, for him selffe and in name and behalffe of the maisters and friemen of the said traid."

That whairas the petitioner, having supplicat your Honours laitlie ffor certifieing of some enormities and brack of good order committed by severall, both of frie and unfrie, of the cordoner calling; and, in particular, against unfriemen who keipes publick shopes on the heighe streit, and againest such friemen as slights and contemnes the deacone, ther meitings, and gives no obedience according to ther oath, the tyme of ther admissione or for certifieing of servants' fies, conforme to the antient custome, unto which supplicatione [may it please] your honours to grant ane gratious and acceptable answer, by ordeanning the supplicant to give in ane list of the persons delinquents, and therafter to give furder answer to the rest of the supplicatioune as the samen with your honours' answer as the end therof beares, and the supplicant holding it his deutie to render your honours ane accompt, according to your ordinance. *Primo,* it is represented that Johne Smythe is ane frieman, and yet ane dispyser and contraveiner of his deacone, and al ordinancees, meitings, and deficient in all duetie; and that ther ar certaine personnes who hes no enterest to leive in this place, nather by tounne, trade, birth, nor breeding, and hes all chopes upon the foirstreitt to the prejudice of the calling contrair to the antient practise, and sells old shoos with new Leddar, coft out the merchandis chopes, vizt., James Johnstonne, George Smyth, Alexander Blackhall, who als is ain unfree breddar; David Keith, who hes ane number of bairnes, and by all appearance will be burthenable to the toune; Patrick Watsone, who contemues the publick meitings and does nae duetie; John Darge, who hede never ony leirning, and is nothing concernit in toune, trade, birth, nor breeding; Johne Beith, who contemnes the meitings, and does noe deutie; Williame Moir, who belongs naither to toune, nor trade by birth nor breading; James Castill, who hes ane number of bairnes, and by all appearance may be burthenable, and belongs naither to the toune nor trade, by birth nor breeding; Alexander Urquhart, ane strainger, and belongs nothing to toune nor trade; Williame Michie, who wes never brede bot, takin up the trade at his awin hands and hes no interest naither in toune nor trade. *Secundo*, as to any bygane neglects of friemen in ther trade deutie—your honours lait ordinance being intimat unto thame—they have promised due performance with all conveinencie without further heiring which (if done) ther sall be no publick heiring any furder. *Tertio*, as to seruands fies it is desyrit and expectit that the deacone and maisteres may have pouer to regulat the samen according to the ancient custome and pryce of victualls for the tyme since they are best accustimnat heirwith. It is therfoir humblie desyred that your honours will be pleased to conteinew to counteinance us in manteining of our friedome and liberties, first by tacking course with the said John Smyth as he shall be found in error; secundo by tacking course to discharge the saides unfriemen from keiping chopes on the heighe streittis, and that selle no shois with new leddar coft out of the Burgh, bot with such as beis brought them by ther imployeres (and that the deacone and the trade put pryce vpon ther work least peiple shud be extortiounat). And that all be discharged the toune who have not enterest nather in toune nor trade by birth or breeding, and that the deacone and maisteris may have power to regulat ther servandis fies as accords. Wherin your honours favor humblie is attendit.

In response to the petition the Council appointed Baillies Mollesone, Gilbert Daly, and "Capitaine" Melvill to make full inquiry into the "haill particulars above wreitin," and to give what redress was deemed necessary.

The traffic in hides and bark was for a long period regulated by the Shoemaker craft. Any person detected bringing rough hides into the city without having made the deacon acquainted with the fact rendered himself liable to a substantial fine. And for the purpose of detecting and preventing infringements on the acts made anent the importation of hides, the deacon and masters of the craft, each in his turn, were posted every Saturday at the ports of the town to watch and apprehend such as attempted to infringe the statutes. From the following act of the craft, passed in 1640, it would appear that the craftsmen were at times somewhat lax in the performance of this duty :—

10th October, 1640.—The said day ye haill nichtbouris and bretherene of ye calling being conveint this daye thay al, with ane voyce and consent be thir present act, that thay sall dewlie keip sic portis of this burghe as thay sall be injoinit upon be ye dekyn, foir apprehending and taking bak againe roche hydis transportit furthe of this burgh be extraneans. And quha beis absent sall pey to ye weill of ye craft vi. schillings and aucht pennies monie, *toties quoties*. And quha beis absent that promises to cum, be thair dekyn and be the officiar, thair Setterdaye aboutte, sall pay 40s. monie *toties quoties*. And to be poyndit preceislie thairfoir, quharupon thai desyreit act to be maid.

Bark, as well as hides,* was a commodity which no merchant burgess could bring into the town, and sell without first making intimation to the Dean of Guild and deacon of the craft, who, when informed of its arrival, examined the quality, noted the quantity, and fixed the price at which it was to be sold. Frequently the deacon, for behoof of the freemen of the craft, made the first purchase ; the remainder, after the freemen were served, being disposed of by public roup.

The barkmill with its multures, and " any uyther dewtie bygane or to cum," was renounced in favour of the Shoemaker craft in 1605 by David Cargill, for the sum of one hundred pounds Scots.

The following is a statute enacted " anent ane bargane of barkis, coft be ye dekyn foir hymselff and in name of ye craft ":—

10th October, 1540.—The said day forsameikle as ye said James Hall, decain, hafing coft ane bargane of barkis fra Alex. Fraser, merchant, Inverneiss, amounting to ane hundrethe boxis or thairby, to ye weill of ye said calling and ye said decain, payable betwixt and ye 15th day of Januar nixt, on ye shoar of Aberdeen, winde and wedder servand, ye saplin barkis at four pundis ye bowe, ye birk barkis at thrie pundis vi*s*. viii*d.* ye bowe, and that of ye weicht contenit in ye standard maid thairanent, and thairfor willit ye nichtbouris of ye said craft to tak their pairts af of his hands, and relieve him of ye pryces thereof at the merchant's hand, qlk. they willinglie imbracit, as ye maist of thair names taken

---

* Many of the shoemakers, it must be remembered, were also curriers, and made their own leather.

T

thairon on ane paiper bearis, quhairupon ye said decain tuik act of curt and instrument.

The craft feeling themselves "molestit and wronged" in the common market by "contriemen anent selling of barks in seiks," they "to prevent both townsmen and countrymen being altogeddar frusterat and wronged" in the matter, got the Council to ordain the Dean of Guild to "cause mak ane sufficient firlot, with ane peck for measuring such barks as sall be brocht to the mercatt of this burgh in tyme cuming." The market was open at "aucht houres" A.M. in the summer, and at "nyn houres" in the winter time. But notwithstanding these precautions a good deal of smuggling went on. In particular, in 1679, "Jon Cowper and Andro Galloway did at their awin hands buy roch hydes cuming heir be sea, baith from the south and north, as als barks, and did inhanse and monopoleiss the samen without offering the samen to the Deine of Gild, quhairby the said shoomaker traid, quho ought to haf hade the first offer of the samen as belanging to their tred, wes now sistit to buy the said comodities fra thame at the second or third hand, att ane deare and great rait, quhilk maid thame unabill to leive be their callings for maintenance of their families, and beireing of burdens with their nichbouris, and to mak and sel their handiwork at the rates and pryces thay formerlie used to doe." Cowper and Galloway had bought "ane parsill of hydes of about fyfteen pound sterling worth of pryce," on the last day of March, and the Trade petitioned to have them ordained to give the said complainers "ane pairt of the said parsill of hydes at the samen pryce thay boucht the samen thameselffis." The Council accordingly ordained that half the hides should be given to the Trade at the price paid by the purchasers and half the expenses they had been at, to which Cowper and Galloway agreed.

At an early period the shoemakers appointed one of their number to act as "clerk to the flesh market," his chief duty being to visit the market every Wednesday and Friday, between the hours of ten and twelve in the forenoon, in order to see that the hides "beis free fra cutting, scoreing, or gashing in the slaying thereof." Previous to 1698, the boxmaster acted as inspector, but in that year the two offices were separated, a salary ranging from ten to two pounds ten shillings Scots being paid to the clerk of the flesh market. Strangers and unfreemen paid a penny for each hide inspected, and freemen a halfpenny, the proceeds going to the poor of the Trade. This impost frequently led to serious contentions and disputes betwixt the fleshers and the Shoemaker Incorporation. The fleshers petitioned the Magistrates to have the custom abolished, and in so far as the amount imposed was concerned the Magistrates gave judgment in their favour by reducing the tax by one half, viz., for freemen, one farthing per hide, and for strangers or unfreemen, one halfpenny, but all the other clauses in the Act were allowed to remain in full force during the pleasure of the Council.

The records of the Shoemaker Trade are more than ordinarily voluminous.* The regular freemen were frequently at law with the cobblers and unfreemen in the neighbourhood of the town, who came to the market to sell their wares, and these disputes are almost all recorded at length ; and they also contain interesting information about the hide trade, the barking and buying of leather, and the difficulties the craft had in preventing the importing of boots and shoes manufactured in the south. The oldest minute-book which contains the acts and statutes of the Trade has the following preface :—

This buik perteinis to ye Cordoner Craft friemen burgess of Aberdene beginine upon ye twentie twa day of Januar, 1634, wharin is conteened sindrie acts and statutes maid be ye deacones and maisteris of ye said craft to be obeseruit and trewlie keepit be ye haill members and bretherne of ye said craft in all tyme comyn be yair gryte aithis sworne to yat effect. Trewlie extracted and drawn furthe of thair auld court buikis of the said craft be Johnne Donaldson, notar court clerk, at command of the said craft.

"The Lord is the portion of our inheritance." ·

The following are the principal acts and statutes :—

ANENT KEEPING THE SABBATH.

Imprimus, it is statut and ordanit foir ye glorie of God yat ye Lordis Sabbothe beis sainctefeit, and yat ye severill houris of prayer and preiching

---

* Some years ago Mr. James Downie, a member of the Trade, transcribed the greater part of the records, but found them too voluminous to put in book form. His MS. has proved of great assistance to me in preparing this notice of the Shoemaker Trade.—E.B.

be precieslie keipit be maisteris, seruandis, prentises, of ye said craft, and
na worke to be wrocht, nor buithe dore oppin, efter ye prayer bell ceiss in
ye morning, and na vaiging nor drynking.   And quha brakis thir present
ordinance sall pay as followis, viz., ye maister vij. s., ye seruand iii. s. ij. d.,
and ye prenteis to be punishit in his personne at ye will of ye dekyn and
maisteris.   And ye maister of ye said seruand to be comptabill yairfor,
efter lauchful tryall and heirupon maid act.

ANENT OBEDIENCE TO THE DEACON.

Item, it is statut and ordanit yat ye haill brethrene sall give dew obedience to ye deacone of ye said craft, baithe in court, comand, and ordinance,
and nane dissobey nor contradict ye said deacone nor ye lauchfull ordinances of ye said craft sett downe be thair ancient predicessouris, and quha
brackis yis ordinance sall be condinglie punischeit at ye will and discretioune of ye deacone and maisteris foir ye tyme.

ANENT SERVANTS AND APPRENTICES.

Item, it is statut and ordanit yat it sall not be leasum to no maister to
receave ony servand or prenteis to work in yair buithe without yai cum
first befoir ye deacone for ye tyme, and mak ye said deacone acquaint yairwith, and quha bracks yis present ordinance shall pey to ye box for ye use
of ye poore ye sowme of thretie shillings Scottis.

Item, it sall not be leasom to na frieman heiroff to accep of ane uthers
seruand undischargit of his former maister, and hes leife askit and gewin,
and quha does in ye contrar of yis present act sall pey to the collecktor ye
sowme of 40s. monie to be peyit and unforgewin.

Item, giff ony sall be fund to inteiss or withdraw ane uther manes seruand
without leive and consent of his awin maister, ye contraveinar sall pey in
4 pundis to ye said craftis box, *toties quoties.*

Item, it is statut and ordanit yat giff it hapens ony personn to give in
ane complent againis ony frieman heirof for not doing of dewtie to yair
seruandis and apprenteiss undir yair chairge, and giff it happens ye maister
to have failzeit in his pairt, he sal be amerciat and punishitt in ane unlaw
of sic monies as ye deacone and maisteris sall modifie according to ye
grauvitie of ye faulte.

ANENT "MADE" WORK.

Item, it is statut and ordanit that it sall not be leasum to no frieman of
ye said craft to bringe hame frae ony pairt within this kingdome ony maid
work to top or sell ye samyn within this burghe, or at landwart mercatts,
and quha contravenes heirintill sall pey fyve markis monie, to ye comon box
for helping of ye poore.

ANENT BUYING WITHOUT THE DEACON'S CONSENT.

Item, it is statut and ordanit that it sall not be leasum to no frieman
heirof to buy ony merchandice belanging to thair craft fra extraneans to his

awin vse, bot that ye samyn sall be coft be ye decain of ye said craft to ye use of ye haill brethrene. Twa—that it sall not be leasom to no pryvate man to buy sic comodities to his awin use bot consent of ye decain, as said is, and quha contraveines heirintill sall pey ye sowme of 40 shillings monie.

ANENT DISMISSING SERVANTS.

Item, it is statut and ordanit, that in caice it sall fall out that any maister of ye craft offer ony injurie offensive to his servandis: in that caice it sall not be leasum to ye servand offendit to remuve fra his maisteris worke vnless he beis compelit be his maister to remuve, and in caice he be so remuvit that he immediatelie thairefter cum to ye deacone and mak him foirseine thairof, vtherwayis the said servand to pay to ye vse of ye poore ye sowme of iij. shilling and 2d., and his remaining in his maisteris service efter he has recivit injurie sall not be prejudicall to him seiking justice, quhilk sall be ministratt to him, quhan and at quhat tyme ye pairtie offendit sall sute for the samyen.

ANENT PROFANITY, CURSING, AND BANNING.

Item, forsameikill as ye deacone and maisteris understanding in thair conventioune throw laik of punishments in tyme past, ye name of God is prophaulie spokin of be rasche aithes, taking his blissit name in vane, and be cursing and banning; for remeade thairof it is statut and ordanit be voyce of ye haill calling, that quhasoever sall contravene this Act, that everie persone how oft he happens to transgress sall pey to ye persone quha happens to be collector aucht pennies scotis, *toties quoties*, for helping of ye poor.

ANENT DRINKING AND LOOSE BEHAVIOUR ON THE LORD'S DAY.

Item, foirsameikill, siclyke, as ye dekyn and maisteris haveing perfyt intelligence of ye lowsniss of ye seruand boyis of ye craft, and of yair skandelous behaviour in vaiging and drynking on the Lordis Sabbothe, contempending God and His ordinances, and neglekting of yair maisteris and behaviour towardis yame. For remede yairof, yat it is statut and ordanit yat everie seruand repare to ye kirk on ye Lordis Sabbothe, afoir and efter nune, with yair maisteris, and heir Godis wird, and yat yay cum oute of ye kirk recompaneing yair maisteris. It sall be askit gif yay cum not, and ane count to be takin on Monondai of yair maisteris, and yair aithis takin yairon gif ye seruandis hes obeyit ye said ordinance. And ye maister of ye seruand contravening without ony lauchful caus, for ilk brak sall pay iii. shillings, quhilk ye maister salbe answerabill for, and he to haue releiff of ye seruandis vaigis.

ANENT OFFENSIVE SPEECHES.

Item, it is statut and ordanit that if it happens ony frieman heirof to offend ane uyther be offensive or scandleous speiches ayther in his awin presence or behind his back, or dois any uyther molestation, ye doar thair-of sall pay to ye comone box ye sowme of fouir pundis by and attour sateis-factioue to ye pairtie griveit at ye will and discretione of ye deacone.

ANENT WORKING ON THE SABBATH DAY.

Item, it is statut and ordanit for ye glorie of God yat quhosoever beis fund on ye Sabbothe day efter ye prayer bell stanis ringin ayer maister or seruand in yair buithes salbe punishitt as followis, viz., gif ye seruand beis working at new schoone, ye saidis to be inbrocht to ye craftis vse ; and gif he beis fund mending auld shoois ye seruand to pey fouir schillingis yairfor to ye collector, or than to tak awaye ye schoone yat beis mendit. And ordains visitoris to be appoyntit for yat effect. And yis act is bot prejudice of ye foirsaid act—anent keiping of ye kirk on ye Sabbothe.

ANENT FEEING APPRENTICES.

Item, it is statut and ordanit yat it sall not be leasom to no frieman heirof to fee nor conduce with ony prenteis to serve for fewir yeirs yan fyve zeirs as prenteis, and ane zeir yair-efter for meit and fie, and quhan he hes servit furthe his haill prenteisschipp, sall serve yair-efter in his progress for uyther thrie zeirs ; quhane he may find best sichte and his comoditie. And that the prenteis beis nowayes acceptit in ye craft as ane frieman or his bill be harde, quntill he have servit completelie ye haill nyn zeirs, and yis act to strik againe thame yat is in present service or to serve heirefter.

ANENT BOOKING APPRENTICES.

Item, it is statut and ordanit that ilk fiall yat happins to cum and serve ony of ye friemen heirof, sall pay to ye collector of ye craft twentie shillings-monie scottis togedder with four shillings to ye clerk foir buiking him. And ilk prenteis to be receavit heirefter be indenture sall pey to ye said collector foir defrayeing of ye craftis adyce the sowme of fourtie shillings scottis monie togidder with four shillings to ye clerk foir buiking ye samen. And sic lyke it is statut and ordanit yat quhatsomever prenteis yat hes servit furthe ye haill zeirs of his prenteischippe, and gif he enter as ane journeyman with ony maister sall pey to ye said collector twentie shillings with four shillings foir buiking ye samen : swa yat he sall pey als aft as he enters with ony maister ; and yat be reasone of craftis with in ye samen have hichtit yair servands and prenteisses entries.

Item, it is statut and ordanit that ye clarke of ye said craft sall mak all indentures betwixt maister and prenteis, and that it sall not be leasum to no maister to give, grant, or subscryve ony back band for fewir yeirs yan is contenit in his indentur—and quha contraveines herintill sall pey x. pundis be ane unlaw; to be takin upp and not for-given—and als it is statut and ordanit yat gif it happens ony prenteis of ye said craft do comitt fornicatioune or adultrie wt-in ye yeirs of his prenteis-schip, in that caice, eftir tryall and prowen yairof, he sall beginne of new againe and serve over ye haill yeirs and paines conteinit in his indentur.

ANENT ENTRY MONEY.

Item, forsameikle as ye deacone and maisteris with consent of ye haill brethrene of ye said craft understanding ye chaipness of intrant friemen creiping in amongst yame for ye compositioune or banquet siller verie far prejudicall to thair comon box and enritching thairof, quhairas uthyer craftis verie far extendis thair compositiounes or banquet siller ; for remeid yairof the deacone and maisteris with consent of ye said craft as haveing power to augment ye saids compositiounes have statut and ordanit yat sic interants yat beis admittit friemen amongst thame in tyme cuming sall pey ye compositiounes following, vizt., the prenteis yat hes servit within yis burt, ye sowme of fourty poundis. And ye extranear or servand yat hes not bein prenteis sall pey ane hundred merks and mair according to ye deacone and maisteris will, by and attour ye regular dewis usit and wont, togidder with twentie shillings peyable be ye new intrant to be given in to ye deacone conveinars box according to ane ordinance maid yairanent. Nayer sall it be leasom to na brethreine of ye said craft to speik in favors of ye intrant for ony mitigatione he wes undir ye pain of ye craftis unlaw.*

23rd January, 1698.—The traid by voyce of court did stricktlie statute and ordain that, in all tyme coming, no prenteis shall be admitted freeman of the said incorporatione for less banquet siller than ane hundreth markes scots money, and no extranean for less banquet silver than six score and ten markes foirsaid. And that to be payed in readie money, or then the deacone and boxmaister for the tyme to be lyable therefor. And also it is ordained that the bill money and sey mony be allowed in pairt of payment of the above written. And that the new entrant shall, in all tyme coming, be quit and free of all expences for drink (except at the three tymes under mentioned), vizt.—first when the entrant puts in his bill, secondly, when the sey is halff perfited, and thirdly, when the sey is past and the haill traid present. And ordains that freemen's chyldring be admitted conforme to the aucient custom and laudable Acts made thereanent. And that no freeman contraveen thir presents, nor come in the contrair hereof in all tyme comeing.

ANENT WEARING HATS AT BURIALS.

Item, it is statut and ordanit that quasomever yat ar in use to weir hattis sall adres them selffis theirwith, orderlie to all burialls as yei happin to be warnit yairto. And quha beis absent frome ye said burialls being warnit laulie yairto sall pey iiijs. to ye deacone of ye craft for ye tyme. And quha brakis yis present ordinance sall pey sex s. viijd. *toties quoties.*

ANENT SPOILING NEW WORK.

Item, it is statut and ordanit yat gif ouy frieman heirof spyle ony new wark to ony personne quhatsumever, and giff ye complaint cums in befoir

---

* This act was ratified in September, 1684.

ye deacone and maisteris, and thay find ye samen vnsufficient, ye pairtie defendand sall pey ane unlaw to ye craft at ye will and discretioune of the deacone and maisters for ye tyme, by and attour sateisfactioune to ye pairtie complainane.*

ANENT FOREIGN SHOES.

Item, it is statut and ordanit that no friemane of ye said craft sall tak vpon hand to tak or receave frae ony person quhatsomever ony Inglis schoone, Frenshe schoon, buittis, panterneil, or stripingis, to sell ye samen in culloirs of his awin maidwork, and quha contraveins this present act sal pey xi. s. monie, *toties quoties*. And that nane buy nor sell new work that is maid outwith this burgh under ye paine foirsaid.

ANENT THE DEACON.

Item, it is statut and ordanit yat ye craft sall choiss about Michealmass, zerlie, ane decain amangis ye sex maisteris, ye maist wysest and vndirstandin manne, yat hes unctioune and pouer to gowerne ye said calling.

ANENT THE TRADES HOSPITAL.

Item, it is statut and ordanit yat quhasomever of ye said craft wilfullie withholds his help of his meanis from ye craftis hospitall sall have no pairt nor portionne of ye mortefeit monies dedicat for yat effect, nayer to have vote in ye choising of ye deacone and maisteris of ye said craft, or admissionne in ye said houss of any frieman.

ANENT BRIBERY.

Item, it is statut and ordanit yat quhasumevir of ye said craft convocats yame selffis for choising of ye deacone befoir ye day of electiounne, or suvornes ony vythir to geirss† ony mane, befoir ye said daye, the doar yairof, quhasumevir he be, sall be convictit in six pundis money, to be inbrocht to ye deacone convenirs box, and giff he have na monies, to be debarit of al vote in ony meiting quhatsumevir—and sic lyke quha peys not yair quarterlie stagis, entries, and convictiounes, sall haue nae vote in ony tym heireftir in choising of ye deacone.

ANENT MEETINGS OF THE CRAFT.

Item, it is statute and ordanit that quhatsomever deacone of yis present craft conveins in his awin houss ayer with his haill craft or with his haill maisteris, to hauld court or meetings anent any affairs of ye craft, and conveines not formlie in yiar convyening houss of ye Trinities—in yat caice ye deacone contraveining of yis present ordinance sall pey to ye deacone conveneris box ye sowme of sex pundis monie *toties quoties*. And yat he pey

---

* On 3rd December, 1633, this act " was ratifit and approvit be voyce of court."

† To oust or throw out.

ye samen withiu fourtie-aucht houris yairefter, and failyeing yairof sall pey ye doubill of ye sowme, and to be poynit yairfor.

Item, it is statut and ordanit that at quhatsumever court beis halden ayther generall or particular within the said conveining house, the court being ance fencit, quhasoever thairefter speikis without leave askit and given sall pay sex shillings money *toties quoties*, and if he refuse salbe presentlie poyndit thairfor, to be inbrocht to the craftis awin box, and gif ony beis refractur to be defraudit of his vote at ony meeting of court till ye samen be obeyit.

Item, it is statut and ordanit that quhasoever persone beis lauchfullie warnit to ony meiting or court quhatsumever, and cumes not at the hour appoyntit, sall pay iiij shillings money, *toties quoties*, to be inbrocht to the deacone's and maisteris' uses. And sic lyke quha pays not thair quarterlie stagis, entriess, and convictiounes sall have no vote at ony tyme heirefter iu choising of the deacone.

ANENT ATTENDING THE "SHOONE MERCAT."

Item, it is statut and ordanit according to auld use and wont that ye deacone of ye said craft sall go ilk setterdaye with ane of ye maisteris to ye comon shoone mercat for ye trying of all unsufficient work repairing yairto. And if ony beis fund in ye said mercat (with concurrance of ye magistrates), to escheat and inbriug ye samen to ye use of ye craft, conform to ane ordinance maid yairupon be ye provost, baillies, and counsell of ye samen in favors of ye said craft.

ANENT "MAISTERSTICKS."

Item, forder, it is statut and ordanit that quhasumever presumes to receave the benifyte of ane frieman sall have twa sey maisteris to awaitt on hym quhill his maisterstick be maid, and to mak ane pair buitts, twa pair shoone, and ane pair slipperis, suffycient work.

ANENT SELLING TO UNFREEMEN.

Item, it is statut and ordanit that quhasumeyer frieman sells to vnfrieman ony sollis, heills, boords, or ony sorte of new leddar, ye contraveneir sall pey to ye weil of ye craft ij shillings, *toties quoties*, as ye samen beis prowin and qualifiet.

ANENT INSUFFICIENT BARKIT LEATHER.

Item, it is statute and ordanit that quhasomever of ye said craft sells to any of ye brethrene insufficient barkit ledder ye contraveiner yairof sall pay to ye weil of ye calling ye sowme of iiij pundis monie *toties quoties* by and attour satisfactionne to ye pairties. And yis act to strik als weil againes yame yat sellis insufficient barkit leddar iu common mercats and fairs as withiu yis burght.

ANENT WEARING HATS AT HEAD COURTS.

Item, it is statute and ordainit yat quhasomever are in vse to weir hattis on yair heids sall adress yame selffis yairwith to all heid courtis formalie. And quha contraveines sall pay 6 shillings and 8d. *toties quoties.*

ANENT SERVANTS BARKING LEATHER.

Item, it is statut and ordainit that no servaud sall have ony fordder libertie in barking, yeirlie, during his abyding with his maister, bot onlie ane hyde and ane skyn, and quha contravenes heirintill salbe lyabill for ye craftis vnlaw, to be weyit by thame, bothe ye maister and servand to pay the vnlaw equallie betwixt thame, in respek ye maister suld not give way to ony fordder than his deu.

ANENT WAGES.

It is statute and ordanit that it sall not be leasom to no frieman heirof to give to ony servand for his wark mair nor sextein pennies scots, excep he beis trainit up in forran countreyeis. And quha brakis thir ordinance sall pey to ye collector in name of ye craft ye sowme of x. markis monie, *toties quoties,* and that ye said servand sall be removit fra that maister and sall go to ane nyther as ye will of ye deacone and maisteris that will keip this present ordinance, qlk act wes maid be consent of ye haill calling.

ANENT OUTSIDE WORKING.

Item, it is statute and ordainit yat it sall not be leasom to no frieman heirof to mak new wark in merchandis' houss, nor work leddar there, bot onlie in friemen's buithis, and quha brakis this present ordinance tha sall be vnlawit and convictit in x. pundis monie, *toties quoties.* And this ordinance to strik agains al inhabitants that resydis in ye toune.

ANENT APPLICATION FOR THE FREEDOM.

Item, it sall not be leasom to no prenteis that hes servit within this burght to seik the benefite to be friemen unto the tyme he serve within this burgh the space of thrie yeirs immediatlie efter the entering of his prenteishipe, and this to staud perpetuallie in all tyme cuming.

Item, siclyke it is statute and ordanit that na extranear sal be receavit as freeman within this burghe unto the tyme he serve the nichtbouris of the tredd be the space of thrie yeirs.

ANENT THE PRICE FOR MAKING SHOES.

Item, it is statute and ordainit that no freemen give mair to ther journeymen and fialls bot only fyve shillings for the pair of menis shooue, and four shillings for the pair of womenis', without any bountie or other benefitis, under quhatsomevir name, cullor, or pretext, and this act to have effect in all tyme to come after Pashe nix, 1664. And quha sall contraveine and do in the contrair, sall pay thrie pounds *toties quoties* for the use of the poore.

ANENT COBBLERS.

Item, it is statute and ordanit that no frieman give out ony worke of quhatsomever sort to ony cobbler or vther unfrieman without their awin buithes at ony tym heerefter, under ye pane of fouir pundis scottis, *toties quoties*, to be peyit in to ye collector's box be ye persons contraveneing.

7th February, 1698.—The traid ordains that in all tyme hereafter no cobler be admitted within the burgh except the supplicant give in ane bill to the court, and that the court get ane voyce thereanent. And this to be observed in all tyme coming.

ANENT FREEMEN DWELLING IN THE SPITTAL.

8th February, 1687.—Item, it is statute and ordanit be voyce of court that ilk freeman of the said traid that dwalls in the Spithill, Old Aberdeen, or any territories about the toune of Aberdeen, shall acquaint the deacon of the craft befoir they fee or conduce aither prenteiss or fiall : and shall be obligit to pay entry-money and quarterlie pennie als freelie in all respects as ane other freeman that resides or dwalls within the toune off Aberdeen conforme to the laudabill lawe and custom. And this to be observed in all tyme comeing, and quha brakis this act to pay 30 shillings *toties quoties.*

ANENT JOURNEYMEN.

30th November, 1696.—The said day the traid did statut and ordain that no journeymen of the said calling sall in tyme comeing mak ony new work within the hous he dwalls in, but onlie in his maisteris schope, excep he have ane relevant excuse, and in caice he beis caught working ony new work contrair to this Act, the said new work sall be attatchit for the vse of the comone box and confiscat therto.

ANENT A PHYSICIAN TO THE INCORPORATIONS.

4th March, 1786.—The said day the trade having taken under their consideration a proposal from Dr. James Davidson, a son of Convener Davidson, relative to his proposal of attending the several Incorporations, their families and servants, and providing them in medicines ; they approve of the plan and agree to make trial of it for one year, and to contribute from the funds of their society three pounds sterling for one year, for paying Mr. Davidson for his attendance, and grant warrant to the boxmaster to pay him accordingly when the other trades do, and agree also to pay what medicines shall be provided by him for the sick.

16th February, 1787.—The trade having heard the proposal anent having a dispensary physician to the trades, they appoint the deacon and boxmaster as a committee to wait on Dr. Davidson, with the committee from other trades, to hear the plan proposed, that the same may be laid before the trade.*

ANENT THE ELECTION DINNER.

16th October, 1792.—The trade, by a very great majority of votes, agree that, in time coming, there shall be no election supper or dinner to be paid by the boxmaster from the trade's funds, it being their opinion that the money so expended may be more properly applied for the support of the poor of the trade, and in future no boxmaster shall be allowed more than ten shillings for incidents with the tenants at receiving their rents.†

A fruitful source of trouble to the cordiners was the importation of boots and shoes into the town from the south. In 1662 a petition was presented to the Magistrates complaining of boots and shoes being brought from Edinburgh and other places, and that "thereby they wer not able to undergoe the public burdens of this burgh nor to interteine themselves nor mantein their severall families, without remeid wer provydit be the Counsell for that effect." The Council appointed and ordained "that no merchant within the Burghe bring to the samen from Edinburgh or any other place within this Kingdom to sell, top, or exchange in their booths or otherways any boots or shoes nor any maid work tending to the prejudice of the forsaid Traid. But that the forsaid Traid injoy and possess the samen, and commoditie redounding thereby, as ther libertie and freedom, with certification to any who sall contraveen to be punishit at the Counsell's pleasure, the freemen of the said traid always furnishing the inhabitants of the Burgh as they sall be imployit with sufficient shoes, boots, and other maid work needful of good and sufficient leather within competent time efter advertisement, at the ordinar pryce and rates set downe yeirly thereanent be the Counsell, wherin if they or any of them be found to contraveene and be deficient the forsaid Act to be void and null and of no effect in all tyme ther-

---

* As nothing further is reported touching the above subject, it seems the matter ended here, and that no appointment was made.

† At the passing of this Act, the deacon (Alex. Hutcheon) became indignant and left the chair, refusing at the same time to sign the minute after it had been inserted in the book, and during the time the clerk was reading the Act he left the hall. Twenty-five remained, who elected George Strachan preses, whom they empowered to sign the same. However, when the boxmaster presented his accounts and was discharged, Hutcheon was again in the chair as deacon, and signed the accounts.

after, and the merchants to have libertie to bring home and
sell shoes or other maid work for the use of the towne as
they sall have occasione, and declaring it to be always leasome
to the merchants to bring home boots and shoes for their own
particular uses allenerly and no further except in caice forsaid."—*Council Register, vol.* liv., *p.* 373.

A strict line of distinction was always drawn between the
cobblers and regular shoemakers.   The cobblers, while recognised by the craft and permitted to share in its benevolent
funds on payment of certain small annual contributions, were
not made freemen or admitted to full membership.   They were
allowed to have stalls in the public places of the town, but
they were prohibited from erecting sign-boards, and were
otherwise strictly restricted to a certain class of work.   From
time to time, however, serious disputes arose, and at last, in
1731, the Trade passed the following statute:—

19th January, 1731.—The trade taking to their consideration the great
loss by the freemen of this trade through the great number of cobblers in
this burgh, and that their keeping of shops to the open street, and also
that the number of them is daily increasing, whereby they enhance a great
part of the work that should be wrought by freemen, they therefor unanimously Statute and Ordain in all tyme coming, such as are already admitted cobblers in this burgh shall pay yearly of quarter-pennies to the
boxmaster, for the use of the trade, sixteen shillings, Scots money.   And
also the trade hereby prohibit and discourage the said cobblers or any of
them from having any shops in any public street of this burgh, and from
putting up signs at their shops, the same being so highly prejudicial to the
free members of this trade.   And the trade do also hereby statute that no
person shall be admitted as a cobbler within this burgh or liberties thereof
on any pretext whatsomever unless such, allanerly, as have served apprenticeship to a freeman of this trade, and that such as have served apprenticeship as aforesaid shall pay to the trade for the liberty to be cobblers such
a sum as the trade shall think proper.

This action on the part of the freemen led the cobblers to
take steps for forming themselves into a separate corporation,
with a deacon, boxmaster, clerk, and other office-bearers; but
the Magistrates, on being appealed to for an interdict by the
Shoemaker Incorporation, declared "that the cobblers of this
burgh are a subordinate part of the society of the Shoemaker
Trade, and depend upon them, and found that it was illegal
and unwarrantable in the cobblers to put up signs or to erect

themselves in a separate society, or have a deacon, boxmaster, clerk, or public box, and therefore discharged all practices in tyme coming under all highest pains that the Majestrates should think fit, and ordained the papers, which they have by way of records, to be destroyed, and appointed the three shillings and sixpence sterling money of their public stock to be distributed among the poor cobblers by the present deacon of the shoemakers; but found that it has been the practice of this and other cities that cobblers have stalls in public places, for working therein at the ordinary work competent to cobblers, and found that the contributions formerly in use to be paid by the cobblers to the boxmaster of the Shoemaker Trade is eight shillings eight pennies Scots per annum, and that the voluntary contributions agreed to be paid among themselves is eight shillings Scots per annum, which would be more properly lodged in the hands of the boxmaster of the Shoemaker Trade, and therefor found it just and reasonable that each cobbler should pay in and contribute yearly sixteen shillings Scots money to the boxmaster of the Shoemaker Trade, and that in lieu thereof the said cobblers, when they became old and unable to work, they shall be entituled to the charity of the Shoemaker Trade, and that the trade shall be burdened with the expenses of burying them when they have no effects for that purpose, and found it just and reasonable that none should be admitted cobblers in time coming but such as are, or shall be, apprentices, or serve as journeymen to some of the Shoemaker Trade, and that each cobbler of quality aforesaid ought to pay of composition at his entry ten merks Scots money, and that the cobblers ought to keep themselves within due bounds, and not encroach upon the freemen. And for effectuating the premises and securing both parties in the above terms, they ordain that an Act should be passed by the Incorporation to that effect, with certification thereof, before the next term of Martinmas, and the Incorporation failing thereof, then the cobblers shall be free of paying any new contributions but only the foresaid eight shillings and eight pennies Scots yearly."—*Trades Papers.*

There were also a class of men known as "Spitalmen"— residents in the Spital portion of Old Aberdeen—who had to make an annual contribution to the funds of the Trade; and residents in the following district were also made to pay :— Well o' Spa, Futtie, Garden Nook, Hardweird, Loanhead, Rubislaw, Hazelhead, Couparstoun, Ruthrieston, Hardgate, Pitmuxton, and Bridge of Dee. These men paid their dues at Candlemas, Ruid-day, Hallow-day, and Lammas Court, and on these occasions they appear to have been hospitably entertained, "Att receiving the spitalmen money £1 15s. 4d."; and "with several spitalmen and single soled men 8s.," being common entries in the books. These men came into the market to sell their shoes, and it was mainly for this privilege that they were obliged to pay dues to the Trade.

The essays prescribed in this craft varied in accordance with the class of shoes that the applicant made. There were men for making single soled shoes and double soled shoes, and no craftsman was permitted to make any kind of shoes except of the description which had been prescribed to him for his essay. The following was the form of entry with regard to the admission of a freeman :—

12th September, 1692.—At Aberdeen the twalt day of September, jaj, vi c., and nynty twa yeiris. In presence of William Strachan, deacone, Alexander Ogilvie gave in his sey : To witt, a pair of single solled shoon and a pair of single pumps with sex pounds scots, of sey money, and gave band to the traid that he should work no other work but single work conform to his sey, and that he should not intyse no frieman's servands to work to him. Whereupon his sey was past, and 100 pounds of failzie to be putt in his band; and he payit the boxmaister fyve markes in compleet payment of his compositione.

Curriers, who were not at the same time shoemakers, have been admitted to the Shoemaker Trade, the essay prescribed being as follows :—

27th Apryll, 1691.—The said day John Denoon gave in his sey to be currier, with sex pundis scots of sey monie, and did offer to be serviceable to the traid, and presented ane cowe hyde, and ane ox hyde, weil dressit, to the contentment of the traid, wherupone his qualificatione wes ordanit to be reported to the Counsell.

In a dispute which arose between the master shoemakers and their journeymen, in 1668, regarding the rate of pay for making boots and shoes, the Magistrates fixed the rate for "ilk pair of best shoes wrocht be them for men, fyve shillings Scots monie. Item, the second sort of men's shoes wrocht be them, ilk pair four shilling sex pennies money foresaid. Item, for ilk pair of best shoes for women, three shilling sex pennies money foresaid. Item, for ilk pair of weemen's shoes of the third sort, two shilling sex pennies money foresaid. Being all good and sufficient work, and which are all to be payed after completeing of the said work respectivlie. And anent that part of the supplicatione relating to restraining of the said journeymen mending and cobbling of shoes within ther owin houss, statutes and ordains that the said journeymen sall begine to ther work with ther imployers at sex houres in the morning and continue untill sex houres in the afternoon, usual and convenient tyme being allowit to them at nyne and twelve houres in the forenoon for refreshment."—*Council Register, vol.* lv., *p.* 107.

The account books of this Trade have been much better preserved than some of the others. From entries that occur in the earlier accounts it is evident that the old books had originally consisted of loose and unruled paper. One quire of paper was all that the Trade purchased at a time, and when filled up another was procured until a certain number had accumulated of sufficient bulk to form a book for binding. In 1694 one of these quires cost the Trade eight shillings Scots (eightpence sterling), and the cost of binding one pound four shillings Scots (two shillings sterling). The following are a few entries taken at random from the accounts:—

1695.—To lyneing to Patrick Gordons coat by ordours .	1 02 08
To deacone Gordone by ordor for lyneing his coat	00 14 00
In deacone Curries at dennar and to the fidlers .	6 13 4
At aireing ye paperis	00 12 00
With ye Conveiner quhan ye box wes paynting .	2 17 4
Quhan ye box wes openit and ye paiperis putt in	00 12 00
Quhan george skeen wes putt in the toolboth in John Smiths house	00 3 00
Att tua tymes wt Clk Davidsone wt the traid .	2 00 00
Att ane ither tyme wt Clerk Davidsone and maisteris	1 11 8
More quhan the marches wes sett up in Clk Davidsons	1 11 3
1697-8.—For a chacke locke to the midd dore of the daske	00 10 00

1702.—To a poore man that his house was burnt, by order	0	4	0
To a destressit tradesman q^{ch} had 4 ribbs broken in his side	0	6	0
To a destressed pooreman come out of Ireland and 8 barnes by order of the Convener . . .	0	6	0
1706.—To a poore woman quho hade borne many children	00	10	00
1712.—To Rot. Coutts, blind, going to London . .	0	8	0
At receiving extraordinars	1	10	0
1714.—For a pair marikin shoes to Dean of Gild officer .	02	06	0
1743.—To Dr. Philips for cutting John Smith's nose .	16	8	0

The wife of a journeyman shoemaker was thus rewarded for bringing forth triplets in 1784 :—

29th June, 1784.—The said day John Forbes represented that David M'Allan's wife had brought furth three children at one birth. The trade, on account of said David being Mr. Forbes's principal servant, grant warrant to the Boxmaster to give him one pound sterling.

The entry for which in the boxmaster's accounts is as follows :—

Paid David M'Allan, journeyman, on account of his wife having three children at one birth, £1.

Forbes afterwards entered the Trade in the year 1792, and died in 1821.

At a very early date the cordiners formed a connection with the church. As already mentioned, they had, prior to the Reformation, a special chaplain for their altar in St. Nicholas Kirk, and when the change of religion took place the craft fitted up "dasks," first in St. Nicholas, and then in Trinity Kirk. In 1741 they fitted up a new "dask," the cost of which is set forth in the boxmaster's accounts as follows:—

DISCHARGE OF MONEY BESTOWED IN BUILDING THE NEW LOFT IN THE NEW CHURCH, ANNO 1706.

Item.—In Ion Burnett's with the clerk anent ane Act	£1	1	0
„ „ Ion Smythe's house on the Counsell day .		0	9	8
„ „ Convenir Patersone's when the Act was granted		0	8	0
„ „ Convenir Douglas' house the sd day . .		0	8	8
„ To Clerk Thomson for the Act, in gold . .		14	4	0
„ In the Convener's anent the Loaft, with several others		0	10	6
„ To Clerk Deans for signing the Act and getting the same		3	1	6
„ To him for ane other Act in parchment . .		1	9	0

U

Item.—At agreeing with the Wrights . . .	£0	16	0
„ With some of the masters and Wrights . .	0	5	4
„ In Convener Whyte's, with the Wrights and several Shoemakers	0	15	0
„ With the Masters and Wrights at communing	1	1	4
„ Of earnest moe to the Wrights . . .	0	14	6
„ With the Clerk anent drawing the Contracts .	0	2	0
„ At desyiring the Convener to be present at contracting	0	3	0
„ At subscribing the contracts before the Convener	0	10	0
„ To the Clerk for writing out pairt of the Contracts	0	14	6
„ In the Convener's when we came from the Baillies for warrant . . .	0	12	8
„ With the Master of Kirkwark in Convener Paterson's	0	6	8
„ With Clerk Deans and Convener Whyte .	0	7	8
„ To the Wrights to buy timber for their paines	266	19	4
„ With the Convener and others at several tymes	0	13	6
„ To the Master of Kirkworks to let the wrights work in the Church	2	18	0
„ Protesting against the Hammermen anent the Crown	0	3	0
„ To Mr. Keith, advocate, for drawing bill anent the Crown	1	16	0
„ With Jon Watson, wright	0	6	0
„ With Clerk Deans in writing the Act anent the Loaft	0	16	0
„ In Convener Paterson's anent the Loaft .	0	8	0
„ In Convener Whyte's that night after the Contracts were subscrybed . .	0	9	0
„ In Clerk Deans' house anent the Acts . .	0	10	6
„ With the Master of Kirkwork and Masons anent the Loaft	0	18	8

(Scots)   £302 19 0

During the execution of the above work the Hammermen Trade gave in a representation to the Magistrates relative to the armorial bearings which the Shoemakers were having executed for the purpose of being put up and fixed upon the front of their newly-erected desk. The Hammermen considered that the Shoemakers had no right to have a crown upon their armorial bearings, but on a reference to the patent granted by the Lyon King at Arms, it was found that the

Shoemakers were as much entitled to the crown as the Hammermen.

In 1854 the Shoemakers obtained a private Act of Parliament to confirm their titles and conveyances, and to regulate the administration of the funds and affairs of the craft. It is drawn in similar terms to the Acts obtained by the Hammermen and the Bakers. For a long time the Shoemaker craft was in very straitened circumstances. Much of its annual revenue was spent in litigation and protecting its exclusive privileges; but about a century ago matters improved financially, and the Trade are now proprietors of part of the lands of Ferryhill, Drywell Park (now Watson Street), Clay Croft (Gilcomston), Well Croft, and part of Marywell Croft, Lochfield Croft, part of Hardweird Croft, part of Queen Street, West North Street, and Shoe Lane; and Dirty Riggs. This last mentioned piece of ground was afterwards called "The Broad Rig and Yaird," and it now forms the North Lodge grounds. In the year 1723 it belonged to Alexander Fraser of Powis, in which year he sold it. It was again sold in 1731 and in 1732; and in 1734 it was purchased by Francis Laflesh, who sold it to the Shoemaker Trade in 1737.

On the panel bearing the arms of the Shoemaker Trade is the following acrostic:—

> S ince Israel thro' the wilderness all past,
> H eavens made them shoos, for 40 years did last,
> O f all that number none did stand in need
> O f a mean latchet, or a sewing thread ;
> M oses, said Ashur, dipt his feet in oil,
> A nd underneath his shoes put brass for toil.
> K ings' daughters' feet by shoos are beautiful ;
> E dom's strong shoos were made of Egypt's bull ;
> R emember still to shoo your feet with peace,
> S o shall we live with concord in this place.

And around the frame are the following lines:—

> As we make shoes for other's feet,
>   Lord grant we may be shoed
> With gospel peace, which is most meet,
>   While here we make abode.

CHAPTER XII.

THE WEAVER TRADE.

WHEN the first grant of trading privileges was made to Aberdeen the weavers and fullers (litsters or dyers) seem to have looked upon themselves as distinctive classes of burgesses, entitled to rank with the wealthier class of merchant burgesses, and certainly superior to the ordinary plebeian craftsmen. In the charter granted to the town by Alexander in 1222, we find that the weavers and fullers or waulkers are specially mentioned as being excluded from the merchant guild—a reservation which also occurs in the charters granted about the same period to Perth and Stirling—and notwithstanding several attempts to break through it, this exclusion was maintained, and the weavers and litsters had to take their place among the rest of the craftsmen.

In 1444 Robert of Petit and William Hunter were sworn in as deacons to the "wobster" craft in Aberdeen—a clear indication that little attention was being paid to the Act of Parliament passed in 1427 putting down deacons, and declaring the meetings of the craftsmen illegal conspiracies.

Although coupled together in Alexander's charter, the weavers and litsters* formed separate societies. The weavers do not seem to have considered it necessary to apply to the Council for a formal Seal of Cause; they were content apparently, with the recognition by the Town Council of their power under Act of Parliament to elect a deacon, which

---

* The weavers and dyers do not seem to have always dwelt in peace and concord, as the following extract would show :—

17th December, 1582.—The said day the provost, baillies, and consall, modifeit the amendis of William Ronaldsone, walker, quha was convict obefoir for the sclandering and mispersoning of David Castell, wobster, to compeer on Friday next the xxi. day of this instant, within the tolbuyht of the said burght, and thair, in face of court and oppin audience, sitting upoun his knees, ask the provost, baillies, and pairtie offendit forgiveness, confessing his falt and offence, revoking the words spoken be him as fales and untriew, promisenand never to do the lyik in tyme coming under the pane of banischement of the toune. —*Council Register, vol.* xxxi., *p.* 86.

WEAVERS [15th May, 1682].—Azure, three leopard's heads erased argent, each having in its mouth a weaver's shuttle or; in the middle chief a tower of Aberdeen. Motto: *Spero in Deo et Ipse facit.*

was done from 1444. In 1536* they entered into an agreement declaring that they would act independently of the Town Council; but the Council would not tolerate this independence, and several offending "wobsters" were tried before the Sheriff and fined for their "strubulence." A few years previously the litsters attempted to do something of the same kind, by declining to join in the Corpus Christi procession, but the Town Council interposed their authority and compelled them to take their place among the rest of the craftsmen.

The weavers made no further effort to separate themselves from the rest of the craftsmen, and on the "sett of the burgh" being established, under which six deacons were annually chosen to vote at the election of Provost and office-bearers, the Weavers formed one of the six crafts on whom that privilege was conferred.

Like the bakers and shoemakers, the weavers were sharply looked after by the Town Council in regard to the price of their work, and at intervals a standard was fixed after the following fashion :—

14th October, 1584.—The quhilk day the provest, baillies, and counsale upoun the greveous complaint gevin in upoun the wobsteris for the gryt and exhorbutant pryces taken be thame for the weyving of all soirtis of claytht extorsenand thairby the inhabitants of this burght, and taking for thair labouris at thair awin pleassour and appetit, express agains guid ordeur, law, and consounce, as the said complaint mair fullelie proportit, quhilk being considerit be thame and haveing consideratioun quhow that the eln of ilk sort of claytht mycht be wrocht be the saidis wobsteris haveing ressonabill proffeit and ganes of the pryces following :—That is to say, the eln of tartan of all sortis, vid.; the eln of carsayis, iiid.; the eln of quhyt plaiding, iiid.; the eln of hewit plaidis of all soirtis, xvid.; the eln of lynning, vid.; the eln of hardene, iiid.; the eln of braid dornick, is.; the eln of narrow dornik, xiid.; and the wobster refusand to observe this statute, and being convick for contraveining thairof in ony poynt to be depryvit of his fredomn; as alswa it was statute and ordanit that na wobster within this burght mak ony clathyt, lynning, or wolne in ony tyme cuming, under the pane of deprivation of him of his fredoume being callit and convict thaerfore.—*Council Register, vol.* xxxi., *p.* 505.

The weavers were continually being annoyed by Old Aberdeen weavers encroaching on their privileges, and various measures were taken to punish the offenders. In 1686 the Weaver Trade of Old Aberdeen compelled one of their number named George Porter, "to restore and give back again ane warped wob quhilk he received from ane certaine person in Aberdene to be wrocht, and that in respect the diacon of the Weaver Traid, with assent of the said traid, did complain to the deacon upon the said George Porter for taking in and resetting the foresaid wob for warping as said is, and this to the effect that peace and unitie in all tyme cuming as has been done in tymes bygane." We have, in connection with the Weaver craft, an instance of the Town Council interposing its authority for the purpose of allowing a new branch of industry to be introduced into the town. In 1597,* they granted to a Fleming, named Michael Wandail, a special per- mission to manufacture grograms, worsets, and stamings, free from any molestation from the Weaver craft, on condition that he trained an apprentice in the knowledge of his business.

In 1772, encroachments by unfreemen having become more frequent, a petition was presented to the Sheriff by the weavers, along with the hammermen, tailors, and shoe- makers, against what they designated the "encroachments of the Old Aberdeen sub-wobs." The Sheriff-Substitute found that "the free craftsmen of the burgh of Aberdeen have the sole liberty and privilege of working craftsmen's wark for the burghers and inhabitants of the said burgh, who bear scot, lot, watch and ward within the same, and that men liv- ing in the suburbs or town of Old Aberdeen, Spithill, or Collidge Bounds, and pairtts adjacent thereto can not work for burghers and inhabitants of the said burgh; and ordains the defenders to desist from working any craftsmen's wark and from carrying out or bringing in either be themselves, wives, bairns, servants, or others in their name, any wark belonging to burghers and inhabitants of the said burgh of Aberdeen, under the penalty of ten pounds Scots money *toties quoties.*" In 1740 an example had to be made of a "bletcher" for encroaching on the privileges of the Trade, and he "bound and enacted himselff that he sall never take in any wark from any other inhabitants of the town or freedom of Aberdeen, to

---

* *Council Register, vol.* xxxvii., *p.* 106.

make the same either by himselff or his servants, under the penalty of one hundred merks Scots."

The oldest minute book of the Weaver Trade is a remarkably interesting volume, and contains a greater variety of statutes and ordinances than some of the others. The preface runs:—"Acts, statutes, and ordinances to be observed and keepit among the brethren of the Weaver Craft of the burgh of Aberdeen in all tyme cuming, sett doun in the year of God, 1591, restivet 1672, and appointed to be keepit."

ANENT KEEPING THE SABBATH.

Item, it is statute and ordained that ilk maister with his family repair discreetly to the church upon the Lord's Day before and afternoon, and continuing till God's worship be ended, and if it sall happen any maister of family be found absent, and cannot give ane lauful excuse for his being absent, then and in that case, he is to pay to the craft threttie shillings and four pennies. In lyke manner each servant that sall transgress the lyke manner they are to pay the lyke sum to the craft, and ane visitour to be appointed for giving true information thereanent, and thereupon made act.

ANENT BEHAVIOUR ON THE SABBATH.

Item, it is statute and ordained that no freeman be fand walking abroad betwixt sermons or aifter sermons, but sall keep within doors decentlie and orderlie, he and his whole family, exercising or meditating upon that they have been hearing (considering it is the Lord's Day) : and if any sall contravene the said Act, master or servant, sall be looked upon as disorderlie, and sall pay to the boxmaster six shillings aucht pennies, and this Act to be observed in all tyme cuming.

ANENT TAKING THE LORD'S NAME IN VAIN.

Item, it is statute and strictlie appointed that none of the craft in any fellowship or company, and especially in ane fenced court, sall tak the name of the Lord in vain : and if it sall happen ony to do, then and in that case, he sall pay to the present boxmaster of the same craft six shillings aucht pennies, and this act to be good.

ANENT BAD WORK.

Item, it is statute and ordained for preventing of prejudice and slander that no freeman of the foresaid craft sall sell nor way put any work whatsoever is made within his own house till first he call for the chosen sworn visitours and show the same unto them ; and if there be any fault found be them with the said work, then and in that case, they are to mak report to the present deacon and maisters that ane speedy course may be taken for preventing of any and such scandals, and if there sall be ane real fault found in the said work, it is to be confiscat by the deacon and his maisters for the use of the craft, and this act to be observed in all tyme cuming.

ANENT THE PRICE OF WORK.

Item, it is strictlie statute and ordained for preventing of slander that ilk weaver within the traid be watchful and accurat in receiving of his work, and not to entrust the same to no servant whatsomever, and if scandals sall arise, then and in that case, he is to have allowed him of ilk work proportionally to witt for every small plaid four ounces, as, also for ilk stone of serg yairn half ane pund, and for ilk stone weight of serge or plaiding ilk stone ane pund, and of a wheeling plaid six ounces, and of each quivering four ounces, or if the quivering be grosser six ounces, and proportionally ilk work equilland ; and this act to be observed in all tyme cuming.

ANENT WORKING ON THE LORD'S DAY.

Item, it is statute and ordained that no weaver, himself, wife, nor servant, nor none in his name sall be found searching and sic work upon the Lord's Day, or any other day, then and in that case, if any sall be found guilty sall pay twentie shillings scots for the first fault, to pay fourty shillings scots, and that to come in for the use of the craft, and this to be observed in all tyme cuming.

ANENT INSUFFICIENT WORK.

Item, it is statute and ordained that if any person sall complean to the deacon for insufficient work, both parties sall be convened before the deacon, his maisters, and the work to be sighted by them, and if the said work sall be insufficiently done ; then, and in that case, the person sall be counted upon the offender's expenses, as also the payment of the work to come in for the use of the craft for the first fault, the second fault double, thirdly to be looked upon as ane infamous neighbour, to be abolished out among the incorporation of the craft, and this to be observed in all tyme cuming.

ANENT DELAYING WORK.

Item, it is statute and ordained that, if work sall happen to be long wrocht, the owner giving ane complaint to the deacon, thereupon the deacon sall convene his present maisters, together with the pairties, and they sall decreet a set time to work the work, then and in that case, if he sall contravene the same, he sall pay to the craft twenty shillings Scots for the first fault, and the next fault forty shillings Scots, and this to be observed in all tyme cuming.

ANENT UNDERTAKING WORK.

Item, it is statute and ordained that no weaver sall tak upon them to lay no work by the loom not having all necessars belonging therunto, and giving cause to the owner to complain to the deacon, he sall pay to the present boxmaster twenty shillings for the use of the craft for the first fault, and to be doubled ; and thereupon made act.

ANENT THE AVOIDANCE OF SLANDER.

Item, it is further statute and ordained for avoiding of slander, that no neighbour sall tak upon them to cut out either webb or plaids to gif satisfaction to the party without the deacon's consent for the suppressing of slander, then, and in that case, if any slander sall arise, they sall pay to the present boxmaster forty shillings Scots, for the use of the craft, and this to be observed in all tyme cuming.

ANENT USING NICKNAMES.

Item, it is statute and ordained that whatsomever weaver of the craft sall use bywords or nickname his neighbouris either out of hatred, malice, or envy, he being lawfully called and accused before the deacons and maisters, and it made out against him, sall pay for the first fault twenty shillings Scots, and his fine to be double, ay and until the offender amend the fault, and this to be observed in all tyme cuming.

ANENT GIVING THE LIE.

Item, it is statute and ordained that whatsomever freeman of the craft sall speak rudely or give the lie or yet speak without leave askit or given in presence of the deacon in an fencit court, or in ane private meeting, he sall pay to the present boxmaster for the use of the craft forty shillings Scots *toties quoties*, and this to be observed in all tyme cuming.

ANENT "SUBWOBS."

Item, it is strictly statute and ordained that no freemen of the craft sall tak upon him or plead for any unfreeman or subwob either before the court, deacon, convener court, or before the magistrates; and furthermore that no freeman of the traid sall tak in hand negatively or positively to plead or speak one for another, then and in that case, if any person or persons sall be found to contravene the foresaid presents to be deprived of any privilege or benefit that they may have of the traid hous until he supplicat the traid, and also to pay three pounds *toties quoties* for ilk tyme this act is contravened for the use of the poor.

ANENT THE PROTECTION OF WIDOWS.

Item, it is statute and ordained with consent of the whole traid in one voice that no freeman within the same sall accept or tak his neighbour's relict, customs until first he enquire at the customar with whom she did work obefore, and she having consented to enquire at her former traidsman concerning her former prices and goodness of work and payment, by so doing it may be ane means to prevent prejudice and to keep up the prices, then and in that case, who sall be found guilty to transgress this present act sall pay into the present boxmaster twenty shillings Scots for the use of the poore, and this to be observed in all tyme cuming.

ANENT DEALING WITH UNFREEMEN.

Item, it is statute and ordained that no neighbour whatsomever of the craft sall tak upon hand directly or indirectly to lend to any extranean or sub-wob graith, reed, or any other material belonging to the weaver trade, then and in that case, if any sall contravene this present act he sall be looked upon as ane unruly member, and sall pay in to the present boxmaster twentie shillings scots for the use of the poore, and to be observed in all tyme cuming.

ANENT FEEING APPRENTICES.

Item, it is statute and ordained that no servant sall be feed out of the deacon's presence that sall stand as effect unless he be presented before the deacon and his old master to be admonished, and that there be no kynd of private promising nor conditioning, but all to be ratified before the deacon ; and if any sall be found to contravene, the same sall pay in to the present boxmaster thirteen shillings four pennies as also that no neighbour of the said traid sall be found to let or lend loomes, but allenarly the sum of sixteen shillings ilk year and none exceed the foresaid sum, then and in that case if any shall be found to contravene, the same sall pay into the present boxmaster the sum of five pounds scots for the use of the poor, and this to be observed in all tyme cuming.

ANENT JOURNEYMEN.

Item, it is statute and ordained that every extranean that comes into the town to fee with any of the freemen sall pay for his entry thirty shillings scots to the present boxmaster, and that within twenty-four hours after his entry to his maister, and that his said maister shall not conceal the same as he sall be answerable and conform to his oath of entry.

ANENT THE SIZE OF PLAIDS, ETC.

Item, it is statute and ordained with the consent of the haill craft for the punishment of vice and the avoiding of slander that no freemen of the traid taks work on hand to mix or putt two sundrie folks yairns in one webb plaids, lining stuff or any other work whatsomever ; in lyke manner, the whole traid hath condesended and agreed upon (and dooth discern) that every fingering plaid sall be eleven ells and ane half of length, three quarters of breadth, and every fuilling plaid eleven ells at the least, and every quivering to be six quarters broad and two ells of length at the least, and this act to be observed, providing always the parties do not agree, and whosoever sall be found to contravene this present act sall pay for his first fault fourty shillings and each fault thereafter to be double, and he to be committed always for an unfaithful member hereafter.

ANENT NIGHT WALKING AND BREAKING SERVICE.

Item, it is statute and ordained that whatsomever journeyman having lawfully feid before the deacon sall happen to break out of his maister's service without leave askit and grantit, or sall be found out of his hous aifter ten o'clock at night sall pay for his brak of service to his maister (for the day) three four (!) pennies, and for night thirteen shillings and four pennies to be payt to the present boxmaster for the use of the poor.

ANENT APPEALING TO THE SUPERIOR COURTS.

Item, it is statute and ordained that whatsomever freeman of the foresaid traid sall mak his redress to any superior judge in meeting not belonging to our own traid, he sall be holden as perjured, and conform to his oath at his entry ; and sall pay for his transgressiou the sum of fourty shillings Scots to the present boxmaster for the use of the poore, and this to be observed in all time cunning.

ANENT PRECEDENCE IN THE KIRK.

Item, it is statute and ordained, the whole traid being convenit for the maist pairt (for the tyme), having taken to their serious consideration the great abuse they have in their church loft be young freemen who presume to place themselves before some old deacons and present maisters, against all equity and sense and reason, tharefore the said haill craft in ane voice has statute and ordained in all tyme to cum, in presence of Doctor William Guild, foundator of the whole traids of this burgh, that the present deacon sall have his own place in the first roome, and next him the old and late deacons in the next roome, and thereafter the present maisters of the said traid carrying office, and last of all everie honest man of the said traid sall have his place conform to his admission, and in case any other young man of the said traid who has not carried office sall contravene this present act, and presume to place themselves in any of the foresaid roomes until the second bell, both forenoon and afternoon, being desired by the present deacon or maisters to remove, before the last bell, to give place to the said deacon and maisters, sall pay twenty shillings Scots to the common box of the said traid *toties quoties* for ilk brak.

ANENT BUYING SPANZIE.*

Item, it is statute and ordained be the deacon, maisters, and hail members of the Weaver Traid that no freeman presume in any tyme hereafter

* The skin of the spanzie was used for making reeds.

to buy any spanzie privately or publicly for their own comoditie from
merchant or stranger, but they sall acquant the deacon of the calling therewith ; and that it is only expedient that the deacon and maisters of the
calling to buy the said spanzie for the use of the foresaid traid, and none
but they only ; and whatsoever person or persons sall be found to transgress the said act sall be halden as perjured, and a braker of his oath at
his entry ; and, further, sall be convicit in ane unlaw of ten pounds Scots
to the present boxmaster for the use of the poor of the said traid, and
never to be looked upon as ane lawful member, and never to carry the
office of ane deacon or maister in tyme to cum, it being lawfully provided
that ilk reedmaker is to have as much spanzie as serves to mak reeds for
the use of the calling, and no more, and ordains this act to stand for a
memorial in all tyme cuming.

ANENT WATCHING UNFREEMEN.

Item, it is statute and ordained with ane unanimous consent of the
said whole traid that everie freeman thereof sall watch and wait unfreemen and to catch them with unfree work, ilk ane tyme and place about,
according to the order of their names as set down in the book, and any
that disobeys and contravens herein sall pay six shillings Scots, to fee and
hire ane other to supply their place in the business *toties quoties*.

ANENT REFUSING TO ATTEND MEETINGS.

Item, it is statute and ordained that everie neighbour of craft who is
lawfully warned and charged by the deacon's officer to court or convention,
then and in that case if the foresaid person sall not give obedience so that
the deacon be constrained for to send and poynd them, or if he or any other
sall deforce the said officer from taking of ane sufficient poynd he sall be
holden as disobedient and sall pay to the use of the craft twenty shillings
scots, and this act to continue firm and sure always.

ANENT WORKING GEAR.

Item, it is statute and ordained that everie member freemen of the craft
sall be sufficiently provided of working gears so that they may be able to
serve the king's lieges according to their aith at their entry, and that it
sall be leisim to the deacon and his maisters to mak search once in ilk year
and to punish accordingly at their pleasure.

Item, it is statute and ordained that all freemen of the said traid sall be
sufficiently provided of weights, back, and broad, and elwand and staks
be of sufficient weight and length, and to be sighted yearly by the deacon;
as also that any neighbour of the traid who sall occupie any of his neighbours work loomes more non ance without leave asked or given, sall pey
in to the present boxmaster twenty shillings Scots money, and this to be
observed in all tyme cuming.

ANENT MEANS TO CARRY ON BUSINESS.

Item, it is statute and ordained with uniform consent and assent that neither extraneans nor prentisses sall presume or be accepted to be freman, until he be in ability with forty pounds beyond that whilk sall mak him freeman, together with an stand of sufficient armour wherein to serve the King's Majesty; as also sufficient work loomes for prosecuting of his handywork, and that he sall refer himself to the will of the Traid in all poynts as effeirs, and this act to be strictly observed in all tyme cuming.

ANENT APPRENTICES' FEES.

Item, it is statute and ordained that whatsomever freeman of the traid sall receive twa prentices sall pay of entries for the first thirteen shillings four pennies, and for the second forty shillings, and upwards if he have any more prentisses; and this to be observed in all tyme cuming.

ANENT THE TRADES PROPERTY.

It is statute and ordained that the whole trades common necessaries such as ane stand of arms, complete with a twa handed sword, nichpiece, and Acts of Parliament, box, writs, bonds, pencills, and staves with all other kynd of necessaries belonging to the said incorporation sall be weill keepit and upholden upon the traids own charges, and likewyse sall be delivered to every new deacon at the tyme of their election, and if any deacon sall pretend any expenses for the keeping of any of those materials, they sall be looked upon as a person doing prejudice to the common good; and if any prejudice sall befall them, to mak them up upon his own expenses, and to pay into the present boxmaster forty shillings for the use of the poor.

ANENT THE BOUNTY TO SERVANTS.

Item, it is statute and ordained that no freeman sall tak upon hand to give to any fiall servant a half of their bounties, but that the fiall sall leave that to his maisters discretion and modification, and whatsomever maister he be that sall contravene this present act sall be holden as contumacious and contravener of good ordour, and sall pay into the present boxmaster forty shillings scots to the use of the poore.

ANENT PAYMENT OF SERVANTS.

Item, it is statute and ordained that no servant sall tak upon hand to go to any of his maisters customers to receive or uptak any money without leave askit of his maister, and in case of necessity the said servant man have nothing to work the work upon, then, and in that case he sall require of his maister some payment to work the same work, and if his maister sall require to give him any, he sall mak his redress to the deacon, and after the deacon having heard and considered with his maister the foresaid premises to determine according to reason, but if the foresaid sall do in the contrair, then he is to pay to the present boxmaster twenty shillings scots for the use of the poore.

ANENT ENTRY MONEY.

Item, it is statute and ordained unanimously with consent of the haill traid that in all tyme cuming every prentiss of the calling who has duly served his maister, being ane freeman, and being an indentur, pay betwixt them, when he is to be received freeman of the traid and supplicat for that effect, he sall pay of composition to the traid of hand money upon the Trinity table the sum of fifty merks annual scots money, and to be free of any banquet, dinner, or anything of that nature to be craven be the traid from him ; and also, that everie extrauear who sall enter freeman of the traid in all tyme hereafter sall pay to the traid of composition and band money as said is the sum of fore score merks usual scots money, and sick-lyke to be free of banquet, dinner, or anything of the lyke nature to be craven of him be the traid, the said prentiss paying ane rex dollar with ane bill and fourty shillings scots money of say and the extrauear the double thereof.

ANENT FINDING BAIL OR CAUTION.

18th February, 1693.—The said day it is statute and ordained by voice of court that no freeman of the said incorporation sall meddle to become cautioner for any freeman's prentiss to the Magistrates of Aberdeen anent his liberation out of the tolbooth of Aberdeen unacquanting the deacon and maisters of the said calling under the failzie of forty pounds scots, to the effect none might prejudice their neighbours of the said traid in tyme cuming.

ANENT " OUTRIGGING " SOLDIERS.

3rd March, 1694.—The said day it is statute and ordained that the journeymen proportionally amongst them refund to the traid such expenses as the traid hath been at for outrigging ane soldier for serving of his Majesties in this present joyntur, and that no freeman give their mark until they pay in their proportions, and whatsomever freeman receives them sall pay to the journeyman he gives wark to, and thereupon required act and instrument.

ANENT VISITORS AT THE MARKET.

5th December, 1690.—The said day the haill court ordains two of the masters, by course, to wait upon the cross weekly for tryall of the insufficient work, and this to continue in all tyme cuming, the two visitours going their course with them.

ANENT INSOLENT SERVANTS.

4th September, 1705.—The said day, the traid considering that, by the indulgence of some of their members towards their servants, the saidis servants were become insolent, therefore, and for redress whereof they statute and ordain that no master give of what shall come with any web or at werping thereof, but ane proportion pairt with the rest of his servants, and as the said shall think fit and convenient, declaring that hereafter all servants whatsomever within said trade shall have no pairt, portion, or concern with any gratuities given to the maister by customers but what allenarly the maister shall give out of goodwill and kindness, and not as aue obligation on him; and ordains the deacon and maisters for the tyme to take tryall hereanent in tyme cuming and punish the transgressors as they shall find reason.

ANENT RAISERS OF TROUBLE.

4th September, 1705.—The said day the court having taken to their serious consideration the great abuses that arises among the members of the said incorporation to the traid's ruin both as to public and privat, and for several other weighty reasons doe therefore unanimously statute, enact, and ordain that any master who shall hereafter make any abuse either in courts, meetings, or without ye samen, the then deacon shall extrude and put out among them such members and fyne and amerciat them conform to the merit of their transgression; and that the transgressor shall not be called to the courts or meetings of the said traid, nor have any concern therein or with any member thereof; certifying every member of the said traid if they be found corresponding with the said transgressors any manner of way untill he shall happen to be again received he shall be amerciat in the sum of fourtie shillings, *toties quoties*, and be holden and repute as ane fomenter cf trouble and division.

Judging from the number of acts passed in regard to insufficiency and delay in the execution of work, the weavers in olden times seem to have been somewhat independent of their customers. The following is a sample of minute which occurs very frequently, binding them to execute orders. The wife in every case is the complainer, she doubtless having the wool to prepare :—

Upon the 16th day of October, 1637, compearit Alexander Still and obliged himself to work to Alexander Findlater's wyff three pair of fingerin plaids betwixt this and the seventeenth day of September, and in the case of failzie of the said day sall pay six prices, whilk is ten pounds, of his awin consent thereto for ilk plaid thereof and thereon made act which is subscribed by my hand.

"To mak and perfect ane sufficient essay within fourty days," or to "mak ane holland wob," was the common form of essay prescribed to applicants for admission into the Weaver Trade. At one time the weavers were very numerous in the city, and their society was the most influential of all the crafts, but the sound of the hand loom has almost entirely ceased, and there are now few practical weavers alive. The rules of admission to the incorporation have in consequence been relaxed; but still an applicant must show that he is engaged in business connected with the sale and manufacture of woven goods.

The first property purchased by the Weavers was the Angell Croft, in 1695. The other properties belonging to this Trade are land at Borrowstown, Parish of Newhills; Whitemyres, part of the fourth lot of the lands of Shetocksley; lands of Pitmuckston; and feus at Craibstone Rig, Gordon Street, Wellcroft, Denburn, and Green.

In addition to a panel containing the arms of the Trade and the following lines and acrostic, there are also hanging in the West Committee Room adjoining the hall two shields with the arms and mantlings boldly carved and coloured :— (see opposite page 292.)

> As the Weavers' shuttle passeth in its place,
> So help us Lord to spend our days in grace,
> That so our hearts may still united be
> To Jesus Christ and all Eternity.

> *W*hen all the arts, crafts, callings, and vocations,
> *E*ven in the world, are censured in their stations,
> *A*dvyse & view ; think weill then altogither,
> *W*ith seriusnes then with your selffs consider ;
> *E*re our industrius works, beyond all Arts,
> *R*espected are, most gainfull in all parts ;
> *S*urely therwith are prince and people clad ;
> Yea, birth day, baptisme, wedlock, buriall-bed
> Of monarchs, princes, Kings and Emperors,
> Ther glorious ensigns, all are works of ours ;
> And that most blessed body of our Lord,
> In lyfe and death was with our works decor'd.
> Then, the Weavers' Art, it is renouned so,
> That rich nor poor without it can not go.

FLESHERS [15th May, 1682].—Gules, three flesher's knives fessways in pale, and on the dexter side an axe paleways, the edge towards the sinister, all the blades proper and hafted argent; in the middle chief a tower of Aberdeen. Motto: *Virtute vivo.*

CHAPTER XIII.

THE FLESHER TRADE.

In the oldest volume of the Council Register we find that after the provost and magistrates had been elected for the year 1399, four *appreciatores carnum* were chosen to appreciate or examine the quality of the flesh sold in the town. This, as may be supposed, is the first mention of supervision by the authorities over the fleshers, who at that time, and for a considerable period after, were the recognised dealers in fish as well as flesh. Again, in 1441, it was statute and ordained by the "avise of the haill counsall, for the commoun gude of the hale commounytie of this burgh," that "na fleschewaris, na nane vther man, nychtbour nor vnfreman, buy ony maner of fische quhill thai cum to the merkate; and yat na man buy to tap agane at the derth to the commownys ony maner of fische quhill the hight of the day be passit, vnder the pavne of viii. s. unforgiffin, and eschete of the fische bot favour." Flesh and fish were sold in the same market, and the regulations that were from time to time issued referred, as a rule, to both classes of victuals, the price of fish being fixed as well as beef and mutton; and anything in the nature of keeping back to create a dearth was punished by forfeiture of the goods so kept back. The earliest regulations enacted in regard to the flesh market were as follows:—

4th June, 1444.—Item, that the fleschowaris dicht and mak clene the fleschous ilke ouke on Friday, and yat thai remove away the huches that arr in to the fleschous, vnder the sammyn payne.

Item, that na man fleschowar within the burgh or withoute sell mutoune derrar than the bouke for ij. s. viij. d. the best that may be gottin, and the remanent their efter be the price, vnder the payne of viij. s. vnforgivin, alsoft as thai trespass.

Item, that na fleshowar of within or withoute tak out of ony mutoune the neris or the nerecress fra the feest of Mychelmess, vnder paye of eschete of the mutoune to the balyies, &c.

Item, that na fleshowar sell fleshe na brek flesch in ony othir place bot the fleschous vnder the payne of viij. s. vnforgivin, alsoft as thai be taynte and eschete.—*Council Register, vol.* v., *p.* 680.

In the following year specific instructions were issued regarding the days of the week on which the fleshers were to slay; and sworn persons were appointed to fix the price and to see that all the flesh was sold in the market place under the Tolbooth. The ordinance is as follows:—

19th April, 1445.—It is ordanit be the counsaile that fra hynce forthwartis the fleschouris of this burgh sal sla ilka Setterdai at evin, or the son gang too, almyskil flesche as sal serue al the ton on Sundai at the leeste, suppose that strangearis come to the tou ; and thai sla on Monoundai the flesche that sal serue on Monoundai and Twisdai ; and they sal sla on Wednysdai that sal serue on Thurisdai ; and they sal sell na flesche quhill it be prisit be the sworne prisaris, the quhilke the alderman and the bailyheis sal bryng to thaim, and thai be warnit quhat time that thair flesche be redy ; and that thai sell na flesche vnprisit, as is forsaid, vnder the payne of tynsal of the flesche, and viij. s. vnforgiffin, and bannysing fra the craft at the third tyme. And it sall be lieveful to the alderman and balyheis for to tak, in absence of the sworne prisaris, ony vtheris gude men of the toune to prise the flesche, makand gude faith tharto. And that thai sell na flesche bot vnder the tolbuth, and at it be kepit in honeste.— *Council Register, vol.* i., *p.* 401.

The right to exercise two branches of trade was objected to by the merchant burgesses in 1518, and the Council, considering that the "guid toune wald not tholl yaim occupie" two crafts, passed the following ordinance :—

23rd October, 1518.—The said day the provost exponit to the toune how it was heavily murmured be the merchants of yis burgh quhow the flessaris of ye samyn occupiet and usit twa craftes that was to thair ain craft of butchering and merchandise ; wherefore ye provost charged Thomas Lavinginstoun and And. Syme, flessaris, whilkis were present for the tyme to shaw the laff of thair craft and to avise betwixt that and Monanday, eightenth day of this instant month, and chose yaim ane of the tua craftis forthwith to remain, certifying yam that ye guid toune wald not tholl yam occupie them baith, and to give answer to ye provost in guid toune ye said day whilk they warned.—*Council Register, vol.* x., *p.* 9.

The fleshers were among the last of the craftsmen to apply for a Seal of Cause, but, like others obtained about the same date, it does not suffer on that account. It is fuller and more specific in its terms, and, as will be seen, gives a clear indication of the extent of the powers delegated to the Crafts by the Town Council:—

Be it kend till all men be this present letters, We, Provost, Baillies, Counsell, and comunitie of the burghe of Aberdene, the comone weill of the samen in that part heid sein, consyderit, and ounderstoud be us. And we being rypelie advysit therupoune to have granted, given, and committed and by the tenor thereof grants, gives, and comits to our lovites neighbours, fleshers, deacons of the craft of fleshers of the burgh for the time and to their successors in all time to come, our full, free, and plain power and authority upon all and sundry occupiers and exercisers of the said craft within the said burgh and freedom of the same to convict and punish the trespassers their unlaws, amerciaments, and escheats to be advised and modified by the foresaid deacons and their successors. And also we ratify and affirm that no freeman shall be made of the said craft tile he be examined by the said deacons or their successors deacons of the craft for the time, and that he be found by them ane sufficient craftsman and made his master stick of wark, and that he be proven worthy by his wark to be ane master and admitted by the deacons for the time and presented to us as ane able person to be made freeman. Sicklike it shall be leisome to the said deacons and their successors with the advice and counsel of the principal neighbours of the said craft to make statutes and ordinances for the common weill of the said craft and good and honor of the said burgh. Givand and grantand to the said deacons and their successors deacons of the said craft for us and our successors all powers and privileges afore written for ever. The said deacons and their successors answering to us and our successors for all and sundry their neighbours, masters, servants, apprentices, and occupiers of the said craft for all faults that lies under their correction gif they leave any sic faults unpunished or punish them otherways than they ought to do of law and good conscience. And that they do justice to all occupiers of the said craft at all times when they are required bot (without) fear or favor. And giff any occupiers of the said craft disobeys or contemns the said deacons or their successors deacons for the time that they complain to us or our successors. And we cause them to be obeyed conform to their power, providing always that the said craft choose no deacons in time coming bot them that be responsal to the town conform to their power, and that they answer to us and our successors for the said craft and all things concerning them and their craft whenever they be required thereto. And we, the said provost, bailies, council, and community shall warrant, keep, and defend all and sundry the premises to the said deacons and their successors as said is by this writ. And attour we will and ordain that it shall not be leisome to any of the deacons above written to do or statute anything above written concerning the evil of the said craft, particularly by himself, but all they shall love, agree, and counsel together in all things they have ado touching the said craft. And sicklike their successors in time coming. In witnessing of the whilks to

this present writ and power and privilege we have caused append our
common seal.   At Aberdeen the twenty-fifth day of April the year of God
one thousand five hundred thirty and four years.

The price of beef and mutton was fixed at stated intervals
by the Magistrates.   On 5th October, 1576, it " was statut and
ordainit that na mutton be sauld in the mercat nor fleschowse
bot of the pryces following, viz., the best mutton buik for xiii
s, and secondar, for xii s and x s, effeiring to the guideness of
the stuff, under the pane of escheating thairof ; and that na
beiff be sauld in the mercat nor in the fleschowse on to the
tyme that the baillies compryse, and put a price thairon
effeiring to the guidness of the stuff, &c.   And that the fische-
mercat be haldin in tyme cuming within the ayrin ring in the
eistheid of the castelgett, and that the said fishmercat nor
fleschemercat be in na way in tyme coming on the Sabbath
day fru the ringing of the first bell afoir noon and efter
noone quhill the sermon be done under pain of escheating of
the fische and the fleche apprehendit to the puir folkis ; and
that nae middinis be sufferit nor permittet to be on the king's
command yett in na tym cuming under the pane of twenty s."
On 8th October, 1656, the price of the best mutton was fixed
"at no higher rait than threttie sex shillings the best sort; item,
the second sort two merks ; the third sort according as the
appreciators sall appoint, under the pains of fyve pund *toties
quoties*.   Item, the best ox beef to be sold at twelff pund.
Item, the second sort at nyne poundis and under, at the
discretione of the visitours under the penaltie forsaid.   Item,
the best ky beef at nyne pounds, the second sort at nyne
merks and under, at the sicht of the visitours under the
penaltie forsaid.   Item, the best vaill to be sold at sex punds ;
item, the second sort at four punds and under, according to
the worth thereof under the pains forsaid.   Item, that flessaris
and slayers of nolt and sheep alsweil to burghe as landwart,
bring their fleshes to mercat with the hyd, heed, tallow,
vncuttit scorit or spoilit vnder the paine of fyve pund the first
fault, ten pounds the second fault and so furth thairefter *toties
quoties* besyds confiscatioun."

The first regular flesh house or killing market was erected
in 1631, as the following entry in the Register bears :—

12th October, 1631.—The said day the prouest, baillies, and counsall thinkes it meit and expedient for the ease of the fleshouris friemen of this burghe, and advancement of this tounes common gude, that a fleshous sal be biggit in all convenience diligence at the back of the new toun hous, on the north syd of the castillgett, and nominates George Moresone, deane of gild, maister of wark to the biggin therof wha is ordanit to provyd materiallis thereto, and the expensis to be disbursit be him thairupon, to be allowit to the said deane of guild in his comfitis.—*Council Register, vol. lii., p.* 31.

It was at the same time ordained "that no fleshour within this burgh shall slay ony nolt, sheip, nor wther gudes, nor bestial wpoun the kingis hie streites, nor withoute housses in tyme comeing vnder the payne of fourtie shillingis to be peyit be the contravenir to the deane of guild, *toties quoties*, as they sal happin to failzie thairin."

About the beginning of the present century frequent complaints were made to the Magistrates about the condition of the flesh market, and an effort was made to improve matters. The Council met on 4th April, 1801, and instructed George Turreff "to employ scavengers, or other proper persons, for the purpose of collecting and cleaning the dung of the slaughter market once every day, and the sale market on the mornings of each Monday and Thursday, and to sell, by public roup, the whole of the said dung frequently, as he may find it necessary; and, after payment of all necessary charges and expenses incurred thereanent, to pay the free rouped price thereof to the boxmaster of the Butcher Trade, to be applied for the benefit of the poor thereof. And the Council farther prohibit and discharge all butchers and other persons frequenting the said markets from bringing any live cattle or carts of any kind into the said sale market, and appoints a turnstile or bar to be fixed at the south and north entries thereof next the Castle Street and Queen Street, and another bar or turnabout to be fixed on the passage between the said two markets, and the accesses or entries made out from any private houses in the Lodge Walk, or other ways into the said market, to be shut up; unless the proprietors shall agree to give the necessary declarations or obligements to the Dean of Guild, in order to prevent such entries from being afterwards claimed as servitudes upon the town's property. And, in order to accommedate the butchers with some convenient place for holding their live cattle before they are butchered, the Council agree to fit up part of the gardens adjacent to the butcher market, belonging to William Naughton and Miss Neilson, how soon access can be got thereto, to be employed as a receptacle for that purpose; and appoint all such butchers as shall take the benefit thereof to pay an addition for that accommodation of ten per cent. upon their respective current prices."

Notwithstanding these regulations, however, the nuisance complained of remained unabated, and in 1804 the Flesher Incorporation appointed a committee to look out a site for a new flesh market. Suitable buildings were erected in Wales Street, where slaughtering has since been carried on under the supervision of the office-bearers of the craft, one of the first regulations adopted being that the boxmaster should " prosecute all those who shall persist in the practice of selling drink."* The Wales Street Market is still the property of the Flesher Incorporation, and forms the main source of their revenue.

In consequence of frequent disputes with the Shoemaker Trade about the inspection of hides, the Town Council ordered the fleshers in 1757 to give access and show their hides to the searchers and visitors appointed by the Shoemaker Trade, and also prohibited them from " selling or exposing to sale any of their hydes until twelve of the clock each mercate day, and that no hydes be carried from the mercate till the same be inspected and searched." The charge made for inspecting the hides was a farthing for each hide belonging to a a freeman, and one halfpenny to an unfreeman, one third of the dues to go to the poor of the Shoemaker Trade. The fleshers were relieved of this impost by an Act of Parliament passed in 1830.

Unlike the other Trades the fleshers did not, when they commenced keeping regular minutes, copy in their acts and statutes from their old register. That such a register was in existence there is no room for doubt, there being references in

* In 1807, about a year after this regulation was in force, a member of the craft was fined for a breach of this regulation.

the existing books to ordinances which were recognised and put in force at a much earlier date. But the old register is gone, and we have only the Acts passed after 1660, from which we make the following selection :—

ANENT UNNEIGHBOURLY CONDUCT.

7th September, 1704.—The said day anent the complaint given in to the court of the unneighbourly disorders and complaints made by several persons of their own members to the ruin and abuse of the craft, for remeid thereof it is ordained and hereby statutes and ordains that any person within the said craft, either master or servant who shall make any complaint to the magistrates of this burgh anent whatsomever concern without the consent of the deacon of the trade for the tyme or forget making their complaint to him shall be liable, and do hereby oblige themselves to pay to the boxmaster of the trade for the use of the trade the sum of six pounds Scots money *toties quoties*, and the said freeman contravening the premises to have no vote nor concern with this trade untill he pay the said sum and be pardoned be the members hereof.

ANENT THE RATE OF WAGES.

7th October, 1668.—The said day it is ordained be the deacon and haill traid that all jurneymen of the flesher traid within this burgh sall serve in the first place only freemen of the said trade as long as they shall have work and employment for them, and that they undertake to serve none untill the freeman be first servit, and that they shall give of wadges for killing and brucking of ilk ox or cow four shillings Scots, and when they do not bruck the beast they shall give only fourtie pennies Scots ; and for killing of every score of sheep ane merk, and ane to the score. And for brucking of everie pairt of bieff whatsomever nothing they do not kill themselves.

ANENT "PACKING AND PEILING" WITH UNFREEMEN.

27th March, 1671.—The said day it is statute and ordained that non of the traid in any tyme coming sall pack nor peill with any unfreemen directly nor indirectlie, under whatsomever colour or pretext under the penaltie and censure of the traid, to be inflicted upon the transgressor, *toties quoties*, as any sall be found to contravene herein.

11th December, 1807.—The trade enacts that in future every entrant shall be bound under the penalty of £25, that he shall not part and peel with unfreemen in all time coming.

ANENT THE DUTIES OF OFFICER.

15th June, 1672.—It is statute and ordanit that in all time coming ilk officer of the traid sall punctuallie keep the dark door in the old church from the ringing of the first bell everie lords day ; and every other meeting whatsomever that the traid sall have ; and to do the dutie punctuallie under the penaltie of six shillings *toties quoties.*

ANENT SELLING BROKEN MUTTON.

5th January, 1675.—The said day it is statute and ordained unanimously be the haill traid that no member thereof sall in tyme coming sell ony mutton in pieces or broken, but only in haill syds or legges conforme to the ordinar practice, and whasomever sall contravene herein sall pay to the boxmaster fourtie shillings Scots *toties quoties* for the use of the craft.

ANENT THE DEACON'S SEAT IN THE KIRK.

6th March, 1680.—The said day the haill trade unanimously statutes and ordains that in all tyme hereafter whoever shall be deacon, that he shall have a forme for his seat in the dask in the old church belonging to the trade keepit for him till the third bell bo rung in, and that the officer whosoever the same shall happen shall attend his deacon and boxmaster anent the keeping of the said seat and attending of him otherwayes conform to his oath under the failyie of twenty shillings Scots for each fault *toties quoties.*

ANENT VILLIFYING THE DEACON.

21st September, 1700.—The said day by voyce of court it is statute and ordained that no person or member of the said incorporation presume to villipend their deacon or give their neighbour the lye, or culuminat or abuse them in presence of the deacon at court or meeting, and whosoever transgresses in the premisses to pay to the boxmaster for the use of the poore fourteen pennies Scots, *toties quoties*, and this to be observed in all tyme coming.

ANENT SERVANTS DEALING ON THEIR OWN ACCOUNT.

16th June, 1722.—The said day the traid, taking to consideration the great damage freemen in the same sustains by servants buying and selling upon their own account, they therefore, that the same abuse and encroachment may be remedied in tyme coming, do be thir presents enact, statute, and ordain that no parent or member of this craft shall allow their sons or servants to buy any goods be themselves or for their own behoof, but only that whatever goods they may happen to buy shall be entirely by their parents or masters orders and for their parents and masters behoof, certifying that any person who shall contravene this act that they will be amerciat in ten shillings sterling for the use of the poor of this incorporations. And that the transgressors parent or master shall be compteable therefor.

ANENT SELLING IN THE MARKET.

3rd October, 1726.—The said day the flesher trade hereby unanimously prohibit and discharge all and every member of the said trade from receiving within their shops, houses, or on their pillars any mercate meat, beef, mutton, or other whatsomever belonging to any unfreeman flesher, and from exposing the same for sale or allowing the said unfreemen to sell the samen within their shops or pillars, and that under the penalty of six pounds scots money to be paid by the contravener hereof to the boxmaster for the time being for the use of the poor without any defalcation or mitigation.

ANENT APPRENTICES.

22nd October, 1739.—The trade appoint that in all time coming every master who shall conduce with a servant for learning his trade shall enter into indenture with the said servant, and that not under the space of five years at least ; and that every servant or apprentice who hereafter shall desire to be admitted freemen without serving the said five years, in case he enter to service and serve under that, these shall noways be admitted freemen on any account whatsomever, and that any man who shall conduce for less than five years, shall be liable for such a penalty as the trade shall think proper.

ANENT SERVANTS DEALING IN THE FLESH MARKET.

16th May, 1761.—The trade, considering the great incroachments and abuses made by the servants belonging to the trade, hereby statute and enact that in all time coming no servant shall have liberty to try or sell in the flesh mercate any fleshes or bestiall for their own account, but only ane calf, the price thereof not exceeding half a crown, and the same not to be exposed till two of the clock afternoon on the mercat day ; and the trade statute that any contravening this act shall be prosecuted with all vigour.

ANENT THE INSOLENCE OF SERVANTS.

10th June, 1769.—It having been represented to the trade by the members thereof that they have been of late insulted and abused with the most insolent and opprobrious language by the servants belonging to the trade ; and the trade having taken the same under serious consideration, were unanimously of opinion that the insolence of their servants had arisen to such a height as no longer to be tolerate, and, unless a stop is speedily put thereto, it will tend to the subversion of the government of the trade, they are, therefore, for remedy of all such abuses in time coming, statute and ordain that upon a complaint being lodgit by any member of the trade against any servant for insulting him in any manner of way unbecoming one of his own servant—on conviction of the offender such servants offending shall for the first transgression be obliged to appear in presence of the trade at their first Court thereafter, and in a most submissive manner ask the complainer and trades' pardon, and declare that he is sorry for the offence, and ask forgiveness of them, and, in case of refusal, to be declared incapable of serving any member of the trade, and be denuded of all privileges arising to him as a servant or apprentice to the trade, &c.

ANENT " SPEAKING " PINTS.

25th April, 1793.—The said day the trade having taken under their consideration that it has been the practice for some time past for entrants to this trade to give what is called speaking pints to the masters and others of the trade, and at the passing of their essay to give an entertainment of meat and drink, of which the essay made a part to the whole members of the trade at a very considerable expense to the entrants, tending to no benefit to the trades funds, or any other purpose but an abuse of money, do therefore hereby statute and enact that in time cuming all speaking pints and entertainments such as have formerly been given by entrants to the members of the trade shall be abolished and set aside, and the entrants shall be at liberty to dispose of his essay* after it is passed at pleasure, and be under no obligation to give any entertainment as formerly, with which practice the trade unanimously and heartily dispense in time cuming.

The essay prescribed to entrants in this Trade has uniformly been "to kill and dress ane sheep in the market belonging to the Incorporation."

Although constituted under a regular Seal of Cause, the Flesher Trade did not share in the privilege of sending their deacon to vote at the annual election of the Magistrates. They attempted to do so on more than one occasion, but on 23rd September, 1721, a minute was passed by the Council to the effect that "for some years bygane the deacon of the Flesher Trade of this burgh has presumed to come up with the trades and vote upon the day of the election of the magistrates and council of this burgh. By the constitution of this place the deacon of the Flesher Trade is not privileged to come up with the trades now to vote on the day of the election, but only the six deacons of the trades and four deacons of the old and new council, which makes ten deacons of trades, and therefore the said magistrates and council unanimously discharges the deacon of the Flesher Trade of Aberdeen, in all time coming, from coming up with the trades of this burgh to the council

---

* Like the bakers, the fleshers had been in the habit of making a meal of the essay

upon the day of the election of the magistrates and the council thereof, and from having any vote therein in all time hereafter."—*Council Register, vol.* lviii., *p.* 720.

When Dr. Guild gifted the Trinity Monastery to the Trades in 1633, no mention was made of the Fleshers in the deed of gift, but, in 1657, Dr. Guild, under the following special agreement, consented to the Fleshers being joined with the others, thus making up the number of the Trades who were to have a common meeting-house and hospital to the present number of seven :—

2nd April, 1657.—Alexander Cruickshank, Deacon-Conveneer. The Court fenced and affirmed. The whilk day, in presence of Doctor William Guild, doctor of divinity and founder of the crafts hospital, and remanent members of the Deacon-Conveneer Court therein convened for the time, that is to say—Alexander Cruickshank, Deacon-Conveneer ; William Chrystie, Deacon of the Hammermen ; William Anderson, goldsmith, late Deacon thereof, and John Gray, saidler, master of the said Hammermen Traid ; John Kenny, Deacon of the Baxters, and Alexander Williamson and Patrick Murray, late Deacons thereof, and masters of the said Baxter Trade ; William Anderson, couper, Deacon of the Wrights and Coupers, John Law and William Scott, late Deacons thereof, and masters of the said traid ; George Morisone, Deacon of the Tailyeors Patrick Norrie, late Deacon thereof, and George Watt, masters of the said trade ; Archibald Hog, deacon of the shoemakers, and Patrick Murray and John Hendry, late deacon thereof, and masters of the said traid ; John Bleinshell, deacon of the weavers, Alexander Clark and George Adam, late deacon thereof and masters of the said traid ; For themselves and in name and behalf of the haill trades of the said burgh COMPEARIT personally Andrew Watson, deacon of the fleshers, and John Craighead, late deacon of the said traid, for themselves and in name and behalf of the rest of the freemen of the said Flesher Traid. And did supplicate the said foundator and haill members of the Deacon-Conveneer Court above named that it would please the said foundator and the rest of the Deacon-Convener Court to accept, receive, and incorporate the said Flesher Traid (being freemen) amongst the rest of the said traids and to have libertie to meet and convene in the conveening house of the said Hospital and to hold courts thereintill as freely in all respects as any of the foresaid traids and hereby the said Deacon of the fleshers and remanent members of the said traid (being freemen) to have the benefit of the said hospital when occasion shall offer ; And generally to exercise all and sundry other privileges as any of the foresaid traids has had or any ways may pretend to have within the said conveening house and hospital. And the said

Flesher Trade being freemen to have also their right to the property and benefit of the hospital and rents belonging thereto, as any of the foresaid crafts in all time coming when occasion shall offer *in omnibus* as in the said supplication of the date foresaid in itself more fully perfects. *Whilk* supplication and the desire of the said Flesher Trade (being freemen) the said and hail remanent Deacon-Conveneer Court thought reasonable. And all in ane voice GRANTED and ACCEPTED the said supplication. Whereupon the said Andrew Watson and John Craighead for the gracious acceptation of the said supplication for themselves and in name of and behalf of the said traid (being freemen) did instantly pay and deliver to Walter Melvill, goldsmith, burgess of the said burgh, present master of the said hospital all and haill the sum of four hundred merks good and usual money of this nation for the use of the hospital and members thereof, whilk sum the said Walter Mitchell granted the receipt thereof. THAR- FOR witt ye lls the said foundator of the said crafts hospital with consent and assent of the said Deacon-Conveneer Court, deacons masters and haill remanent members of the said Conveneer Court above expressed. And we all with uniform consent and assent for ourselves and in name and behalf of the haill traids of this burgh to have give and granted, and be the tenour hereof for us and our successors gives and grants full, free plain libertie and power to the said Andrew Watsone and John Craigheid for themselves and in name and behalf of the said Flesher Traid (being freemen) and their successors to hold courts in the said hospital or con- veening house, and to be incorporate amongst us the rest of the said traids in manner aforesaid in the said hospital, and generally to have access and libertie to any benefit or portion pertaining to the said hospital. Also freely in all respects as any of the foresaid traids has had or any ways may claim or pretend to have thereto in all time coming in any manner of way, with this provision always that at what time it shall happen the said fleshers and their successors to receive and admit any freemen in time to come that the entrant freemen shall pay and give some benefit to the said hospital according to the entrant's ability, and as other traids are in use, to do WHILK above specified the said Doctor William Guild, foundator, with consent and assent of the said Deacon-Conveneer Court and they all with ane consent and assent binds and obliges their successors to ratify and approve of this present act and declaration to the said fleshers and their successors (being freemen) in all time hereafter whomsoever they shall be required for that effect and in sign thereof the said foundator, Deacon-Conveneer, Deacons, and remanent masters of the said Deacon- Conveneer Court for themselves and in behalf of the haill traids of this burgh have subscribed this present act and ratification with their hands, day, place, and year of God above specified. Whereunto the said act being extended on parchment the haill Deacon-Conveener Court and members thereof have subscribed the same, and in testimony thereof the said Deacon-Conveener and Master of Hospital have instantly subscribed the same.

On a picture of the arms of the Trade, painted on canvass in 1829 by " J. Laing, pictor," are the following lines :—

> Whilst we do sheep and oxen slay,
> Frail mankind here to feed ;
> Help's Lord to pray, our Father this day,
> Give us our daily Bread.

From ancient times, our origin we draw,
When priests were cons'crate to keep God's law,
When sacredotal sacrifice and feasts,
Made altars smoak with blood of slaughter'd beasts,
Such as young bullocks, kids, and fatted rams,
Males without blemish, of goats, sheep, and lambs.
When Israel's princes did to Moses bring
Each prince his gift, and peace-offering ;
To dedicate within the sanctuary,
The Tabernacle of the Lord most High,
And all, for that the priests might sacrifice,
Sins to atone for Israel's God to please.
Then, 'twas as first the Almighty taught the way
Rams, bullocks, goats, kids, lambs, to kill and slay ;
Then did our Trade at Heaven's decree commence,
To cleanse Israel from crimes and all offence ;
Our Trade most lawful, ancient, as you see,
Strange, not Heaven's councel, voted so to be.*
Moses and Aron their fingers oft did dye,
With blood of beasts themselves to sanctifie ;
Yea, Aron and his sons were hallowed
With blood of rams, whereon the altar shed :
Moses to hallow, did sprinkle with his hand,
Blood on their garments, as God gave command.
Heaven's monarch sent kind messages to Abraham
To spare his son Isaac, and kill a ram ;
God's angel called, " Stay thy bold hand and knife,
Look, there's a ram, hurt not thy Isaac's life ! "
Both David and Josiah, Judah's Kings,
Made solemn feasts and passover offerings,
And unto God did sacrifice and kill
Rams, bullocks, sheep, kids, lambs, with glad goodwill.
Yea, many more proofs sacred can be given,
Our Trade was taught first, and advis'd by Heaven ;
Let's then with gladness to this author raise,
Our heaven-born souls, him ever more to praise. †

---

* Exod. ch. xxix., v. 9, 16, 18, 20. Num. ch. iv., v. 2, 10, 11, and on and for the end.

† Exod. ch. xx., v. 20, 21. Gen. ch. xxii., v. 10, 11, 12, 13. 2 Chron. ch. xxxv., v. 1, 6, 7, 8, 9, 10, 11.

CHAPTER XIV.

THE ABOLITION OF SPECIAL TRADING PRIVILEGES.

ONE of the results of the Burgh Reform movement, which began to gather force in Scotland about the beginning of the present century, was the abolition of the exclusive trading privileges which had been so long enjoyed by the merchant and craft guilds throughout the country. Owing to peculiar local circumstances, the reform agitation was carried on with intense vigour in Aberdeen, and no class of the community took a more active share in it than the different bodies of craftsmen. They expected to reap many advantages from the opening up of the burghs; they little anticipated that the reform they so anxiously sought for would pave the way for the "disestablishment" of their own particular associations so far as their trading monopolies were concerned. They fondly hoped that, under a reformed system of local government, they would enter on a new era of extended trading privileges and increased powers for regulating the trade and industries of the town. But the reform movement, which they were so active in promoting, did not stop exactly where they expected it would. In its onward march it overtook their own particular trading privileges, and in one "fell swoop" swept away privileges and monopolies which they had enjoyed for nearly seven centuries.*

* As a curiosity we give a copy of one of the last petitions presented to the Magistrates in reference to the exclusive privileges of the craftsmen of Aberdeen :—

Unto the Honourable the Magistrates of Aberdeen The petition of James Clyne, Shoemaker in Aberdeen, present Boxmaster of the Shoemaker Trade, a Incorporation of Aberdeen, for himself, and as representing said Trade,

Humbly Sheweth,

That the said Trade have the exclusive right and privilege of carrying on the Shoemaker Trade of the Burgh of Aberdeen ; that notwithstanding thereof Alexander Ritchie and William Ritchie, Shoemakers, Schoolhill, Aberdeen, carrying on business under the firm of Alexander and William Ritchie, Shoemakers, Schoolhill, Aberdeen ; George Burgess, Shoemaker, Union Street, Aberdeen, and carrying on business under the firm of George Burgess and Company, Shoemakers, Union Street, Aberdeen ; and George Melvin, Shoemaker, Woolmanhill, Aberdeen, have been carring on said trade for sometime past within the

When the reform movement sprang into active life in Aberdeen about 1816, the affairs of the town were in a deplorable state. The Town Council was one of the "closest" in the country; the corporation funds were in a mess; and all classes of citizens united in moving for a radical change. In 1817 the retiring members of the Town Council issued a manifesto stating "that they were compelled to leave the affairs of the burgh in a state of embarrassment, which, as it has been a source of much vexation and distress among themselves, must still prove one of considerable difficulty to those who may be destined to succeed them unless immediate steps are taken to redeem the credit of the corporation." The members of the Council themselves were of opinion that the existing " mode of election of the Town Council and management of town's affairs are radically defective and improvident, tending to give to any individual or party who may be so inclined an excessive and unnatural preponderance, and to foster and encourage a system of concealment under which the most upright and best intentioned magistrates may not be able to acquire a thorough knowledge of the situation of the burgh;" and it was felt that nothing short of a complete change in " the manner of electing the Council, and an effectual control given to the citizens over the expenditure of the town's office-bearers, would effect any good."

Burgh of Aberdeen without being freemen, whereby they have become respectively liable to said trade and petitioner as Boxmaster foresaid in damages and expenses, and in respect they persist in carrying on said trade it is necessary to present this petition for fine and interdict.

May it therefore please your Honar to appoint this petition to be intimated to the said Alexander Ritchie, William Ritchie, and Alexander and William Ritchie, as a company ; George Burgess, and George Burgess and Company ; and to the said George Melvin, on a short inducio, and with or without answers to fine and amerciate them in the sum of ten pounds sterling each in name of damages and expenses payable to the petitioner as Boxmaster foresaid, and as representing and for behoof of said trade. Also to prohibit and discharge them from carrying on said trade or any part thereof within Burgh, under the penalty of ten pounds sterling each *toties quoties* in all time coming, or until they become members of said trade, and also to find them liable in the expense of this application and procedure to follow thereon. According to Justice drawn by   (Signed)   ALEX. ALLAN.

Aberdeen, 10th April, 1840.—Appoints the said Alexander Ritchie, William Ritchie, and Alexander and William Ritchie as a company ; George Burgess, and George Burgess and Company ; and George Melvin to lodge answers to the foregoing petition, if they any have, with the Clerk of Court within three free days after they are respectively served with a double of said petition and of this deliverance by an officer of Court with certification.

(Singed)   J. URQUHART.

A full double served on you the said George Melvin, this tenth day of April, eighteen hundred and forty years, by me,   WILL. WALKER, Town Sergeant.

The Trades appointed a special committee to look after their interests, and numerous were the petitions forwarded by them to Parliament praying for a radical change in the mode of electing Town Councils, and for a redress against what they considered were encroachments by the merchant burgesses on their special privileges.

But when the Burgh Reform Bill of 1833 was introduced, the merchant guilds and craft incorporations throughout the country began to see that their own privileges were to be curtailed. In the form in which the bill passed the House of Commons, the right of deacons of guild and deacon-conveners to sit in the Town Councils was to be swept away; but, mainly we believe through the efforts of the Glasgow Trades House, the bill was amended in the House of Lords, and the deacons and conveners were allowed to remain constituent members of the Town Councils.* An important clause was also introduced in this bill providing—"That nothing herein contained shall be held or construed to impair the right of any craft, trade, convenery of trades, or guildry, or merchant house, or trades house, or other such incorporation severally to elect their own deacons, or deacon-conveners, or deans of guild, or directors, or other lawful officers for the management of the affairs of such crafts, trades, conveneries of trades, or guildries, merchants or trades houses, or other such corporations, but that on the contrary the said several bodies shall from and after the passing of this Act be in all cases entitled to the free election in such forms as shall be regulated by them of the said several office-bearers, and other necessary officers for the management of their affairs, without any interference or control whatsoever on the part of the Town Council thereof."

The abolition of trading privileges took place under an Act passed in 1846, the preamble of which sets forth:— " Whereas in certain Royal and other Burghs in Scotland the members of certain Guilds, Crafts, or Incorporations possess exclusive privileges of carrying on or dealing in Merchandise,

---

* The Deacon-Convener in Aberdeen, unlike those in several other towns, had no seat at the Town Council. He had merely a seat at the Police Board before the amalgamation of the Municipal and Police Departments.

and of carrying on or exercising certain Trades or Handicrafts within their respective Burghs, and such Guilds, Crafts, and Incorporations have corresponding rights entitling them to prevent persons not being members thereof from carrying on or dealing in merchandise, or from carrying on or exercising such trades or handicrafts within such burghs ; and whereas it has become expedient that such exclusive privileges and rights should be abolished, be it enacted, &c." Then follows the enacting clause declaring "that from and after the passing of this Act all such exclusive trading privileges and rights shall cease."*

What is known as the Dunlop Act, which was passed in 1860 for amending the law relative to the legal qualification of councillors and the admission of burgesses in Royal Burghs in Scotland, and under which burgesses can be created on payment of twenty shillings, also provided that " such admission by minute of Council shall not *per se* be held to give or imply any right of title to, or interest in, the properties funds, or revenues of any of the Guilds, Crafts, or Incorporations of the burgh, or any mortifications or benefactions for behoof of the burgesses of such Guilds, Crafts, or Incorporations or their families, or any right or management thereof in any of the said Guilds, Crafts, or Incorporations."

Under a subsequent Act passed in 1876 for the assimilation of the law of Scotland to that of England respecting the creation of burgesses, it was also enacted that " nothing herein contained shall interfere with any law or legal usage by which burgesses are now created or admitted in any burgh, or give or imply any right or title to or interest in any merchants house or trades house or any patrimonial lands, commons, or other properties, funds or revenues of any guild, burgesses of guild, crafts, or incorporations of the burgh, or to or in any burgess acres, or any grazing rights connected therewith, or any mortifications or benefactions for behoof of the members of such guilds, burgesses of guild, crafts, or incorporations, and of their families, or any right of management thereof."

The only special privileges that remained to the craftsmen in Aberdeen after the abolition of exclusive trading privileges,

* For full text of this Act see Appendix.

above those enjoyed by ordinary citizens, were a preferential claim for the admission of their sons to Robert Gordon's Hospital, exemption from the Bell and Petty Customs, and a right to vote for the election of Harbour Commissioners. But even these have gradually disappeared ; and a free craftsman is now, so far as any special rights of citizenship are concerned, practically on the same platform as an ordinary residenter or ratepayer.

CHAPTER XV.

THE FUNDS OF THE SEVEN TRADES.

THE Acts of Parliament mentioned in the foregoing chapter effected a vital change in the work and functions of all merchant and craft guilds. Bereft of their trading privileges, the members turned their attention almost exclusively to provident and educational objects; and in this respect the Aberdeen Trades have been remarkably successful. The individual incorporations have not only added to their capital, but the additional funds, in which all have a common interest, have also been considerably augmented. The following comparative table, showing the amount of the allowances paid to widows, annuitants, orphans, &c., for the years 1837 and 1886, will give an indication of their financial prosperity during the last fifty years :—

	1837.			1886.		
Hammermen	£899	3	6	£1481	4	7
Bakers	237	0	0	1056	1	9
Wrights and Coopers . . .	384	11	0	906	18	1
Tailors	403	14	2	937	4	4
Shoemakers	250	10	10	808	9	11
Weavers	191	9	3	212	6	11
Fleshers	121	18	0	223	7	0
	£2488	6	9	£5625	12	7
Widows' Fund . . .	444	0	0	1224	13	0
Supplementary Fund . .	11	10	0	225	0	0
Trades Hospital . . .	563	7	9	835	4	2
Bursaries	40	0	0	155	11	6
Total . .	£3547	4	6	£8166	1	3

In addition to these sums the Trades pay about £400 per annum of corporation duty; and when salaries, management, and other expenses are taken into account, it will be seen that their present revenue represents a capital of close upon £250,000.

The following is a statement of the present entry monies
to the different Trades, extracted from the Tables of Dues :—

HAMMERMEN.

Entry money at 21 years of age, £120. After the age of 21 entrants
pay, in addition to the foregoing sum, £5 for every year or part of a year
up to 33 years of age, at which age the payment will amount to one
hundred and eighty pounds, which sum is the highest payment for an
entrant of any age to the Trade. Widows' Fund payment extra, according to age, &c. Sons of members who have joined the Incorporation previous to the adoption of the present rules (November, 1886), are admitted
at 21 years of age for the sum of £54, with an entra payment of 20s. for
every year or part of a year over that age ; and to the Widows' Fund,
when above 40 years of age, £2 7s. 3d. Sons-in-law of members who have
joined the Incorporation previous to the adoption of the present rules are
admitted at 21 years of age for the sum of £60 6s. 3d., with an extra payment of 20s. for every year or part of a year over that age ; and to the
Widows' Fund, when above 40 years of age, £4 1s.

BAKERS.

Sons	.	.	.		.	.	.	.	£94 12 3
Sons-in-law	.	.		.	.	.		96 2 3
Extraneans	.	.	.	.	.	.	.	151 13 0½

Extra payment to Widows' Fund above 30.

WRIGHTS AND COOPERS.

Sons	aged 20	.	.	.	.	.	.	£53 13 11
Sons-in-law	do.	.	.	.	.	.	.	57 0 11
Apprentices	do.	.	.	.	.	.	.	80 10 11
Extraneans	do.	.	.	.	.	.	.	91 0 3

Sons, sons-in-law, and apprentices pay £1 10s. for each additional year
of their age above 20, and extraneans £2 12s. 6d.

TAILORS.

Eldest sons, aged 21	.	.	.	.	£40 3 6
Younger do.,	do.	.	.	.	.	45 3 6
Sons-in-law,	do.	.	.	.	.	67 0 6
Apprentices,	do.	.	.	.	.	127 0 6
Extraneans,	do.	.	.	.	.	157 0 6

For every year over 21 an extranean pays £3, eldest son £1, son-in-
law and apprentice £1 10s. ; for every year after 30 an extranean pays
£3 15s. to the Widows' Fund, and after 40, £6 10s. 6d. ; sons over 40
£2 7s. 3d. ; sons-in-law and apprentices over 30, £1 10s. ; and do. over
40, £4 1s.

SHOEMAKERS.

Eldest sons,	under 40	£39 15 7
Do.,	40 and over	42 2 10
Younger sons,	under 40	41 15 7
Do.,	40 and over	44 2 10
Sons-in-law,	under 30	45 2 7
Do.,	30 and under 40 . . .	46 12 7
Do.,	40 and over	49 3 7
Apprentices,	under 30	84 2 7
Do,	30 and under 40 . . .	85 12 7
Do.,	40 and over	88 3 7
Extraneans,	under 30	117 18 7
Do.,	30 and under 40 . . .	121 13 7
Do.,	40 and over	124 9 1

WEAVERS.

Sons, 20 years of age	£44 4 7
Sons-in-law	49 8 7
Apprentices	60 14 3
Extraneans	90 13 7

For every year after 20 sons pay £1 4s. ; sons-in-law, £1 8s. ; apprentices, £1 17s. 4d. ; and extraneans, £2 10s. ; and extra rates to the Widows' Fund after 30.

FLESHERS.

Sons, 25 and under	£41 13 1
Sons-in-law, do.	52 0 1
Apprentices	55 0 1
Extraneans	84 16 1

Extra payment of each additional year of age according to table.

The scale of benefit varies in the different Trades. Annuitants receive from £25 to £70 per annum ; widows, from £20 to £35 ; indigent sons and daughters, from £4 to £6 ; orphans, from £3 to £9 ; while in several of the Trades considerable sums are annually voted by " warrant " in cases of necessity.

The Widows' Fund mentioned in these tables was established in 1771 for the purpose of supplementing the sums given by the individual Trades to the widows of their deceased members. Annual contributions are made to this general fund by the Convener Court and the seven Trades, while a portion of the entry money paid by each entrant is allocated to the Widows' Fund. For a considerable time—in fact, down to 1851—the accumulated capital of the Fund was comparatively small, but greater attention having been paid to this branch of benefit, the stock now amounts to over £30,000, the annual payments, as will be seen by the foregoing table, amounting to over £1200.

LIST OF FACTORS OF THE TRADES WIDOWS' FUND.

1771.	Hugh Gordon.	1805.	George Roger.
1772.	Peter Proctor.	1806.	Nath. Gillet.
1773.	Robert Martin.	1809.	John Chambers.
1774.	William Milne.	1811.	Alex. Watson.
1775.	Patk. Gordon.	1813.	William Nicol.
1776.	Wm. Knowles.	1815.	George Anderson.
1777.	Patk. Gordon.	1817.	Don. McDonald.
1779.	Thomas Taylor.	1819.	James Christie.
1780.	James Hacket.	1821.	John Barron.
1781.	Peter Robertson.	1823.	James Topp.
1782.	James Gordon.	1825.	William Maitland.
1783.	Wm. Donald.	1829.	James Topp.
1784.	Wm. Farquharson.	1831.	George Fullerton.
1785.	James Clark.	1832.	James Topp.
1787.	Thomas Warrack.	1836.	John Fraser.
1788.	Adam Watt.	1841.	James Berry.
1790.	George Craig.	1853.	Charles Robertson.
1792.	James Gordon.	1854.	William Smith.
1794.	Wm. Michie.	1856.	John McHardy.
1795.	Alex. Thomson.	1857.	Robert Thomson.
1796.	Alex. Tytler.	1861.	John Rust.
1797.	James Ramsay.	1862.	Wm. Bird.
1798.	Alex. Hall.	1871.	John Mitchell.
1799.	John Wallace.	1875.	James Thomson.
1801.	David Reid.	1884.	Alex. Nicolson.
1803.	George Smith.		

In 1816 a Supplementary Widows' Fund was established, mainly through the exertions of Mr. John Leslie, goldsmith, a worthy citizen whose hand was visible in many a good work among his fellow-citizens. It is optional for members to join this fund, but the dues are by no means heavy, considering that the annual allowance to widows in the fund is £9. If under thirty years of age, entrants pay £19; if above thirty and under forty, £25; if above forty and under fifty, £30; if above fifty and under sixty, £35; and if above sixty, £40. Baillie James Berry is at present factor of this fund.

We have already referred in a previous chapter to the Bursars' Fund, under the management of the convener, master of hospital, and seven deacons; and, to still further encourage members to provide the best education attainable for their children, several of the Trades have, since the Trades School was given up, established educational funds of their own. The Trades School was for many years a valuable adjunct in connection with the Trades. It was established in 1808, under the following resolutions :—

(1) That the lower rooms of the Trinity House be set apart and fitted up for the schoolhouse, the expense to be defrayed from the fabric money (*i.e.*, money set aside for maintaining the house).

(2) That six pounds sterling be annually paid from the funds of each of the Seven Incorporations, and of the Hospital, making altogether £48 annually—the whole or part of which to be paid as salary to the master.

(3) That the managers of the school shall consist of seventeen, viz. :— the patron, convener, and master of hospital, *ex officio*, and two elected from each Trade. The patron, or in his absence, the convener, to have the casting vote at all the meetings—seven to be a quorum.

When the new hall was built a portion of the building was set apart for the school, where it was conducted with marked success until 1878; but, for various reasons, it had reluctantly to be given up. Owing to the enlarged area of the town, many members could not take advantage of the school; while the passing of the Education Act forced up the cost of maintaining a school to such an extent that the disadvantages and loss became greater than the advantages.

APPENDIX.

CHARTER BY QUEEN MARY IN FAVOUR OF CRAFTSMEN 1556.

MARY, be the grace of God Queen of Scots, to all and sundry our leidges and subjects to whom thir present letters shall come wisheth health ; be it known unto you, because we understand that our most noble progenitors, kings of Scotland, having an consideration and respect that the common wealth cannot long stand without artificers and good craftsmen, and therefore they gave and granted many and divers privileges and liberties unto the craftsmen of the burghs and cities of our kingdom, to witt, that they should choyce principally skillfull men of their own craft, and together superiours and deacons to visite and examine all crafts, and that no extortion be the leidges of our realm against them be used, but that every craftsman should work and labour diligently in his own craft without fraud, guile, evil, or deceit, and that they should make such laws, penalties, and pains as is agreeable and consonant to equitie and right ; And further put the samen to execution against those that offends in their craft, and that the persons daminfied by these craftsmen should be recompenced for their skaith ; Further they gave privileges and power to good craftsmen that should be free burgesses of our burghs to use and sell merchandise as all other merchants of our realm uses, with divers other and sundrie privileges, liberties, and faculties granted to them under the great seals of our most noble progenitors seen and considered be us. The whilk notwithstanding being derogate by the Act of Parliament last holden in the moneth of July the year bypast for certain causes expressed and proposed by the samen Parliament, it was ordained that no deacons from that time should be chosen within the burgh, but that the Provost, Bailies, and Councill of every burgh should choose the best and most skillfull craftsmen in their own craft, and that every one of these persons should be called visitors of their craft, and should be chosen yearly att the feast of Michaelmas, and that no craftsmen within the burgh should bear office in time to come except two be chosen yearly upon the Councill of the burgh, with divers other restrictions as att more length is contained in the foresaid Act of Parliament, from the whilk time of the said Act of Parliament we have found no cause nor reason brought to effect whilk moved our foresaid Act of Parliament unto the samen yea all things to be done by the saids craftsmen moe stablie than before, and therefore not willing to diminish the privileges of our predecessors without an great necessity and just cause, but all things according to equitie and right, granted of old to be restored unto the said craftsmen ; and also designing to remove the dissentions private and publick, hatred and contentions of our merchants and crafts-men dwelling within our burghs, and for certain other just and reasonable causes moving our mind thereto, of our knowledge and proper motion we dispense, and by thir presents dispenses with all and sundry craftsmen of our burghs and cities within our said realm concerning our last Act of Parliament, and all articles and clauses contained in the samen whilk is contrary and obstant to the liberties and privileges, and to the long and continuall possession had by them by virtue of the samen of our most noble progenitors, and we give them place again to use and have deacons of their crafts who shall give their sentences and votes in choycing of men that bears office in burghs, and all sorts of craftsmen should be chosen within the burgh, and they shall use and exercise the samen if they be found convenient and meet for the samen, and they shall bear the compt of the common goods, and they shall be a part of the auditors of the samen, and shall conveen and make lawful statutes and ordinances concerning of their affairs for the keeping of good order amongst craftsmen, and main-taining of good service at their altars, and they shall sell, use, and exercise all sorts of merchandise within our realm and without the same as it shall seem most expedient for them, with all and sundry privileges, liberties, faculties, and customs, and given and granted unto them by our most noble progenitors, used and possessed by them in time bygone, notwithstanding our forsaid Act of Parliament and pains whatsomever contained therein concerning the which we dispense with them by thir presents. Further, we ratifie and approve by thir presents all privileges and faculties given and granted by our most noble progenitors unto the saids craftsmen in times bygone, to be used and exercised by them with form, force, and effect in times to come as they enjoyed, possessed, and used the samen before without any variety. Wherefore we command you and every one of you our leidges and subjects in so far that ye nor none of you presume in time coming to make any impediment, molestation, or obstacle in con-trary of thir presents unto the saids craftsmen enjoying, possessing, and using the liberties, privileges, and faculties prescrived unto them, not-withstanding any Acts, letters, statutes, precepts, or proclamations what-somever made or to be made in the contrary or any pain contained in the samen under the highest pain, danger, or offence whilk ye or any of you may incur or committ in this point against Our Majesty. In witness of the whilk unto thir presents we have commanded our great seal to be affixed at Sterling, the 18th of Aprile, the year of God 1556, and of our reign the 9th year.

COMMON INDENTURE, 1587.

(BETWEEN TOWN COUNCIL, GUILDRY, AND TRADES OF ABERDEEN.)

AT Aberdene the seventh day of July the zier of God ane thousand five hundred fourscore and seven years, we Alexander Cullane, David Menzies, baillies of the burght of Aberdene, and Alexander Forbes, burgess of the said burght, commissionars electit, and nominate be the provost, baillies, council, brethren of gild of the said burght, on the ane part, and George Elphinston, deacon-conveneer, Alexander Ronaldson, baxter, John Duncan, tailor, commissionars chosen, electit, and nominate be the haill craftismen, freemen of the said burght, on the uther part, and Maister Alexander Cheyne, parson of Snaw and commissar of Aberdene, odman and o'man, equally chosen by the saids commissionars anent the decision of the contro-versy afterspecifit betwixt the saids commissionars for the saids parties ; that is to say, Forsameikleas the saids commissionars havand sufficient power of baith the parties foresaid are finally appointit and agreet upon all and sundry the heads after following ; and first, to take away all differences whilk hitherto resultit upon the admission of freemen of craft, and for the establishing of ane perpetual ordor yairanent, we ordane and decerns all persons willing to be made free and incorporate to the fraternity of ony craft, that they sall first present themselffs to the provost, baillies, and council, to be made free burgesses of the said burght ; and gif they mean to leif by their said craft, the said provost, baillies, and council and dean of gild, before ony furder proceeding, sall remit the entrant be their testi-monial to the deacon and maisters of the craft profest be the said entrant, to be examint by them ; and being examint, and not found qualifyt, sall be repellt baith frae the suit of burgess-ship and freemanship of the craft foresaid ; but be the contrar, gif they be found qualifyt be the said deacon and freemen of the said craft, reportand to the provost, baillies, council, and dean of gild, ane sufficient testimonial upon their conscience of the entrant's qualification and hability : that then and in that case they sall be admittit, agreeand for the freedom of the burgess-ship according to the antient use and laudable consuetude of the said burgh ; providing that this clause, viz., *secundem libertatem sue artis*, or sicklike words, signifiand odius restrictions, be not insert in their testimonial, but that the same be done *admissus in burgensem tantummodo ;* and thereafter, notwithstanding of the whilk admission the said entrant sall not have place to work, nor exercise his craft, unto the time he report his testimonial of the said pro-vost, baillies, and dean of gild, under the subscription of the town clark, that he is admitted to be burgess, and present the same to the deacon and

maisters of that craft, who thereafter sall compone with the entrant for
the freedom and free licence to exercise the craft : And be reason sume
doubts resulted amang the said commissionars concerning the composition
of the entrants, it is finally agreet by the saids commissionars and decernt
by them, that the said compositions and blankates be made after the auld
use and custum, and not after the will of the entrant ; bot because consideration aught to be had diversly after the estait and condition of diverse
persons suitars of the freedom ; to wit, giffe the entrant be the eldest son
of ane free burgess, or zit the eldest son of ane free craftisman that hes
past their prenticeship within the said burgh of Aberdene, he sall be free
with the craft for the bancate only ; bot the rest of merchants sons, or
free craftismens sons that hes past their prenticeship within the said burgh
of Aberdene, sall pay forty shilling o'head, with the bancate befoir, allenarly ; and all prentices learning within the said town, and zet being ane
forane, or born out of the said town, as also they that are not freemens
sons, suppose they be born within the town, sall pay ten marks overhead
with the bancate, for their freedums, to the deacon and brethren of their
craft ; sicklike outlands craftismen that are notht born burgesses sons or
freemans sons of the said burgh, neither hes past prenticeship within the
same, but has learnt their craft in ony uther place not within the town,
they sall pay to the deacon and maisters of their craft for their freedom,
at the least twenty marks money foresaid with the bancate as said is ; and
decerns the composition of the money foresaid for the freedum, as is above
expreamt, to be delivert and payt to the deacon of the craft, he to be
answerable for the twa part of the same to the dean of gild and to deliver
the same to him for to be wared and bestowt upon the aid, support, and
help of the common charges of the town, according to the directions to be
given be the provost, baillies, and council of the said burgh to him thereanent ; and the third part of the said composition, with the bankates foresaid, to be distributit an bestowt at the pleasure of the deacons of the
craftis and their brethren freemen aforesaid : And sicklike the twa part of
the composition of the entress of every prentice (whilk is the sum of
twenty shilling) the twa part thereof to be delivert to the dean of gild, and
the third part to the deacons and maisters of craftis, to be usit in manner
and to the effect above expreamt. Secondly, we the saids commissioners
for baith the said parties, *hinc inde*, decerns and ordains that the saids
craftismen sall not meddle with na kind of foreane nor oversea wares, but
to have their shair of timber conform to use and wont, and of salt sa meikle
as serve thair houses allenarly ; and as concerning the bearing of offices of
magistrates, sic as to be provost, baillies, deans of gild, and thesaurers, we
decern that na craftismen sall aspyre thereto unto the time that they be
promotit to be bretheren of gild ; bot prejudice always that it sall be liesom to the said craftismen to choise sax persons of their awin number zierly,
to be upon lyitis of whom the concil sall choise twa thereof zeirly,
who sall have place with the rest of the ordinary auditors to hear and see
all and sundry the town's compts, baith of property and casualitys. Thirdly,

in respect that gryt contraversies hes been at all times betwixt the said parties concerning the using of the traffique and exercise of all kinds of merchandise in general or in special, premisable or notht premisable to the craftismen, where anent we the saids commissionars for the provost, baillies, and brethren of gild, willing all matters debatable to be sattled and put to rest, are content to grant the saids craftismen, likeas be the tenor hereof grants to them, the free use and traffique of barking of ledder, buying of buttir, victual, cheese, sheep, and nolt, lyme, coals, carsays, plaiding, raw claith, hiland grays, mantlings, and linen claith, and to sell and tope the same in all parts within the realm of Scotland as freely as merchants brethren of gild does; and forder, permitts to them the traffiquing of little claith whilk is maid within their awin house allenarly, and na utherways: Of the whilk specialls, grantit in manner forsaid, the said craftismen notht being contentit, in respect of the same was not sufficient recompense, as they alleg't to them, for their refusal of all kind of oversea and forrane merchandries, likeas be the tenor of thir presents we the commisionars for the saids craftismen refuses the same, with divers uther privileges grantit to us and the remnant craftismen be our soveraign lord's disposition, under his Majesty's gryt seal, so that we the saids craftismen and our successors mighten juiss free liberties to traffique only with all kind of Scotis wares; but stop or impediment to be maid to us be the saids provost, baillies, and bretheren of gild in times cuming; and forder, contention appearing for to ensew to the inquetness of the commoun wealth of the said burgh, the provost, baillies, council, and brether of gild, being mov't with natural pity for to put the saids craftismen, being members of their awin commoun wealth, frae forder trouble, on the ane part; and the said craftismen, as neighbors, willing with detfull reverence to obey their said magistrates, ware content on the uther part to referr the samyne to us commissionars *hinc inde* respective forsaid, with power to us, in case of discord, to chise an oversman to discern thereanent as he should think expedient; and after lang reasoning maid *hinc inde* thereupon, we the said commissionars, having power and command of baith tha said parties in manner forsaid, hes reffert, likeas be the tenor of thir presents referrs the decision of the said controversy, formit as afterfollows, to Mr. Alexander Cheyne, parson of Snaw, and Commissar of Aberdene, according to the tenor of the designation within written: viz. Quhidder giff besides the former things agreet and grantit to the saids craftismen, &c., the council and bretheren of gild sall grant the liberty of Scotis wares be nomination of some specialls, and excluding the craftismen from the rest; or giff they sall grant to the saids craftismen the liberty of all Scotis wares in general, reservand certain specialls to themselffes; and I the said Maister Alexander Cheyne, after the acceptation of the samen, having herd and considert the reassonis and allegationis maid be the said commissionars *hinc inde* for baith the parties forsaids, the name of the Lord callt, to whom I maun be answerable this day and the day of judgement, findis, that forsameikleas the merchants and

bretheren of gild has the prerogative and dignity far abone the saids craitismen, in sic sort as they have power to call and accuse, and cause them be convictit and correctit for the transgression of all and sundry the points of every thing, either grantit or notht grantit to them, wharebe the contrair the saids craftismen has notht the like power at all to call, accuse, or pursew the saids merchants bretheren of gild for buying, selling, or toping aither of oversea and forrane wares, or zit of Scottis wares, guides, or geir, considering that all kind of merchandeis whatsumever is free to the said bretheren of gild without question and contraversy ; but namely, because tbe saids craftismen hes consentit and agreet to give and deliver the twa part of all the compositions, as is before expreamt, maid and given to them for the admission of all freemen and receiving of all prentices to their craftis respectively forsaid to the dean of gild, for to be bestowt be him upon the common charges of the town, as is abone rehearst ; wharebe the contrair the saids craftismen might have employed the samen to their awn particular uses, as they had wont to do in times past ; and therefoir I the said Master Alexander Cheyne, with consent and assent of the saids commissionars electit and chosen for baith the saids parties, pronounces and decerns, that the council sall grant, likeas be the tenor hereof grants to the saids craftismen and their successors, the general liberty of all Scottis wares, by and attour the things grantit them, as said is, to buy and sell the samen universally within the realm of Scotland, as they sall think expedient, reservand the specials to the saids bretheren of gild themselffs ; and specially the heads, wares, and form thereof, as after follows, secludand the saids craftsmen and their forsaids therefrae for ever ; viz. That it sall notht be leisom to ony of the saids craftismen or their foresaids to have the handling of ony stappil guides, whidder the same be Scottis or forrane wares ; but that the only use of handling of the samen, that is to say, packing and peiling of fish, hydes, skin, and woll, sall properly appertain unto the merchants bretheren of gild allenarly, but prejudice always to the said craftismen that they be not stopit to buy and sell the said wares in smalls in ony part within the realm, as said is ; and the saids craftismen in speciall to buy, sell, and tope sameikle wool as they sall cause be wrought respective in their houses ; ·
and sicklike reserves to the said bretheren of gild, to have the only power to transport Scottis wares in schipps boats, either be sea or be land, in forrane countries, there to traffique therewith, and the saids craftismen notht to have power to do the same, neither directly nor indirectly ; providing always that it prejudge notht the saids craftismen and their foresaids to traffique, buy, sell, and tope all manner of Scottis wares in general (excepting as is befoir excepted) within the realm of Scotland, and they never to be callt, accust, nor convictit for the samen, bot to be free thereto, as said is ; and but prejudice of the privilege of ledder barkers in buying of rough hydes in all parts within the realm, and barking and selling of the samen, as said is ; and privilege of coupars according to auld use and wont : Providing also that gif it sall chance the said craftismen and their

successors to be teachit and learnt in making of woolens, sautings, silks, taffities, or ony kind of stuff that hes notht been maid of auld within the realm of Scotland, bot of lait throw the incoming of strangars within the country, that it sall not be leisum to the craftismen to sell the samen, except it be their awin handy wark, and that in haill pieces, (dispensand always with them to sell and tope in small or gryt their said handy wark of seyis, worsetts, linings, and single sergis, but stop or impediment :) And anent the transgression of the said points, or any of them above rehearst, giff it sall happen ony of the saids craftismen and their foresaids, in times cuming, to be callt and accust for the transgressing of the heads and points afore inhibite to them, as is abone expreampt, they being convictit therefoir, to be unlawt according to the antient laws of this said burgh : Providing always, that it sall notht be leisum to condemn the alleagt contraveener upon ane bare suspicion in ony sort, bot be sufficient tryal maid and had be witnesses unsuspectit and undefamt, either merchant or craftisman, purging themselffs be their corporal aith of partial counsell. And finally, it is ordaint, that baith the said parties, merchants and craftismen, present and to cume, inviolably observe, fulfill, and keep this present appointment and decreet of every head, clause, and article therein contain, likeas we the saids commissionars and oversman foresaid ordains them to do the same, and the practique and execution thereof to be and begin the day and dait of thir presents, and to continue as an perpetual law in all times coming : And for the better observing, keeping, and fulfilling of the premises, we the saids commissionars and oversman are content and consents that the designatiou written on the uther side hereof, and this present decreet, be insert and registered in the buikes of council of Aberdene, as also in the commissary buikes of Aberdene, alswell *ad perpetuam rei memoriam*, as also to have the strength of ane confest act and judicial decreet, with executorials of poinding and horning the one, bot prejudice of the other to pass thereon upon ane single charge of four days warning : And forder ordains, that the procuratorys and mandates given to the saids commissionars be registrate in the said commissar's buikes in like manner, *ad perpetuam rei memoriam* ; and giff need bees, consents that ane act of parliament sall be procurit for ratification and approbation of this present appointment and decreet for to stand as ane perpetual law betwixt the parties foresaid and their successores respectively for ever, and to that effect constitutes and ordains discreet men, &c., and ilk ane of them conjunctly and severally our lauchfull and undoubted procurators, to compear for us and iu our name before the said commissar, provost, and baillies forsaid, as also in presence of the lords of parliament, to the effect forsaid, *promitten, de rata, &c.*

In witness of the whilk we the said commissionars and o'man, in sign and taken and fortification of our decreet and appointment foresaid, hes subscrivt the samen as after follows, day, year, and place foresaid, before thir witnesses :

Maisters George Barclay, Richard Irvine, Gilbert Bissset, John Kennedie, Robert Paip, Thomas Mollysone, James Davidsone, and James Ogstoune, notars public.

Sic subscribitur,

Alex^r. Cullan, Commissionar, w^t my hand.
David Menyzies, commissionar, w^t my hand.
Alex^r. Forbes, w^t my hand.

George Elphinstone, saidlar, John Duncane, tailor, and Alex. Ronaldsone, baxter, with our handis at the pen, led be the notars underwritten at our commandis, becaus we cannotht wret ourselffis.

Ita est Mag^r Robertus Paip notarious publicus ac testis in præmissis de mandatis dictorum Alexandri Ronaldsone, Georgii Elphinstone, et Johannis Duncan, scribere nescien, ut asseruerunt ad hæc manu sua rogatus et requisitus per dictos commissarios.

Ita est Alex^r Donaldsoun co-notarius in præmissis rogatus et requisitus per dictos commissionarios ad hæc manu propria.

Maister Alexander Chene, comiss^r of Aberdene, w^t my hand.

CHARTER OF CONFIRMATION

By KING CHARLES the FIRST under his Great Seal, ratifying
a MORTIFICATION by DOCTOR WILLIAM GUILD to
the Free Craftsmen of Aberdeen. 1633.

Translated from the original Latin, by P. J. Anderson, LL.B.,
Aberdeen, 1887.

CHARLES, by the grace of God, King of Great Britain, France, and
Ireland, Defender of the Faith, TO ALL good men of his whole land,
clergy and laity, Greeting : KNOW YE that we, with express consent
and assent of our well-beloved cousin and councillor, William Earl of
Morton, Lord Dalkeith, etc., chief treasurer of our kingdom of Scotland, our
collector and comptroller, and of our beloved cousin, John Lord Stewart of
Traquair, our treasurer-depute in the said offices, and of the rest of the
lords commissioners of our exchequer of our said kingdom, have fully considered a CERTAIN CHARTER, donation and mortification therein contained, made, given and granted by our beloved Mr. William Guild, preacher
of the Word of God at Aberdeen, to the free craftsmen of Aberdeen : of all
and whole that place and monastery of the Holy Trinity of the said burgh,
belonging heritably in feu farm to the said Mr. William, with all and
sundry the houses and buildings thereof, together with the church and
churchyard of the same, yards, orchards, greens, and pertinents whatsoever,
lying within the said burgh of Aberdeen, and the sheriffdom thereof ; as
also of the ministry of the same place, with all and sundry lands, annual rents,
fruits, profits, emoluments, and duties whatsoever, now belonging, or which
were of old known to belong, to the foresaid monastery, wheresoever [they
lie] within the burgh, or in the fields without the burgh, with the tenants,
tenandries, services of free tenants of the same, and their sundry other pertinents ; that the same place, with the revenues, may be an hospital for old
poor craftsmen of the burgh aforesaid, as specified in the said charter ; to
be held of us and our successors in pure and perpetual alms and mortmain
for ever : [the said charter], at our command seen, read, and inspected, and
diligently examined, being whole, entire, not erased, not cancelled, nor
suspected in any part thereof, in form as follows :—

"TO ALL and sundry who shall hear and see the present letters, Mr.
William Guild, preacher of the Word of God at Aberdeen, Greeting in Him
who is the true salvation of all.

"KNOW YE that I, to the glory of God, for the comfort of the needy,
and to afford to others a good example of charity towards the poor,
whom our Lord Jesus Christ has to the end of the world left amongst us,

Z

and recommended to us, to be fed, clothed and cherished, HAVE FOUNDED, gifted, and perpetually mortified to the free craftsmen of Aberdeen, and, by this my present charter, do found, gift, and perpetually mortify, to the same: ALL and whole the place and monastery of the brethren of the Holy Trinity of the burgh of Aberdeen, belonging to me, the said Dr. William Guild, heritably in feu farm, with all and sundry the houses and buildings thereof, together with the church and churchyard of the same, yards, orchards, greens, and pertinents whatsoever lying within the said burgh of Aberdeen and the sheriffdom thereof ; as also, the ministry of the same place, with all and sundry lands, annual rents, fruits, profits, emoluments, and duties whatsoever, now belonging, or which were of old known to belong, to the foresaid monastery, wheresoever [they lie] within the burgh, or in the fields without the burgh, with the tenants, tenandries, services of free tenants of the same, and their sundry other pertinents ; that the same place, with the revenues aforesaid or afternamed, may be an hospital for old poor craftsmen of the burgh aforesaid, to be sustained and supported in the same, who shall be of good fame, and not reduced to poverty through their own vice, or especially through drunkenness and extravagance.

"AND THEREFORE, in order that none be brought into that hospital or enjoy the fruits of this mortification save good pious and sober men, I ORDAIN as patrons, a preacher of the Word of God at Aberdeen (whom the deacons of the six crafts shall choose from the number of their own pastors), with the deacon-convener ; who shall associate to themselves six men of good fame, prudence, and piety (one from every craft), whom they shall bind with a solemn oath, one by one, that they nominate these whom they judge most worthy to be presented and admitted ; of which number it shall be lawful to the foresaid minister of the Word of God (with the deacon-convener), to admit him who shall seem most worthy to them, and be approved pious and sober by others, not for supplication or for bribe, but only out of charity, as they shall answer to God in the day of their appearance.

"LIKEWISE, in order that care be taken of the building, of the revenue, and of those admitted into the hospital, I ORDAIN, that on the same day on which the deacon-convener is chosen, a director, or master and caretaker of the hospital be chosen by the said minister of the Word, deacon-convener, and other deacons—a man, diligent, pious, and able to exercise that office, and who shall yearly give an account of his diligence, care, and faithful administration to the foresaid minister of the Word of God, deacon-convener, and other deacons of the crafts, in the week preceding the new election of the deacon-convener or deacons.

"I WILL also, that no woman dwell in the said hospital (although the wife of one that is admitted), or stay therein for a moment ; and that no one who is admitted wander in any way forth thereof through the town or streets ; and that they all be always clothed with gowns of a single and decent colour ; MOREOVER, that the said beadmen be subject and obedient to the commands and admonitions of the foresaid director, and that they be an honest, godly, and peaceable conversation. And if any of them wander without, or be troublesome within to any of their comrades, or commit any other fault, or be found disobedient, or a breaker of the rules of this mortification, he shall be punished in his person, or removed from the hospital, by the said director, who, however, in this case shall take the advice and consent of the foresaid minister of the Word of God and deacon-convener, who have, and by these presents shall have power, one poor man dying or removing from the said hospital or being otherwise withdrawn, to choose and put in another poor man in his place, in form aforesaid.

"I WILL also, that they be always present at the Sunday and weekly sermons (unless they be confined to their beds by sickness), as also at the public morning and evening prayers (especially in summer). ALSO, I ordain that in their own chapel a portion of the Word of God be read twice daily, and prayers offered up by a suitable reader (who shall have fifty merks paid him therefor yearly), to be properly chosen by the patron, which service shall be between nine and ten in the morning or forenoon, and between three and four in the evening or afternoon : and whoever (except through sickness) shall be once absent, let him be admonished ; if twice, punished by the director ; and if thrice, removed from the hospital.

"I WILL also, that one of the foresaid poor men be janitor of the said hospital weekly, having the keys of the doors and gates thereof (except the keys of the private rooms) ; and keep this order—First, in the morning, he shall open the outer gate and the door of the house and chapel at half-past seven hours, that they may go to public prayers in the church, or to hear a discourse, and at that same hour shall ring the bell a little, that by ringing thereof the rest being awakened may make themselves ready for the foresaid exercises : Next, the same janitor shall ring the bell regularly about the ninth hour in the morning, and the third hour in the evening, to summon the rest to hear prayers and the reading of the Scriptures in the chapel : And from thence they are to go to their own private rooms, and use their trade till the eleventh hour in the forenoon, and the sixth in the evening, and then they shall assemble in the common hall, and under a common president dine and sup together, the hebdomadar always publicly giving thanks.

"TO BE HELD AND HAD the foresaid place, with all and sundry its houses, church, yards, and pertinents whatsoever, as also the lands, annual rents, fruits, profits, and emoluments whatsoever, pertaining to that monastery, wheresoever [they lie], and mortified by me ; from me and my heirs, by the said poor and their successors who shall be put into the said hospital, of our Lord the King and his successors ; in pure and perpetual alms and mortmain for ever : with full power, faculty, and authority, to the said poor, by their director and caretaker of the hospital aforesaid, to exact, crave, uplift, and receive the annual rents from the persons due therefor, and, on failure of payment, to compel them by the common law,

and to do, use, and exercise, all and sundry other things which shall be
needful or convenient for obtaining receipt and payment.

"RENDERING therefor yearly and daily, the said poor, and their
successors dwelling in the said hospital, to our Lord the King and his
successors, as also to the burgh of Aberdeen, and to the magistrates,
ministers, and other inhabitants thereof, the offerings of devout petitions.

"RESERVING to us, during all the time of our life, the power of the
patronage and direction in all things, as shall seem to us most expedient
therein.

"IN WITNESS WHEREOF, to this my charter, written and subscribed with my hand, my authentic seal is appended, at Aberdeen, the
sixth day of the month of June, in the year of our Lord, one thousand six
hundred and thirty-three, before these witnesses, Mr. Thomas Melvill,
Minister of the Word of God at Dyce; Mr. Walter Anderson, Minister
at Kinellar; and Mr. William Ogstone, Minister at Kinnethmont."

WHICH CHARTER above-written, donation and mortification therein
contained, in all its points and articles, its conditions and forms and circumstances whatsoever, in all and by all, in like form and effect as aforesaid,
we ratify, approve, and, for us and our successors, for ever confirm.
FURTHER, with express consent and assent aforesaid, for the great
regard which we have for the glory of God, and the help and support of
the said poor, of our own certain knowledge and free will, we have OF NEW
given, granted, founded, gifted, mortified, disponed, and by this our present
charter have confirmed, and by the tenor thereof do give, grant, found,
gift, mortify, dispone, and for us and our successors for ever do confirm: All
and whole the foresaid place and monastery of the brethren of Holy
Trinity of the said burgh, with all and sundry the houses and buildings
thereof, together with the said church, churchyard, yards, orchards, greens,
and pertinents whatsoever, lying as aforesaid ; as also the ministry of the
said place, with all and sundry lands, annual rents, fruits, profits, emoluments, and duties whatsoever, now belonging, or which were of old known
to belong thereto, as well within the burgh, as in the fields without the
burgh, with the tenants, tenandries, services of free tenants of the same, with
all their pertinents, with all right, title, interest, and claim of right, property
and possession as well petitory as possessory, which we, our predecessors or
successors, had, have, or in any way may claim or pretend to have thereto,
or to any part or portion thereof, or to the maills, fermes, profits, and duties
of the same, for any years whatsoever bygone or to come, by reason of ward,
relief, non-entry, escheat, forfeiture, recognition, purpresture, disclamation, bastardy, reduction of infeftments sasines or retours, revocations,
or Acts of Parliament whatsoever, or by other laws, practices, or
constitutions, of this kingdom; renouncing and upgiving the same, with all
action and instance thereanent, for us and our successors, now and for ever,
with the paction of not seeking, and with supplement of all other defects, as
well not named as named, which we, for us and our aforesaids, will to hold

as set forth at length in this our present charter : TO BE HELD AND
HAD of us and our successors, in pure and perpetual alms and mortmain
for ever: RENDERING therefor yearly and daily, the said poor, and their
successors dwelling in the said hospital, to us and our successors, and to the
said burgh of Aberdeen, and to the magistrates thereof, the ministers, and
other inhabitants of the said burgh, the offerings and prayers of devout
petitions. IN WITNESS WHEREOF, to this our present charter we
have ordained our great seal to be appended.—WITNESSES, our well-
beloved cousins and councillors, James Marquis of Hamilton, Earl of
Arran and Cambridge, Lord Aven and Innerdale, &c. ; George Earl of
Kinnoul, Vicount Dupplin, Lord Hay of Kinfauns, High Chancellor of our
foresaid kingdom of Scotland ; William Earl Marischal, Lord Keith and
Altrie, Marshall of our said kingdom ; Thomas Earl of Haddington, Lord
Binning and Byres, Keeper of our privy seal ; William Viscount Stirling,
Lord Alexander of Tullybrodie, our Chief Secretary ; our beloved familiar
councillors, Sir John Hay of Laud, Clerk of our rolls, register, and council ;
Sir George Elphinstone of Blythswood, our Justice Clerk ; and Sir John
Scott of Scottistarvett, Director of our chancery, knights. At Holyrood
House, the twenty-fourth day of the month of June, in the year of our
Lord, one thousand six hundred and thirty-three, and of our reign the
third.

[*Endorsed.*]

Sealed at Haly⁴.
Primo Julij 1633.

[Signed]   W. Sybbald.
             Gratis.

Writtin to the great seall.
Primo Julij 1633.

[Signed]   Scottistarvett.
             Gratis.

Aberdeine ye 22 Maij 1656. Producit be Patrik Murray, Deacon, and
ane Minut takine and Recordit in the books of Excheq', Conforme to the
sea actis of parliament y'anent.

By me.

[Signed]   W. Purves, Cls.

DECREET OF DECLARATOR

AFFECTING TRADES HOSPITAL CHARTER

(PRONOUNCED 10TH MARCH, 1803).

At Edinburgh, the tenth day of March, one thousand eight hundred and
three years, Anent the Summons and Action of Declarator, raised and
pursued before the Lords of Council and Session, at the instance of the
Reverend Dr. James Sheriffs, first minister of the City of Aberdeen,
patron ; John Leslie, Goldsmith, present Convener of the Trades ; John
Baron, Master of the Trades Hospital ; and the following persons, Deacons
of the Seven Incorporated Trades, all of the said City of Aberdeen, viz.,
John Leslie, Robert Spring, William Bartlet, Andrew Mennie, John
Fraser, George Lawrance, and Alexander Harrow ; as also the following
other persons, being the remaining members of the Convener Court of the
Incorporated Trades of the foresaid City of Aberdeen, viz., William
Cowie, George Smith, George Angus, William Roger, John Blaikie, Robert
Watson, William Donald, Thomas Greig, Alexander Cooper, John Gordon,
Roderick Macdonald, John Keith, David Wyllie, William Reid, George
Taylor, Arthur Farquhar, James Farquhar, James Coutts, William
Hendry, Junior, Joseph Berry, Andrew Hall, Robert Donaldsou, and
William Spark : Against the following persons, being the whole present
Members of the Seven Incorporated Trades of the City of Aberdeen, viz.,
Here follows a list of the various Members of the different Trades, con-
sisting of :—63 Hammermen, 38 Bakers, 50 Wrights and Coopers, 40
Tailors, 63 Shoemakers, 33 Fleshers, and 34 Weavers—in all 320 Members.
Which Summons maketh mention, That, whereas, on or about the year
one thousand six hundred and thirty-three, Dr. William Guild, then one
of the Ministers of the City of Aberdeen, by a Deed of Mortification,
dated in that year, mortified to the poor Tradesmen of the City of Aberdeen, the place or Monastery of the Holey Trinity of the Burgh of Aberdeen, and certain other subjects therein described, to be an Hospital for
the poor old Tradesmen of the said Burgh, who were to be kept and
maintained in the said house under certain conditions and regulations
therein expressed. And, whereas, by a certain other Deed of Mortification
executed by the said Doctor William Guild, upon the fifteenth September,
one thousand six hundred and fifty-five, he obliged him and his heirs to
pay Five thousand Merks, or in the option of his heirs to mortify a house
in the Castlegate of Aberdeen, for the purpose of entertaining three poor
boys, Craftsmen's sons, as Bursars in the New College of Aberdeen. And
he appointed the said Mortifications to be placed under the management
of the first Minister of Aberdeen, as patron, the Deacon-Convener and

Deacons, and a master of Hospital to be named by them. And to be managed according to certain rules and regulations therein set down. As the said Deeds of Mortification in themselves more fully bear. And, whereas, the subjects contained in the first Deed of Mortification, before recited, do now consist of the Trinity Hospital, and the whole grounds contiguous thereto, as now possessed by the pursuers. The Causewaymen's Croft. The price of Thorneybaulkridge, sold in the year seventeen hundred and forty-two, amounting to one hundred pounds sterling. The few duty of Ferryhill, payable by the Master of Mortifications of Aberdeen. The few duty of Potwater, payable by the Treasurer of Aberdeen. The few duty of William Smith's house in the Exchequer Rowe of Aberdeen, and a few duty of the Lands of Craigbowie, payable by . . . . Horne. And, whereas, after the date of said Deeds of Mortification, John Turner, of Dantzig, mortified an annuity of Eight pounds six shillings and eight-pence Sterling, payable out of the Rents of the Estate of Turnerhall, and Dr. Patrick Sibbald mortified the sum of Three hundred Merks both for the maintenance of Depauperate Freemen of the Incorporated Trades in the said Hospital, and that the subjects and funds of the second of said Mortifications do now consist of the foresaid House in the Castlegate of Aberdeen, called the Bursar's house, which is now under lease for a term of years. And whereas various other donations and Mortifications were made to the Incorporated Trades of the said City of Aberdeen, and a variety of funds do now belong to them separate and distinct from the said Mortifications before specially recited, and, Whereas, for sometime the funds of the first Mortification before recited were applied to the main-tenance and support of Depauperate Tradesmen of the said city, who lived and resided in the said Hospital, and were guided by the rules and regula-tions laid down in the foresaid Deeds of Mortification. But for some con-siderable time, owing to the change of the times and manners of the people, many of the regulations stipulated in the original Deeds of Mortification have been found inexpedient and in many instances impracticable. In so much that no one person entitled to the benefit of those charitable Institutions has come forward to claim or will accept thereof according to the literal conditions of the mortifications. On which account the Managers for a long time by gone have been in the custom of distributing the proceeds of said Mortifications amongst the poor Tradesmen of the City, living out of the house, along with the other funds belonging to the said Incorporated Trades, and under the management of the pursuers as the Convener Court thereof. And, Whereas, this mode of distribution and management has been followed for many years without interruption or challenge, and has been attended with much use and benefit to all parties till lately That some of the Tradesmen of the City made application to the Magistrates of Aberdeen praying to have the pursuers prohibited from any further application of these funds, except according to the express and most strict Interpretation of the regulations laid down in the original Deeds of Mortifications before specified, and that the Interference of the said parties to Challenge the present system of management of the fore-

said funds has been attended with the most hurtful consequences. Inso-
much That for a year past the different poor Tradesmen of the City of
Aberdeen, who are entitled to aid from their Poors funds, have received
little or nothing, and no distribution whatever of these funds, has, during
that space taken place, and whereas It is not only inexpedient, but in so
far as no person will accept of the foresaid Charitable Institutions on the
conditions specified in the original Deeds of Mortification, It is impracticable literally to follow all the rules and regulations therein laid down.
Therefore the pursuers as managers of the several Mortifications and funds
before mentioned are desirous to have it ascertained by Decreet of the
Lords of Council and Session, what course, in the circumstances of the
case they ought to follow, and to have the extent of their powers Regularly
adjusted and defined. Therefore the foresaid persons being the whole
present members of the seven Incorporated Trades of the City of Aberdeen,
Ought and Should be called and conveened before the said Lords of
Council and Session to hear and see the nature and extent of the power of
the pursuers, and their successors in Office Managers of the said funds, and
the rules and regulations which are to be observed thereanent specially
ascertained and defined. And it Ought and Should be found and Declared
That so far as any of the conditions and regulations specified in the original
Deeds of Mortification have become impracticable That the same should be
held *pro non scripto*. And more particularly The following Regulations
which have been unanimously agreed to and adopted by the pursuers as
managers of said Mortifications ought to be Ratified and confirmed by the
said Lords, and it Ought and Should be Found and declared in terms of
said regulations, that the whole of the subjects and funds therein before
specially described as included under the first Deed of Mortification of the
said Dr. William Guild with the annuity mortified by John Turner of
Dantzig, and the sum of Three hundred merks mortified by Dr. Patrick
Sibbald for the maintenance of Depauperate Freemen of Trades of Aberdeen, should in all time coming be kept separate and distinct in the Master
of Hospital's accounts from all the other funds under his Administration.
That they should be constantly under the sole management and direction
of the patron, Conveener, Master of Hospital, and seven Deacons of the
Incorporated Trades, and be applied to the uses and purposes and in the
manner mentioned in Dr. Guild's deed of Mortification so far as is now
practicable. That when there is room or accomodation in the Hospital for
any depauperate Freemen, Every person of unexceptional moral character
entitled to and applying for the benefit of the Hospital funds shall be
apprised that he will be received into the Hospital under the conditions
specified in the said original Deed of Mortification. And as for some years
past no person has been found willing to live as a Beedman in the Hospital,
In case persons properly qualified and desirous of admission into the said
Hospital shall not be found after every endeavour has been used for that
purpose for the space of two years, Then the managers shall have it in
their power to distribute the revenue or profits of the aforesaid funds in
such way and manner as they may Judge most beneficial to the poor

tradesmen of the whole Incorporated Trades, they being always persons of the description and character required by the original Deed of foundation. But that the funds should never be applied but for the support of Beedmen in the Hospital when such can be found. It being also understood that the Trades should still have right to hold their meetings in the Hospital as they have hitherto done. And with respect to the other funds under the administration of the Master of the Trades Hospital, It ought and should be found and declared That they should continue under the management and direction of the patron and others Members of the Conveener Court as formerly and be distributed among the poor of the Trades as they shall think proper and expedient, But with and under these express conditions, viz. :—That all sums paid to, or expended in maintaining a House Keeper in the Hospital shall be charged against these funds, except when there are Beedmen in the house, in which case a part of the expense shall be charged against the funds mortified by Doctor Guild, That the Conveener Court shall not be obliged to admit every person to the benefit of the Hospital funds who has been admitted to the benefit of the funds of the separate Trades, but shall have the sole power of Judging and determining what persons Ought to be so admitted, and every person applying to be settled on the funds of the hospital shall be obliged, along with his petition, to produce a certificate of his moral character to the satisfaction of the said Conveener Court, And Finally That in case at any time the revenue of the funds mortified by Dr. Guild, John Turner, and Dr. Patrick Sibbald shall be insufficient for the maintenance of the Beedmen that may happen to be in the Hospital, and the other necessary expenses, then the deficiency shall be made up from the other funds under the Master of Hospital's Adminis-tration. And Lastly, In regard to the Bursars house mortified by Dr. Guild's second Deed of Mortification before mentioned It Ought and Should be Found and Declared That after the expiry of the present Lease thereof, It should in future be always let by public roup, for a space not exceeding seven years at a time, after three consecutive advertisements in the *Aberdeen Journal.* That no person shall be admitted to the benefit of that foundation unless he produce proper certificates of his answering the description therein, That two months previous to each sitting of the College due intimation shall be given by the Master of the Hospital to the Deacons of the several Trades to be by them communicated to their respective corporations what burses on this foundation are open for Candidates, and that when no candidates properly qualified do claim the benefit of these burses, the free rent of the house shall be applied for extinguishing the debts affecting the house and for increasing the fund ; and in case of a proper observance of the rules and regulations above set down, the said haill Defenders, and all others, their successors or those claiming in their right, Ought and Should be Prohibited and Discharged in all time coming from further challenging, troubling, or molesting the pursuers and their successors in Office there anent. And anent the charge given the Defenders in virtue of the foresaid Summons, by Messengers-at-Arms, to have com-peared before the said Lords upon two certain days, now by gone, to have answered at the instance of the Pursuers in the said matter, and to have heard and seen the premises verified and proven, and Decreet and sentence given furth and pronounced therein in manner to the effect and with certification lybelled. As in the said Summons and Executions thereof at length is contained. The Pursuers compearing by Mr. Adam Gillies, Advocate, their Procurator, and Alexander Barron, one of the members of the Conveener Court of Aberdeen, and as such inserted in the Summons as a Pursuer, Compearing by Mr. Robert Craigie, Advocate, his Procurator, who for him produced in presence of the said Lords, a Disclamation by him as a Pursuer of said action, and requesting his name to be delete from the list of Prosecutors, addressed to Alex. Youngson, Esq., Writer to the Signet, and dated at Aberdeen, the Third day of February, Eighteen hundred and three. And the Defenders being by virtue of the foresaid Summons lawfully summoned to said action in manner foresaid oft-times called, but failing to appear. The which foresaid Summons, Executions thereof, Compearance made for the Pursuers, and desire of their Pror after insert, Compearance made for Alexander Barron. Together with the absence of the Defenders and haill other steps and circumstances of the said matter, being all at length read, heard, seen, and considered by the said Lords, and they therewith well and ripely advised : The Lords of Council and Session aforesaid have Found and Declared and hereby Find and Declare, That so far as any of the conditions and regulations specified in the original Deeds of Mortification by Dr. Willm. Guild have become impracticable, they are to be held *pro non scripto*. Ratified and Confirmed, and hereby Ratify and Confirm the following regulations which have been unanimously agreed to and adopted by the Pursuers as managers of said Mortification ; and Found and Declared, and hereby Find and Declare that in terms of said regulations that the whole of the subjects and funds herein before specially described, as included under the first Deed of Mortification of the said Dr. William Guild, with the annuity mortified by John Turner, of Dantzig, and the sum of Three hundred merks mortified by Dr. Patrick Sibbald for the maintenance of depauperate Freemen of the Trades of Aberdeen, shall in all time coming be kept separate and distinct in the Master of Hospital's accounts from all the other funds under his administration. That they shall be constantly under the sole management and direction of the patron, Conveener, Master of Hospital, and seven Deacons of the Incorporated Trades, and be applied to the uses and purposes and in the manner mentioned in Dr. Guild's deed of Mortification so far as is row practicable. That when there is room or accommodation in the Hospital for any depauperate Freemen, Every person of exceptionable moral character entitled to and applying for the benefit of the Hospital funds shall be apprised that he will be received into the Hospital under the conditions specified in the said original Deed of Mortification, And as for some years past no person has been found willing to live as a Beedman in the Hospital, in case persons properly qualified and desirous of admission into the said Hospital, shall not be found after every endeavour has been used for that purpose for the space of two years, Then the managers shall have it in their power to distribute the revenue or profits of the foresaid funds in such way and manner as they may Judge most beneficial to the poor Tradesmen of the whole Incorporated Trades, they being always of the description and character required by the Original Deed of Foundation, But that the funds shall never be applied but for the support of Beedmen in the Hospital when such can be found. It being also understood that the Trades shall still have right to hold their meetings in the Hospital as they have hitherto done. And with respect to the other funds under the administration of the Master of the Trades Hospital Found and Declared and hereby Find and Declare, That they shall continue under the management and direction of the patron and other members of the Conveener Court as formerly and be distributed among the poor of the Trades as they shall think proper and expedient. But with and under these express conditions, viz., That all sums paid to, or expended in maintaining a house keeper in the Hospital shall be charged against these funds except where there are Beedmen in the house, in which case a part of the expense shall be charged against the funds mortified by Doctor Guild. That the Conveener Court shall not be obliged to admit every person to the benefit of the Hospital funds who has been admitted to the benefit of the funds of the separate Trades but shall have the sole power of Judging and determining what persons Ought to be so admitted, and every person applying to be settled on the funds of the Hospital shall be obliged, along with his petition to produce a certificate of his moral character to the satisfaction of the said Conveener Court. And Finally That in case at any time the revenue of the funds mortified by Dr. Guild, John Turner, and Dr. Patrick Sibbald shall be insufficient for the maintenance of the Beedmen that may happen to be in the Hospital, and the other necessary expenses, Then the deficiency shall be made up from the other funds under the Master of Hospital's Administrations. And Lastly in regard to the Bursars house mortified by Dr. Guild's second deed of Mortification before mentioned Found and Declared, and hereby Find and Declare That after the expiry of the present Lease thereof It shall in future be always let by public roup for a space not exceeding seven years at a time, after three consecutive advertisements in the *Aberdeen Journal.* That no person shall be admitted to the benefit of that foundation unless he produce proper certificates of his answering the description therein. That two months previous to each sitting of the College due intimation shall be given by the master of the Hospital to the Deacons of the several Trades, to be by them communicated to their respective Corporations what burses on this foundation are open for candidates, and that when no Candidates properly qualified do claim the benefit of these burses, the free rent of the house shall be applied for extinguishing the debts affecting the house and for increasing the fund ; And in case of a proper observance of the rules and regulations above set down : Prohibited and Discharged and hereby Prohibits and Discharges the haill Defenders and all others their successors or those claiming their right in time coming from further challenging, troubling, or molesting the pursuers and their successors in office thereanent. Because after Elapsing of the diets of compearance contained in the foresaid Summons the same was called in common form, and in regard there was no appearance then made for the Defenders the Summons was Ordained to be inrolled in the Regulation Roll, which having been done accordingly the same in course thereof was called in presence of the Lord Woodhouselee Ordinary in the Outer House upon the said Tenth day of March One thousand eight hundred and three years the date hereof, when Mr. Robert Craigie Advocate Procurator for the said Alexander Baron Represented, That the present process had been raised in his name without his consent or approbation. That on the contrary he highly disapproved of the procedure and then produced a signed disclaimation. To which Mr. Adam Gillies Advocate the Pursuers Procurator answered That altho Mr. Baron had thought proper to disclaim the process yet the other Pursuers were entitled to proceed therewith so far as they were interested, and repeated the Libel and Craved Decreet at their instance in terms thereof. And the Defenders being not only lawfully Summoned to said Action in manner foresaid, but also the said day several times called by a Macer from the Barr, as use is to have compeared and defended, but being still absent and failing to appear, The Lord Ordinary Allowed the name of Alexander Baron as a Pursuer to be withdrawn from the Process ; And Decerned at the instance of the other Pursuers conform to the conclusions of the Libel. And so the said Lord Ordinary and by him the Lords of Council and Session aforesaid Gave and Pronounced Decreet and Sentence in the said matter, Finding, Declaring, Ratifying, Confirming, Prohibiting and Discharging in manner foresaid, and ordain Letters of Horning on fifteen days charge and all other Execution necessary and competent to pass and be direct hereon inform as Effeirs. Extracted upon this and the Twenty three preceding pages By this for the Record. (Signed) Ja. Colquhoun, 6th April, 1803. Clerk's fees marked paid and Dect. compared. (Signed) John Alexander. Extracted on this and the Thirty two preceding pages, by me, Deputy Keeper of the Records of Scotland. Declaring that the word "which" on the seventh line counting from the top of page eleven hereof was delete before authentication.

(Signed)   JOHN C. CHRISTIE.

DONATIONS AND BEQUESTS TO THE SEVEN INCORPORATED TRADES OF ABERDEEN.

YEAR.		MERKS.	STERLING.
1633.	1. Dr. William Guild—The Place and Monastery of the Holy Trinity, with sundry annual rents -		
	2. Do. The Penny Rig Croft - - - - - -		
	3. Do. Cassiman's Croft - - - - - -		
	4. Do. Murray's Croft - - - - - - -		
	5. Do. Thornybank Rig - - - - - -		
	6. Do. Teind Barn - - - - - - -		
	7. Do. The Bursars House - - - - - -		
1644.	8. Sir Thomas Crombie of Kemnay - - - - -	500	£27 15 6
	9. Geo. Robertson, son of H. Robertson, cordiner -	100	5 11 1⅓
	10. Jean Guild - - - - - - - - - -	150	8 6 8
	11. Rev. John Gregory, Drumoak, Jean Guild's son-in-law - - - - - - - - -	100	5 11 1⅓
	12. Jane Spence Herald - - - -	150	8 6 8
	13. William Gray, elder - - - -	100	5 11 1⅓
	14. Walter Cochrane, baillie -	50	2 15 6⅔
	15. Gilbert Hervie, burgess - - - - -	50	2 15 6⅔
	16. Robert Ferguson - - - - - - -	100	5 11 1⅓
	17. Andrew Burnett - - - - - - - -	100	5 11 1⅓
	18. George Peacock - - - - - - - - -	150	8 6 8
	19. Patrick Jack, younger - - - - - -	100	5 11 1⅓
	20. John Lichten - - - - - - - - -	50	2 15 6⅔
1663.	21. George Davidson of Pettens - - - - -	300	16 13 4
1688.	22. John Turner, Dantzic, burden on the Lands of Tipperty - - - - - - - - -	150	8 6 8
	23. Andrew Craighead, flesher, half of Stott's Hole -	Value not known.	
	24. Archibald Beans, litster, 400 pounds Scots, laid out on the other half of Stott's Hole - -	600	33 6 8
	25. Robert Cruickshank, house at back of the Town's Hospital - - - - - - - - -	Value not known.	
	26. Elspet Donaldson, relict of James Milne - -	100	5 11 1⅓
	27. James Davidson, merchant - - - - - -	100	5 11 1⅓
	28. Agnes Grub, relict of James Watson - - -	150	8 6 8
1691.	29. Alexander Adam, M.D., Anstruther - - -		1 2 2⅔
1698.	30. Dr. Patrick Sibbald - - - - - - - -	300	16 13 4
	31. George Gladstaines, pewterer - - - - -	300	16 13 4
	32. William Ord, wright - - - - - - -	450	25 0 0
	33. James Christie, tailor, convener - - - -	100	5 11 1⅓
	34. James Milne of Blairton - - - - - -	300	16 13 4
1700.	35. Alexander Galloway, merchant - - - -	500	27 15 6

YEAR.		MERKS.	STERLING.		
1704.	36. James Leonard, weaver, tenement in the Green -	Value not known.			
1711.	37. James Douglas, mortification for Baker Trade -	350	£19	8	10⅔
	38. Robert Gordon, merchant - - - - - - -	50	2	15	6⅔
	39. Robert Smith, tailor, convener - - - - -	50	2	15	6⅔
1716.	40. James Purdie, skinner in Edinburgh - - - -	50	2	15	6⅔
	41. Alexander Mitchell and Spouse - - - - -	500	27	15	6
	42. George Massie and Spouse - - - - - -	100	5	11	1⅓
	43. Robert Morgan - - - - - - - - - -	100	5	11	1⅓
1720.	44. Alexander Smith, shoemaker, convener - -	100	8	6	8
1724.	45. Alex. Williamson, chaplain to the Viscount of Arbuthnot - - - - - - - - -	50	2	15	6⅔
1726.	46. John Falconer, wigmaker - - - - - -	300	16	13	4
1734.	47. David Jaffray - - - - - - - - - -	200	11	2	2
	48. Alex. Robertson, tailor - - - - - -	100	5	11	1⅓
1736.	49. James Milne, tailor - - - - - - - -	500	27	15	6
	50. Rev. John Moir, rector of West Tanfield, Yorkshire - - - - - - - - - -	1000	83	6	8
	51. Jean Mercer (Mrs. Provost Mitchell) - - -	1000	83	6	8
1737.	52. Mrs. Mitchell - - - - - - - - - -	100	5	11	1⅓
1738.	53. John Straton - - - - - - - - - -	75	4	4	0
1739.	54. Margaret Duncan, school mistress - - -	200	11	2	2
1742.	55. John Leslie, weaver, convener - - - - -	150	8	6	8
1745.	56. Alexander Massie - - - - - - - -	225	12	10	0
1753.	57. John Fraser, merchant - - - - - -	500	27	15	6
1754.	58. Helen Gifford, relict of James Thom, tailor -	360	20	0	0
1756.	59. John Taylor, clerk to the Trades - - -	500	27	15	6
1760.	60. William Gerard of Stonehouse, Stirlingshire -		150	0	0
1769.	61. Mrs. Norrie C. Smith, relict of J. Norrie, tailor -		60	0	0
1781.	62. Agnes Fowler, spouse of James Mackay, merchant		243	0	0
1790.	63. John Nicol and his Spouse, Helen Wilson - -		100	0	0
1803.	64. Mrs. John Cushnie, shipmaster - - - - -		200	0	0
1823.	65. Deacon William Bain, weaver - - - - -		100	0	0

CHARTER BY CHARLES I. IN FAVOUR OF ABERDEEN
TRADES, 1641.

CHARLES, be the grace of God king of Great Britain, France, and Ireland, Defender of the faith—To all and sundrie our leidges and subjects to whose knowledge thir presents shall come greeting. Be it knowne unto you all, because we understanding our most nobell progenitors kings of Scotland haveing consideration and respect to the commonwealth and peaceable governance of our said kingdome of Scotland and that without artificers and good craftsmen ane well ordered commonwealth cannot long stand ; For that cause they have given and granted all and sundrie privaledges and liberties to the craftsmen of all our burghs in our said kingdom especiallie to our said burghs of Edinburgh, Pearth, Dundie, and Aberdeen as by the gift granted to them under the great sealls of our most nobill progenitors doeth appear. Lykeas our dear good dam, of worthie memorie, Queen Mary by hir majesties gift and donation granted to the craftsmen of Edinburgh, Pearth, Dundie, and Aberdeen in anno 1556, gave the craftsmen who are free burgesses of the saids burghs the liberties of power and privaledge to sell and use all manner of merchandies within and without this our kingdom of Scotland, as they should think most expedient for them, together with dyvers other privaledges and liberties to the craftismen of the saids burghs mentionat in the said gift as the same of the date foresaid under her majesties great seall at more lenth bears. As alsoe our dear father King James the sixth, of eternall memorie, granted the lyke liberties and privaledges to the craftsmen of the forsaid burghs and ratified and confirmed all other former privaledges, liberties, and faculties whatsomever as by the gift thereof under his majesties great seall, bearing date at Dalkeith the second day of Julie, 1581 years, more clearlie doeth appear. It is theirfor humblie supplicated be the craftsmen of our said burgh of Aberdeen as they who are only interested and injured in their saids privaledges contrair to our saids nobell progenitors, their royall privaledges and gifts granted be them as saidis that the lyk gift may be granted unto them by us under our royall hand and seile. Witt ye theirfor us and for sundrie other reasonable causses moeving us to have ratified, granted, and given, and be the tenor heirof ratifies, gives, and grants to all and sundrie the craftsmen our loyall subjects of our said burgh of Aberdeen, all and whatsomeveṝ liberties, privaledges, and faculties granted of before to them or any of our burghs within this our kingdom by our saids nobell progenitors and speciallie to use and trade all manner of merchandice within and without this our kingdome of Scotland, also freelie in all respects as any of our liedges, craftsmen of the said burghs of Edinburgh, Pearth, and Dundie ever hath been in use for to do, dispensand and be the tenor heiroff dispenses with and dischairges all acts whatsomever, decreits, statutes and proclamationes made or to be made in the contrair, and all paines contained in the same or any of them. Wheirfor we command and chairge you and everie one of you our liedges and subjects, that you nor none of you presume in tyme comeing to make any impediment or molestation in contrair of thes presents unto the craftsmen of our said burgh of Aberdeen for enjoying and possessing the liberties and privaledges concerning their crafts and trade of merchandices, as said is, notwithstandeing of any acts, decreits, statutes or proclamationes made on the contrair or any paines contained in the same under all highest paine danger and offence which you, or any of you, may incur at our hands. To the witnes wheirof we ordaine our great seall to be appendit heirunto and lres to be dirrect hereupon in forme as effeirs if need beis. Subscryved be our royall hands at our palace of Halyruid House, the 14th September, 1641.

ACT OF PARLIAMENT ABOLISHING EXCLUSIVE TRADING PRIVILEGES, 1846.

WHEREAS in certain Royal and other Burghs (in Scotland) the Members of certain Guilds, Crafts, or Incorporations possess exclusive Privileges of carrying on or dealing in Merchandize, and of carrying on or exercising certain Trades or Handicrafts within their respective Burghs ; and such Guilds, Crafts, or Incorporations have corresponding rights, entitling them to prevent Persons not being Members thereof from carrying on or dealing in Merchandize, or from carrying on or exercising such Trades or Handicrafts, within such Burghs : And whereas it has become expedient that such exclusive Privileges and Rights should be abolished : Be it therefore enacted by the Queen's most Excellent Majesty, by and with the Advice and Consent of the Lords Spiritual and Temporal, and Commons, in this present Parliament assembled, and by the Authority of the same, That from and after the passing of this Act all such exclusive Privileges and Rights shall cease, and it shall be lawful for any person to carry on or deal in Merchandize, and to carry on or exercise any Trade or Handicraft, in any Burgh and elsewhere *in Scotland*, without being a burgess of such Burgh, or a Guild Brother, or a Member of any Guild, Craft or Incorporation : Provided always, that in lieu of the Stamp Duties of One Pound and Three Pounds now payable on the admission of any Person as a Burgess, or into any Corporation or Company in any Burgh *in Scotland*, for the Enrolment, Entry or Memorandum thereof in the Court Books, Roll, or Record of such Corporation or Company, there shall from and after the passing of this Act be paid on every such Admission a Stamp Duty of Five Shillings.

II. And be it enacted, That notwithstanding the Abolition of the said exclusive Privileges and Rights all such Incorporations as aforesaid shall retain their Corporate Character, and shall continue to be Incorporations, with the same Names and Titles as heretofore ; and nothing herein contained shall anywise affect the Rights and Privileges of such Incorporations, or of the Office Bearers or Members thereof, except as hereinbefore enacted.

III. And whereas the Revenues of such Incorporations as aforesaid may in some Instances be affected, and the Number of the Members of such Incorporations may in some Instances diminish, by reason of the Abolition of the said exclusive Privileges and Rights, and it is expedient that Provision should be made for facilitating Arrangements suitable to such Occurrences ; be it therefore enacted, That it shall be lawful for every such Incorporation from Time to Time to make all Bye-Laws, Regulations, and Resolutions relative to the Management and Application of its Funds and Property, and relative to the Qualification and Admission of Members, in reference to its altered Circumstances under this Act, as may be considered expedient, and to apply to the Court of Session, by summary Petition, for the Sanction of the said Court to such Bye-Laws, Regulations, or Resolutions; and the said Court, after due Intimation of such Application, shall determine upon the same, and upon any Objections that may be made thereto by Parties having Interest, and shall interpone the Sanction of the said Court to such Bye-Laws, Regulations, or Resolutions, or disallow the same in whole or in part, or make thereon such Alterations, or adject thereto such Conditions or Qualifications, as the said Court may think fit, and generally shall pronounce such order in the whole Matter as may to the said Court seem just and expedient; and such Bye-Laws, Regulations, or Resolutions, subject to such Alterations and Conditions as aforesaid, shall be, when the Sanction of the said Court shall have been interponed thereto, valid and effectual and binding on such Incorporations; Provided always, that nothing therein contained shall affect the Validity of any Bye-Laws, Regulations, or Resolutions that may be made by any such Incorporation without the Sanction of the said Court, which it would have been heretofore competent for such Incorporation to have made of its own Authority or without such Sanction.

TABLE OF SCOTS AND STERLING MONEY.

SCOTS.		STERLING.		
1 Penny	equal to	£0	0	0 1-12th
1 Bodle	„	0	0	$0\frac{1}{6}$
1 Plack	„	0	0	$0\frac{1}{3}$
1 Shilling	„	0	0	1
1 Pound	„	0	1	8
1 Merk	„	0	1	$1\frac{1}{3}$
100 Merks	„	5	11	$1\frac{1}{3}$

INDEX.